THE RECORDS

OF

AMERICAN

BUSINESS

Edited by
James M. O'Toole

THE SOCIETY *of*
AMERICAN ARCHIVISTS

CHICAGO

The Records of American Business Project was supported in part by a grant from the Division of Preservation and Access at the National Endowment for the Humanities, an independent federal government agency. Additional support for the project was provided by the Minnesota Historical Society and the Hagley Museum and Library.

THE SOCIETY OF AMERICAN ARCHIVISTS
600 S. Federal, Suite 504, Chicago, IL 60605
312/922-0140 Fax 312/347-1452
info@archivists.org
http://www.archivists.org

Printed in the United States of America

Library of Congress Cataloging-in-Publication Data

The records of American business / edited by James M. O'Toole.
  p. cm.
  Includes bibliographical references and index.
  ISBN 0-931828-45-7 (alk. paper)
  1. Business records—United States—Management. 2. Business enterprises—United States—Archives. 3. Corporations—United States—Archives. 4. Archives—United States—Administration. 5. United States—Commerce—History—Sources. I. O'Toole, James M., 1950-   .
HF5736.R3625 1997
651.5—dc21   97-24781
                                                                        CIP

⊗ The paper used in this book complies with the Permanent Paper Standard issued by the National Information Standards Organization (Z39.48–1984)

Contents

Acknowledgments

The Records of American Business Project (RAB) has proven a remarkable enterprise. Some projects are born and continue under a lucky star, and this is definitely one of them. Since its inception as a proposal from Mark Greene and Todd Daniels-Howell in 1992, RAB has grown and developed an international constituency that has greatly expanded its impact and its products. The importance of the work has been validated at every turn, and the project's products have involved important contributions from many people.

A major portion of The Records of American Business Project was funded by the National Endowment for the Humanities (NEH). Support of staff at NEH was welcome and important; this volume was suggested by Jeffrey Field, Deputy Director of the Division of Preservation and Access. Former program officers Barbara Paulson and Karen Jefferson helped shape the project and provided critical advice during its early stages.

This volume is the first in many years to focus on the records of business. We are especially grateful to each of the essay authors; they are a stellar group whose willingness to prepare essays in the midst of many commitments was immediate and critical to the project's success. Particular thanks must go to James M. O'Toole, who as the book's editor brought his considerable skills to establishing the volume's place in archival literature and ensuring its relevance to communities outside the world of business archives. We are also grateful to Teresa Brinati, Director of Publications for the Society of American Archivists, whose expertise, counsel, and good humor made the book's production a pleasure, and to SAA Executive Director Susan Fox for her support and enthusiasm for this project.

The opportunity to bring together the two institutions with the largest holdings of business archives in North America—and thus the greatest impetus to refine and redefine the appraisal and use of corporate records—has been one of the benefits of the RAB Project. The complementary but not always overlapping interests of the Hagley Museum and Library and the Minnesota Historical Society have enriched the project's discussions and informed its conclusions.

At the Minnesota Historical Society the RAB Project could not have achieved success without the support of the society's director, Nina Archabal, and Assistant Director for Library and Archives, Lila J. Goff. The society's Executive Council, which includes many business executives among its members, was also important to this process. The leadership and support of former society president Kennon V. Rothchild remains enormously important in efforts to enhance the role of business history.

The Director of the Hagley Museum and Library, Glenn Porter, was an enthusiastic supporter of the project. From the beginning he saw the importance of opening a dialog between business historians and the archival community. Philip Scranton, Director of the Center for the History of Business, Technology and Society, and Associate Director Roger Horowitz, helped shape our thoughts about the future of business history and business archives.

To those who have advised the RAB Project as members of its various committees, and at professional meetings past counting, we express our deep appreciation. It is our belief that this book will enrich and expand discussions on the place of business and its history in the ever smaller and more interdependent world in which we live.

James E. Fogerty　　　　　　　　　　*Michael Nash*
Minnesota Historical Society　　　　Hagley Museum and Library

Foreword

James M. O'Toole

This book is about the records of American business—and it's not.
The authors have drawn on their varied experience to describe the
current state of business records in the United States and the archival
programs that care for them. Whether from the perspective of an archivist who works as a part of the organization producing the records
or from that of an archivist in an outside repository—both views are
represented here—these authors address the special challenges of documenting the complex phenomenon that is American business. At the
symposium sponsored by the Minnesota Historical Society and the
Hagley Museum and Library in April 1996 (at which some of these
essays were first presented) and since, these authors have thoughtfully
considered the range of issues involved in preserving the evidence of
business enterprise, a subject that is at once well known and poorly
understood. For those whose archival responsibilities include the care
of this kind of documentary material, these essays will, the authors
hope, provide insights, advice, and encouragement.

At the same time, these essays have a wider applicability and
importance. Though writing particularly about American business, the
authors explore issues that are of pressing, day-to-day concern to all
archivists. The challenges of preserving and making available the documentation of contemporary human activity may be seen in especially
sharp relief by business archivists, but those same challenges are
equally familiar to archivists who manage the records of, for example,
higher education or religious life or even the papers of individuals and
families. All archivists and curators face problems of bulk, privacy
and access to information, the evolving role of documentation in human
affairs, and the changing nature of the record itself. Thus, those in

other archival settings who have no direct responsibility for the care of business records can profit from the discussions presented here. The best advice is this: every time the word "business" appears in these pages, simply substitute the word "academic" or "religious" or the descriptor that applies to your own setting. That translation will prove easy and apt.

What are the issues explored here that all archivists must face? Several stand out. First is the question of the placement of the archives program in relation to the activity or organization it is designed to serve. Many businesses have chosen to establish their own internal archival programs. In such cases, the corporate archives is placed within the company itself—just where on the organizational chart varies considerably from case to case—to provide systematic care for the company's documentation at all stages of the records life cycle. In such arrangements the corporate archives can play a central role in meeting the broad information needs of the company. While not unconcerned with the needs of researchers outside their parent organization, archivists who work inside a company focus their attention on demands that come from within their own institution. Many other businesses, by contrast, have chosen to place their records with universities, historical societies, or other archival repositories. In such cases, the archives stands apart from the company, preserving these business records as part of its larger efforts to document a particular geographic area or realm of human activity. This external repository is perhaps better positioned to make its collections available to users of the records from outside the company structure, but it must nonetheless commit itself to serving the companies whose records it holds.

Though the question of the "correct" organizational placement for business records—inside the company or with an outside archives—is sometimes passionately debated, the dichotomy is a false one. There is not, and there should not be, a single, one-size-fits-all answer. In-house archives have the advantage of working in the midst of the organization whose records they care for. They are thus positioned to play a central role in managing the firm's information resources, one of the most valuable commodities any company possesses. They are also able to intervene early to guard against the loss or destruction of crucial documentation. At the same time, they may be subject to pressures that work against the successful completion of the archival mission. The business, after all, is established to do and accomplish things other than the preservation of records as such: records are always likely to be seen as merely a means to some other end. Archives and records programs may thus be seen as "luxuries" that can be abandoned when times are hard. Moreover, institutional loyalties sometimes lead company officers to think—inaccurately—that the destruction of documentation better serves company interests than the preservation and use of that information. Records professionals must therefore always be prepared to educate company personnel on the importance of good records practices.

Archivists in so-called collecting repositories who preserve records from outside the business environment may have the advantage of a more neutral stance toward the phenomena they are trying to document. They are also in a position to encourage the use of business records by a wide clientele of researchers. They must guard, however, against separating themselves from the concerns of the companies whose records they acquire. If they define their role narrowly, these repositories may be seen as being too distinct from the businesses' own interests or, even worse, as working at cross purposes with them. Questions of access to sensitive company information, including trade secrets and other vital business information, for example, must be carefully addressed in any gift or deposit agreement so that both the business and the archives retain one another's full confidence. Collecting repositories must also suppress a predatory attitude that selects only the "good stuff" from a company's records, leaving the apparently more problematic records to their own devices.

Archivists managing other, nonbusiness kinds of records face these same dilemmas. Many religious organizations and congregations, for example, have established their own internal archives programs, while others have placed their records in the custody of local and regional historical societies or with a college connected with the parent denomination. Both arrangements can be successful. In the former case, the congregation's records remain close to the center of its community life, where they can be used to address practical matters of "this-worldly" administration and to reinforce the spiritual life of the group. In the latter case, the group's records receive the professional care they might not get amid more pressing demands on resources for the devotional, educational, and social welfare programs of the religious body. Similarly, many cultural organizations have faced the same decision: several American symphony orchestras, for instance, have established successful in-house archives programs, while others have chosen to place their records with a local library or historical society. Like the business organizations addressing this question, these nonbusiness institutions have had to strike a balance, weighing the benefits of in-house custody with the costs involved, weighing the benefits of outside custody with the separation of the records from direct institutional control. Enough examples of high-quality archival efforts of both types exist so that archivists in all sorts of institutions can draw on them in their own decision making about records. In the essays that follow, many of the authors have addressed this larger issue, and the cases they present can inform the thinking of all archivists.

A second concern that cuts across these essays and applies to archivists of all kinds is the crucial matter of the appraisal of records. Early archival theory presupposed that deciding which records had sufficient value to warrant retention in an archives and which did not was the responsibility solely of those who created the records. The archivist had to maintain a strictly neutral stance, carefully preserving the records once they had come to the archives but not influencing the decisions about which would survive and which would not. Throughout most of the twentieth century, however, archivists have been assuming a progressively more active role in shaping documentation. Modern-day records are so voluminous and complex that deliberate means for identifying their long-term value are essential: if the survival of high-quality documentation is left to chance, the archival record of all aspects of society will be spotty and inadequate. Without careful analysis, valuable information will be lost while information of passing significance (or no significance at all) is saved.

For these reasons, appraisal has been the subject of continuing and lively discussion among archivists in the last twenty years, and several of the essays in this volume contribute to that discussion. Moving far beyond the intellectual framework best articulated by Theodore Schellenberg, which sought to identify what were called the evidential and informational values in records, archivists today are articulating new foundations for making appraisal decisions. Some have elaborated models which call for a sophisticated decision-tree of analysis, weighing not only the information content of the documents themselves but also the practical and policy implications of appraisal actions for the archives and for the parent body. Other writers have called for planned, multi-institutional, and cooperative strategies for preserving documentation. Still others have argued the merits of shifting attention to a broader analysis of the functions performed by the organization or individual producing the records. Only after those core functions are understood, this argument goes, will archivists be able to identify the records that best document them. Then archivists will more confidently be able to approach the massive compilations of data and make better selections. Gone from all these new approaches is the notion that appraisal is nothing but a vaguely defined "art," an intuition that the archivist develops only with practice, or a mystical sixth sense for knowing valuable records when one sees them.

Some archivists have found this ongoing discussion confusing and troubling: "can't we just agree on the *right* way to do appraisal," they seem to say, "and get on with it?" Others, however, find in these debates a healthy sign of intellectual vigor in the professional conversation. Given the complexity of modern life and the consequent complexity of its records, the search for a simple, universally applicable approach to appraisal is wrongheaded. Rather, all archivists should join the debate, testing the several models in their own settings, identifying the strengths and weaknesses of different approaches, revising those models, or developing new ones of their own. Many of the authors represented in this volume have done just that, and they have done so, it should be noted, not in pursuit of a pure theory of appraisal but rather to solve very immediate problems. A new consensus may eventually emerge, but for the moment all archivists are helped by a mental world in which a thousand appraisal flowers bloom.

The authors of the essays presented here have focused their work on appraisal of records in corporate settings, but their insights apply equally well to other archival situations. Archivists who must confront the massive files of their organization's accounting department, for example, do not care whether they are the accounting records of a for-profit business or those of a modern American university. Archivists faced with decisions about legal files of cases and contracts might not be able to tell whether they come from a modern multinational corporation or a religious community with missions around the world. Archivists appraising personnel files may be unaware of (and even unconcerned with) what those personnel actually do for their employer: are they factory line workers, or are they state government employees? Archivists who seek to preserve information about the role of their institution in the wider community may be selecting the records of the city's largest employer or the records of the museum or cultural institution that gives that locality its distinctive character. Archivists who preserve the personal papers of local citizens may be less concerned with what those papers actually talk about—is it the financial bottom line of the individual's company or the success of an author's latest novel?—than with the responsibility to preserve adequate and important documentation and to guarantee its usefulness.

A third challenge affecting all archivists is that posed by the impact of modern computer technology on the very processes of making and keeping records. Three decades ago, computers were huge, cumbersome, and expensive machines; today, they are compact, lightweight, and affordable devices which individuals may even hold on their laps while riding in trains or airplanes. In the next three decades, some futurists predict, computers will get even smaller, so much so that we will all be wearing them on our clothes and plugging them into far-reaching networks to which we gain access by stopping at something that looks like a phone booth. However that may be, the electronic revolution of the late twentieth century has had a dramatic impact on the production and use of records. Where financial information, for instance, was once kept in large and heavy ledger books, it exists now in the ether of "virtual documents," assembled and disassembled on a flickering screen in response to particular demands. Archivists accustomed to managing records that have a clear, material existence—records that one can hold in one's hands and read with the naked eye—have thus necessarily had to accommodate themselves to records that have few tangible characteristics and can be read only with the intervention of specific kinds of hardware and software. At the same time, archivists have begun to explore and use automated techniques for the management of their collections, applying specially developed formats and data bases to improve familiar archival tasks. Whether dealing with archival records that are themselves in electronic format or using electronic means to manage traditional paper records, archivists today are on the front lines of changing technology and its impact on modern life.

Such issues are framed with particular clarity in business settings. After all, it is in business organizations that the pace of technological change, spurred on by the desire to remain profitable and competitive, has been particularly rapid. High-tech firms have come into existence, at once helping to spread the availability of the technology and using it in their own work. The computer has become ubiquitous, however, because its applications can be useful in any number of settings, and for this reason all archivists face its challenge and its potential. It may be able to manipulate large quantities of business information, but it may also be the most efficient means for keeping a school's student transcripts. It speeds the delivery of all goods and services, whether they are the products of industrial manufacturing or tickets to the latest "megashow" at the local museum. Whether the e-mail messages it carries have been written by a corporate executive, a doctor in a health center, a member of Congress, or a cloistered religious is entirely immaterial (both figuratively and literally!) to the computer. The connections it makes possible to large-scale networks, most notably the World Wide Web, are everywhere: once the preserve only of corporations and other substantial institutions, today even grade-school children seem to have their own Web pages. The archivist who seeks to capture and preserve these communications and records, if they have enduring value, must become familiar with the nature of electronic records and the possibilities for automated control of records. In this, nonbusiness archivists have much to learn from their colleagues in corporate settings.

The technology of modern life may be daunting to some, but more familiar will be another of the concerns of all archivists: the importance of defining and serving a range of clienteles or "publics." Archivists know that theirs is essentially a service profession, that they do everything they do to preserve valuable information so that it will be useful to someone—or, more precisely, to a long list of someones. The identification, appraisal, arrangement, description, and preservation of records are important tasks not in themselves, but only insofar as they allow others to draw on that information to answer questions large and small, personal and collective, practical and cultural. In the past some archives defined their user clientele narrowly, concentrating their energies on the allegedly "serious" scholar, as if archives were bothered by too many unserious people crowding their facilities. At the same time, many archives adopted a fundamentally passive stance toward their users: the archives held valuable collections, and if anyone wanted to use those collections they had to find out about them and come in of their own accord. Today, thankfully, both of these attitudes have begun to change. Most archives now recognize that if they had to wait for the visits of those serious scholars (usually thought of as academic researchers, especially in history) they would be very quiet and lonely places indeed. Many archives have also begun to embrace the responsibility to spread an awareness of what materials they hold and how they can be used. Through the implementation of active programs of outreach, some of them designed for very nontraditional groups of archival users, today's archives are redefining their clientele in a healthy, more open and democratic direction.

Business archives are participating in this reexamination of archival services and the consequent redirection of professional effort. Those who perform their archival responsibilities from inside a corporate setting must of course be primarily concerned with serving the needs of the parent body, its officers and personnel. As a result, their approach to the traditional archival tasks must keep those demands uppermost in view. In their programs of arrangement and description, for example, they must strive to achieve intellectual and physical control over their holdings both rapidly and effectively. Producing finding aids that are works of archival art is less important than gaining control over large amounts of documentation rapidly. Providing complete information to company officers when they need it is the primary goal: in such immediate circumstances, it is little exaggeration to say that those company officers are the archives' only clientele. With the passage of time, however, as many records lose their pressing administrative applicability, they may also be made available to users from outside the company. These may be students or scholars investigating the role of the company in its community or in the industry of which it is a part. Such users help place the company in a larger context and, in many cases, spread the firm's name and reputation. Access to certain records by these outside researchers may understandably be restricted, but users and archivists alike have found ways of cooperating with one another to mutual benefit.

Archivists who collect business records into repositories outside the company must also work to meet the needs of their users. They must balance the interests of the companies whose records they acquire—legitimate interests in privacy, trade secrets, and confidential data—with those of the researchers who depend on the archives to preserve information of wider significance. These archivists face the additional burden of standing in between the company and researchers when the interests of those two groups come into conflict. Researchers, for example, may seek access to information sooner than company officials would like. While archivists in collecting repositories cannot really be the "broker" in such cases, fully representing the interests of one group to the other, the archivists do in some senses stand in the middle, and they must therefore define their role carefully. Spelling out clearly the terms under which access to a company's records will be accorded is critical, and this helps the archives serve both its traditional clients and newer ones. In the same way, repositories must think of new ways to broaden their user base to ensure better understanding of American business and the other phenomena they seek to document.

All archivists face these same issues. Those who document an institution from the inside—whether the institution is a business firm, a university, a hospital, a museum, a religious organization, a state government, or any other kind of corporate body—must take as their first concern service to that institution. University archivists do not preserve the architectural drawings of the buildings on campus because those buildings are examples of certain architectural styles—though they may be. Rather, the archivists preserve those records because they are of immediate practical benefit to the university when a roof leaks or when repairs are underway. A museum archivist does not provide access to administrative and curatorial records because the history of the museum's collecting policies may be a subject of study for an art historian—though the records may be precisely that. Rather, the archivist organizes those records because they are crucial in establishing the museum's legal rights and responsibilities and in decision making about future policies. The religious archives does not preserve the records of the orphanages and social welfare agencies run by its denomination because those records are important to future genealogists—though the records are surely that. Rather, the archives preserves those records because of the legal significance they have both to the institution and to the individuals involved. In all such cases, serving the primary clientele of the archives in no way precludes serving a wider clientele too.

In the same way, archivists who collect the records of such institutions in outside repositories balance the interests of many different kinds of researchers. The respository that collects architectural records must accommodate the possibility that these records will be used in ways the archives might think of as "nontraditional." The researcher who comes to the archives for help may be not the academic scholar who uses them under the controlled conditions of the research room, but the engineer or contractor who takes them to the building site to oversee emergency repairs. The archives that collects administrative and legal records from a museum or other institution may face the prospect of a court subpoena when the matters discussed in the records become the object of litigation. Religious archivists who hold adoption records from church-related institutions may find themselves on the front lines of enforcing rules governing privacy that have been established by law—even when the archivists themselves may personally disagree with the substance of those laws. In all cases, the archives must be deliberate in identifying its many clienteles and in serving their needs as fully as possible. Because business archivists—whether in corporate settings or in collecting repositories—face these issues every day, their experience has much to tell other archivists, regardless of administrative setting.

Successfully balancing these interests points, finally, to the importance archivists should place on building alliances of all kinds. In the past, too many archives thought that they had to "do it all" on their own. In institutional settings, the archivists too often thought that they were isolated, bravely carrying on the fight for the preservation of records with less than completely adequate support. As a consequence, they often sought the patronage of a particular company officer who would promote the archives' services and programs. This was fine while it lasted, but support for the archives, if too narrowly defined, could disappear amid reorganizations, mergers, and downsizing. At the same time, archivists in outside repositories thought that their base of support was well defined but confiningly scholarly—important and interesting in an intellectual sense but generally lacking the clout (not to say the cash) to be of much help when times were hard. Even worse, archivists in collecting repositories too often fell into competition with one another, wasting energy and resources on attempts to acquire certain collections before their professional colleagues in other repositories could get them. At the same time, archivists working within company structures occasionally looked on archivists in outside repositories as scavengers who would "steal" collections from their "rightful" home within the company. All such attitudes, developed in isolation, are a waste of professional energy.

Given the complexity of modern business and the records it produces, archivists are better served by sustained efforts to build alliances across the board, with one another and with those who have different perspectives on the records of American business. Support for archival endeavors has been traditionally uncertain and generally inadequate: we do not have the resources to squander on professional competition of any kind. Instead, united efforts to spread awareness of the importance of archival work to company personnel are needed. Cultivating the support of the company's personnel, of the research community broadly defined, and of other archives and records professionals is an essential task. Only if alliance building comes to be seen as part of the core of archival services—equal in importance to appraisal, arrangement, description, preservation activities, and all the other familiar archival tasks—will archivists be able to meet the multifarious challenges of modern records. There is a consensus in many quarters that, driven significantly (thought not exclusively) by changes in recordkeeping technology, the nature of information in modern society is undergoing a transition similar to the earlier transitions from orality to literacy and from purely manuscript literacy to print. If that is indeed the case, archivists will have to work closely with one another and with related professionals. Otherwise, the work of archivists will become obsolete and irrelevant—not completely unnecessary, perhaps, but surely not worth much investment of resources.

In this important area as in the others, archivists in a range of settings have much to learn from their colleagues who work with business records. Business archivists who have maintained programs within companies have important experience they can share on how to nest a concern for company records within a parent body that may or may not have been predisposed to do so. Case studies of successful archival programs in business can teach much to those who are trying to encourage archival awareness and activity in other institutions (cultural, educational, religious, social) where concern for records as such may seem secondary. Case studies of collecting repositories that have achieved solid and trusted connections with the businesses whose records they preserve can offer both encouragement and practical strategies to repositories seeking these connections with other kinds of institutions. Those who have built broad alliances—involving company officers, researchers, and other interested parties—to preserve business records can show the way to those seeking to form similar alliances in other settings. The presence of the profit motive in business, while surely important, hardly makes the archival lessons learned in that setting irrelevant to other archivists. In fact, it may be taken as encouragement. If business archivists can build support for their programs even in a world in which, because of the ever-present bottom line, archives seem a "hard sell," how much more easily will other institutions, for whom the profit motive is less critical, be able to build their own programs?

The professional world in which archivists live is often thought of as a highly compartmentalized one, and this is normal enough. All professions establish their identity by defining who is a member of the profession and who is not; for this reason, some emphasis on the distinctions within the archival community is inevitable and even healthy. Too great a concentration on difference, however, leads to an unfortunate tendency to build walls between professional subspecialties and to think that the experience of one particular group has nothing to say to that of another. The essays presented in this volume are an effort to carry on a conversation that explores the more important common ground. What, we may wonder, can an archivist caring for business records say to an archivist caring for other kinds of records? The answer may be everything.

Introduction

Business and American Culture: The Archival Challenge

Francis X. Blouin, Jr.

"The chief business of the American people is business" stated Calvin Coolidge. Though this quote is often cited in a variety of ways to support a variety of perceptions about the nature of American culture, I think the observation is worth noting again as a preface to the important collection of articles that follow in this volume. For the entire history of this country the institutions of business enterprise have formed the basic infrastructure through which goods and services have been distributed. In more recent decades, however, it seems that business enterprise has exerted a broader set of influences in the areas of culture, values and social organization.

Yet despite the enormous impact of these institutions in American life, comparatively little is known about them. This is partly due to trends in academic history that should have an interest in issues of this kind but that have not focused on business institutions. It is also partly due to the fact that when compared to other institutions (political, religious, educational, etc.) there is very little documentation with which to work.

The essays in this book address issues of documentation from a variety of perspectives and are thus enormously important if we are going to have any success in assembling more information on the nature of business enterprise in this country. In this introduction I want to explore first what exactly we mean by *business*. It is a term that permeates all of the articles, but it is not necessarily defined in the same way. I then want to introduce the articles grouped around several

key issues and conclude by drawing some broader implications from
the articles as a whole.

As a word, *business* has come to mean many things. Many of the
articles focus on business as for-profit institutions that are organized
to produce and/or distribute goods and services. While this definition
is valid and for the most part classic, I think using it for archival
purposes poses the danger of relegating these institutions to marginal
status when held up against political institutions that seem so fundamental to American life. I would argue that business enterprise in the
latter half of the twentieth century has emerged as much more central
to our understanding of the conduct of our individual and collective
lives over time. If that argument is accepted, then knowledge of the
issues explored in this volume becomes fundamental to our ability as
a people to come to a full historical understanding of our national
heritage. Thus, the need to document these business institutions, despite the enormous obstacles, becomes more compelling.

The origins of business enterprise are rooted in the critical social
requirements for a system of institutions to facilitate the distribution
of goods and services. When these institutions were small, then the
capacity of business to affect this distribution of those goods was se-
verely limited. However with the consolidations of the late nineteenth
century based on new concepts of mass production and distribution,
product domination in specific economic areas became more common.
With the development of advertising, the source of demand shifted
from individual taste to what emerged as a combination of individual
interests and the strength of the advertised message. Business enterprise could shape its market.

It is in its capacity to understand and shape its market that business
enterprise has become more of a defining presence in American life.
Over time the process of advertising became a well-honed science. The
delivery of the message was often based on considerable research and
analysis of taste, attitudes, and inclinations. As a result the message
became more powerful, the process of influence stronger. The capacity
of visual media to deliver the message in a crisper and sharper format
compounded the ability to get the message out. Shapes and images that
defined notions of a preindustrial culture increasingly shared space with
the industrial arts. New icons arose that provided a sense of time and
place. Values, too, were increasingly shaped by the powerful messages
designed to shape and reflect consumer attitudes.

If the medium was not entirely the message, the power of the
media came to be recognized to the point that the media industry itself,
largely through delivery by aural and visual means, could construct
images of enormous influence and distribute those images to the population as a whole through TV, radio, and cinema in a matter of days.

The media industry in particular moved beyond a narrow business role as a purveyor of goods and services to become a more pervasive institution defining culture and values.

Business enterprise has also had enormous impact on social organization and perceptions. For the consumer, the ownership of products had come to define a way of life and position in society. Moreover, for the worker, position in a corporate organization's structure frequently defined position in society as a whole. As corporate models of organization were increasingly applied to institutions that fell outside the more traditional definition of business such as those devoted to education and culture, then these organizational-based notions of social position became increasingly pervasive.

With innovation in transportation and communication, business enterprise has moved beyond a national context. The global links put some business enterprise beyond the reach of particular nation states. If we have a global community at all, it is one that is defined as much by the infrastructure of business enterprise as any other factor. Business enterprise now not only moves goods and services, but also promotes images and products that homogenize values and perceptions.

I do not mean this to take on the aura of a coordinated and directed movement because it all evolves within a system of fierce competition where some institutions rise and others fall, sometimes with great speed. Rather, I want to identify trends that go beyond the fate of individual entrepreneurs and corporate organizations. This is all to underscore the importance of the study of business, the importance of assembling the historical records of these institutions, particularly those that are in a position to have influence on these larger trends.

When a reader finds the word *business* in the articles that follow, the reader should consider both broad and narrow definitions of the term as it relates to contemporary society. In the broad sense of the term, business is an institution that defines culture and values. In the narrow sense it is a set of organizations that have structure and purpose focused on the delivery of goods and services. The articles that follow present a host of challenges among the most vexing in the archival profession. Many repositories have chosen to collect historical records in other areas rather than to face the difficulties inherent in these challenges. Even repositories for inactive records within business institutions struggle to define the role and function of archives. The challenges presented in these papers fall into three main areas: appraisal, use, and technical considerations. These are fundamental issues.

The process of the archival appraisal of any kind of modern record is extremely complex. The articles on appraisal in this volume present a variety of approaches and perspectives. Because business records are private, the challenge to archivists to assemble a credible record of business institutions is particularly difficult. The strategies identified here seem to depend upon how the author perceives what indeed a business is. Christopher Baer focuses on the particular with an emphasis on the individual firm. Bruce Bruemmer focuses on the functions of firms in an attempt to identify certain broader principles that transcend particular firm behavior. Timothy Ericson, while drawing on functional analysis, argues for selection of material beyond the corporation itself. By articulating this strategy he sees the firm as but a part of a larger economic system. Mark Greene and Todd Daniels-Howell essentially agree with all these definitions and try to weave a very pragmatic course of action through the mound of documentation that can result. How archivists appraise records often depends on a vision of the final product. This is in response to questions such as What does this collection tell us? What is the important material in this collection? What can this material be used for? In coming to grips with these varied appraisal issues, the reader must choose a particular framework for consideration of what constitutes business.

From a somewhat narrow institutional perspective, Baer looks at business in terms of four points he considers crucial: strategy, structure, detail, and function. This is in essence a view of documentation from within the firm. He discusses each of these concepts in terms of appraisal, and in doing so he provides a framework for understanding institutional behavior.

In working through the records of a firm, he looks for evidence of corporate strategic thinking and subsequent implementation of particular ideas. Strategies may be focused on reduction of risk, or may be concerned principally with short-term profit in anticipation of a report to stockholders. In any case, understanding corporate strategy is key to understanding the history of firm behavior and the records generated in that process.

Baer also emphasizes the importance of understanding the structure of the firm. For some firms this is a simple matter. For others, usually the most influential, these structures are complex, hierarchical, and bureaucratic. He notes that in complex organizations, natural persons give way to artificial ones. Therefore the corporate record provides one perspective while managerial records can provide quite another.

He does not limit his analysis to broad issues of corporate organization. He recommends searching for evidence of detail, a concept he borrows from Schellenberg's notion of informational value. For Baer, detail is about product detail or detail on individuals. This is the sort of information that is useful to the corporation itself. He concludes that detail is what converts modern business archives into an information resource. This can have an impact on the definition of a corporate archives program. This point anticipates a division that will be sharper in subsequent articles in this volume.

The application of functional analysis to the process of appraisal is a theme that reoccurs in this volume. Baer, with his very intimate knowledge of the workings of several firms, is able to offer a matrix that is particularly useful and is consistent with his firm-oriented discussions of strategy and structure. Where strategy and structure seem to focus on the essential function of an enterprise, functional analysis emphasizes the breadth of activities.

There is a general point in the Baer article that is useful to keep in mind when reading others in this volume. He notes that modern business culture is not terribly devoted to the past. Rather, modern management is focused more on the future, on the need to reinvent, to move with the times. As a result, business does not see value in emphasizing past glories or achievements—though as Philip Mooney shows the past can be useful in marketing. Any archival activity within the firm usually arises from a concern over records management and legal compliance rather than any corporate conception of historical importance and impact.

Bruce Bruemmer and Timothy Ericson take a broader view of the universe of documentation that constitutes the archives of American business. Bruemmer draws from the important work of Helen Samuels in emphasizing functional analysis and documentation strategies. As he notes, functional analysis for corporations can be a tricky business. The profit motive is a powerful determinant in identifying what are core functions. How a corporation perceives its own functions may be simply a matter of the bottom line. The healthier the corporation, perhaps, the broader the view of function. Therefore, internal and external perceptions of function need to be defined so as to be clear on the exact nature of any documentation plan that results. This gets to the essence of my initial question—what exactly is a business within the context of modern American life? Who then determines what the real functions of a business are?

Timothy Ericson also takes a broader view of the business enterprise. He has defined several issues relating to the process of finding documentation. His solution is creative and important. He suggests searching for documentation external to the firm. I find this particularly intriguing since archivists are now in the digital age. Given the difficulty in assembling the inactive records of corporations for archival purposes, why not search data bases and other sources to bring together archival information on these firms or associations? The challenge then seems to be to assemble information from the archival and the public record. While this approach needs to be further developed, it does address a concern that while business creates an enormous amount of documentation, the extent to which that documentation contains substantive information and or summary information may be a problem. Other good summary information can be found in sources outside the firm. The challenge is then to access this information and to bring it together in some coherent package. Some combination of internal documentation and information generated externally can be a better source for understanding the impact of the work of a firm on society and culture.

Mark Greene and Todd Daniels-Howell offer a more pragmatic approach in their "Minnesota Method." They are interested in determining the extent of the records universe as a context for more strategic decisions on the selection and retention of material. Like Bruemmer they are mindful of the practical realities in the process of assembling archival collections relating to American business. They select among companies and then select within the documentation of those companies. The system is a process of determining levels of documentation and then refining priorities regarding what needs to be done.

Their approach to appraisal differs in particular from that of Baer. Where he emphasizes a particular firm, the Minnesota model uses whole industries as a point of departure. This is of course an approach that will only work within the context of a huge research repository for historical records.

Greene and Daniels-Howell do not emphasize the broader political or social impact of the activities of particular firms or industries. But they are clearly conscious that the universe of documentation relevant to understanding the role of business is vast. They propose a very systematic approach to selecting what may be ultimately of most use.

Appraisal is an issue of critical importance. Given the complexities outlined by Baer and Bruemmer, Ericson and Greene and Daniels-Howell are quite right to emphasize the importance of the total universe of documentation in the selection of business records of long-term value. Given the various conceptual and institutional orientations of the various authors it seems appraisal is less an exact process in this context and far more dependent on the nature of the institution collecting the records and the orientation (i.e. preconception of what in fact business is) of the individuals doing the appraisal.

The ultimate purpose of appraisal is to foster the use of business records. Anticipation of use of materials is another way to get at the central question here—what is business and why is it important? Several of the articles focus on the use of records and follow very different lines of thought.

As evidence of use, Michael Nash provides a broad survey of the best of business history written over the past 70 years. He quite rightly points out that there has been important scholarship in this field and that this scholarship has been based on business archives. He cites the early business biographies that sought to ennoble institutions of enterprise after decades of attack. He also cites the broader studies that set particular business firms in a larger context or conceptual framework. Many of these have focused on the role of business in American life. Some explored the social and cultural consequences of corporate growth. Others centered on the growth of the firm as a managerial and structured enterprise. In any case these latter studies used a variety of sources and went beyond a concern with a single firm. The emphasis was on the bigger questions of impact, role, and function.

While interest in the history of business and enterprise has never been central to the concerns of academic historians, Nash notes that studies have appeared recently on social structures within firms and on the role of regulation in the history of particular industries. However, it is particularly interesting to note how little serious historical attention has been given to an institution in American life of such importance and influence.

Nash's point is that there has been a broad interest in the history of business institutions. The argument in his paper that is less explicit is that these broader studies rest on the availability of collections that have been shaped to serve scholars with these interests. The language of the Nash article is quite in contrast to that of Philip Mooney who presents points of equal value and importance that lead to a very different set of conclusions. Mooney argues for the importance of archives to the corporations themselves. He stresses several myths that seem to prevail about why, or even whether, archives can succeed in the corporate environment. Mooney reminds readers that indeed the business of business is business. There is a set of expectations within a profit-driven firm that forms the basis for evaluation of corporate services. Who uses the archives is then an internal administrative issue within the firm. One can conclude from his article that corporate archives can perform a function and should be able to survive, if they are able to meet certain kinds of corporate expectations. Archives can indeed result from this kind of approach. However, one needs to recognize that in terms of orientation, focus of service, nature of collection, and overall mission, the archives Mooney describes are very different than those implied by Nash. This perspective is reinforced in the article by Marcy Goldstein. She is even more explicit about the particular corporate functions that can and should be informed by carefully identified archival material.

This difference, implicit in Nash and explicit in Mooney, seems to reveal a tension in the business archives community. This is addressed squarely by Karen Benedict in her article, which goes beyond the subject of use. However, her article is important, I think, to recall in this context. The issue for Benedict is that of placement of a corporate archives. Who can do it best? Where should they be? Obviously some archives are found within firms, others are found in research repositories. Because I argue that business is a very broad concept that is relatively unstudied, I would stress that the documentation of such a complex set of institutions cannot follow any prescribed conceptual or structural model. Persuaded by both the Nash and Mooney arguments, I can only conclude that business archives, if they are to flourish at all, will do so under a variety of conceptual and administrative frameworks, which because of practical concerns will need to limit the possibilities for documentation. The broad array of use that has been identified for corporate archival records would suggest that our general understanding of American business will rest on a pluralistic approach to collecting over a variety of institutions. It seems only through this approach that the needs of a clearly diverse group of user constituencies can be met.

Appraisal and use are at the core of the archival challenges inherent in business records. However, other authors in this volume point to specific challenges arising from the nature of archives in our own time. These issues all revolve around the problems and possibilities of new technologies. Richard Cox points to the problems of electronic records, James Fogerty extols the possibilities of oral history, and Ernest Dick explores issues relating to visual media.

Richard Cox peers into the future anticipating the inevitability of corporate organizations that will rely increasingly on communication in digital form. He rightly points out that this will have a huge impact on our traditional notion of corporate strategy, structure, function, and processes. He argues that the paper trail of particular decisions and actions has not generally been terribly revealing of intention and motive. Cox suggests that digital communications may result in more complete documentation if the archivist knows where to find it. This raises the basic question (often stated in legal terms) of how interested corporations themselves are in any notion of completeness of the record. Without doubt new technologies and new applications of technologies will require a reexamination of the processes of documentation in large organizations. Marcy Goldstein extends this perspective to the center of the operations of business themselves. She urges that the business archivist move from a more traditional custodial role to take on the role of an information manager. The possibilities for archivists to assume this function are clearly enhanced by new technologies. However, she does not see this as a convenience of technology. Rather, she emphasizes knowledge management as an operational mindset within a corporate archives. She pushes beyond the traditional notions of appraisal and assembly of documentation to urge consideration of what she calls the "documentary probe." The focus of such a probe yields useful sets of information somewhat independent of traditional concepts of organization by provenance.

James Fogerty and Ernest Dick provide important perspectives on documentation not usually associated with a traditional view of corporate archives. Oral histories gathered after the fact can be of critical importance in filling gaps in the record or the story. Fogerty's notion of aggressive use of oral history is interesting and can combine with Ericson's notion of gathering documentation beyond the bounds of internal recordkeeping processes. Fogerty offers a very challenging view of oral history that goes beyond the concept of a casual reminiscence. Ernest Dick aptly points to sound and visual records as sources of information in areas where the records are either lost or too voluminous. The notion of a film on manufacturing process can substitute for a variety of transactional records. This is a concept that needs further study.

John Fleckner looks at business history in its very broadest sense. He notes that the process of consumption of the goods and services generated by business enterprise produces not only documents of importance but also artifacts and images. Writing from the perspective of a museum, he notes that the surviving artifacts and historical images have encouraged a popular curiosity about the products and the processes of manufacture and distribution. From the museum perspective, he argues for the importance of these artifacts as a point of departure for popular appreciation of this dimension of our history and culture.

The issues raised in the articles that follow provide important and well-conceived perspectives on the challenges facing those who have responsibilities for the administration of the archives of American business enterprise, broadly conceived. The challenges can at times seem overwhelming. However, it is only by recognizing the enormous importance of business enterprise in American life and culture that the scope of the challenge seems worth the energies involved. The articles that follow collectively form a framework to assist those who rise to this very important challenge.

1

Business History and Archival Practice: Shifts in Sources and Paradigms

Michael Nash

There has always been a complex relationship between historical scholarship and the keeping of archival records. This has been particularly true in the areas of business history and business archives—disciplines that emerged together during the 1920s and 1930s, and have continued to have a symbiotic relationship. Business history—the history of the firm, industrial sector, or the American business system—has always been dependent on the availability of firm and trade association records. Before these kinds of primary sources were accessible, scholars interested in economic questions had to use aggregate economic data which, for the most part, was only available through government documents or other public sources. Using materials of this kind, they were able to write about macroeconomic issues such as the behavior of competitive markets, price movements, trends in national income, consumer expenditures, capital investment, and labor market participation. This is what came to be called economic history. However, without company records, historians could not explore microeconomic questions, nor could they reconstruct the central role that the firm, its entrepreneurs, and managers have played in American economic life.

The relationship between business archives and business history has been a reciprocal one. Business historians need firm level records in order to understand the business decision-making process. Archival collecting has in turn always been strongly influenced by the types of questions historians ask. For example, after the publication of Alfred Chandler, Jr.'s prizewinning and tremendously influential books *Strategy and Structure* (1962) and the *Visible Hand* (1977) archivists began to acquire records documenting the modern, bureaucratically organized, decentralized corporation. Collecting tended to focus on the papers of top management. During the past decade, as business history moved away from this structural and functional approach and has begun to focus on the impact that culture, politics, and society have had on the American business system, archivists have modified their collecting policies in order to document the impact of these external factors on the firm.

The Business Historical Society

As a discipline, the origins of modern business history can be traced to the founding of the Business Historical Society (BHS) at the Harvard Business School in 1925. Its organizers were economic historians, librarians, and historically minded business people who aimed to change the focus of economic history. Instead of studying macroeconomic questions: market behavior, government finance, the impact of the tariff, economic growth, and the distribution of wealth, the founders of the BHS were interested in the history of the firm and entrepreneur. As part of its mission the BHS sought to preserve and make business records available to scholars. The society had the support of many prominent business people of the day who believed that industrialists were being unfairly portrayed in the scholarly and popular literature. The Gilded Age and the Progressive Era had seen the publication of such muckraking classics as Henry Demerest Lloyd's *Wealth Against Commonwealth* (1894), Upton Sinclair's *The Jungle* (1906), and Ida Tarbell's *History of the Standard Oil Company* (1904). It was assumed that a scholarly approach to business history, based on archival research in business records, would serve as a counterbalance to this literature.

Under the leadership of William Brett Donham, dean of the Harvard Business School and Norman Scott Brien Gras, who became the first Strauss Professor of Business History, the society embarked on a systematic search for business records. The George F. Baker Library at Harvard University (named for the president of the First National Bank of New York and a founding member of the Business Historical Society) was designated as the repository for the collections that the society anticipated acquiring. Other founding members included:

E. H. Gary (United States Steel Corporation), Charles Francis Adams (Union Pacific Railroad), Charles Schwab (Bethlehem Steel), Herbert N. Straus (R. H. Macy & Company), Arthur Lehman (Lehman Brothers), Charles Belden (director, Boston Public Library), Arthur H. Cole (assistant professor of economic history, Harvard University), Herbert Hoover (secretary of commerce), and Clarence Brigham (American Antiquarian Society).

From the beginning the founders of the society saw that there was a reciprocal relationship between the writing of business history and the collecting of business records. This was made clear in its statement of purpose:

> The primary purpose of The Business Historical Society, Inc. is to encourage and aid the study of the evolution of business in all periods and in all countries. Further to formulate the results of such investigations and studies and publish them in such form as to make them of service to the business community, necessitates adequate tools for such investigation. This means the collection of all possible original records, data, etc. having to do with the beginning and progress of American business and depositing this material at some center accessible to all.[1]

The society thus had a dual purpose, to preserve business records and promote the writing and understanding of business history. Most of the scholarship sponsored by the Business Historical Society was conservative and probusiness in orientation. This brought business historians into intellectual conflict with the progressive synthesis that dominated the historiography of the interwar years. This clash of interpretations may have contributed to the widening of the gulf between business and economic historians. The ideological divide deepened after the classical synthesis began to break down and scholars like Thorstein Veblen, Richard Ely, and John Commons began to gain influence within the field of economic history. These progressive economists and sociologists were interested in asking questions about class, income distribution, the role of the state, protective legislation, and labor relations; issues that the members of the BHS sought to ignore.

Norman Scott Brien Gras played a critical role in defining business history as a discipline distinct from economic history. An English economic historian by training, Gras was a charismatic figure and soon attracted a small group of students to the Harvard Business School. For Gras, business history was the study of the firm and the entrepreneur, while economic history was the study of public economic policy and collective economic behavior. Under Gras' leadership, the Business Historical Society became a professional association and its *Bulletin* was transformed into a journal rather than a newsletter and catalog of archival acquisitions. During the depression of the 1930s, when it was extremely difficult to secure academic employment, Gras' students were often hired to write business histories that corporations used for public relations purposes. This access to the business community facilitated archival collecting.

While the Baker Library claimed to have aspirations to collect nationally, it tended to focus on New England. The first sizeable collection that it acquired was several hundred volumes relating to the Rhode Island entrepreneur, Samuel Slater, who is widely recognized as the founder of the New England cotton textile industry. By 1932 it had acquired more than 500 collections including the papers of John Hancock, George Henry Corliss (whose steam engine symbolized the Philadelphia centennial exhibition of 1876), records of the Middlesex Canal Company, and the Boston and Albany and Boston and Worcester Railroads.

During these years, the New England textile industry was a major focus of the early Baker Library collection, and its history became the central narrative for business historians. The story revolved around the rise of the textile industry in Lowell and Lawrence, Massachusetts, and the transformation of these factories into modern mass production facilities. Studies of the production systems of the great New England firms described the triumph of the joint stock company, the factory system, and the bulk, staple system of manufacturing. As Thomas Cochran has observed in *Frontiers of Change*, this model began to break down in the late 1950s and early 1960s when the Hagley Museum and Library in Wilmington, Delaware, began to collect records from Mid-Atlantic firms. Once these records were made available, scholars started to raise questions about the New England model as they discovered vital centers of manufacturing in New York, Pennsylvania, and Maryland. This demonstrated that the Lowell joint stock company was not the only path to economic development.[2]

At the Harvard Business School during the early and middle decades of the century, business history proceeded in the Gras tradition. The primary aim of business history was seen as being the study of "the processes by which individual business enterprises adjusted to internal and external forces impinging on top management."[3] According to Gras, the major areas business historians needed to explore were (1) the form of organization imposed on the firm by public law (proprietorship, partnership, or corporation); (2) the relationship between ownership and managerial control; (3) internal organization or managerial structure; (4) administration and business decision making which he identified as taking place at the top of the organization chart; and (5) line functions such as production, finance, and sales.[4]

Gras believed that business historians should begin by studying "individual firms or companies—the elemental cell in business organization." The history of an industry was also a legitimate subject of study. However, he asserted industry studies needed to wait. Since he did not approve of using macroeconomic sources such as census and custom house records to draw generalizations about industrial sectors, Gras believed that it would take at least 25 years before business historians could begin to think about synthesis. It would take that long to build a sufficient monographic literature.[5]

Gras gave considerable thought to the problem of business history sources. He recommended that archivists begin by trying to locate annual reports that included financial statements and descriptions of plant, equipment, and organizational structure. Then he suggested searching for accounting records documenting individual transactions, which, according to Gras, were "the details concerning the business that [was] actually done." After that, historians were encouraged to examine the minutes of board of directors and executive committee meetings and correspondence of executive officers with particular emphasis on the corporate secretary and treasurer. Gras thought that company magazines and labor union records might be worth looking at, but he observed that "in general, such records commonly fall short of expectations." Finally, trade catalogs, newspapers, and records describing hearings before congressional committees were "useful sources."[6]

The Harvard Studies in Business History

The Harvard Studies in Business History, a series that was launched in 1931 with the publication of Kenneth Porter's biography of John Jacob Astor, followed by Henrietta Larson's biography of Jay Cooke (1936), and N. S. B. Gras' *The Massachusetts First National Bank of Boston, 1784–1934* (1937), was an effort to put the Gras methodology into practice. These monographs and the 39 others that followed were, for the most part, biographies of entrepreneurs or administrative histories of individual companies. They were all based on a close reading of business records, usually the minutes of board of the directors and executive committee meetings, correspondence of top management, and financial records.[7] The authors had access to internal corporate documents and received financial support from the company which had the right to review the manuscript before publication. Funding for this work was handled through the Business History Foundation, a nonprofit foundation incorporated in New York City but administered by the Harvard Business School. Occasionally, when it was believed that a particular book might appeal to an audience beyond the academy, the Business History Foundation sought to publish it through a commercial house.

The best of these Harvard studies were Ralph Hower's histories of the advertising agency N. W. Ayer (1939) and the New York department store, R. H. Macy's (1946), and Ralph and Muriel Hidy's history of the Standard Oil Company of New Jersey (1955).[8] The focus of these works was the firm, its internal operations, administrative policies, and managerial methods. They analyzed the policies of major company executives, trying to understand the transition from a personal style of management to a more institutionalized system of administration and the corresponding tendency to separate ownership from management. There was very little attention paid to labor, technology, or the relationship between the firm and the larger culture and society. This was business history as seen from the perspective of top management. Even in the cases of Macy's and Ayer's, there was no effort made to study the relationship between the firms and their customers or to evaluate the impact of sales and advertising strategies on consumers or society. In fact, in his introductory essay to the Macy's history, N. S. B. Gras explicitly stated that Hower did not intend to study the impact of advertising and changing style on the retail industry. He claimed that these questions could never be studied scientifically and, therefore, historians needed to concentrate on administrative policy and managerial procedures. Hidy and Hower, however, did try to situate their firm studies in the context of the development of industrial capitalism. Their work represented a conscious effort to refute the robber baron thesis and rehabilitate the reputation of leading business executives. Business historians, however, were unable to make a significant dent in the dominant historical paradigms of the progressive synthesis. Part of the reason for this failure was their lack of interest in situating business history within a larger context in such a way as to address the dominant historiographical discourse that was concerned with the impact of economic inequality and class relations on American politics.

This approach to business history was reflected in the appraisal policy of the Baker Library. When looking at the inventories of the collections acquired during these early years, one is struck by the fact that nearly all the materials described are either papers of top management or financial records. This top down approach to appraisal left little room for acquiring informational records, or even departmental level records describing functions such as advertising, public relations, political lobbying, or personnel.

Despite Gras' efforts to build bridges to the American Historical and American Economic History Associations, business historians continued to operate on the margins of academic life. This was partially due to the fact that most of them had appointments in business schools rather than in history departments, and historians were suspicious that business sponsorship tended to influence the way business history was written. While Gras and his associates maintained that the writing of company history was the foundation for a general history of the American business system, this general history was never written and the individual company histories never included the kind of synthetic analysis or attempt at generalization that would make them appealing to anyone but the specialist, or the business school professor looking for a case study. The few mainstream scholars who were aware of this literature concluded that it had very little relevance to their work.

As early as the 1930s, some business historians, notably Arthur H. Cole, head of the Baker Library, were expressing dissatisfaction with the way business history was being practiced. Cole concluded that the Gras approach "had the rather significant defect of leading nowhere." "The studies did not add up."[9] These monographs did not appear to be pointing toward synthesis or larger macroeconomic conclusions. As the Great Depression deepened and scholars began to look for explanations in the economic and business history literature, many became disturbed by the lack of conceptual focus that made these studies largely irrelevant insofar as policy makers were concerned.

Committee for Research in Economic History

In 1940, Arthur Cole took the lead in creating the Committee for Research in Economic History (CREH), which sought to bring together business and economic historians who were interested in studying entrepreneurship from both a theoretical and public policy perspective. Cole and his CREH colleagues believed that the entrepreneur was the major agent for economic change and that business historians needed to adopt this as their conceptual framework. After CREH settled on this new research agenda, Cole turned his attention to a search for grant support. From the beginning, the Rockefeller Foundation was the main target of Cole's fund-raising energies. Executive Director Joseph Willets shared Cole's interests and concerns. He believed that if business history could transcend its narrow focus, it could make a contribution to public policy. Cole was encouraged by Willets' support and began making plans to submit a grant proposal. As part of this process, CREH needed to define its research program with some precision. In an October 8, 1940, report, the committee, chaired by Cole, set forth a research agenda. Clearly influenced by the economic crisis of the 1930s, it declared that in addition to the entrepreneur, the research program should focus on the business cycle, foreign trade, and the role played by government in stimulating economic development.[10] Cole and his colleagues realized that such an ambitious research agenda would require a renewed commitment to business archives, with particular emphasis on the modern period, 1890 to 1940. If business historians were going to make their work relevant to public policy, they needed get out of the nineteenth century and begin to transcend the boundaries of the individual firm.

The discussion about research agendas led to debates about archival appraisal strategy. Cole noted that during the "last 50 years there has been some very formidable business records acquired by the Baker Library. However, librarians and custodians [had] no guidance for selections—no rules for evaluating material." According to Cole, the Baker Library was now facing a space crisis. The committee concluded that establishing principles for selection would assure that valuable historical documents would be preserved, while records that were of no use to historians could be destroyed. The CREH membership believed that such an approach to selective retention of business records required cooperation between archivists and business historians. If archival appraisal was to proceed, "good economic historians [had to be] connected with the archives."[11] In the fall of 1941, the committee submitted a $300,000 grant proposal to the Rockefeller Foundation. It was funded and provided a source of money for fellowships that supported a generation of scholars pursuing projects in business or entrepreneurial history.

During these years CREH became actively involved in the effort to preserve business records. Thomas Cochran of the University of Pennsylvania, who had been commissioned to write the history of Pabst Brewing Company, and Shepard Clough, a European economic historian at Columbia University who was writing a history of the Equitable Life Insurance Company, argued that business executives should be urged to maintain their own historical records in usable form. They maintained that this would not only be of great long-run benefit to the company, as it would preserve corporate memory, but would relieve research libraries of this expensive task. In 1943, a small grant was secured from the Social Science Research Council to explore the possibilities and attempt to persuade business people to establish in-house archives. A committee chaired by Thomas Cochran and including Edward P. Farley, chairman of American-Hawaiian Steamship Company, Roy Foulke, vice president of Dun & Bradstreet, and Emmet J. Leahy, director of the United States Naval Records Archives, established a National Records Management Council to do the appraisal work and contract for storage space. The original idea was that once the collections were organized both the corporations and scholars would have access to these research materials. However, while records preservation did improve, many of the companies did not welcome scholarly access and this arrangement soon fell apart.[12]

Despite this setback, by the late 1940s the committee had set up a Research Center in Entrepreneurial History at the Harvard Business School. The aim was to shift the focus of historical inquiry from the individual firm to the larger sociological grouping of people who were identified as businessmen in order to tell the story about the role that the business system played in American life. Cole hoped that this could be done by asking questions about the place of businessmen in society and the role that the "human factor" played in economic development. Through the center he encouraged scholars to investigate issues such as how railroad entrepreneurs, who were among the nation's first salaried managers, differed from wool manufacturers, who, for the most part, were owner-managers; and how family background, education, and early career choices made by entrepreneurs affected their business careers. Defined this way, entrepreneurial history became interdisciplinary, drawing on economics, sociology, and anthropology.[13]

Cole argued that entrepreneurial history should be the sociological study of the "economic functions of entrepreneurship." He also sought to encourage the pursuit of larger questions about the nature of business bureaucracy, profit, business ethics, sources of capital, and the development of rational modes of communication and control. Cole was not interested in a catalog of the particulars, but in reconstructing the general patterns of business development. He hoped to integrate business history with studies of intellectual history, society, and culture. His objective was to develop a comprehensive theory of entrepreneurship that would explain the dynamism of the American business system. His goal was to shift the thinking about entrepreneurship from viewing it as "an individual personal thing" toward conceiving of it as "a characteristic of organized systems of behavior."[14] Scholars needed to investigate the entrepreneur within a social context. Where did they come from? Where did business innovation come from, and how was it diffused throughout the economy? Where did entrepreneurs get their ideas and business concepts?

Cole wanted to celebrate the role of the entrepreneur and integrate the concept of entrepreneurship into economic theory, establishing a kind of middle ground between economics and sociology. The major contribution of the entrepreneurial school was to recognize that business was part of a larger society and it could not be studied in isolation. There needed to be an awareness that there was a relationship between business practices and social and cultural values. However,

this proved to be a slippery concept, as was the whole idea of entrepreneurialism. How was this to be defined? Could its success or failure
be measured? How were historians to assess the success of a firm,
industry, or overall economic system? In the modern era, which has
been characterized by a separation of ownership from management,
how important was the entrepreneur? Should the focus be on the salaried manager and the firm as a bureaucratic system? Thus, despite
the excitement generated by CREH's efforts to redefine business history and generous Rockefeller Foundation funding, the literature of the
1940s and 1950s remained limited in scope and failed to generate
interest outside of the small circle of scholars who defined themselves
as business historians. Even when the ranks of business historians
came to include Allan Nevins and Thomas C. Cochran, the discipline
continued to occupy a very marginal position within the historical profession.

Thomas Cochran's 1953 book, *Railroad Leaders, 1845–1890: The
Business Mind in Action* was one of the most influential studies to
emerge from Cole's center. Cochran's aim was to demonstrate that
understanding the history of business and the "thinking of business
leaders" was one of the keys to the American past. His study was a
systematic analysis of the ideas and attitudes of a homogeneous group
of American businessmen, or a kind of intellectual history of business.
Cochran analyzed the world view, value system, and business philosophy of 60 railroad executives. This was an attempt to understand "the
psychology of the business leader as a social type." In his first chapter
he argued that the reason historians had neglected this important subject was that "leading entrepreneurs seldom left large collections of
letters deposited in libraries for perusal by graduate students." However, the fact that they were relatively inarticulate did not diminish
"the social importance of the thinking of business leaders."[15] Cochran
decided to focus his study on railroad leaders because the Chicago,
Burlington and Quincy and the Illinois Central Railroads had recently
deposited their historical records at the Newberry Library in Chicago.
Since railroads required long distance written communications in order
to operate, it appeared that there would be letters written by the railroad presidents that could provide a window into their thinking on
business issues.

Cochran studied the ideas of the railroad leaders about business
practices, managerial problems, external relations, and general social
issues. He analyzed the correspondence left by the leaders of the big,
well-managed western railroads in order to study the "ethics or spirit
of developing capitalism." He studied the letters exchanged between
the railroad entrepreneurs and top level administrators and described
the interactive social systems that developed between these two

groups. When he was finished he had taken notes on more than 100,000 letters and concluded that he had captured the railroad executive's conception of his social role. Cochran was particularly interested in the growth of managerial power, which he saw as being part of a trend that A. A. Berle and Gardner Means had identified in their classic work on the separation of ownership from management.[16] He realized the limitations imposed by his reliance on the correspondence of top level management, recognizing that this type of source would not reveal the impact of the ideas and activities of the railroad leaders on American society or its various social environments. His book did explore the most important change in the history of business institutions, the transition to big business and "professional entrepreneurship." Cochran discovered that nineteenth-century railroad executives were primarily interested in profit, security, and growth, and as leaders of America's first large-scale business organizations, they developed systems to evaluate performance according to standardized bureaucratic criteria.

As David Sicilia has pointed out, Thomas Cochran studied business as a social and cultural phenomenon.[17] He drew on the discipline of sociology for conceptual ideas about mass group behavior and social norms. Cochran emphasized the relationship between behavior (innovating acts) and environmental factors. For him, entrepreneurial history was a search to identify value systems and character traits that led entrepreneurs to seek innovation, be tough minded, and take risks. Cochran's railroad leaders were conservative, both politically and economically. Their world was largely static and their value system changed little during the nearly half century of his study. Cochran found little evidence that pointed to the impact of external factors (public pressure, government, or labor) on the world of the railroad men. Primarily interested in the impact of culture as opposed to market forces and technology on business behavior, understanding the world view of the railroad leaders was for Cochran a problem in intellectual history. His main sources, cited in more than 90 percent of his footnotes, were the more than 100,000 letters written by 60 top railroad executives.[18] It is possible that if he had consulted the papers of line managers, engineers, and superintendents from the middle levels of the organization chart he may have found more evidence about the ways in which economics, labor, bureaucratic imperatives, and technology shaped railroad operations. These sources were not available, and these were not questions Cochran was interested in.

Structure and Function—The World of Alfred Chandler, Jr.

Alfred DuPont Chandler, Jr., whom many consider to be the father of modern business history, approached his work from a perspective that was very different from that of Thomas Cochran. He believed that modern management and the rise of the decentralized corporation were the keys to the success of the American economic system. As a graduate student, Chandler was a fellow at Harvard's Center for Entrepreneurial History, but he soon began to question the Cole and Cochran framework. Instead of concentrating on the entrepreneur, he believed that business historians needed to study the corporation as an organization. He was particularly interested in the rise of the vertically integrated firm and the impact of organizational change on market performance. Chandler's writings, which included *Strategy and Structure: Chapters in the History of American Enterprise* (1962); *The Visible Hand: The Managerial Revolution in American Business* (1977); and *Scale and Scope: The Dynamics of Industrial Capitalism* (1990), transformed business history as it introduced a theoretical model—the dynamic relationship between corporate strategy and corporate structure—that would prove extremely influential in both the academic and business worlds.[19] His work, which won the Pulitzer and Bancroft Prizes and finally brought business history into the main stream of historical discourse, influenced a generation of scholars in Britain, France, Germany, Japan, and Italy. It also made a significant impact on the disciplines of economics, sociology, and management science as well as history.

Chandler's interest was in the "big question." What were the dynamic factors in the growth of the American economy and its business system during the late nineteenth and early twentieth centuries? His answers were (1) the rise of the railroad, (2) the development of concentrated urban markets for industrial and consumer goods, (3) the emergence of mass production technology, (4) the rise of organized research and development.[20]

Strategy and Structure is an analysis of the business decision-making process. Chandler argued that companies changed their overall direction (strategy) when forced to by competitive pressures. He further argued that strategic changes were only likely to succeed if accompanied by dramatic changes in organizational structure. *Strategy and Structure* had a profound impact on students of business administration. Almost immediately after it appeared, required courses in all the major business schools were built around this concept. Consulting firms such as McKinsey used *Strategy and Structure* to teach clients about the timing of strategic change and the need to adjust organizational structure accordingly. Translated into dozens of languages,

Strategy and Structure found its way onto the shelves of thousands of managers.

In 1971, Chandler and coauthor Stephen Salsbury published a long biography of Pierre du Pont.[21] This book, which was really a long strategy and structure case study, described the building and administration of the modern DuPont and General Motors Corporations.

Chandler then turned his attention to studying the development of the professional salaried manager. In *The Visible Hand*, he argued that managerial decision making had replaced Adam Smith's impersonal marketplace as the principal allocator of economic resources. He showed how modern big business (multiunit enterprises) replaced small traditional firms when administrative coordination permitted greater productivity, lower costs, and higher profits than coordination by market mechanisms. He went on to demonstrate that with the rise of big business, a managerial hierarchy was needed in order to realize the advantages of vertical and horizontal integration. As management professionalized, there was a separation of ownership from control. Chandler believed that when career managers became increasingly technical and professional in their training and orientation, they tended to emphasize long-term growth over short-term profit (an observation that has certainly been questioned in recent years).

Chandler sought to influence the thinking of economists who, he believed, were preoccupied with static equilibrium theory and abstract mathematical models that did little to explain business behavior. He sought to substitute empirical evidence drawn from archival sources, such as business records, for econometric modeling. Alfred Chandler was extraordinarily influential. His work not only helped to define the concept of corporate strategy for business executives but set the agenda for a generation of business historians. In the more than three decades since the publication of *Strategy and Structure*, the Chandlerian model dominated the business history literature as the evolution of the large modern firm, the rise of big business, and the role of the salaried manager became the major themes.

In *Scale and Scope* Chandler proposed a comparative, international model to explain the dynamics of industrial capitalism. In a study of three major western economies (the United States, Great Britain, and Germany), nations that together accounted for two-thirds of the world's industrial output during the years between 1880 and 1945, he used concepts such as economies of scale and scope to explore the history of competitive managerial capitalism. The focus was again on manufacturing firms during the second Industrial Revolution. Chandler argued that effective management optimized the organizational capabilities of the firm as it coordinated the autonomous, self-contained operating units that formed the modern multidivisional corporation. Chandler attributed the decline of British industry to its failure to "develop organizational capabilities necessary to compete in global markets." British firms, which for the most part remained family controlled, did not develop functionally differentiated management organizations. On the whole, they remained smaller and more personally managed than their American and German competitors. Their inability to integrate limited their available capital and ability to modernize technologically.

In Germany and the United States, entrepreneurs made the necessary investments in production facilities and large-scale organization to exploit the economies of scale and scope. In both these countries the founding entrepreneurs shared decision making with senior managers that they recruited, developing the organizational capabilities necessary to expand both at home and internationally.

As Francis Blouin and JoAnne Yates have observed, Chandler's work had significant implications for archival appraisal.[22] It clearly demonstrated that the multidivisional firm was a bureaucracy dependent on written records. Managers gave written directives to those who reported to them, relied on formal policy and procedure manuals, and received information from subordinates in written form. The typical Chandlerian firm generated thousands if not tens of thousands of cubic feet of records: reports to the board of directors, minutes of executive committee meetings, department and divisional reports, records of operating departments, internal and external correspondence from all levels of the organization chart, interoffice memoranda, advertising and public relations records, personnel files, and series upon series of financial records. These records document the operation of the multidivisional firm in exquisite detail as they describe the process of strategic decision making, changes in organizational structure, and all aspects of operations. Since the multidivisional firm, like all modern bureaucracies, generates such huge quantities of records, appraisal is the key to managing corporate archives of this type. The task of the archivist becomes one of separating records of historical value from those that are purely transactional in nature, while keeping in mind JoAnne Yates' call to preserve evidence of the internal communication systems.

For historians studying the internal operations of the firm, the records of the large modern corporation present a wealth of source material. Alfred Chandler and those business historians who have adopted his theoretical framework have themselves made extensive use of these records; between 25 and 35 percent of the footnotes in Chandler's work refer to business records. This figure is far lower than in Thomas Cochran's work as Chandler tended to rely on published sources including company annual reports, contemporary books and articles, newsletters, trade journals, and government documents. Most of his references to business records (between 80 and 90 percent) are to executive officer correspondence, the same kinds of sources used by Thomas Cochran. Chandler also relied on records from other levels of the organization chart. Managerial report files and internal correspondence from both staff and line departments are cited throughout his works. The internal memoranda, through which managers directed the work of their subordinates and reported to their supervisors, provided him with much of his evidence about corporate organization. Like Cochran and most other business historians, Chandler made virtually no use of financial records.[23]

During the past 30 years, while Chandler's strategy and structure model was being widely adopted as part of the business school curriculum, there has been an increasing recognition of the "present value of corporate history," particularly in the strategic planning process and as a repository of corporate culture. However, the citation study that was done in conjunction with this project revealed that students of business administration, organizational behavior, and corporate communications rarely use business records even when dealing with historical subjects that adopt the Chandlerian vocabulary. In the journals that were reviewed for this study there were many references to the work of Alfred Chandler, but virtually all of the citations were to secondary literature, oral history interviews, or personal observations. It appears that, at least as of this writing, only historians have the internal fortitude required to do research in business records.[24]

The History of Technology

Many scholars from the maturing discipline of the history of technology have adopted the Chandlerian framework in an effort to understand the relationship between science, technology, and corporate strategy. Chandler's work pointed historians in this direction as he identified technological change as the major factor that led to the rise of the modern corporation. Technology provided the necessary precondition for mass production and mass marketing since it enabled business leaders to take advantage of the economies of scale and scope.[25]

In recent years, there have been a number of important books that have analyzed the impact of science and technology on the modern corporation. The transition from inventor-entrepreneur to institutionalized industrial research has been explored in Thomas Hughes' 1971 biography of Elmer Sperry (the founder of the Sperry Corporation, one of the leading science-based companies in United States) and Reese Jenkins' 1975 study of Eastman Kodak. David Hounshell and John

Smith's 1988 history of research and development at the DuPont Company, George Wise's study of General Electric, and Leonard Reich's *Making of American Industrial Research: Science and Business at GE and Bell* (1986) describe the role that scientific research played within the modern corporation. These monographs trace the relationship between science and corporate strategy, and the impact of external factors such as competition and antitrust regulation on corporate research and development. Internal issues explored include the balance between pure and applied science; the relationship between scientific and commercial considerations; the ways in which scientists were recruited and trained; protecting proprietary information; publication policy; and the relationship between corporate and university research programs.[26] As one would expect, these studies draw on the records of the industrial research laboratory, but they also rely on executive committee minutes and reports, papers of upper-level management, and departmental records, which describe the role of scientists and engineers within the corporation and the way top management viewed the research laboratory. Histories of particular projects are often documented in special compensation files that describe how the corporation rewarded scientific innovation. In many cases, oral history interviews with managers and research scientists supplement the written record. In the aggregate, between 35 and 57 percent of the citations in these history of technology studies are to business records, with managerial correspondence accounting for more than half of this total. Records of research and development laboratories account for a significant number of citations (approximately 10 percent of the total).[27]

The increasing prominence of the history of science and technology has had a significant impact on archival practice. The 1983 report of the Joint Committee on the Archives of Science and Technology, *Understanding Progress as Process*, and the follow-up study published by the Massachusetts Institute of Technology have sensitized archivists to the importance of scientific records.[28] However, as of this writing there is still no general agreement about appraisal standards particularly in the areas of laboratory notebooks, patent records, and technical reports.

The Breakdown of the Chandlerian Synthesis

In broad outlines the work of Alfred Chandler and of those scholars whom he influenced describes the triumph of the American economic system. It is a story in which modern technology and effective management result in increasing productivity and economic growth. Under Chandler's influence, business history grew increasingly self-

confident and far less isolated from other historical disciplines. However, while the strategy and structure model increased the discipline's
analytical depth, many business historians continued to write and
think about the history of business without considering social, cultural,
political, or even economic context. Reading this literature one would
never suspect that there were workers in any of the Chandlerian firms,
or that the political state had any impact on the firm or the business
system. Beginning in the middle 1970s, the American economic system entered into a long period of decline—a crisis of competitiveness
that depressed living standards for all but the most skilled and well-
educated members of the labor force. It was this decline that led some
scholars to take issue with the Chandlerian synthesis and its apparently Whiggish interpretation of American business and economic history. This reevaluation has been driven by the current debates about
"the crisis of mass production" and the perception that the large American corporation may by the 1980s have become an uncompetitive
industrial dinosaur. During this period some went so far as to argue
that the solution to America's economic problems may lie in a return
to a system of craft or batch production.

In their best-selling book, *The Second Industrial Divide: Possibilities for Prosperity* (1984), economist Michael J. Piore and political
scientist Charles Sabel argued that an economic strategy of "permanent
innovation" based on an ability to respond quickly to changing market
conditions through the flexible use of plant and equipment and the
skills of a highly trained work force, may be the key to American
competitiveness and economic growth.[29] This conceptual framework
led historians to explore the role that small business had played in
American life. Scholars like Philip Scranton and John Ingham have
demonstrated that well into the twentieth century, significant sectors
of the economy continued to be characterized by craft or specialty
production.[30] In industries like clothing, jewelry, and machine tools,
most firms did not adopt assembly line techniques emphasizing
throughput, standardization, and scientific management, but instead
relied on systems that allowed them to manufacture according to customer specification and to adapt quickly to changing market conditions. This system, which Scranton has called flexible specialization,
put a premium on the talents of skilled workers who retained a good
deal of autonomy and control over the production process.

Small Business and Its Records

The types of firms that Philip Scranton and John Ingham studied
are organized and function very differently then the Chandlerian firms.

Small speciality producers tend to have flatter organizational structures, with far fewer supervisors and middle managers. Since there is
only infrequent written communication between various layers of management, there is much less systematic documentation of internal administrative matters. In small businesses, most written communication
is with outside suppliers and customers. Thus, instead of documenting
internal organizational changes, records tend to describe the process
by which the firm responded to customer demand—producing on specification and designing products with a flexibility necessary to succeed
in an ever-changing marketplace.

Specialty producers tended to cluster in industrial districts—machine shops in North Philadelphia, clothing manufacturers in New
York City's garment district, Trenton potters, and Paterson, New Jersey, textile manufacturers. This made it possible to build complex
interfirm networks that yielded external economies and reduced the
risk and costs of product diversity. In these industrial districts, complex contracting relationships linked suppliers to producers of product
intermediates, and finally to manufacturers of the final consumer or
producer good. In many areas, efforts were made to institutionalize
these relationships, and this often resulted in the creation of trade
associations that regulated pricing decisions, quality standards, and
marketing strategies.

Documenting industrial districts and interfirm connections through
the records of these local trade associations is a critical part of any
strategy to document the history of small business. Trade journals and
trade catalogs are also important sources for information about industrial districts, marketing and distribution networks, and local trade
associations. Historians like Scranton and Ingham usually rely on this
type of documentation rather than on firm records, since small businesses usually have few surviving records—typically a handful of volumes of financial records and sales correspondence. A citation study
of Philip Scranton's two major books, *Proprietary Capitalism*, which
describes the history of Philadelphia's textile industry in the years
between 1880 and 1885, and *Figured Tapestry*, which takes the story
through 1941, shows that less then 10 percent of his footnotes refer
to firm records. Trade journals, industrial directories, government documents, and contemporary newspapers account for almost 65 percent
of the sources used.[31]

Putting People Back In

Scholarship describing the history of small business has begun to
refocus historians on the role of the entrepreneur and the concept of

corporate culture, areas that were largely neglected during the Alfred Chandler era. In an 1989 *Business History Review* article, Harold Livesay argued that dynamic entrepreneurs are still the key to business success even within large corporations. Louis Galambos' 1992 article, "Theodore N. Vail and the Role of Innovation in the Modern Bell System," and the books by Robert Garnet, George David Smith, and Neil Wassermann in the Johns Hopkins/AT&T Series in Telephone History demonstrated the lasting impact that creative leadership, entrepreneurial initiative, and shared values had on one of America's most successful corporations. These studies describe the ways in which Vail, chief executive officer of the American Telephone and Telegraph Company at the turn of the century, created a corporate culture that emphasized innovation, technology, and customer service, values that resonated with those of the dominant culture of the Progressive Era. Under Vail's leadership, AT&T became one of the United States' most technically advanced firms, a leader in productivity, with a mission to bring universal service to the country. In spite of the fact that AT&T operated in a highly regulated environment, Vail managed to make it into a cutting-edge, science-based company, which, until the breakup of the 1980s, represented almost everything that was right with the American economic system.[32] The Johns Hopkins/AT&T telephone series, which focused on Theodore Vail and the corporate culture he established, foreshadowed some of the issues that business historians have recently begun to explore. Scholars are now moving away from a purely structural and functional view of firm behavior.[33]

Instead, they are attempting to place the history of American business into a larger cultural context. Values, culture, and social change have become major themes. Olivier Zunz's *Making America Corporate*, is about the making of the modern middle-class or white-collar, salaried manager who was so central to the development of the modern corporation, but who remains such a shadowy figure in the work of Alfred Chandler.[34] Approaching his work as a social historian with an interest in class formation, Zunz describes how managerial capitalism created a new value system or work culture upon which the success of the bureaucratically organized corporation depended. His book, which links corporate growth to the formation of a middle class, is based on an analysis of the records of McCormick Company, International Harvester, Ford Motor Company, Metropolitan Life Insurance Company, the Chicago, Burlington and Quincy Railroad, and E. I. du Pont de Nemours. Zunz relied on the correspondence of middle-level managers and sales agents, personnel department records (including payroll data), organization charts, internal newsletters, and records from the research, engineering, and advertising departments. He made particularly good use of the letters that the sales agents wrote to their supervisors at the home office to understand the world and values of the emerging strata of middle-class managers. Zunz's work relies on firm records, but to a lesser degree than the strategy and structure studies. Only one-quarter of his footnotes refer to business archives. He also consulted a wide variety of printed primary and printed secondary literature which describes the impact of social change on the corporation and the new managerial class.[35] *Making America Corporate* illustrates the ways in which studies that relate the history of American business to larger social and cultural trends need to use business records in conjunction with sources that are external to the firm.

Business, Gender, and Race

Business history, as it is usually written, has focused on middle- or upper-class white males. The literature has paid relatively little attention to the questions raised by social historians about the ways in which gender, race, and class have shaped the American experience. This has begun to change in recent years as some scholars are now seeking ways to combine the concerns of women's history with the concerns of business history.[36] Most women in business operated small enterprises such as beauty parlors, grocery stores, millineries, and dressmaking shops. However, concerns about gender are also embedded into the structure and operation of the large corporation. Business historians are now attempting to incorporate women into their narratives by exploring how ideas about manhood and womanhood helped to define business and workplace organization. In *Engendering Business* (1994), Angel Kwolek-Folland argues that the Chandlerian synthesis, which implies a "rational, progressive interpretation of economic and business growth," ignored the role of gender. This influential book shows how "turn of the century gender roles built on the nineteenth-century notion of separate spheres" to shape ideas about womanhood and the ideal office worker. As business became increasingly dependent on clerical workers, the all-male office staff was transformed into a predominately female clerical work force. This changed the network of social relationships within the corporation in ways that were not always in harmony with the rationalization of business practices. Job descriptions and the physical spaces of the workplace were often organized to reinforce gendered behavior and expectations even when this did not result in maximizing efficiency. Kwolek-Folland analyzes the complex relationship between the "ideological and behavioral changes" in women's and men's roles and work, and how this shaped the organization and functioning of the modern corporation. Instead of a rational, hierarchical model rooted in neutral firm strategies as described by Chandler, Kwolek-Folland sees a complex process of accommodation among managers, workers, and customers "rooted in different class and gender expectations." Notions about female secretaries as office wives, the linking of gender stereotypes to particular jobs, and the association of scientific management with masculinity raise questions about the nature of bureaucratic rationalism in the corporate office.[37]

During the course of her work, Kwolek-Folland consulted the archives of a number of banks and insurance companies that employed large numbers of women in clerical positions. She did research in the records of the Provident Mutual Insurance Company, the Equitable Life Assurance Society, Metropolitan Life Insurance Company, and New England Mutual Life Insurance Company. As one might expect, she was particularly interested in the files that document employment policy. She also relied on employee magazines, newsletters, and public relations literature. Photographs depicting the way interior spaces were designed in large corporate office buildings were particularly important sources. Again, as with Olivier Zunz's work, firm records account for a relatively small percentage of the footnotes (14 percent with another 13 percent of the citations referring to company publications such as employee magazines and newsletters). External documentation including contemporary books and articles, trade journals, newspapers, and government documents account for nearly 30 percent of Angel Kwolek-Folland's footnotes.[38]

Writing the history of African American business presents some of the same methodological problems that Angel Kwolek-Folland encountered. Again, for the most part historians are dealing with very small firms that generated few records. Scholars, therefore, are almost completely dependent on external sources. When working in this setting, the boundaries between business history, social history, and historical sociology often blur. John Ingham has made good use of local African American newspapers and government documents in order to reconstruct the history of the African American business experience in the South between 1880 and 1929. Advertisements and news articles provided him with information about black entrepreneurs, their sources of capital, markets, and relationship to the African American communities and larger society. Ingham's work built on the classic sociological studies of Abram Harris, E. Franklin Frazier, and W. E. B. Du Bois, which defined the research agenda for several generations beginning in the 1920s. These works are still extremely useful as they describe the role that black businessmen played in the African American community during the early years of the twentieth century. They

also provide valuable source material and sociological data for the
business historian.[39]

The History of Advertising

Scholarship on the history of advertising describes many of the
same social and cultural issues that Angel Kwolek-Folland and Olivier
Zunz explored. The advertising industry has probably done more to
shape America's values, belief systems, and iconography than any
other single national institution. As a result, advertising history operates at the intersection of business, cultural, and social history.

In their innovative and influential studies, Roland Marchand and
T. Jackson Lears have described the ways in which the American
business system has shaped fashion, taste, and our material culture.[40]
Using the records of advertising agencies like J. Walter Thompson, N.
W. Ayer, and Batten, Barton, Durstine, and Osborn as well as those
from corporate advertising departments of firms such as E. I. du Pont
de Nemours and the General Electric Corporation, Lears and Marchand place the history of advertising into the wider context of American cultural history. *Advertising the American Dream* (1985) and
Fables of Abundance (1994) analyze the ways national advertising depicted concepts of progress, modernity, the good life, mass society,
gender, class, and race in order to reconstruct the "folklore of industrial society." These studies also explore the way advertisers created
a "symbolic universe where certain cultural values were sanctioned
and others rendered marginal or invisible."[41] While both Marchand
and Lears would be the first to admit that advertisements are distorted
prisms through which to view American society and culture, they have
demonstrated the ways in which they can be used in conjunction with
other types of records, particularly market research studies and correspondence between advertising agencies and their clients, to study
the history of mass marketing and the consumer society.

Like the works of Zunz and Kwolek-Folland, Lears' and Marchand's work relied heavily on external sources. Only 8 percent of the
footnotes are to firm records with 81 percent of the citations referring
to printed primary materials, mostly trade journals and contemporary
newspapers and magazines. This is in striking contrast to the sources
used by Ralph Hower in his 1939 history of the advertising agency
N. W. Ayer. In Hower's institutional study referred to above, 45 percent of the footnotes were to business records and 13 percent to oral
history interviews done with company executives.[42]

Business and the State—Labor and Government

Politics and the conflict and accommodation that has characterized the struggle among business, labor, and government provide another perspective for understanding the relationship of the American business system to the larger society. Most historians see this story as a chapter in the "search for order" and the rise of the administrative state.[43] To use Robert Collins' words, beginning in the 1890s American business made a "conscious effort to build a corporate socio-political order" that would blunt social tensions and the excesses and inefficiencies of laissez-faire capitalism, stabilizing the market economy and the political system. The modern relationship between business and the state was initially defined in the Progressive Era and the 1920s and refined in the 1930s and 1940s. In response to the depression and war, a system of "countervailing forces" that recognized labor as a legitimate interest group and the government as the broker between business and labor was established. This accommodation lasted until the 1980s when changes in the world economy and the balance of domestic political interests destroyed the so-called New Deal order.[44] The history of government regulation and antitrust policy is well described in Ellis W. Hawley, *The New Deal and the Problem of Monopoly* (1966); Colin Gordon, *Business, Labor, and Politics in America* (1994); Martin Sklar, *The Corporate Reconstruction of American Capitalism* (1988); William H. Becker, *The Dynamics of Business Government Relations* (1982); and Thomas McCraw, *Prophets of Regulation* (1984).[45] These studies also construct the modern corporate commonwealth, which would attempt to reconcile the individualist, free enterprise tradition with the need to regulate business and achieve a degree of economic security for all. The Roosevelt and Truman solution was Keynesianism and the politics of growth based on union recognition, high wages, and aggressive internationalism. During these years the interests of business were often represented by national business organizations (the National Association of Manufacturers, the National Civic Federation, the Chamber of Commerce of the United States) and the large trade associations. Their records, along with those of the federal regulatory agencies and personal papers of the major political and economic leaders of the Roosevelt, Truman, Eisenhower, Kennedy, and Johnson administrations, have provided source material for the literature on business and the state. Firm records, while valuable for identifying the views of business leaders, account for only 18 percent of the footnotes.[46]

Much writing about business and the state focuses on the Progressive and New Deal eras. These times saw changing patterns of labor relations that by the end of the Second World War resulted in a kind of social compact between business and labor. This pattern tended to be characteristic of the large corporations that Chandler studied. Many of these companies responded to the changed political climate brought about by the New Deal and regulatory requirements of the National Labor Relations Act by establishing industrial relations systems based on bureaucratized personnel practices. Some historians have also shown that the need to stabilize the marketplace in certain highly competitive industries such as clothing and coal led to a species of "regulatory unionism," an effort to bring about price stability through industry-wide collective bargaining agreements.

The changing nature of the American industrial relations system is described in the works of David Brody, David Montgomery, Sanford Jacoby, Lizabeth Cohen, Susan Porter Benson, and Walter Licht.[47] This new industrial history relates changes in technology, business strategy, work culture, workplace organization, and scientific management to larger trends in American economic and political life. Both business and trade union records have been used to describe the impact of business decision making on workers at the point of production. This literature blurs many of the traditional boundaries between business and labor history. For example, a citation analysis of David Brody's seminal book *Steel Workers in America: The Nonunion Era* (1960) shows that well over half of the sources for the first section, which focuses on the economics of the steel industry, refer to business archives: executive committee correspondence, board of directors minutes, annual and financial reports. In later chapters about the mill towns, immigrants, and industrial unionism, the balance shifts to union sources.[48] In addition to using materials of these types, scholars have begun to analyze carefully personnel department records, including employee case files, in order to reconstruct the world of the worker.

This survey of the business history literature, which is backed up by a citation study that analyzed more than 67,000 footnotes in 50 major business history monographs and 5 leading journals, has definite implications for archival collection development and appraisal practice. In all, approximately one-third of the citations analyzed in our study were to business records, 29 percent were to secondary works, and 37 percent were to printed primary works (annual reports, trade journals, internal newsletters, etc.). In spite of substantial shifts in the focus of historical writing, the type of records used by scholars has been remarkably stable over time. Managerial correspondence is clearly the most important source of information for business historians (53 percent of the business records citations). Another 16 percent of the citations were to departmental records, mostly research and development, advertising, public relations, and personnel. Executive committee and departmental reports are also frequently cited. Not surprisingly, given how difficult they are to use, financial records are hardly ever referred to (1 percent of the citations), while board of directors and executive committee minute books were cited only slightly more often (2 percent of the citations). This may reflect the fact that corporate secretaries record only the most basic information in official minute books, which tend to be written in a way to minimize potential liability rather than to inform.

What is most striking about this study is that over time, there appears to be a declining reliance on archival sources. This may reflect the fact that a growing literature presents historians with more secondary works to cite. Most of the monographs that were published in the Harvard Studies in Business History during the 1930s, 1940s, and 1950s relied heavily on firm records (between 50 and 60 percent of the footnotes). This was not surprising because most of these monographs were relatively narrow administrative histories. The authors usually had unrestricted access to company records, and there was very little other relevant material available. Of all the monographs studied, Thomas Cochran's *Railroad Leaders* was the most heavily dependent on business records. As noted above, 94 percent of Cochran's footnotes refer to managerial and executive officer correspondence. In the work of Alfred Chandler and his disciples between 30 and 50 percent of the footnotes refer to business records. (These tend to be more generally dispersed throughout the organization chart.) In some of the more recent studies that describe the history of small business or attempt to place the history of business into a larger social, cultural or political context, the proportion of footnotes represented by firm records is quite small (between 10 and 20 percent): when studying the impact of external social and cultural change on the American business system, scholars must rely on research materials that are external to the firm. These typically include trade association records, trade journals, and government documents.

Given recent trends in business history, archivists need to reexamine their traditional focus on the firm and begin to think about how best to document the place of the business system in American society. This may involve adopting a strategy that makes a systematic effort to collect records from entities such as industry trade associations, industrial districts, professional organizations, design and public relations consultants, law firms specializing in corporate work, lobbying groups, advertising agencies, political action committees, and business advocacy groups. These organizations provide structure to the interfirm networks that connect business to the larger society. Their records can potentially provide the sources that scholars are seeking in order to document the relationship between business, culture, politics, and society.

Endnotes

1. George A. Rich, "Our Primary Purpose," *Bulletin of the Business Historical Society* (June 1926): 1–2.

2. Thomas Cochran, *Frontiers of Change: Early Industrialism in America* (New York: Oxford University Press, 1981).

3. Arthur H. Cole, "The Impact of a Large Collection of Business Literature," *Harvard Library Bulletin* 15, no. 2 (April 1967): 180–199.

4. N. S. B. Gras, "What is Business History," *Bulletin of the Business Historical Society* (October 1944): 87–91.

5. Ibid., 73–78.

6. Ibid., 82–86.

7. Julie Kimmel and Christopher McKenna, citation study done in conjunction with the Records of American Business Project and on deposit at the Hagley Museum and Library. This study, which was done by two graduate students in business history at Johns Hopkins University, analyzed more than 67,000 footnotes in 50 monographs that were identified as being important to the business history literature. Five scholarly journals: *Business History Review, Technology and Culture, Labor History, Journal of Social History*, and *Journal of American History* were scanned for articles relating to business or industrial history. Sources were classified into five broad categories: printed primary, secondary, manuscripts and archives, oral histories, and court cases. Within the manuscripts and archives category they were classified by type of business organization, department, record type, and whether they were organizational archives or personal papers. Hereafter cited as "Citation study."

8. Ralph M. Hower, *The History of an Advertising Agency: N. W. Ayer & Sons at Work, 1869–1949* (Cambridge: Harvard University Press, 1939), and *History of Macy's of New York, 1858–1919* (Cambridge: Harvard University Press, 1946); and Ralph and Muriel Hidy, *Pioneering in Big Business: The History of the Standard Oil Company (New Jersey)* (New York: Harper & Brothers, 1955).

9. Cole, "The Impact," 186.

10. Report, October 8, 1940, Records of the Committee for Research in Economic History, Acc. 1479, Hagley Museum and Library, Wilmington, Del. Hereafter cited as CREH Records.

11. Conference on Economic History Research, September 23, 1940, CREH Records.

12. Unpublished memoirs of Thomas Cochran, Acc. 1651, Hagley Museum and Library.

13. Stephen A. Sass, *Entrepreneurial Historians and History: Leadership and Rationality in American Economic Historiography, 1940–1960* (New York: Garland Press, 1986), 107–154.

14. Hugh J. Atkin, "The Entrepreneurial Approach to Economic History," in *Approaches to American Economic History*, eds. George Rogers Taylor and Lucius F. Ellisworth (Charlottesville: University Press of Virginia, 1971), 9.

15. Thomas C. Cochran, *Railroad Leaders, 1845–1890: The Business Mind in Action* (Cambridge: Harvard University Press, 1953), 3.

16. Adolf A. Berle, Jr. and Gardiner Means, *The Modern Corporation and Private Property* (New York: Macmillian, 1937).

17. David Sicilia, "Cochran's Legacy: A Cultural Path Not Taken," *Business and Economic History* 24, no. 1 (fall 1995): 27–40.

18. Citation study.

19. Alfred Chandler, Jr., *Strategy and Structure: Chapters in the History of Industrial Enterprise* (Cambridge: MIT Press, 1962); *The Visible Hand: The Managerial Revolution in American Business* (Cambridge: Belknap Press of Harvard University Press, 1977); and *Scale and Scope: The Dynamics of Industrial Capitalism* (Cambridge: Belknap Press of Harvard University Press, 1990).

20. Alfred Chandler, Jr., "The Beginnings of Big Business in American Industry," *Business History Review* 33 (spring 1959): 1–33.

21. Alfred Chandler, Jr. and Stephen Salsbury, *Pierre S. du Pont and the Making of the Modern Corporation* (New York: Harper & Row, 1971).

22. JoAnne Yates, *Control Through Communication* (Baltimore: Johns Hopkins University Press, 1989); Francis X. Blouin, Jr. points out this theme in Chandler's work in, "A New Perspective on the Appraisal of Business Records; A Review," *American Archivist* 42 (July 1979): 312–320. See also JoAnne Yates, "Internal Communication Systems in American Business Structures: A Framework to Aid Appraisal," *American Archivist* 48 no. 1 (spring 1985): 141–158.

23. Citation study.

24. As part of the citation study the following journals of business administration were reviewed: *Harvard Business Review, Academy of Management Journal*, and *Journal of Business Communications*.

25. Louis Galambos, "Technology, Political Economy, and Professionalization: Central Themes of the Organizational Synthesis," *Business History Review* 57 no. 4 (winter 1983): 471–492.

26. Thomas Parke Hughes, *Elmer Sperry: Inventor and Engineer* (Baltimore: Johns Hopkins University Press, 1971); Reese V. Jenkins, *Images and Enterprise: Technology and the American Photographic Industry* (Baltimore: Johns Hopkins University Press, 1975); David A. Hounshell and John Kenly Smith, Jr., *Science and Corporate Strategy: Du Pont R & D, 1902–1980* (New York: Cambridge University Press, 1988); George Wise, *Willis R. Whitney, General Electric and the origins of U.S. Industrial Research* (New York: Columbia University Press, 1985).

27. Citation study.

28. Joint Committee on Archives of Science and Technology, *Understanding Progress as Process: Documenting the History of Post-War Science and Technology in the United States*. (Chicago: Society of American Archivists, 1983); Joan K. Hass, Helen Willa Samuels, and Barbara Trippel Simmons, *Appraising the Records of Modern Science and Technology* (Cambridge: MIT Press, 1985).

29. Michael J. Piore and Charles Sable, *The Second Industrial Divide: Possibilities for Prosperity* (New York: Basic Books, 1984).

30. Philip Scranton, *Proprietary Capitalism: Textile Manufacture at Philadelphia. 1800–1885* (Philadelphia: Temple University Press, 1983); *Figured Tapestry: Production, Markets, and Power in Philadelphia Textiles, 1885–1941* (New York: Cambridge University Press, 1979); and "Diversity in Diversity: Flexible Production and American Industrialization, 1880–1930," *Business History Review* 65 (spring 1991): 27–90; John N. Ingham, *Independent Mills in Pittsburgh, 1820–1920* (Columbus: Ohio State University Press, 1991); Michael Nash, "Small Business, Manufacturing, and Flexible Specialization: Implications for the Archivist," *American Archivist* (forthcoming).

31. Citation study.

32. Harold C. Livesay, "Entrepreneurial Dominance in Business, Large and Small, Past and Present," *Business History Review* 63 (spring 1989): 1–21; Louis Galambos, "Theodore N. Vail and the Role of Innovation in the Modern Bell System," *Business History Review* 66 (spring 1992): 95–126; Robert W. Garnett, *The Telephone Enterprise: The Evolution of the Bell System's Horizontal Structure, 1876–1909* (Baltimore: Johns Hopkins University Press, 1985); Neil Wassermann, *From Invention to Innovation: Long-Distance Telephone Transmission at the Turn of the Century* (Baltimore: Johns Hopkins University Press, 1985); George David Smith, *The Anatomy of a Business Strategy: Bell, Western Electric, and the Origins of the American Telephone Industry* (Baltimore: Johns Hopkins University Press, 1985).

33. For a provocative theoretical article see Kenneth Lipartito, "Culture and the Practice of Business History," *Business and Economic History* 22 (1993): 92–104.

34. Olivier Zunz, *Making America Corporate, 1870–1920* (Chicago: University of Chicago Press, 1990).

35. Citation study.

36. Joan W. Scott, *Gender and the Politics of History* (New York: Columbia University Press, 1988); Wendy Gamber, "Gendered Concerns: Thoughts on the History of Business," *Business and Economic History* 23 no. 1 (fall 1994): 129–140.

37. Angel Kwolek-Folland, *Engendering Business: Men and Women in the Corporate Office, 1870–1930* (Baltimore: Johns Hopkins University Press, 1994), 7–14.

38. Citation study.

39. See John N. Ingham, "Prejudice, Pride and Profits: African-American Business in the South, 1880–1929" (research paper presented at the Hagley Research Seminar, Wilmington, Del., March 10, 1994); W. E. B. Du Bois, *The Philadelphia*

Negro (Philadelphia: University of Pennsylvania Press, 1899); E. Franklin Frazier, *Black Bourgeoisie* (Glencoe, Ill.: Free Press, c1957); Abram Harris, *The Negro as Capitalist* (Philadelphia: University of Pennsylvania Press, 1936); Willard B. Gatewood, *Aristocrats of Color: The Black Elite, 1880–1920* (Bloomington, Ind.: Indiana University Press, 1990); Alexa B. Henderson, "Richard R. Wright and the National Negro Bankers Association," *Pennsylvania Magazine of History and Biography*, January, 1993: 51–81.

40. Roland Marchand, *Advertising the American Dream: Making the Way for Modernity, 1920–1940* (Berkeley: University of California Press, 1985); Jackson Lears, *Fables of Abundance: A Cultural History of Advertising in America* (New York: Basic Books, 1994).

41. Quotations are from Lears, *Fables of Abundance*, 1–17.

42. Citation study.

43. Robert Wiebe, *The Search for Order, 1877–1920* (New York: Hill and Wang, 1967).

44. Robert Collins, *The Business Response to Keynes* (New York: Columbia University Press, 1981), 1–2; John Kenneth Galbraith, *American Capitalism: The Concept of Countervailing Power* (New York: Houghton Mifflin, 1956).

45. Ellis W. Hawley, *The New Deal and the Problem of Monopoly* (Princeton: Princeton University Press, 1966); Colin Gordon, *Business, Labor, and Politics in America, 1920–1935* (Cambridge: Cambridge University Press, 1994); Thomas McCraw, *Prophets of Regulation: Charles Francis Adams, Louis D. Brandeis, James M. Landis, Alfred E. Kahn* (Cambridge: Belknap Press of Harvard University, 1984); Martin J. Sklar, *The Corporate Reconstruction of American Capitalism, 1890–1916* (Cambridge: Cambridge University Press, 1988); William H. Becker, *The Dynamics of Business Government Relations* (Chicago: University of Chicago Press, 1982).

46. Citation study.

47. David Brody, *Steelworkers in America: The Nonunion Era* (Cambridge: Harvard University Press, 1960); David Montgomery, *The Fall of the House of Labor* (New York: Cambridge University Press, 1987); Lizabeth Cohen, *Making a New Deal: Industrial Workers in Chicago, 1919–1939* (New York: Cambridge University Press, 1990); Sanford M. Jacoby, *Employing Bureaucracy: Managers, Unions, and the Transformation of Work in American Industry, 1900–1945* (New York: Columbia University Press, 1985); Walter Licht, *Working for the Railroad: The Organization of Work in the Nineteenth Century* (Princeton: Princeton University Press, 1983); Susan Porter Benson, *Counter Cultures: Saleswomen, Managers, and Customers in American Department Stores, 1890–1940* (Urbana: University of Illinois Press, 1986).

48. Citation study.

2

The Evolving Role of
In-House Business Archives:
From Tradition to Flexibility

Marcy G. Goldstein

This essay will explore how recent changes in marketplace imperatives and information technology have begun to alter fundamentally the role of in-house business archives. Traditionally, a business archives' main purpose was seen as preserving and providing access to a company's historical records—a custodial role at best. Today, in many corporations, archives are recognized as serving a business purpose. They are part of an information and communications system that encompasses the management of both current and historical records in paper and electronic forms. As George David Smith and Laurence E. Steadman pointed out in their classic article, "Present Value of Corporate History," "a company's history contains its heritage and traditions, which managers need to understand if they are to see the present as part of a process rather than as a collection of accidental happenings."[1] Viewed in this framework, the corporate archives is the repository of the corporate memory, preserving documents that are needed for administrative, legal, and fiscal purposes and can be used for strategic planning, advertising, public relations, research and development, and litigation support.

As archivists have sought to broaden their roles, they have found new constituencies. Many managers are now recognizing that in the new information-based corporation, archives, whether they are in electronic or paper form, are an important asset. If properly administered the archives will contain the record of the intellectual property produced by professional staff, whether they be scientists, engineers, lawyers, business administration, advertising, or public relations specialists. These ideas and work products are valuable resources that need to be preserved and under appropriate circumstances, made available throughout the organization. The archives also preserves evidence of past decision making, strategic planning, corporate policies, procedures, and the structure of internal communication. Companies are now recognizing that under imaginative administration, the old file room has real value. Managing records creatively and making them available to a larger internal audience is an important corporate function which can transform boxes of raw data in dusty files into useful information that can serve as a knowledge base for managerial decision making.

To support this evolving role, business archivists need to move away from their traditional custodial roles and become "knowledge managers," using machine-readable archival descriptions to relate records to business needs. These descriptors can be designed to incorporate information about both provenance and subject content. For example, an archival description of a memorandum from Theodore Vail, president of AT&T at the turn of the century, analyzing the rationale for developing a system of "universal service," proved to be useful to the attorneys defending AT&T in the antitrust suit of the 1970s and 1980s, since it related the origins of universal service to the impracticality of setting up a competitive marketplace for telephone services. This spoke to the central issue of the case. Thus, the archival description of the Vail memorandum gave it a versatility beyond its original purpose.

New methods of description, organization, and retrieval are being developed to anticipate changing business needs and take advantage of emerging technological opportunities. In the pages that follow I will describe my experiences in several high-technology organizations, which sought to define a new, dynamic role for a corporate archives within the new business environment.[2]

The New Business Environment

In the 1980s and 1990s, large corporations have begun to abandon the classic, hierarchical "command and control" structure and have adopted flatter modes of organization with far fewer levels of middle management.[3] Business leaders have sought to create organizations where the "line of sight" to the customer is as direct as possible, with the ability to adapt quickly to changes in the marketplace. The aim is to create large corporations that are able to function with the agility of small companies.

In 1988, Peter Drucker wrote about this revolution in the structure of business. He argued that in the late twentieth century the real work of a business is being done by functional workers who actually are specialists in their jobs, and by the highest levels of management who make strategic decisions.[4] In the past, one of the main functions of middle managers was to pass information up or down the organization chart so that corporate executives could standardize bureaucratic practices, get the necessary feedback from those who reported to them, and control the work of their subordinates. As JoAnne Yates has observed, "procedures, rules, financial, and operational information were documented at all levels, making organizational rather than individual memory the repository of knowledge." In the bureaucratically organized corporations that dominated American business in the early and middle years of the twentieth century, thousands of linear feet of records were generated by staff and line departments in order to document decision making and work flow. These records were preserved in a centralized way that mirrored the hierarchical corporate organization.[5]

In the Information Age, the computer has taken over much of this role as conduit of information. As a result, during the past decades we have seen many layers of middle management gradually eliminated as their control function has been taken over by the computer. Some of them have been replaced by professionals with specialized skills, but these are not middle managers in the traditional sense. Rather they function as coordinators of professional staff who operate with a good deal of autonomy.

These changes have had a profound impact on corporate structure and records systems. In the modern corporation, traditional departments and divisions are much less important than they used to be. Instead, we have task forces, working groups, cost centers, profit centers, rotating performance specialists—small semiautonomous units, self-governing units, and many other similar structures that cut across traditional departmental lines. To complicate matters further, these new types of organizational structures tend to be ephemeral, often lasting no longer than the life of a project. They dissolve without leaving a paper trail as they are seldom around long enough to become part of the formal records management system. Today, even traditional departments rarely have formal meetings with written minutes. Communications often take place electronically, an increasing proportion of the corporate record is in machine-readable form, and the tendency is to evermore aggressive records destruction schedules. With corporate strategy putting a premium on fast decision making, it is getting less possible to document activities in written form.

Such new corporate strategy and structure pose new demands for documentation and information that, in many companies, are redefining the role of the corporate archivist. With records control systems becoming increasingly decentralized at a time when the importance of information is widely recognized, the archival function becomes the key to preserving organizational memory. In many companies the archivist may be the only person who is concerned with the overall corporate record. The challenge is to respond to changes in record-keeping practices and the revolution of information technology. In an era when organization charts change so rapidly that some companies don't even issue them any more, tracking the relationship between corporate structure, function, record group, series, and provenance has become increasingly difficult and peripheral to the needs of the business. Many archivists have, therefore, moved away from using the organization chart as a guide to appraisal, arrangement, and description and have instead adopted a functional approach. AT&T's use of project, function, or individual name as the defining nomenclature of a collection and the documentary probe, a technique developed by Bruce Bruemmer and Sheldon Hochheiser of the Charles Babbage Institute, Center for the History of Information Processing, may provide the best way to identify historical issues that need to be documented by corporate archivists. The advantage of these approaches is that they allow archivists to focus on the function and the informational content of a record group, rather than on departmental organization, which is constantly changing. Instead of beginning by looking at organizational structure, the documentary probe starts by identifying a company's important products and seeking "historical, organizational, and documentary information from all facets of a company in order to aid in the identification of historically valuable records." A documentary probe may generate an "informational collection" whose provenance is unclear since it includes records from various departments, divisions, and task forces. These collections can be organized to reflect the nature of the probe, which may have centered around a product, service, or activity of a team leader. Descriptors can relate the content of the collection to the larger corporate structure and functions that are documented elsewhere.[6]

By adopting techniques like the documentary probe, corporate archivists can become more proactive. This is one way to build archival collections that document the new corporate world. Rapid turnover of personnel including top management, and the accelerated pace of acquisitions, mergers, downsizing, spin-offs, divestitures, and reengineering all have the potential to create a loss of continuity and control. Archivists need to respond to these challenges as the keeper of the organization's memory, assembling collections that provide a way for new employees to learn about the corporation, its policies, procedures, decision-making processes, values, culture, and traditions.

Mission of the Archives

The AT&T experience provides a good example of the role that history and archives can play in the corporate world. During the past two decades, as AT&T moved from the "age of telephony" to the "age of information," competitive pressures and political forces have shaken its tradition of public service and benign bureaucracy to the core. Since the 1970s, AT&T has been in the process of reorganizing its structure from a function-oriented to a market-oriented organization. New technology, government legislation, and market forces have forced the corporation to develop a breed of entrepreneurial manager. The 1982 court-ordered divestiture resulted in the separation of the competitive from the noncompetitive parts of the business—the regional Bell companies from the remainder of the corporation. Prior to divestiture and the organizational restructuring that came in its wake, AT&T consisted of roughly four main entities: (1) AT&T Corporate Administration; (2) Western Electric (the manufacturing unit); (3) Bell Laboratories (research and development); (4) the regional Bell operating companies. The 1984 reorganization resulted in a restructuring into new companies and, later, business units and divisions. Acquisitions of National Cash Register and McCaw further modified internal structure and now "trivestiture" is again splitting the corporation along new structural lines.

The AT&T archival program played an important role as corporate officers attempted to manage this traumatic change, trying to retain the old service ethic and emphasis on quality while nurturing a new spirit of entrepreneurialism. Early on, Charles Brown, chief executive officer at the time of the divestiture, decided that it was important to carry out a thorough historical analysis of the reorganization.[7] At the same time AT&T commissioned three scholarly monographs that were designed to trace the history of the corporation from its beginnings in the nineteenth century.[8] Corporate executives believed that during a period of profound change, both employees and the general public needed to be reacquainted with the history of AT&T and the historical rationale behind its monopoly status. This was part of a campaign to improve the company's image and influence the debate about divestiture. Also, it was believed that corporate managers, who are going to have to become increasingly responsive to marketplace pressures, could learn much by studying AT&T's entrepreneurial beginnings, its encounters with a competitive environment during the late nineteenth and early twentieth century, and its successful efforts to master new technologies. This history project was housed in the AT&T Archives with archives staff designated to support and manage it. The project provided the archives with substantial visibility within the corporation and reinforced its importance.

After the project came to an end, the newly reorganized archives staff was determined to remain a vital part of the reorganized company. They transformed the Archives Center into a central source of information to serve a company that was becoming increasingly decentralized. During a period of rapid organizational change and corporate downsizing, the AT&T Archives absorbed roles that would otherwise have disappeared as departments were reorganized. For example, the AT&T Archives provided access to internally generated technical and interoffice memoranda, a job previously handled by another department with at least four separate locations. In another instance, the AT&T Archives functioned as a repository for published journals and provided copies of articles for internal customers. During this period, the AT&T Archives absorbed the work of nearly 40 positions from several departments. New responsibilities included management of executive biographies, retention of internal publications, response to external requests for information, and corporatewide oversight of photographs and films. Studies conducted by the Special Libraries Association[9] and an internal analysis conducted by AT&T's Organizational Design Group compared the activities of the AT&T Archives and other business archives. The AT&T Archives had nearly twice as many responsibilities as other similar company archives.

Reengineering projects at Microsoft and Sandia illustrate the same ability of archives staff to act as beacons of continuity and communicators of change. Microsoft's and Sandia's archives have reinvented themselves, changing from repositories of mementos and limited documentation to vibrant centers of valued information.

If the archives is to become a vital center for corporate information, archivists need to think about how to develop new missions, uses and processes for appraising, describing, and using archival information for current and future business needs. What kinds of information and materials do corporate managers need? What records document the way the corporation was organized and functioned? What kinds of informational collections are useful? What records are most appropriate to document past decision making? How do archivists play a proactive role in assuring that the records of important task forces and working groups are preserved? Can we fill in the gaps in the written record by making creative use of oral history?

Changes in corporate structure and the revolution in information technology have not only had a dramatic influence on the way information is generated and stored but have the potential to shape archival practice. As businesses become more decentralized and personnel turnover accelerates, keeping control over an organization's records becomes a critical corporate function. Departments that have traditionally been responsible for their own records no longer have the permanency they once had. This makes it all the more imperative for businesses to establish a centralized archival repository. The computer has clearly had a profound effect on the current information environment. It also may provide the key to solving some of the archival community's current dilemmas, allowing us to keep track of corporate functions and relate them to changing corporate structure. The computer enables the archivist to function not only as a repository of information but as a manager of knowledge, of intellectual property in the service of the organization. Modern technology allows us to describe the content and provenance of records in such a way as to link archival information to corporate needs. For example, most companies file medical records by the name of the patient-employee. Using the computer to describe the individual record more fully than is possible with manual systems, the archivist can also identify the employee's occupation as well as their location. Thus, data about a particular illness can be researched, and computerized descriptions can produce "knowledge" linking the illness to a particular work location, a faulty ventilation system, or the proximity of research laboratories that may be working with toxic substances. This is an example of turning data into knowledge for a business purpose, in this case, health and safety.

The traditional mission for the archives was to document the origins, organization, and development of an institution. One of its main purposes was to preserve historical records so that they would be available if the company decided to commission a history to celebrate its 50th or 100th anniversary. From time to time these collections were made available to outside historians. As George David Smith and Laurence Steadman have pointed out, these histories, while they had some utility for public relations purposes, treated the company's past as a static given, events to be commemorated, rather than as part of an analytic effort that could help "diagnose problems, reassess policy, measure performance and even direct change."[10]

Few companies today are interested in establishing a history program in order to produce a coffee-table book, and even fewer will commit internal resources to an archives that they perceive as serving primarily a cultural mission. Business archives need to advance the mission of the company and serve the current and future needs of the business.

Business Uses

Strategic Planning.   Strategic planning, deciding on long-term goals in order to seek competitive advantage, is the most important function of corporate management. It is the process by which a company makes business decisions about how to allocate resources of capital, facilities, and personnel. As part of the strategic planning effort, executives need to consider the history of their company in which their experiences may be limited. To plan for the future, they must know why certain policies or organizational structures were put into place. What was the historical context that led to the adoption of a particular strategic initiative? What were company managers trying to accomplish? How has the situation changed over time? Is it appropriate to reevaluate a policy in light of changed circumstances? Can success or failure be measured in light of the original objectives? Does the company's present structure reflect current corporate strategy or is it an historical artifact? Preserving the records of the strategic planning process as well as collateral documentation describing the impact of the strategic plan is essential if company managers are to have the necessary perspective to evaluate their successes and failures. In the current business environment it is important to have this type of information in an accessible format. This history, which is larger than the individual manager's own experience, provides the context that needs to be considered as new policies are formulated. Managing change with a sense of continuity has become a central corporate challenge and one in which the archivist can play a central role.

Litigation Support.   Lawyers tend to be heavy users of business archives. This is not surprising because court briefs are often extended historical arguments that attempt to explain why a particular company policy or project was legal and justifiable within the historical context in which it occurred. For example, corporate defense counsel involved in asbestos litigation usually try to argue that company managers did not know that asbestos was a carcinogen until well into the 1960s. Similarly, attorneys working on patent infringement cases like the Sperry-Honeywell lawsuit (1971-1973) that sought to resolve the question of patent rights to the digital computer, often need archival records to argue their cases, particularly when litigation revolves around essentially historical questions, like who invented the first electronic digital computer.

Business archives provide documentation on patent rights, trademarks, and other forms of intellectual property that the corporation may need to defend its rights in court. Lawyers are usually very cautious about keeping documentation that they know is vulnerable to the discovery process and can be subpoenaed. However, a well-organized corporate archives provides the resources to defend the company. In the era of the copying machine and the computer, lawyers can never be sure who has access to what documents. An efficient archives makes it possible for them to mount a well-documented defense and minimizes the likelihood that they will be surprised in court. For this reason lawyers need to work closely with the archivist to ensure consistency of retention practices within the corporation and to make sure that in appraising documents, the archivist aligns archival policy with legal strategies.

Public Relations and Advertising.   The public relations community is both a rich source of information (internal publications, photographs, press releases and newsletters), and a heavy user of archival collections. In many companies, the archives was established to fulfill a public relations function, and the archivist reports to the head of the public relations department. For example, the DuPont Company established its Public Relations Department in 1938 in order to combat the negative publicity that it had received in the aftermath of World War I when a Senate investigatory committee labeled the company as a "merchant of death." In order to counter this image, the advertising and public relations firm Barton, Battin, Durstine and Osborne developed the phrase "Better Living Through Chemistry," to create a new, positive image for the company. This campaign drew heavily on historical photographs that traced the history of DuPont's contributions to American defense, as well as its innovative work with plastics and textile fibers. This effort, which sought to depict the positive role that DuPont had played in American life for nearly a century, led to the establishment of a corporate archival program. A company museum was also created during this period.

Historical materials are also useful to illustrate the ways in which the company has been a good corporate citizen and a reliable business partner. The archives can be a good source of positive images that can be used to counter the bad press that all companies receive at least occasionally. In many companies there is a very fine line separating public relations, institutional history, and product advertising. These connections become clear when examining the case of Wells Fargo Bank, which has long used the Concord stagecoach as its corporate symbol. This is part of an ongoing effort to utilize the bank's history to identify Wells Fargo with the positive values of the Old West. As Dr. Harold Anderson, vice president of the Wells Fargo History Department pointed out, "in a relatively undifferentiated market like financial services, in which most institutions have similar products and services, marketing and advertising are key competitive elements." In this context, "history is an important corporate asset" as advertising professionals use historical images to differentiate their company from the competition and instill a strong sense of customer loyalty.[11] For example, from 1986 to 1987, Wells Fargo created a series of five 30-second television commercials that depicted the bank's use of precision gold standard balances in the nineteenth century. This historical image of a Wells Fargo agent using these scales to measure the gold that he was receiving from a California miner was designed to illustrate the company's reputation for reliability, its commitment to account for customers' money in a precise way, and its use of the best available technology.

AT&T used a similar strategy in a recent television advertisement that was designed to remind the public of its roots as an entrepreneurial small business with a long history of technological innovation. This advertisement featured the handwritten notebook of Alexander Graham Bell's assistant, Thomas A. Watson that documented the first intelligible sentence transmitted over the telephone. The famous words, "Mr. Watson, come here; I want you," provided a powerful image for television audiences, reminding them that AT&T was a science-based company with a long history of innovation.

Corporate speech writers often find ideas for executive speeches in the archives and can also use the archives to verify factual information. Maintaining up-to-date biographies of top corporate officials is also an invaluable service the archives can provide. Public relations departments may ask the archives to respond to certain types of questions from the general public and, therefore, ask the repositories to keep lists, timelines, and product and service information on hand. Archives staff also assemble packets of historical information that can be useful when companies are seeking to expand investment opportunities and markets abroad. These public relations packages typically trace the history of the company in a foreign market in such a way as to emphasize shared cultural values. They also describe past business dealings and technological exchanges in ways that make future joint ventures seem attractive.

Where a corporation has had a history of commercial relations in a foreign market, highlighting this past experience can be effective. For example, when AT&T was attempting to expand its business in the Pan-Asian market, it found it useful to publicize the fact that during the post–World War II years it had developed the concept of "Quality" (the use of measurements to assess customer satisfaction, product quality, and continuing improvement). This idea is usually associated with Japanese manufacturing. Reminding the Japanese and the American public that this concept had its roots in Bell Laboratories and Western Electric projects during the late 1940s proved to be a useful marketing tool. In today's global economy, foreign customers are sensitive to a business's commitment to cultural diversity. Diversity within a business can be emphasized through the use of multicultural images in corporate brochures and publications that appeal to an international audience.

Finance.   The financial officers of the corporation may be interested in keeping vital records in a temperature- and humidity-controlled environment. They look to the archives to preserve a company's oldest ledgers and make them accessible when documentation needs to be produced. Determining what financial information needs to be kept permanently is also important. Archivists, however, can often play more than a custodial role. In one corporation, after the archivist indexed a series of medical records, the finance department was able to identify excessive charges that had resulted from the health insurance company's use of a national rate-base rather than local rates that were considerably lower. As a result, the corporation quickly found another insurance vendor. Archival records of vendor contracts, when collated nationally, provided the information necessary to cut corporate medical insurance costs.

Research and Development.   Preserving R&D records can assure that the results of past research efforts, which were often conducted at great expense, can be made available to current generations of scientists and engineers who may be able to utilize experimental data generated by their predecessors. There are times when research efforts do not lead to profitable product development, but laboratory reports might be useful to future generations of researchers who may be attempting to solve similar technological problems. For example, in the 1960s, Bell Laboratories attempted to develop a "picturephone." This never resulted in a viable product, but the research and development effort proved to be useful a decade later when Bell Laboratories developed the technology associated with teleconferencing. At that time, scientists and engineers made good use of the laboratory reports and notebooks that were generated by the "picturephone" project. If AT&T had not had an archival program, the results of this past research might have been lost.

Product Managers, Trade Shows, and Exhibits.   Product managers can use archival records or pictorial materials to compete for market shares in both local and foreign markets. Product managers who were marketing the AT&T pay telephone used materials from an AT&T Archives' exhibit on the history of the pay telephone in order to promote product identification. The exhibit displayed various iterations in the development of the public pay telephone from a replica of the original, not invented by AT&T, to the most modern version offering visual images as well as sound transmission. The exhibit continues to circulate, years after its initial creation. The archives of a corporation can frequently help to create an exhibit for a trade show using artifacts and copies of interesting photos and documents. Visual images, in particular, are important to anyone organizing local or international trade shows.

International Market Penetration. Entering global markets can be difficult especially where existing local products with high name recognition exist. Historical documentation that can help to differentiate a business in a foreign market can make the product or service look more appealing. When a corporation has had a history in a foreign market, documenting and publicizing this relationship can make the corporation appear less like a strange foreign entity and more like a friend of long-standing. For example, one archives created a poster of its products sold in international markets and had it translated into at least five other languages. Foreign visitors were delighted to receive the poster, and product managers used the posters in international product ventures. Wells Fargo's museum distributed brochures in eight different languages to make their exhibits accessible to a large number of foreign visitors.[12]

Corporate Culture. Business archives are the repository of corporate culture. Many archivists are now playing an important role in employee orientation programs as corporations are recognizing the value of making staff aware of the company's history, culture and traditions. The idea is to instill staff with a pride in the company, its accomplishments, and the contributions that it has made to society so that they will recognize that their jobs have an importance that goes beyond the day to day routine. This is particularly important in the current environment of restructuring, downsizing and reengineering that has led employees at all levels to question the "psychological contracts" or informal understandings between worker and employer.[13] Establishing new "psychological contracts" is difficult and transforms even long-time employees into newcomers. Archives staff can play a central role in this process. Mere symbolism and slogans are not enough to cushion the effects of radical change. It is crucial for corporations to ease the transition to new styles or policies by providing evidence of the need for change couched in positive terms that emphasize the company's accomplishments, traditions, and culture. In her article on corporate culture,[14] Denise Rousseau discusses the importance of laying the groundwork for change by elaborating on past achievements; paving the way to new successes by celebrating past successes, before actually implementing changes. Symbolism is important. Exhibits and retrospective articles on company achievements can smooth many transitions. Linking a distinguished past to a distinguished future can strengthen employee morale and give confidence that success lies ahead. It can also help to get a corporation through times of crisis by revisiting events that have bound the staff together.

Especially helpful is documentation on social service and community-related activities of employees and the organization. Several telecommunications and public service companies have used advertisements that publicize community-oriented services especially during times of natural disasters. Other corporations have encouraged participation of their employees in events such as the Olympics to demonstrate the human side of the company, the camaraderie of its personnel and the implication that this atmosphere can withstand future reengineering or downsizing. The accomplishments of the individual can be celebrated in such a way as to instill a sense of pride in the entire corporation.

Documenting Individual Achievements. Documenting the achievements of outstanding employees is an effective way to boost morale and let employees know they are valued in a graphic and highly visible way. Exhibits can help to do this as well as photographs and articles in internal publications. In science-based companies celebrating awards such as the Nobel Prizes encourages pride in one's colleagues and by association, in the larger corporate community. Oral histories can also illuminate individual achievements.

Inquiries from the General Public. Since the archives document the growth and achievements of a corporation, it is in a particularly good position to answer questions from the public about the business. The archives can prepare packaged responses for student and other outside requests. Many companies provide information for students, recognizing in them future customers with appreciative parents and teachers. Teachers may also want to know something about how the business works. The archives can help employees with presentations for student groups. Some corporate archives have also reproduced historic products, images and packaging. This nostalgic look at the past can keep the image of a business in the public eye. In addition, the archives may find it can generate its own "products," depending on the nature of the enterprise. There are many examples of business archives—Coca-Cola, Nabisco, and Hess Gasoline—reproducing historic labels, bottles, packaging, or product images in order to tell the public about the company's accomplishments and contributions to society. Recent Coca-Cola advertisements that depict the ways in which Coca-Cola was distributed to the American soldiers during the Second World War are a good example of this genre.

Centralized Documentation and Internal Communications. An archives can save an organization time and money by providing access to documents in a central location—avoiding searches for materials dispersed over a wide employee population, and eliminating duplicate storage. For example, several large companies centralize their photographic resources. The staff is educated to go to a single source to obtain a photograph so less time is spent searching other sources. Several groups can use the same photograph for different purposes, saving the cost of rephotographing an image. A photograph of women in a laboratory setting may be used for a variety of purposes: for affirmative action documentation; for recruiting women workers; for a newspaper article on the particular person in the photograph; or for legal purposes to verify the type of equipment used in the laboratory. All of the above uses can be supported if the archives skillfully anticipates potential needs and uses those needs as the foundation of its collection policies.

The approach to archival management described in this essay shows how the work of business archivists can contribute to the bottom line. In the present environment of tight budgets, increasing competition for resources, and political pressures, archivists working in a variety of settings need to be more responsive to marketplace imperatives. This may be the time to innovate, to let new technology help us develop the skills that will ensure that business archives are seen as valuable resources—as knowledge management centers and not historical warehouses.

Endnotes

1. George David Smith and Laurence E. Steadman, "Present Value of Corporate History," *Harvard Business Review* (November–December 1981): 164.

2. The views expressed in this article are based on my work with such high-technology organizations as Bell Laboratories (Lucent Technologies), Microsoft and AT&T, consulting relationships with several international law and economics firms, and participation on the High Tech Committee (initiated by the Smithsonian and consisting of leading-edge technology companies, including Bell Laboratories, Microsoft, Hewlett Packard, Texas Instruments, Motorola, Cray, DEC and Sematech). In addition, my views have been influenced by the study of "knowledge management" in a variety of other environments such as museums and libraries and through discussions with W. D. Penniman, former head of the Special Libraries Association, and Michael Nash of the Hagley Museum and Library.

3. The "command and control" structure appeared in the years following the American Civil War and evolved further after World War I. "Command and control" relied upon the basic assumption that military methods of achieving missions and conducting work were successful and could be applied to general business practices.

4. Peter Drucker, "The Coming of the New Organization," *Harvard Business Review* (January–February 1988): 45–53.

5. JoAnne Yates, *Control Through Communication: The Rise of System in American Management* (Baltimore: Johns Hopkins University Press, 1989), 271.

6. Bruce H. Bruemmer and Sheldon Hochheiser, *The High-Technology Company: A Historical Research and Archival Guide* (Minneapolis: Charles Babbage Institute, Center for the History of Information Processing, 1989), 103.

7. Robert G. Lewis, "The Bell System Divestiture: A Project to Analyze the History," *The Business History Bulletin* 1, no. 1 (summer 1988): 7.

8. Robert Garnet, *The Telephone Enterprise: The Evolution of the Bell System's Horizontal Structure* (Baltimore: Johns Hopkins University Press, 1985); George Davis Smith, *The Anatomy of Business Strategy: Bell, Western Electric and the Origins of the American Telephone Industry* (Baltimore: Johns Hopkins University Press, 1985); Neil H. Wasserman, *From the Invention to Innovation: Long-Distance Telephone Transmission at the Turn of the Century* (Baltimore: Johns Hopkins University Press, 1985).

9. The SLA conducted several annual surveys of libraries and archives. These may be available from the SLA for various years.

10. Smith and Steadman, "Present Value of Corporate History," 165.

11. Harold P. Anderson, "Banking on the Past: Wells Fargo & Company," *The Business History Bulletin* 1 (fall 1988): 9–12.

12. Smith and Steadman, "Present Value of Corporate History," 12.

13. Denise Rousseau, "Manager's Journal," *Wall Street Journal*, August 12, 1996, A2.

14. Ibid.

3

Archival Mythology and Corporate Reality: A Potential Powder Keg

Philip F. Mooney

> *Identifying new opportunities and then converting those opportunities to reality requires strong business-assessment skills and tools.*
> *Value-based management makes us all think about creating value in everything we do, every day, at every level of our Company. In an age where everyone has the same information at the same time, the advantage goes to the people who can take that information and quickly put it to effective and profitable use.*
>
> *June 1996*

With these two position statements, executives at the Coca-Cola Company outlined the philosophical underpinnings of a business strategy that will govern the allocations of financial and human resources into the twenty-first century. For an archives program to successfully function and prosper in such an environment requires a disciplined and somewhat unconventional application of traditional archival principles directed towards measurable results. Unfortunately, many practicing business archivists either fail to recognize the inherent reality of similar operating systems in their organizations or are incapable of adapting their archival practices to a changing corporate culture. The inevitable result is a stagnation in the growth and development of business archives over the last two decades with little hope for a reversal of this trend in the foreseeable future. Extending the analogy even further, the archival community, taken as a whole, has adopted a myopic view of their roles and responsibilities within their parent organizations that has detrimentally affected administrators' views of the value of archival functions and the respective resources required to support them.

Concepts such as "intelligent risk-taking," "thinking outside of the box," "working with a strategic focus," and "fostering a learning environment" are familiar elements in the lexicon of contemporary business. They serve as guiding principles and measuring sticks in reviewing group initiatives, achievements and budgetary resources. With few exceptions, the archival community has continued to operate in an insular fashion, either refusing to acknowledge the existence of evolving corporate management schemes or steadfastly holding to traditional procedural methodologies. The predictable result is that corporate archival programs, if they exist at all, are underfunded, understaffed and underutilized.

Central to this divergent set of operational perceptions is a series of archival myths that have been perpetuated through the years both in the professional literature and in the training accorded aspiring archivists. For at least the last two decades, authors and educators have suggested approaches to the administrative use of corporate records that have been flawed if not totally unfounded. At this critical juncture in the development and preservation of corporate archives, it might be appropriate to look at some myths that have gained acceptance through the years against the realities of life in the corporate world.

Myth #1.   Many corporate archives are developed to be helpful in providing perspective to the conduct of the daily affairs of business. Executives and senior managers will review and analyze past initiatives, policies, and programs, assess the historical record and develop best-business practices based on documented success stories.

An article produced by William Overman in the January 1959 issue of the *American Archivist* provides this rationale for the development of the Firestone Archives, the first recognized corporate program in the United States. According to Overman, Harvey Firestone, Jr. believed that company records not only were useful tools for the development of a planned company history, but also "that certain records would be of value to management for reference in making decisions regarding current business problems as they arose."[1] The underlying assumption here is that this program offered valuable information for the formulation of contemporary policies and procedures. If that assertion is true, why does Firestone continue to operate today without benefit of an archives?

Reality #1.   The reality of the situation may be found in the same article where reference is made to an approaching 50th anniversary celebration. In all probability, the impetus for development of a historical collection was a single, seminal event that required historical documentation for an appropriate execution. However, when the immediate, quantifiable reason for archival support disappeared, so too did the archives.

In real terms, company employees rarely think of the archives as a source of contemporary information. By its very nature it stands as a repository of "past" information, data that is irrelevant to the realities of a competitive marketplace. The only way that the records become a tool in the contemporary marketing mix is for an advocate to promote their use with supporting evidence of meaningful results. Motorola and Wells Fargo effectively use permanent exhibits as brand-building activities and key components in the development of their respective corporate cultures. Nabisco, Disney, and other consumer goods companies frequently use archival resources to produce nostalgic promotions with broad consumer appeal. A merchandise-licensing program at the Coca-Cola Company annually generates revenues in excess of $7 million from merchandise using imagery drawn from its Archives Department. In all of these situations, the archivist has either assumed the cloak of heritage marketer or has developed a network of satisfied clients who actively endorse the value of corporate memory and the relevant resources attendant to it. Otherwise the role of the archives would be short-lived and event-specific.

Myth #2.   Companies understand and appreciate the role of history within the corporation. History helps to establish corporate culture within the organization and to define common objectives.

Harold Anderson of Wells Fargo argued in a 1982 special issue of the *American Archivist* that with the development of internal corporate archives "the lessons of history are being organized as building blocks to the future." Echoing a similar theme, George David Smith and Laurence E. Steadman wrote in the *Harvard Business Review:* "A company's history contains its heritage and traditions, which managers need to understand if they are to see the present as part of a process rather than a collection of accidental happenings. Perceiving a company in this way can enhance a manager's ability to plan for the future."[2]

Reality #2.   There is very little hard evidence to support this thesis. Corporate culture is an evolving process driven by the technological and consumer trends rather than a "this-is-the-way-we-have-always-done-it" approach. Only if the archival program has the capacity to project its resources in programs that are relevant to the lifestyles of the business's consumers will it be successful. The archives must contribute to the bottom line in a direct or indirect fashion, but in either case, the results must yield hard numbers.

Some of the traditional measurements used to capture the archival contributions have included trademark and patent protection, customer/client support, and nostalgic promotions, but the difficulty in the analysis lies in the imprecise nature of value calculation. The use of records to defend proprietary patents and trademarks would appear at surface level to have a compelling financial payback, but the actual use of corporate records for this purpose is small at most institutions.

From a strictly managerial perspective, it might be cost-beneficial to hire contract historians to research trademark and patent issues on an "as-needed" basis rather than to absorb the overhead of a departmental operation. The remaining elements outlined above are essentially intangible assets. There is general agreement that some value exists in each of the categories, but it is much more difficult to assess the precise nature of the contribution.

Corporations are ahistoric by their very nature. Their success or failure is governed by the degree to which they generate positive financial results in regularly defined intervals, usually on a quarterly basis and certainly on an annual one. Analysts, stock portfolio managers, shareholders, the business media, and consumers will evaluate performance and issue report cards from these respective positions. The constant challenge to management is to continue to produce strong financial numbers, signaling a healthy and growing enterprise. Any failure to focus on the delivery of positive numbers and on business growth invites a strong negative reaction from the client base, which endangers the corporate body and the management group that governs it. Is it any wonder that history plays such a small role in this process?

Value-based management is simply the latest corporate term used to describe the ongoing need to quantify the contributions that an internal archival program makes to the bottom line. In previous iterations, "zero-based budgeting" and "cost justifications" characterized a similar process of focusing all corporate activities against the costs associated with executing them. A return-on-investment calculation determined whether the project, task, or function received the requested level of funding.

In most contemporary business planning cycles, operating units must annually present both a short- (12 months) and long-term (3 to 5 years) plan that include proposed initiatives, deliverables or results, and a listing of resources required to successfully complete the plan. A review panel consisting of senior executives, line managers, and strategists review all proposals and decide which projects are most strategically aligned with overall corporate objectives. Only when an archival program can align its programs and resources with the contemporary impetus of marketing programs can it expect to receive appropriate levels of support. Most often the archives falls into the "nice-to-have" category that is acceptable during years of prosperity, but is dangerously expendable in periods of economic stress.

Business archives in the 1990s must accept the premise that their existence in the corporate structure requires them to model their behavior after their departmental associates. Job number one requires that documentation of contributions to the financial well-being of the parent body be maintained and distributed to decision makers. Every task and project undertaken should produce statistical data that justifies the activity. Public relations departments use advertising tables to compute the value of articles and media coverage generated by the department; consumer information centers and marketing research groups have developed sophisticated tracking systems to measure the success of products and promotions; advertising executives can determine the penetration and effectiveness of commercial messages to segmented markets. In a similar fashion, archival professionals need to develop more precise tools to measure bottom-line contributions and to focus energies on those areas where results are evident and documentable.

Rather than relying on the quantitative statistical reports that many archivists use to justify their programs, qualitative evaluations of project results provide more meaningful data to asses performance and value. Mirroring corporate models, such reports should include cost analyses of resources employed against results attained. Though the archival function frequently operates in a supporting role, it is possible to develop an accounting structure that recognizes and measures the contributions of all parties. Many archivists are familiar with the concept of establishing an "in-kind" or "overhead" fee in developing grant applications. Similarly, a model business evaluation system would recognize the archival contribution to projects and programs on a percentage basis, thereby providing a clear picture of the archival component that management could use in assessing performance.

Myth #3. Corporate archives have experienced healthy growth over the last 20 years reflecting a heightened interest in the maintenance and administration of an internal history department.

Reality #3. The reengineering of American corporations over the last two decades and the economic upheaval caused by acquisitions, divestitures, and wide-scale downsizing of staff positions have virtually eliminated any growth potential for the business archives. From 1975 to the present, the number of archivists claiming affiliation with a business has remained static, while a number of major programs have closed their doors.[3] Included on the casualty list are the notable collections of Sears, Eastman Kodak, United Technologies, Boeing, Arco, Educational Testing Service, and International Harvester (Navistar).

Management may accept the notion that a historical record helps to establish core values, create a shared business philosophy, and serves as a useful public relations tool from time to time, but the perception also persists that history and historical research is a commodity that can be purchased as needed. The rise of the historical consulting business as an on-demand service mirrors a larger trend in management theory that asserts that businesses need to focus on their core productive functions in developing organizational structures and in allocating the overhead that accompanies each of those functions. All other services, from accounting to human resources, can be purchased as needed from a host of providers. The unstated corollary to that position is that these same services can be discontinued, discarded, or reallocated as the needs of the business require without the burdensome issue of separation packages that may come into play with permanent staff.

Given this environment of managing lean and mean in an ever-changing marketplace, prospects for a corporate archival renaissance are bleak. Private consulting groups will have enormous impact over the quality and quantity of records preserved and on their physical location. They speak to business in a language that corporate managers understand, and their focus is task-specific, time-sensitive, and goal-oriented, qualities that many practicing archivists have not acquired.

In a recent paper delivered at the Records of American Business Conference, a revised version of which is published in this volume, business consultant Karen Benedict suggested a strategy of encouraging business enterprises to remove their historical files from the corporation and to donate them to historical agencies and universities who have the staff and training to properly care for these materials and make them available in some form to the public. While her proposal was strongly criticized by a few business archivists in attendance, it offers a very pragmatic and creative solution to a problem that will not disappear. Few corporations will be willing to make the investments required to maintain an internal archives program. The return on investment simply is not there.

The archival community needs to decide on an approach to this dilemma. From a philosophical and emotional standpoint, archivists can and should continue to encourage a corporation to consider establishing corporate archives programs and hiring professionals to administer them, but at the pragmatic level, other options must also be advanced. Regional business centers, contract archival services and storage, more formalized support for businesses from the Society of American Archivists and regional archival organizations, and benchmark models for corporations to review provide some additional initiatives that might help capture business records that otherwise will be consigned to the shredder.

From an internal perspective, business archivists and consultants need to be very focused in their approach to history. They must be aggressive self-promoters, seeking every opportunity to sell the use of the archival record for business enhancement. From exhibits, promotional publications, and employee orientations to licensing, public relations, training, and outreach, archivists must view the archival function from a multifunctional, universally proactive perspective. To achieve success and financial stability, the archivist must adapt to the business environment and constantly seek new opportunities to market its resources and service to its constituents.

The archival community can also play an important role in helping practicing archivists better understand the realities of work life in an environment where Dilbert may be more relevant than Schellenberg. Sponsored seminars, workshops, and publications on both the regional and national level might help to focus archivists' thinking towards results-oriented activities and provide platforms where case studies and "best practices" might serve as useful guides for strategy formulation. The Archives Management Roundtable offers one existing resource for information sharing on such issues, but there needs to be a broader dissemination of learning to a much broader audience. The myths and realities of the corporate world have parallels in the academic and nonprofit sectors. Enlightened archivists will take note of them and pursue action plans that will insure continued support of the archival mission.

Endnotes

1. Quoted in William D. Overman, "The Pendulum Swings," *American Archivist* 22 (January 1959): 4.

2. Harold P. Anderson, "Business Archives: A Corporate Asset," *American Archivist* 45, no. 3 (summer 1982): 264; George David Smith and Laurence E. Steadman, "Present Value of Corporate History," in *Corporate Archives and History: Making the Past Work*, eds. Arnita A. Jones and Phillip L. Cantelon (Melbourne, Fla.: Krieger Publishing Company, 1993), 163–164.

3. The 1975 *Directory of Business Archives in the United States and Canada* (Chicago: The Society of American Archivists) listed 195 institutions. By 1990 the number of corporate archives listed in the directory had dropped to 158.

4

View from the Inside: Corporate Executives and the Records of American Business

Edward G. Jefferson, Dolores Hanna, and Michael Miles

Archivists, historians, and other users of business records often proceed as if their views on value and permanence are the only important ones. That is hardly the case. Critical to the preservation of records of business is the support of the corporate executives. While business leaders are inevitably concerned with the products, services, and financial stability of the companies they lead, they are also well aware that the history of those enterprises is useful in such varied work as marketing, employee training, and the development of corporate image. In the excerpts that follow, three executives discuss their views of the way in which a sense of history is integral to the company mission. These personal reflections convey a clear sense of why each believes in the value of corporate memory.

History: An Indispensable Resource
Edward G. Jefferson

Edward G. Jefferson was president and chief executive officer of the DuPont Company from 1981 to 1986. Born in London, England, he holds a doctorate in chemistry from King's College, University of London. Joining DuPont in 1951 as a research chemist, he served in a variety of research and technical positions before assuming general management assignments during the 1960s. Under his leadership the company supported the research and writing of *Science and Corporate Strategy* (Cambridge University Press, 1988) by David Hounshell and John Smith. This history of research and development at DuPont drew on the DuPont Company archives at the Hagley Museum and Library. Jefferson made the following observations in a discussion of his views on the importance of collecting and presenting corporate history.

Science and technology have had such a large role in shaping our society that we cannot expect to understand our world without study of the history of science. Believing historical studies to be valuable to the chemical industry, I decided, in 1982, to support development of a history of research in the DuPont Company that would be not the traditional anniversary book or public relations-type history but a scholarly work of lasting merit and credibility.

Histories do not contribute to profits, so one might ask why we supported this work, devoting time, effort, and funds to work with historians. Several considerations helped me make this judgment. Fundamentally, a good history is its own justification. History is an indispensable resource for the advance of society, and its importance is one of our shared humanist values. DuPont research has made key contributions to science and technology. Those of us who have been part of DuPont's research tradition realize that it is not enough to say simply that the company invented nylon, neoprene, Teflon, and other products. The scientific work that led to these developments, the organizational approach to the work, and often the resilience and sense of purpose of the scientists and engineers can help guide and inspire research in the future.

But why should such a history be a scholarly work, as opposed to an in-house production? There are several reasons. First, for a history to remain credible and of permanent value to society it is best it be a work of scholarship. An important function of a civilized society is to develop and preserve an understanding of its culturally important institutions. Corporate research in the Bell Laboratories of AT&T, or the laboratories of General Electric, DuPont, and many others is just such a resource both for the corporations and society as a whole.

Second, to the extent that people have an awareness of history, they often take it for granted—or worse, confuse it with reportage and chronology. History is more than a recounting of dates and events. It is, as the classical writers understood, "philosophy learned from examples." Its methodology is no less demanding than that of any other discipline. It is not reasonable to expect excellent results from someone who is not trained in its art and practice.

I expect the DuPont research history will show our research managers how past problems were solved, and they will see how many of the issues we are wrestling with today are not unique to our time. Organizational concerns such as centralization versus decentralization have surfaced again and again. It is doubtful that a company writer would view our research from the historian's perspective and be able to place it in an appropriate social context.

Third, as valuable as a scholarly approach to corporate history is for an internal audience, it is essential if the end product is to have credibility outside the company. If we are producing our history for society's benefit, then we must do so on society's terms. And society, particularly the opinion leaders we are trying to reach, will view anything less than a rigorous, professional history as corporate vanity—however well intended and informative it may be. It makes little difference that the commentators and institutions who make such judgments may have more than a tinge of vanity themselves. As a practical matter the burden of proof is on us.

Is it important for us to reach opinion leaders? Of course it is, especially for the chemical industry. Of all the industries grounded in the scientific tradition, ours is probably the least well understood. People learn about us primarily through the news media or through the works of writers who discuss our activities—past and present—in a manner that serves their personal agendas.

We complain, and rightfully so, that the criticisms leveled against the chemical industry are naive and unsophisticated. We find it hard to accept that the critics are being honest with themselves and with the public. Many otherwise well-informed people still see major corporations as monoliths of secrecy and power. There is little appreciation of the human drama, creativity, and teamwork that underlie the key technological advances that have come from our industry. There is little awareness that the achievements of corporate scientists and executives can stand comparison to their counterparts in universities and government. Brochures and advertisements will not correct these misperceptions, but by carefully documenting our histories, we can show that the motivations, problems, and accomplishments of corporate science and engineering are worthy of serious inquiry and examination.

Good history is not going to change things overnight, but it will help. By establishing an authoritative record that serves as a reference, we can temper the more sensational accounts. William J. Reader's two-volume history of Imperial Chemical Industries, for example, has had just such an effect on subsequent studies of ICI.

More importantly, such histories will eventually find their way into the discourse of academics and political leaders. Alfred D. Chandler's works, for example—of particular value to historians of science, technology, and business—have also influenced the thinking of traditional historians. The idea of history as primarily political history is giving way to a broader view of the subject in which the history of science and technology is treated as an essential element. Without the study of corporate histories, the story of science and technology in our century will be told inadequately or not at all. Should we permit such a deficiency to persist, we will be passing up an opportunity to place knowledge of industrial science where it belongs—in the mainstream of American intellectual thought.

We have a responsibility to ourselves, to science, and to society to see that the history of corporations is effectively recorded. The corporate organizations in which so many have spent long and fruitful careers are worthy of respect and understanding, because the science and technology coming from our laboratories have made a positive contribution to the world. We have a responsibility to ourselves and to those who have preceded us to inform others of these accomplishments. If by neglect we imply that our histories are unimportant or if we subject them to unscholarly treatments, we then have no defense against those who would seek to diminish our achievements.

Our responsibility to science is somewhat different. The history of science and technology is a rapidly growing field. Its potential is so important in an advanced technological society that the National Endowment for the Humanities suggested that a course in the history of science and technology be a compulsory element of a liberal education. There exists an opportunity to have the story of industrial science told and assimilated by the next generation so that it becomes part of their world view.

Finally, we have a responsibility to society. Our companies are institutions of importance to society, and we believe that our science has made a contribution to a better life for the people of our time. If we agree that society has a need to understand the impact of these developments, then it follows that the only way this understanding will emerge is if the story of industry is told.

Once that history is appreciated, we can look for certain benefits. Among them is a better understanding of how policy decisions of government affect developments in industry, which in turn shape the world in which we live. It is generally believed, even by informed laymen, that government impact on the chemical industry began with the Environmental Protection Agency. DuPont's research history has revealed that government laboratories, antitrust legislation, and tax policy have had an impact on the direction and scope of our research for many decades.

Kraft Foods, Inc.: An Interview with Dolores Hanna
Dolores Hanna

Dolores Hanna had just retired from her position of Senior Trademark Counsel at Kraft General Foods, Inc. (now Kraft Foods, Inc.) when she made the following comments in 1990 as part of an oral history interview with Elizabeth Adkins, Kraft's corporate archivist. Hanna joined Kraft General Foods' predecessor, Kraftco Corporation, in 1973 as trademark counsel. Prior to that she was a partner in the law firm of Fitch, Even, Tabin & Flannery.

ADKINS: I know that you were very involved in helping getting the Archives started at Kraft. When did you first think about putting an archives together? What kinds of things made you think it would be a good idea?

HANNA: I had always felt that a special department was needed, whether you called it Archives or not, that could work with the law department in looking through corporate records, trying to verify certain folklore stories and myths that were constantly arising. In my close association with the public relations department, the two departments were constantly confronted with copy that had imminent deadlines, but contained statements that we were both concerned about and which we could not easily and accurately verify. In the past some of the verification had taken the form of, "I found this information in a previous company publication." As we examined those previous company publications, we were able to determine that no verification of accuracy had ever occurred. There were several stories that we did take time to look at very carefully and learned that they were totally inaccurate, in fact embarrassingly inaccurate. So we refused to permit those stories to be used thereafter. All of this took a great deal of time which neither the PR department nor the law department had available. So we discussed among ourselves the need to have a separate group set up to keep records and to be able to check and verify. The idea of an archives started emerging from all of this. I heard about other organizations that had archives and I had discussions with people who would tell me that the establishment of something like an archives would be very useful and that many corporations saw the need for it, even though they might talk about it only in terms of company records that were never to be destroyed and that could be used then for verification purposes. Once or twice we had management

consulting groups or other groups suggest an archives and
at one time, we had a formal presentation made to us. However, senior management was not initially enthusiastic
about the idea. No one wanted to create a budget or to
increase staffing in a non-income producing area. I still
selfishly had wanted some kind of a department created
because I saw that there was less and less time that anyone
could devote to assisting certain projects. For example, we
had periodic anniversary marketing programs, like the
PHILADELPHIA BRAND cream cheese 100th anniversary. We spent too much time trying to assist the brand
managers and others to get information to made exciting
stories that were true for the anniversary.

One day at a meeting I attended, there was a cocktail
party preceding the meeting and I met a consultant who
helped organizations establish archives programs. I told her
to send me some materials, so that I could look them over
and talk to some people. I showed the material she sent me
to a number of individuals in the law, advertising, and public relations departments. I said, "Can't we reactivate an
interest in this again? If I could be assigned a little bit of
money to do some investigation, I could at least get a proposal." Someone finally assigned some money so I could
pay her and that's how it started. She sent us a proposal,
with various alternate ways that we could move ahead. Then
a presentation was arranged to be made to what was then
called the management policy committee. The consultant
made a suggestion which we thought would be a good idea.
We decided to talk about it in terms of a limited project,
so it wouldn't be so permanent and threatening. If after that
limited period of time it didn't work out, that would be the
end of it and there wouldn't be any real big final commitment. Well, that worked. It was accepted as a three-year
project with a review every six months or a year.

Our next problem was finding space to house the Archives. We wanted the Archives to be on the premises. We
thought that it would have a greater effect and impact if it
was accessible for people to drop in and use. That way
people would always be conscious of it. We almost got
space for it on the floor where engineering was located,
which is now the fourth floor in the new building. But space
was tight and that didn't work out. We finally agreed that
we would go off-site, because we would have more space
that way, and we would have the Archives attached to

enough corporate groups so that its visibility wouldn't be lost. That's how it all started. It caught on immediately and people saw its value and used it on a regular basis, so we dropped this three-year project idea and the questions never arose again. It just continued as a permanent department.

ADKINS: Mike Miles was, I believe, a supporter of the idea.

HANNA: Yes. Mike Miles fortunately had a good marketing and advertising and promotion background and saw the value of having facilities available to people within those groups. He wasn't thinking in the terms necessarily that I was, in helping with litigation and verification, but he saw the value of it as a unit that was useful on a day-to-day basis, and not in the case of extraordinary events. He just assumed that it was a department that everyone should have access to and could use.

ADKINS: I've always been struck that Kraft got its archives started right, in a fairly big way, as opposed to getting into it gradually which so many companies do.

HANNA: Our luck was that we had a good consultant. She had various proposals, but all of them envisioned a real archives. When the facts and figures were there, and compared to other things that were being done within the company, suddenly that amount of money, time and effort didn't seem that extraordinary. So it was very wise to have put it all on the table at once and not to let it just grow quietly and topsy-turvy. The other fortunate thing that the consultant recommended was that we not just promote someone from within the corporation that had no background or training or understanding of what an archives is; instead, we went out to professionals.

In this discussion, I hope that I did not make it sound as if I was the one who started the Archives. I wasn't. A number of people had an interest, but someone always had to keep them interested and push them ahead, and I think that I did that. I wouldn't let the subject die, but the others were the ones who had the power and the authority to make it happen. If they didn't believe in it, regardless of what I said, it wouldn't have happened. We just all believed that it was a good thing.

ADKINS: I think it was helpful that there was a variety of people, and a variety of departments, who were interested.

HANNA: The director of advertising recognized the value of main-
            taining all those records that he tried to maintain indepen-
            dently; the senior management in the public relations
            department saw the value of it for disciplines within the
            corporation that had nothing to do with the law. That's what
            helped.

ADKINS: Did the Archives then come to serve the function you had
            envisioned? Did it give you the kind of help you had hoped
            for?

HANNA: Yes. What we had to do was recognize that some of the
            answers that the Archives provided with the material it had
            at hand wouldn't necessarily be evidentiary type of answers
            that you would have to have in a court of law, but you had
            to accept that. We couldn't have answers that were always
            without questions or without some reasonable doubt. We
            had to understand that any archives, no matter how efficient
            and what materials it had, could provide answers only to a
            certain point. Like a computer, you get answers only based
            on what you've put into it. The Archives has to continue to
            encourage people to provide it with materials so that when
            at a future time answers are needed, it has those materials
            from which to draw. No matter how innovative or creative
            the archivist is, it can't find answers if it doesn't have any
            clues as to where the answers might be. So I think it has
            to continue to be certain that the kind of information it
            needs for future answers is provided to it.

            That's hard to do. Just as an example, we should always
            be aware of the Archives at the end of litigation. Maybe
            that's something you will always have to approach the law
            department and ask about: Is there anything that was as-
            sembled in current litigation that should be retained for
            archival reasons? The current trend now with lawyers is to
            destroy more than to save; that is the trend because of the
            requirements of discovery and the demand for production
            of documents. You may want to ask that question on a reg-
            ular basis before the lawyers physically destroy everything.

            Every time there is any kind of anniversary or a project,
            and you are the ones who have provided the material, you
            should make sure that everything that's been provided is
            returned to you and that you have a good record. I know
            that this seems foolish with all the promotional work that
            is done, but I think it would be smart if you could retain a

lot of the materials that are used in promotions. They will be even more valuable in the future.

Philip Morris Companies, Inc.: An Interview with Michael Miles
Michael Miles

Michael Miles, former CEO of Philip Morris Companies, Inc., made the following comments in 1994 as part of an oral history interview with Elizabeth Adkins, Kraft's corporate archivist. Before starting as Philip Morris's CEO in 1991, he had been CEO of Philip Morris subsidiary Kraft General Foods, Inc. (now Kraft Foods, Inc.). His association with Kraft General Foods started in 1982, when he was hired as president of Kraft, Inc., a predecessor company. Prior to that he was senior vice president of foods at Heublein, Inc. and chairman of Kentucky Fried Chicken Corporation worldwide.

ADKINS: Not long after you started as president of Kraft, you were approached with the idea of starting an archives. From all accounts, you responded favorably to the idea. What gave you an appreciation for the concept of an archives?

MILES: That's interesting. As I remember it, that's a decision for which I would claim almost 100 percent credit.

ADKINS: Really?

MILES: Yes. When I was at Kentucky Fried Chicken, there was a very strong corporate culture built around Colonel Sanders there . . . or perhaps I should say business culture, because it encompassed the franchisees as well. I discovered fairly early on that no one had made any effort to preserve any Colonel Sanders memorabilia or to preserve anything that described the startup of the company. I thought it would be a shame if any business with such a colorful figure and with so much interesting history didn't make some effort to preserve it. So, I initiated a project to set up, not only an archives, but also a Colonel Sanders museum, which I think is still in existence in the corporate headquarters in Louisville. I also commissioned a film to be made about the Colonel's life. Unfortunately we ended up doing it on a sort of a wing and a prayer budget, so it's not the best film of its kind, but it has been used a number of times since the Colonel passed away, to reinstill the Colonel's spirit in the organization. On hindsight, it was one of the best public affairs and corporate affairs investments we ever made.

Some of my interest in this sort of thing may have even traced back to Leo Burnett. In my early years, Leo Burnett (the man) was finishing his career, and the agency went to some lengths to insure that a lot of his memorabilia was preserved, some of his speeches were recorded and some films were made.

When I got to Kraft, I discovered a very strong culture, to some degree built around an individual person, J. L. Kraft, but including a lot of very interesting other people as well. As was the case with Kentucky Fried Chicken, no particular effort was being made to preserve and protect. We painted portraits of chairmen and hung them in the boardroom, but no effort was made beyond that. I'm pretty sure it was my idea to set up an archives and to try to begin to collect some historical material, so that some period of time down the road, people who were interested could look back and understand what was going on. It never occurred to me when we got the project going that Kraft would become part of Philip Morris. Kraft's future culture and history will be inextricably intertwined with Philip Morris' and, to some degree, the history of Kraft will be less interesting than if Kraft had remained a stand-alone company. But, still and all, I think having an archives is very important.

5

Strategy, Structure, Detail, Function: Four Parameters for the Appraisal of Business Records

Christopher T. Baer

One of the chief impediments to dealing with the records of modern business is their bulk and complexity, but the appraisal of business records is a process only occasionally talked about and not well understood. Literature on business records is either excessively general or focused on specific firms or record types.[1] The few firms that have been the subject of in-depth, published appraisal studies thus far have been simple organizations with shallow management structures engaged in extractive industries.[2] The most ambitious and promising project to date, the study of high-tech company records undertaken by the Charles Babbage Institute, works at the other end of the spectrum

Portions of this article were developed as a product of the author's participation in the 1986 Research Fellowship Program for the Study of Modern Archives administered by the Bentley Historical Library, University of Michigan, and funded by the Andrew W. Mellon Foundation, the National Endowment for the Humanities, and the University of Michigan. The author gratefully acknowledges this assistance and would also like to thank Michael Nash, Joan Warnow-Blewett, and JoAnne Yates for their helpful comments and suggestions.

with a young industry whose structures and processes may not be typical of business as a whole.[3]

The appraisal of American business records is further complicated by the fact that they tend to be preserved in two markedly different environments, the in-house corporate archive and the collecting repository. Simply comparing the *Directory of Business Archives in the United States and Canada* (82 pp.) and *Standard & Poor's Register of Corporations, Directors and Executives* (2856 pp.) is sufficient to prove that only a tiny minority of firms, clustered in a few sectors, opt for professionally run archives,[4] and the reality of firm mortality makes record loss inevitable. Despite the successes of corporate archives, collecting repositories will continue to play a role, if only to deal with undocumented sectors, dead or dying firms, and individuals. As a result, however, business records tend to end up at the two extremes, in corporate archives that are essentially private and internally driven and in repositories that are essentially public and client-driven.

Appraisal and Archival Theory: Some Preliminary Observations

Recent years have witnessed a renewed debate over what constitutes valid appraisal theory and practice, generally conducted between the Canadian proponents of archival theory on the one hand and the heirs of Schellenberg on the other.[5] The American position, as I see and accept it, is that the relationship between appraisal and traditional archival theory is dialectical, not dependent.[6] Archival theory evolved to safeguard the integrity of documents that had come into archives through processes that were seen as outside the archivist's purview and thus examined superficially if at all.[7] Appraisal, on the other hand, is essentially an exercise in cost-benefit analysis.[8] Historically, appraisal emerged as a means of bringing large bodies of records that had accumulated in storerooms rather than archives under something approximating traditional archival control.[9] The appraisal archivist must weigh a variety of costs and benefits, realizing that they are rarely equally distributed.

The theorists are perfectly correct in their determination to protect the integrity of records. Applying the concepts and concerns of a discipline external to the records indeed threatens to transform a benignly indifferent archive into a partisan brief or a set of research notes. On the other hand, the pragmatists are also right in their concern for cost burdens and their responsiveness to patrons who can directly or indirectly influence institutional policy and funding.[10] Concerns for integrity and concerns with cost are thus in constant tension that may be resolved in any number of ways, but not without some violence to one or both sides. Either way, a choice must be made.

Despite their disagreements on other issues, most Canadian and American authorities concur that one way of making sure that our choices are well grounded is to focus on the circumstances of records creation and purpose.[11] Terry Cook, following cues from Hugh Taylor, has also called for shifting the focus in appraisal to the mind of the records creator,[12] an essential exercise in the modern archives or collecting repository, where the distances, physical and mental, between the records creator and the archivist are apt to be quite large.

In a dialectical appraisal scheme, the archivist is thus obliged first and foremost to think somewhat like the records creator when in the integrity mode and, like the whole range of his or her clients (with one eye on the budget), in the cost-benefit mode. However, it should be borne in mind that the ability to fathom how, for example, physicists work and what sort of records they create is not (contra Eastwood) the same as the ability to do physics.[13] Much of the requisite knowledge can be learned directly from careful observation, consultation, and experience. This is how the clerks and secretaries who handle the records produced by others learn what they need to know about records' structure and function and is, indeed, the manner in which all sorts of professionals assess the needs of their clients.

How, then, is the archivist to think like the creator of business records, or more exactly, to understand the values, special expertise, needs, and purposes that go into such records' creation? The archival theorists would have us search for properties common to all businesses. Given the fact that the latest *Standard Industrial Classification Manual* lists 71 major categories of business firms, each with multiple subdivisions,[14] this looks like no easy task.

I will here propose that the best intellectual map to this seeming maze can be found in the four parameters of the title: strategy, structure, detail, and function. Collectively, they provide the basis by which the archivist can come to understand the activities of business and thus the content, meaning, and significance of business records. Most, if not all, of what an archivist needs to know on the subject can be subsumed under these headings. This knowledge is the essential qualification when loading both pans of the appraisal balance. On the one side, the parameters form the framework for understanding the purpose and significance of business actions. By illuminating the circumstances behind records creation, they enable the archivist to protect the integrity of an archive in a more precise, nuanced, and defensible way. On the other side, by explicating the original purpose of business records, they can form a more reliable basis for extrapolations regarding continuing or future uses and usefulness. As will

Figure 1. The Four Parameters

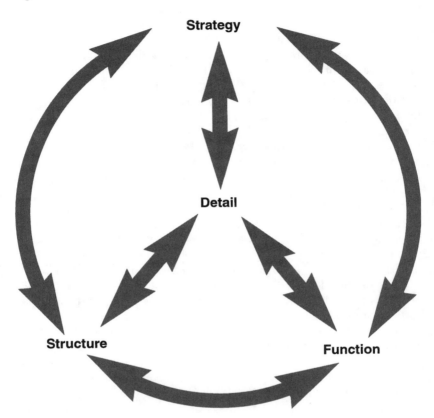

be seen, the subject remains a complex one, and the bill of particulars is quite large. Even so, this scheme appears to be the most
parsimonious one for explaining the multitude of business phenomena and forms.

Unfortunately, like many archival terms, my four parameters are
commonplace words that can mean many similar but different things
in different disciplinary contexts. Structure and function already have
wide archival usage. I will use *function* to mean elemental purposes
and the step-by-step actions required to achieve them. *Structure* will
be used here in its business school sense of organization of the firm
or what archivists would usually call *external structure*.[15] *Strategy* is
another business school concept and is here used in a somewhat
looser way to refer to both strategy and tactics in the military sense.

Detail here is a relative term that refers to the level of specificity and completeness peculiar to a particular record. However, the same type of scale (analogous to the variable powers of a microscope) can also be applied to the other three parameters, each of which may be analyzed at ever finer and finer levels of detail. The relationships among the four parameters are displayed in Figure 1. Why there are four parameters and not two or five will be developed in the argument that follows.

I will treat each of the parameters and the body of scholarship supporting them in turn. Although the diagram is closed, and no parameter the leading one, I will begin with strategy because that is where I began my investigations. The presentations on strategy and structure are reasonably complete. To do justice to function in business records would require a separate and rather large work. The importance of detail emerged in the course of the present exercise and requires further development. These two sections are offered in the way of provisional and preliminary observations. Collectively, this analytical scheme is offered as a substitute for the traditional Schellenbergian nomenclature with which archivists are familiar. However, with one important exception, I will treat only the integrity side of the appraisal dialectic, so that this much of the model should be compatible with archival theory. A similar analysis of the principles and mechanics of actual use would be required to complete the equation, an approach more fruitful than the minute categorization of value.[16]

The analytical framework that I propose here emerged in typically pragmatic American fashion in response to specific difficulties presented by the appraisal, arrangement, and description of the records of large modern firms[17] and by the close observation of similarities and differences in a wide variety of business records. My approach, therefore, grows out of the particular holdings and institutional goals of the Hagley Museum and Library and, as a guide to practice, is directed primarily at archivists in other collecting repositories who are less likely to have had direct experience in or access to the business world. Corporate archivists can and do learn these things by direct immersion. This presentation also focuses on coping with accumulations in a repository environment, although the same principles can be applied to understanding current and future records. Unlike previous published studies, it is based on archives from several different firms varying in age, size, and complexity. Many of the examples are drawn from one of the largest, most complete, and most complex archives, that of the Pennsylvania Railroad (PRR).[18] Together, these archives represent variations in all four parameters over the past two centuries.

Strategy

Although there is evidence that some business leaders have consciously thought in strategic terms since at least the mid-nineteenth century, modern concepts of business strategy were first developed at the Harvard Business School in the early 1960s. Until that time, management training focused on individual business functions, such as production, marketing, or finance. Emphasizing strategy broadened this focus to embrace the enterprise as a whole and its interaction with the external environment.[19] This same need to make sense of a complex array of functions is what recommends the concept of strategy to the archivist. It was in this Harvard environment that Alfred D. Chandler, the most influential American business historian of the 1960s, 1970s and 1980s, developed his paradigmatic treatment of the interplay between strategy and organizational structure in the evolution of the large modern firm.[20] Chandler's work had obvious archival implications and was quickly transmitted to the profession, first by Francis X. Blouin, Jr.,[21] and then by another business historian, JoAnne Yates of MIT.[22] These ideas were in the air when I first began thinking seriously about business records and seemed to have great explanatory power. I thus began with the proposition that what Schellenberg called evidential value and what is most worthy of protection in business archives is equivalent to evidence of strategy and structure.

Just as I moved away from such a simple formulation, it was also a mistake to call this approach "Chandlerian" as I once did. Chandler's goal was to explain the development of contemporary forms of big business. Strategy and structure are broader concepts that grow directly out of the nature of business activities and are not the exclusive property of a particular historiographical school of interpretation.[23] Using the concepts to understand business behavior and records creation is not tantamount to simply selecting those documents that support the writing of "Chandlerian" history. Rather, it allows the archivist to enter the various mental and organizational frameworks within which the creators of business records operate, thus allowing him or her to understand the records on their own terms, independent of the interpretive structures of Chandler or any other user.

Let us therefore approach the concept of strategy through the more general typologies created in business schools. In doing so, it is worth remembering that strategy is largely a practical affair, not a philosophical exercise or a social science. The many descriptive schemes are by no means mutually exclusive. For example, Table 1 lists nine basic strategic alternatives and Table 2 lists six determinants of strategy. All of the basic strategies actually appear in combination.[24] These lists are taken from the more generalized literature of the 1970s and

Table 1. Basic Strategic Options

1. Concentration on a single business.
A. Seek greater market penetration.
B. Move into new markets.
C. Develop new or better products for present markets.
2. Horizontal integration.
3. Vertical integration.
4. Diversification.
A. Concentric or product.
B. Unrelated or conglomerate.
5. Joint ventures.
6. Innovation.
7. Retrenchment.
8. Divestiture.
9. Liquidation.

After Arthur A. Thompson, Jr. and A. J. Strickland III, *Strategy and Policy: Concepts and Cases* (Dallas: Business Publications, 1978), 61–83.

early 1980s and focus on what might be termed the life cycle of the firm. In many respects, they are more relevant to the archivist's concerns than the more specialized recent literature on strategy that focuses, not unexpectedly, on competition.[25] Michael E. Porter's "Five Forces," the reigning paradigm in recent competitive strategy (Figure 3), are in many ways more useful for the study of industry structure.[26]

Another senior business historian, Louis Galambos of Johns Hopkins, has produced a succinct description of the major strategic objectives of American business leaders since at least the mid-nineteenth century. First, they have sought market control with the aim of reducing risks and increasing profits. By freeing themselves from short-term market pressures, executives have been able to carve out a "rather large area in which they could exercise discretionary behavior." They have also pursued efficiency, primarily through innovation. These two objectives were sometimes complementary and sometimes not, so that the act of management becomes a continuous balancing act or compromise. Generally, American CEOs have opted to trade some amount of efficiency for the larger goal of market control and stability, for example, settling for oligopoly rather than monopoly.[28]

Another useful concept is that of strategic levels. The overall or root strategy bridges a series of supporting strategies for each of the separate activities needed to implement it. Each of the supporting strategies in turn generates specific operating strategies that define the specific means of carrying out actions in the marketplace.[29] Strategic thinking and contributions are thus not confined to the top of the

Table 2. Determinants of Strategy

1. Product-market opportunities.
2. Organizational competence and resources.
3. External threats.
4. Personal values and aspirations of managers.
5. Societal constraints and social responsibilities.
6. Organizational personality/corporate culture.

After Thompson and Strickland, *Strategy and Policy*, 47–57.

organization chart. Furthermore, although strategy is normally considered a conscious planning for the future, it may emerge in a cruder form, as the resultant vector of many separate, uncoordinated actions, revealed as a pattern only in retrospect.[30]

Business Records as Evidence of Strategy. Some strategies may translate directly into the documentary record in a relatively straightforward way. Integration, diversification, joint ventures, retrenchment, divestiture, and liquidation all have legal components that produce specific documents such as articles of incorporation, merger agreements, stock-purchase and interest-guarantee contracts, operating leases, deeds for the purchase and sale of property, bankruptcy proceedings, regulatory appeals, and articles of dissolution. However, strategic thinking and behavior take place in a zone of freedom outside the constraints of law and much will therefore elude capture in such purely juridical record types. This is true not only of modern firms, where complex internal dynamics are usually at work, but also of earlier, simpler forms of business.[31]

Innovation is a particularly difficult matter to grasp. It is entirely misleading to make simplistic equations between innovation and specific records such as patents. Innovation may manifest itself not only in what is normally thought of as technology, but also in managerial organization, advertising, marketing, public relations, labor relations, or practically any other aspect of a firm's activities. Innovation may fail just as easily as it succeeds. Furthermore, most historians of business and technology agree that the majority of corporate innovations are incremental, "unobtrusive, unannounced, unobserved, and uncelebrated."[32] Breakthrough innovations are more likely to occur in small, flexible, risk-taking firms, but large firms are more successful at managing and systematizing incremental innovation, often buying and perfecting the work of others.[33]

The determinants of strategy are even less comprehensible from single records or record types. Records creators, after all, are actors in specific circumstances where common knowledge, assumptions, and beliefs can remain unstated. Product-market opportunities may be obvious or not. A sense of organizational resources, well known to the actors, may have to be recreated from an array of statistical series. Organizational competence, corporate culture, or the personality of decision makers may be recoverable only through analysis of style in texts or subtle visual cues in photos and graphics. External threats and societal constraints may be unspoken and described only outside the archive, recoverable only from other sources of information on the same time period or events.

Nevertheless, the concept of strategy provides one of the best tools to guide the reduction of business archives through selection. Its importance in this respect is twofold. First, it makes manifest the thought processes of business managers, the nature of choice in a dynamic market system, and the constant unfolding of technical and managerial change in ways which archival notions drawn from other spheres of thought do not.[34] Secondly, strategic choices cause certain business functions to be emphasized over others in specific ways, so that strategy provides a valid basis for deciding which actions, and thus which records, are more important than others. For example, a firm may pin its hopes of success on production, or research, or marketing. A marketing-oriented firm may go after the high, low, or middle ends of the market. It may emphasize low cost, or exceptional quality, or follow-up service, or create image and brand loyalty through creative advertising.[35]

Perhaps the most important thing that an archivist needs to do in first approaching a business archive is to develop an understanding of how the firm operates in a strategic sense. The business school literature gives a rudimentary sense of what must be identified and how to read the records, but there is no simple formula. Even with short starting lists of basic variables, the number of permutations is quite large, and every strategic history is in a sense a random walk through space and time. Strategy is above all particularistic. Companies like Ford and General Motors have made and sold very similar things in very different ways.[36] The strategic approach prompts the archivist to discover the particulars in the evidence at hand and to select accordingly.

Structure

Archivists have long dealt with the concept of external structure in their analyses of records creation. Addressing this issue in the domain of business records is complicated by a duality in the structure of large modern firms, a division that grows out of the evolution and maturation of the corporate form of organization.

From Proprietor to Corporation: Structure as Real or Artificial Persons. The first aspect of firm structure is what we might call its legal or constitutional structure. Business activities of all sorts may be carried on by both natural or juridical persons. The former may be individual proprietors or members in a simple partnership. Proprietorships and partnerships and their associated forms and procedures can be traced back to twelfth and thirteenth century Italy. They were the norm in American commerce and manufacturing well into the nineteenth century, but by the 1980s, proprietorships were significant primarily in agriculture and personal services, and partnerships primarily in legal services and accounting.[37]

Partnerships, which were governed only by the common law of contracts, had inherent limitations. Successful, long-lived partnerships like E. I. du Pont de Nemours & Company or the Baldwin Locomotive Works required a dedicated, self-perpetuating core of members who could reconstitute the firm following the death of each partner, raise sufficient capital among themselves, and be willing to expose themselves to full liability for debts.

New forms of business enterprise that would overcome one or more of these obstacles had appeared as early as the sixteenth century. The simplest was the limited partnership, which made silent partners liable only to the extent of their investment in return for depriving them of an active role in management. English common law did not recognize the limited partnership, but individual American states copied the practice from the French beginning in 1822. Nonetheless, it remained a minor element in American business until the 1870s, while entrepreneurs instead adopted and refined the corporation.[38]

Although there were several types of corporate bodies in ancient Rome and medieval Europe, American corporation law developed as a homemade response to practical problems driven by the needs and energies of businessmen themselves.[39] Precedents in Roman public and private law, canon law, or tribal life in the German forests were largely "discovered" in the late nineteenth and twentieth centuries by intellectuals either hoping to force the corporate genie into the state's bottle or defending business interests against the state.[40]

One type of business corporation with indisputable influence on more modern forms emerged in the mid-sixteenth century following the rise of the national monarchies in the states of northwestern Europe. Joint-stock companies with easily transferrable shares preserved the company from the vagaries of death and inheritance and allowed greater flexibility in raising capital without the restrictions on management present in the limited partnership. Most importantly, a charter or letters patent from the sovereign established the company as an artificial person in law and usually conferred state patronage in the form of special grants or monopolies. The use of joint-stock companies in the British Empire was restricted after the collapse of the South Sea Bubble in 1720.[41] In the future United States, however, business "corporations" were occasionally chartered by the local assemblies in contravention of common law. Some received legislative encouragement short of a formal charter. Many were merely unincorporated joint-stock companies or private associations that were little more than partnerships, with or without transferrable shares.[42]

In the United States, because of the federal system, powers of incorporation were vested in the states as preexisting sovereigns. Provision for federal incorporation was purposely omitted from the Constitution and, while understood to be implied in the other powers, was little used.[43] As a result, there were as many corporation laws and policies as there were states, with only interstate competition and the federal courts acting to produce some degree of uniformity. Americans made far greater use of the corporate form than Europeans, particularly in New England, where nearly 1,900 business corporations had been chartered by 1830.[45]

Between 1811 and 1875, incorporation by special act was gradually superseded by incorporation by general act, whereby a direct grant from the sovereign was replaced by filing articles attesting to compliance with certain general conditions with a state executive department.[46] The first general laws were usually designed to encourage infant industries. Laws of the 1840s and 1850s continued this process and were generally structured to the needs of purely local enterprise.[47] The last states to adopt general laws did so against a backdrop of post–Civil War scandals and growing anti–big business sentiment, and their statutes imposed certain restrictions across the board.[48] In transportation and finance, the earliest types of business to be incorporated on a regular basis, the first movers were safely grandfathered in their special charters, but manufacturers, now rapidly expanding the scope of their enterprises, were not so fortunate. The result was a renewed interest in the limited partnership, which was subject to minimal regulation. The great Carnegie companies all functioned under the Pennsylvania Limited Partnership Act of 1874.[49]

Business quickly developed other ways of combining companies to form large enterprises. One was the trust, which could hold the shares of smaller corporations and limited partnerships formed in several states, the most famous example being the Standard Oil Trust of 1882. However, the Standard was dissolved by the courts of Ohio in 1892, and the trust form was never widely adopted.[50] Another form was the holding company. The first pure holding companies, over forty in number, were chartered by special act in Pennsylvania between 1868 and 1872.[51] In 1888, New Jersey amended its general law to permit the regular formation of holding companies and also liberalized its rules governing mergers. Additional restrictions fell over the next few years, culminating in New Jersey's revised general law of 1896 that gave directors a free hand in shaping a corporation's power and eliminating nearly all of the traditional common law restraints on corporate activity.[52]

Delaware followed suit in 1899 and, after a temporary progressive roll back in New Jersey from 1913 to 1917, moved into the lead. Delaware law was further revised in 1915, 1927, 1929, and 1967, giving managers almost unlimited power vis-à-vis shareholders.[53] With the advent of more liberal charters, large and medium-sized firms that were still regular or limited partnerships converted to the corporate form between 1890 and 1915, including Carnegie Steel (1892), DuPont (1899), and the Baldwin Locomotive Works (1909).[54] The transition from a partnership to a closely held corporation whose shares are not regularly traded is often a change of legal form only. Most corporations are small, and most are privately held, including such sector leaders as Hallmark, Inc., and Mars, Inc.[55]

Having thus far concentrated on the process by which corporations are formed, it must be noted that corporation law always provides for their extinction. Corporations can be extinguished by simple change of name, by merger, by bankruptcy and sale, by expiration of charter, by revocation of charter, and by liquidation. The first three generally transmit the property and chartered powers to a successor or successors unimpaired. Corporations can also dispose of assets by lease or sale and become dummy or shell companies whose only value is the franchise itself.[56]

Businesses that pursue the various growth strategies are generally not single firms but an interlocked system of companies that are constantly evolving. Companies that operate networks, like railroads or public utilities, are usually pyramids of geographic-specific firms whose consolidation over time is complex and drawn out. The Pennsylvania Power and Light Company has about 1,300 predecessor and subsidiary companies; the Penn Central Corporation had over 1,500.[57] Industrial companies with liberal, post-1890 charters, on the other hand, have few geographical or functional constraints, and the number of separate charters required to reach large size is significantly smaller. The Bethlehem Steel Corporation (New Jersey 1905, Delaware 1936) has about 425 predecessors and subsidiaries.[58] The modern industrial corporate charter is better thought of as an abstract box into which anything may be placed and to which any label may be affixed. The contents and label may be changed with the ease of a conjuror's trick simply by signing a few pieces of paper.[59]

In sum, the evolution of the legal structure of the firm since the mid-nineteenth century has generally followed managers' quests for market control, stability, and efficiency rather than the niceties of ancient legal traditions. In the early nineteenth century, Justice Joseph Story broke with British precedent, which treated business firms and municipalities together as "public" corporations, to group businesses with charities as "private" corporations. The Supreme Court in 1886 invested business corporations with all of the claims to liberty and property rights enjoyed by individuals under the Fourteenth Amendment. The law discarded the entire tradition of *ultra vires*, which held that corporations could only act within narrow stated powers without forfeiture, and abandoned the idea that they could only act under a corporate seal.[60] The most far-reaching New Deal reforms were generally focused on certain classes of firms, particularly public utilities. The more general corporate reforms relied primarily on greater openness and disclosure while leaving managerial autonomy largely intact.[61] How that autonomy was used is reflected in the second aspect of business structure.

The "Organization Man"—Structure as Managerial Revolution. The Bethlehem Steel Corporation could move undisturbed from its 1905 New Jersey charter to its 1919 Delaware charter in 1936 because internal managerial structure is semi-independent of the firm's overall constitutional structure. In many respects, the essence of Bethlehem lay not in the pieces of paper that ratified its existence but in the will and group feeling of Charles Schwab and his "boys" who composed the top management. Corporation and partnership laws prescribe only a minimal organizational framework, such as the difference between general and special partners, the vesting of ultimate authority in a board of directors elected by the stockholders, and sometimes the creation of a minimal number of executive offices, usually a president, secretary, and treasurer. The working structure of the firm, what managers generally call "the organization," is created by the decisions of the proprietors or managers, usually in an ad hoc fashion.[62] While managers were able to secure legal advantages in their quest for market control and efficiency, they actually achieved their goals through their organizations.

Like constitutional structure, managerial structure also evolved from the individual proprietorship, but in different ways. Business school authors recognize at least five organizational types as shown in Table 3. There is no simple progression between types. Rather, a given firm may follow one of many paths, the most common of which are shown in Figure 2. However, the process is an evolutionary and cu-

Table 3. Basic Organizational Types

1. Simple.
2. Functionally departmentalized.
3. Holding company.
4. Multidivisional.
5. Global.

After Jay Galbraith and Daniel A. Nathanson, *Strategy Implementation: The Role of Structure and Process* (St. Paul: West Publishing Company, 1978), 118

mulative one, and it is not possible to pass from the simplest to the most complex form in a single bound.[63]

The single proprietor is a jack-of-all-trades. Conducting business over distance, however, requires the service, first of correspondents and then of agents who may be either contractors engaged on retainer or paid employees. The latter tend in time to become functionally specialized, as does the main office staff of clerks and bookkeepers. As the number of managers and clerks expands with the scale of the business, the functionally departmentalized (F-form) firm takes shape. At the same time, a group of managerial generalists (or, if you will, specialists in management[64] itself) becomes necessary to coordinate and integrate the activities of the growing army of functional specialists.[65]

Depending upon the nature of the business, firms may be further departmentalized along geographic, process, market channel, or client lines. Geographic departmentalization tends to require the duplication of staff functions (accounting, personnel) at the regional level so that these special support skills are available on the spot. Process departmentalization follows the steps of the production process (blast furnace, open hearth, rolling mill, and fabricating shop in steel companies). Market channel departmentalization follows the different markets in which the firm participates (dividing wholesale and retail sales), while client departmentalization follows customer or user groups (freight and passenger traffic, domestic and industrial customers).[66]

The loci of power and lines of authority in functionally departmentalized firms can take many forms. The CEO may be a creature of the board or the board a rubber stamp for the CEO. There may be a line-and-staff system where the generalist at each managerial level has a separate staff of functional specialists.[67] Either vertical or horizontal lines of authority may be emphasized, or it may be a matrix system with neither vertical nor horizontal links predominating. There may be special project staffs or task forces created outside normal departmental lines.[68]

The structure of the Pennsylvania Railroad, which pioneered the functionally departmentalized and line-and-staff forms, assumed its

Figure 2. Evolutionary Sequences

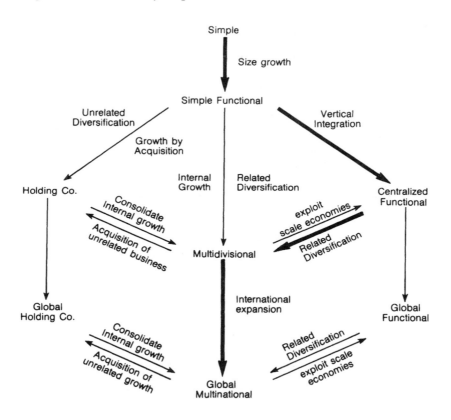

After Galbraith and Nathanson, *Strategy Implementation*, 115.

basic shape between 1857 and 1880. Over the succeeding years there were about 15 functional departments and 60 geographical divisions on 4 hierarchical levels. Primary functions associated with transportation tended to be geographically departmentalized on the line-and-staff system, while others like purchasing, real estate, and engineering design tended to be centralized at headquarters. Departmentalization tended to proceed in two ways, first by subdivision following the increasing division of labor, and second by direct creation to cope with new technologies like electricity or computers or changes in the political and regulatory environments. When such new functions had to be tackled, they were often assigned to special assistants, consultants, or small bureaus before blossoming into full departments.[69]

Firms that pursue strategies of vertical integration or diversification are soon faced with the problem of coordinating radically different businesses and most adopt the holding company, multidivisional, or global forms. In the holding company form, a small headquarters loosely controls a series of decentralized profit centers.[70] The subsidiary units of a holding company are each separate corporations, although for management purposes officers of the holding company may hold dual or multiple appointments with subsidiaries. This type of control ensures that more of the subsidiaries' activities are documented in the records of the parent than when parent and subsidiaries are entirely separate.

The conglomerate diversification popular in the 1960s and 1970s produced a structure with stricter separation between officers of the parent company and its subsidiaries. The conglomerate structure in particular tends to foster a portfolio management style in which top management opts for profit maximization and becomes completely divorced from involvement with particular products or processes.[71] Subsidiaries and their records are bought, sold, or traded like simple chattels, so that a complete documentary record, much less a complete archive, never exists at any one time or place.

The more robust multidivisional or M-form, a key American innovation epitomized by DuPont and the post-1925 General Motors, is tighter than the holding company form and is designed to improve efficiency in the face of complexity. The organization of the parent company itself is decentralized. Typically, each product line or market is handled by a semiautonomous unit or division that acts like a separate, functionally departmentalized firm. A central office provides support services and coordinates the work of the company as a whole.[72]

For example, the DuPont reorganization of 1919 created a Production Department further divided by product line (explosives, cellulose, dyestuffs, paint, and chemicals) with a Service Department for the welfare work, supplies, and technical services associated with production. Auxiliary departments handled sales, finance, law, purchasing, development, engineering, and research. As further refined in 1921, the industrial departments were made completely autonomous, and the Service Department moved from the industrial to the auxiliary departments. The sales function was decentralized across the production departments, but an Advertising Department was created to handle the one sales-related function requiring centralization.[73]

Frequently, the divisions of an M-form company begin life as separate corporations, are acquired by the parent during the course of integration or diversification, and eventually become mere managerial units of the parent company. At any one time, a large concern may have several subunits at each evolutionary stage.[74] Following the diversification and mergers-and-acquisitions movements that began in the late 1960s, the number of divisions in the largest firms has also mushroomed from about a dozen to well over 50.[75] In recent years, many multidivisional firms have evolved into global ones, producing multiple products with their various business functions distributed among many countries. The typical global form is a matrix of product, functional, and geographical units whose records may be subject to a variety of legal systems and, like the conglomerate, never accumulate in a single place under single control.[76]

Corporate versus Managerial Records. Since corporate structure is legally determined, the law typically specifies the keeping of certain records. For ordinary partnerships and unincorporated joint-stock companies the basic document is the contract establishing the firm, while for incorporated bodies it is the charter, letters patent, or articles of incorporation. General incorporation and limited partnership acts and special corporate charters often mandate the keeping of additional records, but these have always been few in number.

Nineteenth century special charters generally required the keeping of minutes of stockholders' and directors' meetings, regular account books, and records of the purchase and sale of shares, both to protect stockholders' rights and as a crude form of regulation. For example, Pennsylvania's 1814 Bank Act required stock certificates with the corporate seal, annual statements to the stockholders and the state, and state inspection of books. The charter of the Schuylkill Navigation Company (1815) required minutes, stock certificates and transfer books, and account books. That of the Philadelphia & Reading Railroad (1833) dropped the explicit reference to accounts but added an annual statement to the stockholders. That of the PRR (1846) required that the annual report be published. As legal restrictions on corporate activity were curtailed, so too were the number of mandated records. The 1874 limited partnership law required only a subscription book, and the general incorporation law required only regular proofs of the election of directors.[77] The 1915 Delaware law required only the keeping of stock ledgers.[78]

Such basic documents, what I will call corporate records, have to be kept for the life of the corporation and any successor that inherits its rights and obligations. For this reason, these records, which define the legal existence of the company, plus copies of charters, letters patent, articles of association, deeds, agreements, and mortgages form the backbone of corporate archives. Functionally, such records are usually housed in the corporate secretary's and treasurer's or comptroller's offices.

Since managerial structure is not legally determined, there are far fewer strings attached to the creation and preservation of what we might call managerial as opposed to corporate records. Government regulation and taxation mandate the creation and preservation of some types of records,[79] but most managerial records are the natural outgrowth of unregulated activity, particularly the communications between specialists and generalists, between managerial levels, between the field and headquarters, and between those inside and outside the firm. Only in the heavily regulated railroad industry did a government agency, the Interstate Commerce Commission, go so far as to prepare exhaustive and binding records retention schedules, and these were gradually jettisoned even before the agency's recent abolition.[80]

Corporate and managerial records only become differentiated when natural persons begin to give way to artificial ones. In a simple partnership, the only thing analogous to a corporate record is the contract establishing the partnership itself. A dividing line is crossed with the development of transferrable shares, which demands not only that a record of stock transfers be kept but also regular minutes and accounts so that investors or their representatives can monitor the activities of the firm. This occurs in early joint-stock companies that are not recognized juridical persons as well as in true corporations.[81]

Managerial records vary widely with structure. In the case of a single proprietor or partner who handles a wide range of activities and decisions, memory may reside only in the individual brain and most information may be transmitted orally. Written records may be minimal: jottings in a journal, quickly scribbled receipts, a few formal legal documents.[82] The need to deal with customers and clients at a distance generates correspondence that puts argument on paper and is richer in detail. The supervision of agents requires even more explicit directives and reports.[83] As agents evolve into formal, functional departments, the written record naturally becomes more comprehensive and systematic. When preserved, this richness enables the user to recover more of the dimensionality of who did what, how, and why than can be obtained from the skeletal corporate records.

Once a given threshold of specialization has been passed, managerial records become a reflection of managerial structure, the content being shaped by prescribed duties and lines of authority. Experience with the PRR, where we actually analyzed all the changes in the organization, confirms that most charts and manuals are simplifications in which certain elements of the organization are emphasized to the exclusion of others. They particularly fail to show the gestation of new departments within old ones or the use of consultants. Likewise, internal communication is far more complex than the lines shown on a typical organization chart. It is thus inadvisable to write off the records of entire organizational units simply on the basis of a chart. All units may contribute, albeit unequally, to strategic decisions or may collect significant information. However, all units also perform housekeeping functions, records of which have traditionally been discarded.[84]

Specialists and Generalists: The Records of Complex Managerial Structures. The records of the simpler types of firms are for the most part easily understood once we have grasped the rudiments of their relatively straightforward structures and functional clusters. The change of scale and complexity in F-form and M-form companies creates problems for the archivist just as it does for corporate managers.

The records of managers in functionally departmentalized firms are evidence both of the act of management and the specialized function or functions being managed. The act of coordination cannot be separated from the specifics of that which is being coordinated. The records of the highest official charged with managing a particular function will typically constitute evidence of that function in its most condensed form.

The process of integrating disparate functions is more complex because such integration does not take place simply at the top. A particular CEO may choose to be kept informed of everything, and another may choose to be relieved of these burdens and play a ceremonial or inspirational role.[85] Furthermore, cooperation among functional specialists is essential in appropriate ways at all levels of management.[86]

Take the case of the terminal improvements constructed by the PRR in Philadelphia between 1925 and 1952, a $60 million construction project. A special engineering office was created reporting to a committee headed by the executive vice president. The Real Estate Department had to acquire the necessary land. The Legal Department handled condemnations and negotiated the restrictions imposed by the municipal authorities. The special engineering office handled the actual design, parts of which were contracted to an outside architectural firm and a consulting engineer but with constant input from the regular

Engineering Department and the Operating Department, which would take over the facilities upon completion. The president would be kept informed and intervene when appropriate from time to time.[87] Such close cooperation produces a record which is both fragmented and has a high degree of redundancy. While the files of the special engineering office contain the most complete overall record, the files of each of the cooperating officers have the most complete record of their particular contributions.[88]

Since the divisions and headquarters of multidivisional companies are themselves functionally departmentalized, the general nature of records is the same for both types of firm, and all of the same caveats apply. If anything, multidivisional and global firms delegate more strategic decision-making authority to their divisions than functionally departmentalized firms give their lower-level units.[89] Whereas in the F-form some departments perform primary and some facilitative functions, in the M-form all divisions are theoretically equal, and the functional mixes occur within the divisions themselves.

The examples of the Pennsylvania Railroad (F-form) and DuPont (M-form) suggest that rapid structural change occurs more readily in certain parts of the organization and at certain times. Structure is particularly fluid in the formative stages of an organization and in periods of stress accompanying rapid growth or decline. In the case of the PRR, the formative period occurred from 1849 to 1857. The period of greatest growth, when the line-and-staff system was perfected, occurred in the years 1867 to 1874. Times of crisis included the 1917–23 period associated with federal control and the post-1952 descent to bankruptcy. In the case of DuPont, the formative period of the corporation occurred in the years 1902–05. Important periods of growth and crisis were associated with the 1907–12 and 1947–62 antitrust prosecutions, the 1915–21 diversification from explosives to other chemicals funded by World War I profits, and the post-1974 changes spawned by the energy crisis, the Conoco acquisition, and the biotechnology revolution.[90]

Another salient feature of structural change is that it tends to occur more frequently at the upper levels of the organization. The basic functions of the firm, it would seem, are quickly created and just as quickly lopped off in response to technological change or market forces but are otherwise stable over long periods.[91] In contrast, the upper part of the structure that coordinates and provides support services is constantly changing. Generally, the upper levels of an organization also take more cognizance of individual executive talents and grant greater individual freedom. It is here that needed expertise may be brought into the firm in the form of special staff vice presidents, special assistants, and consultants.[92] Since the records of top and middle managers contain the evidence of complex decision making and present data in its most refined and summary form, this structural fluidity at the top complicates the task of appraisal and, again, rules out a too-simple reliance on a few manuals and charts.[93]

Owners and Managers: Another Structural Duality. In the transition from small to big business, management typically becomes separate from ownership.[94] This can occur in one of two ways. A firm may lease the management of its properties to a larger firm in return for rents or royalties. In this case, the original owners remain as corporate officers but surrender all powers of management short of approving actions of the lessee in regards to property, collecting the rent, and disbursing it as dividends. The firm thus becomes little more than a private investment club, a transition reflected in its records. This pattern is most common in transportation and communication networks, where early entrants may acquire extremely valuable franchises and can avoid risks by becoming *rentiers*.[95]

More typically, salaried professional managers seize all the real power from an increasingly faceless mass of passive or indifferent investors who are unable or unwilling to control the board of directors. The need to raise large capitals from a broad range of contributors and the increasing need for special technical expertise either prevent the owner-entrepreneur from retaining control or passing it on to the next generation. While this is indeed one element of the modernization of firm structure, there are significant variations. The Pennsylvania Railroad was captured by professional managers at the age of five, but the rival New York Central remained a private fief of the Vanderbilts for twenty years, and family influence persisted for another 70.[96] The last du Pont family CEO retired in 1973.[97] In the contemporary business world, one need only mention Bill Gates, Sam Walton, or Rupert Murdoch.

In short, the owner-manager relationship is also evolutionary in nature and can follow many paths and take many forms. Many of the archives at Hagley come from firms with long histories of family ownership.[98] On this basis, I would have to conclude that the nature of the work, firm size, the degree of complexity and specialization, and the internal distribution and concentration of power all have a greater bearing on the records than the simple distinction between owners and managers. Autocrats still have to bark orders to subordinates and colleagues still have to confer whether the business is "all in the family" or not. One obvious difference is that owner-managers are less likely to compartmentalize their "business" and "personal" lives than bureaucratic managers, so that the records of each are more or less intermingled. Complete understanding requires the complete record.[99] Another obvious characteristic of family businesses is the tendency to fill executive positions exclusively with family members on the basis of relationship, ability, and interest and to find places for less talented relatives. Again, however, the relationship to structure is not that clear-cut. Family practices persisted at DuPont through two generations of structural change and technical innovation, and the PRR hired by family from the locomotive to the executive suite.

Unlike a family firm, widely held public companies will generate voluminous quantities of stock transfer books, stock ledgers, canceled certificates, plus requests to replace lost certificates, proxies, and other stockholder mailings that shade off into junk mail. What matters here, however, is not the identity of every last stockholder, but that of the largest and most influential ones and, perhaps, the average one. Paradoxically, complete stockholder records are more interesting (and manageable) for closely held or family companies where they give clues to the relative clout and balance of power among a small group of owners.

The separation of ownership and management in records is generally independent of the separation of ownership and management in the firm. Evidence of ownership tends to fall into the skeletal corporate records and that of management into correspondence and reports, regardless of whether owners and managers are two separate sets of people. One exception seems to occur when owners and managers are split into warring factions jockeying for control. Such disputes can permeate both the entire organization and the documentary evidence. Previously passive owners may take on management in proxy fights and hostile takeovers. Feuds, possibly unrelated to the actual business, may divide owner-managers in family firms.[100]

Records Top to Bottom: Structural Level and Hierarchy. The pursuit of growth strategies also leads to the development of hierarchies. The expansion of relatively thin managements into top, middle, and bottom levels, further refining the division of labor, proved essential in the quest for corporate efficiency.[101] Decisions can be made at the most appropriate level, relieving top managers of unnecessary burdens. As top managers secure greater freedom to maneuver, they are usually obliged to delegate some of that freedom to subordinates. Business generally tends to grant greater autonomy to lower organizational units than government. Such autonomy increases rapidly above the supervisory grades, and the documentary record changes accordingly. Generally, employees at and below the supervisory grades perform repetitive tasks and the records generated by this activity tend to be standardized forms in which the data is strictly regulated. As one enters the bottom levels of management, however, these forms progressively give way to records that are more open and fluid and in which the author exercises increasing freedom and choice. "Fill-in-the-blanks" forms are replaced by the business letter, memorandum, and special report.[102]

Just as successive levels of an organization usually act as filters preventing the top from being overwhelmed by unnecessary data and decisions, so the archivist should selectively filter records in descending the hierarchical ladder. The specifics will be dictated by where decision-making power lies in the particular organization. Obviously, a firm run by a single autocrat can be documented with greater emphasis on the top than one with a collegial management style, but autocrats are usually succeeded by bureaucrats at some point, and even dictators need henchmen. While informality and structural flux are not unexpected in emerging or restructuring firms and industries, with or without the computer, there is still a top and, in large firms, recognizable functional divisions. In all situations, decision-making power and functional authority are probably superior indicators of relative importance than simple titles or position on an organization chart.

The PRR experience tends to confirm the traditional view that everything important in an organization will be discussed and recorded somewhere in its upper and middle levels. However, it is erroneous to equate this simply with the CEO or vice presidents or headquarters. It is essential to consider the records of middle management and particularly that level directly below the top, where a majority of problems are solved. It is here that the flows of information are most concentrated in the crucial act of mediating between top and bottom. One should particularly consider the offices of each of the chief functional specialists responsible for production, engineering, sales, law, and so forth, and the generalists who coordinate their activities. In a firm with geographical, product, or market-channel subdivisions, one should consider at least the first level of such divisions as well as the headquarters. This is not to say that everything, or even something, should be preserved from each office. Rather, it is to urge the advisability of considering records of top and middle management as a whole until the precise nature of interdepartmental cooperation and records redundancy can be determined.[103]

This approach might be termed "modified top-down" in that it begins at the top but continues working downward until the strategic lode peters out, usually somewhere on the border of middle and bottom management or, functionally, just above where actual decision-making power ends and supervisory authority begins. This is consistent with the caveats of other writers on business records, notably Yates.[104] There remains the question of what it might leave out.

Externalities and Context: Structure, Firm, Industry, and Society. Beyond the structure of the firm, there is the structure of the larger industry of which it is a part. Since knowledge of overall context is an essential element of appraisal, the archivist should have at least some understanding of these larger relationships. This is where Michael Porter's "Five Forces" is most useful (Figure 3). These forces determine the intensity of competition and profitability in a given sector and exert a powerful influence on firm strategy and structure. Most important are the barriers to entry (Table 4). Low barriers to entry, as in such extractive industries as bituminous coal mining, tend to produce a wide array of firms and periods of fierce competition and high firm mortality. High barriers, as in automobiles or consumer electronics, tend to produce a concentration of very large firms (oligopoly) and managed competition.[105] Government actions, including incorporation policy, subsidies, antitrust, and more or less restrictive regulations, constitute powerful barriers to entry and are one point of contact between an industrial sector and the larger society. Naturally, general knowledge of this overall social context always plays an important role in appraisal.

In our analytical framework, most externalities are easily subsumed within the larger concept of strategy under such headings as product/market opportunities, external threats, societal constraints, or the personal values of decision makers.[106] Managers interact constantly with customers, suppliers, all levels of government, competitors, allies, and trade or professional associations, and managerial files are as much records of dialogues with outside parties as internal flows of data and commands.

However, since record preservation in the private sector is haphazard, the files of one firm may contain unique evidence of the many others with which it interacted and may merit retention on those grounds alone.[107] Records of interaction with government bodies would again pass the strategic test but are more likely to be duplicated in public archives. However, they are also likely to contain unique evidence of the firm's private reactions and deliberations that are excluded from the public record.

There is misperception that by concentrating on strategy and structure as appraisal parameters, we are focusing on business as business to the neglect of its social context; by concentrating on the top, we are ignoring the bottom.[108] This is not the case. However, the concern is historiographical and not properly archival, equating "strategy and structure" entirely with the Chandler School of business history. Since much post-Chandler business scholarship (not to mention other subfields of history) stresses the social dimension, this advocacy is natural, but it is really part of the larger phenomenon of historians clamoring for desirable source material. As such it belongs on the use side of our equation and is somewhat out of place in a treatment of archival integrity.

Figure 3. Porter's "Five Forces"

After Michael E. Porter, *Competitive Strategy: Techniques for Analyzing Industries and Competitors* (New York: The Free Press, 1980), 4.

Table 4. Barriers to Entry in an Industry

1. Economies of scale.
2. Product differentiation (Brand loyalty).
3. Capital requirements.
4. One-time cost of product substitution.
5. Access to distribution channels.
6. Cost disadvantages independent of scale (patents, know-how, location).
7. Government policy.

After Porter, *Competitive Strategy*, 7–13.

However, the charge is a serious one and merits an answer. First, the concepts of strategy and structure as outlined here make ample room for all sorts of externalities and sociopolitical factors. While one user may interpret evidence of strategy and structure in a Chandlerian fashion or in some other, partial way, the full range of such evidence is usually inextricably bound up in specific actions regarding products and processes that usually have some social dimension. It is also worth noting in this context that ordinary people can and do interact with business in a variety of capacities at any managerial level. Based on the PRR and other Hagley examples, a strategy-based approach focused on top and middle management levels can reasonably hope to capture such social-context interactions as customer complaints, hiring policies, work rules, paternalistic labor practices, collective bargaining, strikes, grievances, and lawsuits.

On the other hand, an archive cannot be other than what it is as defined by the acts that brought it into being. It tells the truth in the way that Jenkinson described.[109] Business archives are fundamentally about business, about the production of goods and services and buying and selling, not exercises in pure science or the liberal arts. The social connections of an enterprise can be no more than those required by its particular activities and the values of the persons behind it. Obviously, a large firm with many employees and a highly specialized management structure making a highly visible or essential product will have broader and deeper sociopolitical roots than a small firm with few employees making an obscure product for a limited market.[110] Likewise, the complete evidence of any bilateral or multilateral relationship will rarely end up in one place, and contextual research of necessity cannot be concluded on the basis of a single archive. Of course, collecting repositories may elect to focus on socially engaged firms or nonbusiness perspectives, but again, that is a matter of clients and use, not of an archive's internal integrity. Indeed, the whole point of this exercise is to put such choices on a firmer footing.

We may also safely conclude that a firm's internal structure, whatever the form, is a relatively minor element compared to strategy or the external competitive environment represented by Porter's "Five Forces." In fact, structure can be easily identified and documented in a minimum of space. It also seems obvious that the intricacies of structure will be more interesting and relevant to those who will end up working closely with them, MBAs and students of management, for example, rather than students of social theory or macroeconomics. Yet, while it is logical to destroy superfluous evidence of a simple and self-evident structure, complex management structures have evolved for important, strategic reasons. It is unwise to destroy evidence of them simply because they are not universally interesting.

Detail

Focusing on Information. The concept of "detail," or more fully, "level of detail," may be unfamiliar to most archivists though it is a property of all records. I gradually became convinced of its importance while trying to analyze what might lie behind Schellenberg's "informational value." Just as "strategy and structure" seemed to offer a more nuanced explanation than evidential value, detail, a design concept,[111] seemed to be essential to understanding physical objects. Informational value has generally been applied to information about persons, places, and things. Furthermore, things play a critical role in most businesses, whether as products or as production machinery. However, it soon became apparent that detail is a general property of all records, not a synonym or substitute for informational value. Detail is about information, though, and does explain something important about the first part of Schellenberg's term and why persons might value it.

To grasp the concept, we might consider the differing levels of detail, present in views of the Jovian moons, from that of Galileo the astronomer to the latest images from *Galileo* the spacecraft, or the different powers of magnification in microscopy. With a low level of detail, a complex world is reduced to a featureless disc of light and shadow. With an electron microscope, we can begin to see the molecular structure of what we normally perceive as undifferentiated matter. Increasing the level of detail requires increasing the amount of information. The superior images from *Galileo*, for example, are produced by greater quantities of information sent back in digital form. Full detail is tantamount to mapping the world on a scale of one-to-one, that is, producing an exact replica that is literally complete "in every detail."

Records, of course, even the plans from which complex objects are replicated, are rarely representations at the scale of one-to-one. They are abstracts, representations in which that information deemed essential to the purpose is emphasized and nonessential information dropped out. Abstracts can be made of abstracts in turn, but at some point the amount of information lost will change the picture. We will no longer be able to see the volcanoes on Io or the underlying structure of crystals.

Why is detail important? We could cite the old saw about God being in the details, generally associated with the architect Mies van der Rohe,[112] but why might this be so? Detail about material objects is important because matter is refractory. It resists human attempts to manipulate it at will. If it does not actually abhor a vacuum, it demands a certain completeness. One cannot produce, say, a working automobile without meeting in full detail all of the requirements for fuel delivery, combustion, power transmission, traction, suspension, and so on. Consider also the number of decisions that had to be made to design and launch Windows95. Inattention to detail, as in the case of the O-rings on the space shuttle, may prove catastrophic.[113] These examples begin to suggest what types of detail might be more important than others. Detail about individuals is important because human beings themselves are refractory. They literally have minds of their own, and some evidence on the nature of those minds will be essential to understanding interactions, especially, in the case of business, with employees and customers.

It is worth noting that the level of detail present in a record is exactly sufficient for its original purpose or function. Receipts and notes will contain the names of the parties and the amounts debited or credited. Working drawings contain precisely that information necessary to construct an object in all its particulars, while presentation drawings contain exactly that information needed to "sell the product." Minutes of a meeting will include only a digest of those events deemed to be essential to have "on the record." Information regarding general wage rates, hiring, and firing is likely to be recorded on a work history or employment record form, while the specific wage payments will be entered in payrolls, information on pension or medical plan participation on still other forms, and so on.[114]

I will here propose a new take on appraisal as the selective pruning, not simply of superfluity, but of detail. In a sense, this is what archivists have been doing all along without thinking in these terms. It is an essential but risk-laden task. How much detail is enough, and of what kind? One person's essential detail is usually someone else's superfluity. How do we make workable compromises? The problem is compounded by the fact that the finer the level of detail, the more specific it becomes and the more limited its purpose. It seems equally clear, however, that a world purged of detail is a world of stick figures rendered in black and white. Rather, every discipline and craft is structured around a sense of what constitutes pertinent and meaningful detail.

Detail, by definition, resides in particulars and thus works against the theorists' yearnings for holism and universality in archives. Detail is what converts modern archives into information. Old constructs, being aggregates of details, are easily decomposed into information and recycled in almost organic fashion. Relevant detail is simply extracted and recombined with other details into a new construct, the rest being discarded. The end result could be next year's Ford Taurus or this essay.[115] Thus, detail is inseparable from use, and only use renders detail meaningful, whether it be the O-ring in liftoff, the evening lottery drawing, or the points in an argument.

Unfortunately for the archivist, use is simply the need of a particular user, and these are wide ranging when it comes to matters of detail. Most of the accusations levelled against archivists and their appraisal methodologies have their origin in this fact. For persons doing historical restorations, practically nothing less than full detail will suffice, because a specific object has to be recreated in its totality, including patterns of use and cultural associations.[116] JoAnne Yates demanded samples of all sorts of forms from all over many different organizations.[117] Genealogists and family historians may desire all the available facts on particular individuals.[118] Others may be thankful for less, and still others frustrated when the purposes of the record creators are a poor match for their own.

In attempting to answer the question of how much detail is enough, the archivist is really seeking to determine when or if the original use is likely to reoccur and how subsequent use may be different, and so will not require the same level of detail. For example, the type of detail needed to build an automobile (full plans and specifications, the proper tools, production skills) will be quite different from the details needed if we only wish to remember its physical appearance. In that case, a few photos may suffice. An entirely different set of details will be necessary to understand the technical and social aspects of automobile use, for example, what it was like to go cruising in a '57 Chevy in 1960.

Detail in Business Records. While the archivist needs to pay attention to the level of detail in all business records, it typically becomes critical in two situations. The first corresponds to the parallel problem of deciding to extend documentation to lower structural levels. Most records with a high level of detail are typically generated close to the point of production, sales, and such activities or at the interface between managers and those they manage. Most grow out of the actual process as it is being performed or in regular upward reporting.[119] Detailed records of products, processes, and transactions may be retained as legal proofs, as a hedge against future liabilities, as part of continuing obligations for service or maintenance, as portfolios advertising past accomplishments, or simply for reference. They may also be discarded as easily as last week's window display or radio commercial.[120]

Thus a need to preserve a high level of detail on some or all aspects of a firm's activities implies a corresponding need to select documents from the lower levels of the organization, extending, in principle, to the individual work station, the shop floor, and the salesroom. The practice of corporate archives and collecting repositories tends to diverge on this point, with the former preserving details on certain activities following institutional dictates, and the latter preserving somewhat different details on other activities in response to outside clients. Neither would probably take matters to the extreme of preserving canceled payroll checks, requisitions for office supplies, or sales slips. Such differences in practice are a matter of "detail," not principle.

Second and perhaps more important is the interplay between detail and use. Archivists are perhaps most familiar with the detail in various kinds of personal and legal case files. Business records will also include whole classes of documents that are more valuable for their detailed and specific descriptions of employees, property, buildings, machinery, products, and transactions than, for example, what they have to tell about the broader actions of the firm. Records of specific products may be essential for understanding innovation, but they may also be used for comparative studies of the product itself (e.g., the evolution of television). Documents of physical plant layout may be essential for understanding how efficiency is obtained through greater throughput[121] but may also be used for purposes as different as studying factory design in general or for historic restorations. Documents of individual transactions with workers may illuminate the firm's implementation of labor policies or may be used as grist for subjects as different as labor and family history. In sum, anything that is designed and produced must be worked out in detail and embodied in some sort of record.[122]

The level of detail in business records poses additional problems in that it is often the expression of highly specialized technical processes. They may be expressed in mathematical or nonverbal "languages" or employ technical jargon.[123] To some extent, the summarizing process that occurs as this information is transmitted upward serves to partially translate such languages into the vernacular. Just as often, however, such summaries may act only as a gloss that cannot readily be divorced from the original document without loss of meaning.[124]

Another important characteristic of records with high levels of detail is how they naturally aggregate into populations or sets according to their purposes and circumstances of creation. Production records will cover all of the products or their variations, often by product line or by individual factory; personnel records will group all employees usually by plant or department; laboratory reports present all the experiments or projects broken down by laboratory, research team, or type, and so on.[125] Each series thus constitutes a coherent population with certain internal variables.

Herein lies the rub, for without technical knowledge approaching that of the records creator, it may not be possible to determine exactly what those variables are. Such a misunderstanding can lead to entirely inappropriate records selection, such as uncritical reliance on random sampling, "famous case," or "fat file" approaches.[126] It is worth noting in this regard that social scientists tend to be more interested in similarities, but it is the subtle differences that most engage the intelligence of practicing technologists[127] (and managers or automobile dealers for that matter). Detail is fundamentally about particularities and differences, and it is essential to know which differences are most significant within a given population and what constitutes an exceptional or representative case.

One possible way out of this impasse is, again, to rely on the natural filtering process that managers apply to certain classes of detailed records. Middle and top managers will receive summaries appropriate to their needs: grievances appealed as opposed to all grievances filed, construction projects above some threshold of complexity and cost, monthly or annual summaries of earnings, expenses, and output, and so on. They will not, of course, be whole populations.[128]

The question to be asked, therefore, is to what extent does an anticipated use require whole populations. The two areas of business records where secondary users of detailed data are most likely to desire something close to whole populations contain evidence of the individual products and productive "machinery" connected with the firm's main line of work (PRR rolling stock, Ford autos, RCA radios) and of individual employees and officials. Generally, raw accounting records of modern businesses cannot be used without duplicating the efforts of the firm's legion of accountants, and the summaries those accountants prepared for senior management will be adequate for most purposes.

Function

It should be clear by now that understanding strategy and structure are not enough. Structure is particularly problematic as a guide to the appraisal of business records, since we have seen that structure tends to be extremely fluid in times of start-up and crisis. The underlying functions, on the other hand, tend to be more constant, and this brings us back to what might have easily been our starting point. Functions both precede and interpenetrate structure, as the very term *functionally departmentalized* makes clear, and they are also the chess pieces of the business strategist. Functional analysis should also reveal underlying similarities across a wide range of industries.

Functional analysis of business records has a long but uneven history.[129] The first full treatment that showed promise of serving as a model, the JCAST studies, actually focused on science and technology in an academic setting but seemed applicable to business.[130] This promise has born fruit in the admirable work of Bruemmer and Hochheiser on the high-technology company. How can this be extended to cover all or most firms and not simply a few that are new, exciting, and research driven?[131]

I can do no more here than present a preliminary analysis of business functions. I began by looking at existing archival models and the structures of functionally departmentalized firms[132] and distilled those lists into a scheme of five basic business functions (Table 5), which, I believe, can describe all business activity to the level of understanding necessary for archival work. There are also three functions that the sovereign exercises upon business firms, which they do not perform themselves. Functions, as verbs, require objects, which I have reduced to eight (Table 6).

This is my proposal for what amount to the "atoms" of business activity. Following this chemical metaphor, what we actually encounter in everyday life are the equivalents of compounds and mixtures.[133] Generally, every function can control and combine with those below it on the list. Every function can engage more than one of the objects. Every function also imparts something distinctive to the records that arise from it. Thus, I would propose that every record of management, every record of design, and so on, have some underlying similarity, however subtle, regardless of what is being managed or produced. Likewise, the same function wedded to different objects will yield records that, while fundamentally similar, will differ according to the nature of those objects.

Let me make a few suggestions as to how such a framework would work in practice. Science-based research and development and scripting a commercial are both species of design. Accounting is one expression of the maintenance of capital, and locking up valuables in a safe is another. The Four Seasons restaurant on Park Avenue engages in batch production, while McDonalds engages in mass production, and so on.

These five functions may also be considered basic units because, I would propose, nearly every business engages in all of them regardless of which function is the primary one, even if only at a superficial level and for a very brief time. Even a small retail firm will have to design the way in which its wares are displayed or advertised and then produce the shelf arrangement or ad copy. On the other hand, not all

Table 5. Business Functions

A. JUDGMENT:

  1. MANAGEMENT:
        Planning
        Organizing
        Staffing
        Directing
        Coordinating
        Reporting
        Budgeting

  2. DESIGN:
        Conceptualizing
        Defining/redefining
        Experimenting
        Modeling
        Testing
        Refining
        Perfecting
        Presenting

B. IMPLEMENTATION:

  3. PRODUCTION:
        Transforming
        Segmenting
        Combining/assembling
        Handling/routing/moving
        Wasting

  4. EXCHANGE (PURCHASES/SALES):
        Soliciting/advertising
        Pricing
        Negotiating
        Contracting
        Expending/collecting
        Receiving/delivering

  5. MAINTENANCE:
        Recording/numbering/auditing
        Adjusting (includes complaints, claims, grievances)
        Repairing
        Protecting (includes health, safety, security, insurance)
        Proselytizing
        Rewarding/motivating/punishing
        Symbolizing

C. SOVEREIGN-SUBJECT FUNCTIONS:

  1. CREATING
  2. REGULATING
  3. TAXING

Table 6. The Objects of Business Functions

A. INPUTS:

    CAPITAL
    LABOR
    PROPERTY/RESOURCES
        Real property and improvements
        Moveable property/chattels
        Intellectual property
        Legal rights and privileges
    SKILL

B. DOMAINS/ACTORS:

    THE POLITY
        The sovereign(s)
        "The public" (as an abstraction)
        Other interests (nonmarket adversaries)

    THE MARKET
        Patrons (superiors)
        Competitors/collaborators (peers)
        Customers (inferior-independent)
        Suppliers/subcontractors (inferior-dependent)

    THE FIRM
        As an entity or "black box"
        As structure
        Shareholders/partners
        Directors
        Managers
        Other salaried employees
        Wage workers

C. OUTPUTS:

    THE PRODUCT
        Custom-produced
        Batch-produced
        Mass-produced
        Continuous-flow-produced

of the subdivisions will be present. In small or simple firms they may be collapsed within the mental activity of the proprietor. Rather, the subdivisions have been chosen to alert the archivist to precisely those salient features of the activity that must be understood in order to comprehend the form and purpose of the records that arise from it. They are, in sum, the basic vocabulary of business records.

Let us see how this works by giving a very cursory look at design.[134] Design begins with conceptualizing some problem and its proposed solution. This is fundamentally a mental act, and if simple enough, the first stages of design may never be embodied in an external record. However, the idea of conceptualizing alerts us to the importance of finding the first recorded embodiment of this process, whether it be a conceptual sketch, equation, outline, proposal, or first draft. Such records may be notoriously ephemeral, like the legendary doodles on napkins or envelopes. To understand the design fully, we must then track it through subsequent refinements and tests, such as controlled experiments, thought experiments, mathematical or physical modeling, ending with the formal presentation documents and the client's reaction to them. This process holds true whether the object of design is computer software, a jet fighter, a cereal package, or a television commercial; only the concepts and tests are different.

Five other postulates must be offered in this brief presentation. First, the scheme prioritizes functions by setting judgment over implementation and both over maintenance.[135] This follows from the role of strategy in controlling functions and would not be true in passive, nonstrategic settings. In business, conscious, deliberative acts are more important for understanding the enterprise than essentially autonomic ones, but not exclusively so. Second, within the firm itself, management rules by definition. It will, however, be driven by either design, production, or exchange, which should be considered the next most important function. Third, in preserving the record of lower functions, we should give primary emphasis to their intersection or interpenetration with higher ones. Fourth, all other things being equal, polyfunctional documents are probably more significant than monofunctional ones. Fifth, an archive is not complete unless all functions are documented to some degree. While all archives are incomplete by chance or design, the functional matrix provides a scale for evaluating which are less complete than others.

Function by itself, however, is no more the answer than provenance. It seems unlikely to me that even a function-use quotient can be the sole yardstick for selection, particularly in the critical area of appraising managerial files. What is needed is a perspective that reflects all the forces that have shaped the organization and its archive as a whole and enables the archivist to distinguish the relative significance of specific decisions, actions, projects, or events that cut across or integrate simple functions. For this, something like strategy, a dynamic concept inherent in the life of the organization itself, is essential, and so the circle is closed.

Applications and Implications

The Four Parameters in Appraisal: Some Examples. To examine how our four parameters may be used in actual appraisal, it is necessary to return to our original equation. By themselves, they can tell us what needs to be protected to preserve the integrity of the archive. While they also speak to original use and usefulness, they of course cannot say much about the specific user needs and policy decisions that actually govern records retention, which are determined by institutional context.

In the following example of the PRR appraisal, that context was a group of collecting repositories dedicated to preserving documents for the study of the past and answerable to a variety of clienteles, including academic historians, public historians, amateur historians, preservationists, and hobbyists. The object was thus to select documents in a way that maintained the integrity and coherence of the archive in the face of demands from multiple interest groups. The project proceeded on the assumption that the best documentary representation of the firm was one full enough to permit the analysis of its past actions in some depth from a variety of viewpoints. This implied preserving a high level of detail of the "higher" functions. A different context would have produced a different solution, as in the case of Bethlehem Steel, whose archive was a miscellaneous collection of interesting facts, images, and memorabilia assembled for public relations purposes and sharply skewed to the interests of its patron CEO.

Selecting evidence of structure was rather straightforward. The corporate structure of most large firms is so complex that corporate secretaries generally prepare manuals to identify all the components. When not available, the same information can be extracted from minute books and agreement files. Organization charts, organization manuals, and internal directories were selected as evidence of managerial structure, as were departmental files covering managerial structure at levels below that of the general charts. Of course, the record series themselves constitute fuller, if more diffuse, evidence of both corporate and managerial structures, particularly in such characteristics as job titles, forms of address, signatures, covers, binders, and stamps.[136]

Applying the concept of strategy to a particular archives requires that we use the generalities of Tables 1 and 2 as a mental template with which to compare the actual records, a process which may be as simple or complicated as the case demands.[137] In the PRR case in particular, it was relatively simple to devise a strategic profile from existing printed sources before actually examining the archive.[138] Many other corporate archives which Hagley has accessioned have come with printed historical sketches or company histories, which, even if created for public relations purposes, are capable of being read as evidence of strategy.[139] Oral testimony from participants or witnesses can be used for relatively recent events.

In the PRR case we were able to identify in advance, through simple background reading, all episodes of change in market penetration, integration, diversification, and retrenchment. Innovation proved a bit more difficult, but it was possible to produce a mental outline of technical innovations in road and equipment and of managerial and procedural innovations in business practice. This was not the equivalent of writing a monograph on the subject, but it was necessary to recognize, for example, that the Walschaerts valve gear was a successful innovation at the turn of the century and the Caprotti valve gear a generally unsuccessful one about two decades later without having to know any further particulars.

Consideration of function was part of the appraisal at every level. At the broadest, we could easily determine that the company was driven by engineering (design) and operations (production). Consequently, those functions were given priority, and we were able to focus on records from those parts of the structure where they were carried out. Considering the significance of management as a function in its own right led us to prefer the files of the administrative heads of functional departments. We then paid particular attention to the functional responsibilities of subordinate officers.

The concept of detail was likewise employed in close connection with the other three. We retained a greater level of detail, measured both by more documents and descending to lower structural levels, for those offices that carried out the leading functions. Similarly, we retained greater levels of detail, measured by both record volume and redundancy for different viewpoints, for those actions and projects of greater strategic importance.

Applied to corporate records, the concepts reinforced the standard decision to retain all annual reports and board and committee minutes, all of which contain ample, if skeletal, evidence of both strategy and structure. Dockets and other papers associated with board meetings typically give fuller evidence than the official summaries. The strategic test can also be applied to central corporate files of contracts, leases, and agreements. Those concerned with the creation, acquisition, divestiture, and dissolution of firms, with intercorporate alliances, market expansion, and innovation were selected, in the PRR case, over thousands of agreements for private sidings and pipe and wire crossings. Note that service contracts for things like electric light, telephones, or computers may be evidence of innovation when these things are first employed and of substantially less significance thereafter.

For such corporate records as general account books, stock transfer books and stock ledgers, the strategic test permits periodizing the records. Stockholder records lose their strategic importance at the point at which the typical stockholder can no longer directly influence events, providing the large stockholders who still can do so can be identified through other sources like summary lists. Typically, this occurs either when stock ownership becomes widespread, indicated by a massive increase in record volume and the use of anonymous brokers' accounts, or when a company is transformed into a tightly-controlled subsidiary of another.

General account books fail to pass the strategic test once evidence of strategic options, usually contained in nonnumerical annotations, can no longer be extracted from them. (Note, however, that the design of an accounting system itself may constitute an innovation.) In the railroad case, this occurred with the imposition of standard Interstate Commerce Commission (ICC) accounting rules and the development of summary accounting forms. Account books were retained under a complex formula that included the period of start-up, the point at which a firm lost its independence by becoming a PRR subsidiary, and the availability of summary ICC Form A's (usually beginning in 1888/89). No account books were kept for modern, wholly owned subsidiaries under 10 miles in length, but all books were kept for unbuilt lines and nonrailroad subsidiaries, which were not required to submit summary reports to the ICC.

As should be expected, the concepts were of greatest value in appraising managerial records, particularly the file-level selection of mixed-value, departmental administrative files. Here we found abundant evidence of both the determinants of strategy and most strategic options. In the case of the PRR, we retained the CEO's files in their entirety, although they might well have been reduced to about 75 percent. The records of the chief line officer, the vice president of operations, had sustained major losses, but about 50 percent of the surviving material was retained. In fact, the most thorough and significant coverage of events was preserved in the records of the functional staff department heads reporting to the VPO: the chiefs of transportation, personnel, and motive power, and the chief engineer. There was substantial communication overlap between these specialists, but unique information on each of the specialties existed in the files of the other officers. The fullest account of events in the field was found in the records of the second-tier line officers, the regional vice presidents, and general managers.

To learn how the concepts were used in greater detail, let us consider the settled-case and subject files of the Legal Department, reduced by selection from 6,100 to 850 feet. A consultant independently approached by one of the participating repositories, a legal historian, suggested selecting those cases that were precedent setting. The suggestion was understandable but completely wrongheaded. This is simply not what the practice of a railroad legal department is about. Precedent-setting legal cases are documented in law reporters and law reviews. The actual records are primarily about facilitating corporate operations, much of which involves rather mundane claim, regulatory, and real estate work.

Using both "strategy" and "structure," we retained subject and case files that grew out of corporate competition, the struggle over government regulation, or the attempts at technical or market innovation. We likewise retained files on the origin and demise of corporate entities, particularly complicated bankruptcies and liquidations, and on those companies that constituted some kind of diversification or change of direction. We also retained records of major rate and service proceedings to compensate for the nearly total loss of records from the Traffic Department, where more comprehensive data on these subjects would normally have been found. The "fat file" principle proved to be a good indicator of importance, but some fat files failed the strategic test and were discarded.

The only records selected exclusively on the basis of a high level of detail were those relating to individual pieces of equipment, individual buildings and structures (comprising together the productive technology of railroading), and individual workers. In selecting records of workers, we chose the most comprehensive groups in terms of both temporal span and depth of coverage, the registers and case files of the company's sick and death benefits plan—the Voluntary Relief Department (VRD). These included both work histories, medical histories, and sociological data and met the test for whole populations. The other major class of records on individual workers were grievances, which contain evidence on work relations and processes. Here we retained all of the central files of the General Manager's Labor Board and the system and regional Joint Reviewing Committees, but for the sake of detail we also retained subpopulations of bottom-level grievances sampled both geographically and by trade. Payrolls, which had been held on fifty-year retention and filled an entire room, were not retained. The data, simply name and payment arranged chronologically, was too thin relative to bulk, and information on wage rates is available in published sources.

Registers and drawing sets were retained for all equipment (primarily locomotives and cars). Most maps and drawings of individual buildings were not available. The former were retained by one of the repositories to serve special clienteles, the Railroad Museum of Pennsylvania, which has the company's collection of historic equipment and model builders. Both of these categories require close to full detail. Detail short of that needed for complete replication was also selected in the design files for each class of equipment and of major components (brakes, wheels, air-conditioning systems), as well as all major structures and construction projects. Much of this is design and performance detail and passes the strategic test as evidence of innovation. Minimal detail, usually dates of build and modification with some indication of layout and appearance, was selected for minor examples of basic building types (stations, yards, roundhouses, shops, signal systems). This tended to reflect the actual record structure, with thick files for large projects and minor projects arranged geographically in thin, locality files. (Locality files also contained evidence of interactions with local communities.)

It is worth noting that the standard forms that Yates advised archivists not to ignore were not retained by the PRR in any quantity for more than the short term. This is consistent with Hoskin and Macve's idea that such forms are as much disciplinary as analytical in intent. Some examples, although by no means a representative sample, were preserved by being imbedded in managerial files, but these tended to reflect higher-order activities such as requests for capital expenditures or special investigations rather than repetitive daily or weekly returns.

Some breakdowns of the ratios of selected portions to whole series obtained by using these parameters in appraising the PRR archive may be useful. As noted above the CEO's files were rated at 100 percent. By structural position the results were as follows: staff vice presidents and department heads, 40.8 percent; headquarters staff below department head level, 8.8 percent; total headquarters, 21.3 percent; chief field line officers, 11.1 percent; lower field officers, 8.6 percent; total field officers, 9.8 percent. By functional department the results were as follows: relief, 61 percent; tests, 32.2 percent; personnel, 31.8 percent; special services, 30.5 percent; motive power, 29.5 percent; finance, 24.2 percent; accounting, 20.2 percent; operations, 16.4 percent; legal, 10 percent; engineering, 7.5 percent; purchases & stores, 2.5 percent; real estate, 0.6 percent. Aggregating the functions more broadly the results are: capital, 22.3 percent; labor 48.5 percent (17.8 percent excluding VRD case files); technology, 20.3 percent; production/operations, 16.4 percent; law, 10 percent; real property, 0.6 percent. On average, about 15-20 percent of top and middle managers' files were deemed suitable for permanent retention under this process. The overall retention rate of all records present was about 2.5 percent.[140] These percentages compare favorably with other appraisals.[141]

The use of these concepts, being more faithful to the purposes and modes of records creation, should satisfy most future users. Is this assertion any more correct than the similar claims made by the Jenkinsonians? The effectiveness of this approach to appraisal has not been quantified, but ten years of servicing the PRR archive suggests that it has met most, if not all, of the demands placed upon it. I know of only one instance in which a selection decision actively deprived a researcher of desired data, and this was a hobbyist whose particular interest we had decided not to satisfy up front.[142] Most of the disappointments flowed directly from accidental losses or the company's prior records retention policies. Most, though not all, of these would have been met had the records survived to undergo the same appraisal process. There seems to be a general match between this approach and the demands of most researchers.

While it is likewise not possible to quantify integrity, I believe that it has been maintained to the best degree possible and certainly in a more careful manner than the corporate successors would have done. Basic evidence of all the corporate entities in the system has been preserved, as have been all major elements of the managerial structure. Records of functional departments have been preserved in amounts roughly proportional to their relative importance in the hierarchy. The same is true of the evidence of activities and projects within individual departments and offices. The records have not been reduced to a brief for Chandler, Yates, Hoskin, or any of the other individuals who have used them.

A few other observations on use may be illuminating. As expected, the managerial records receive the most use. The corporate records are consulted much less frequently, and only the annual reports, minutes, board papers, and internal corporate history manuals are used with any regularity. Of the managerial records, those falling under the *technology* heading are used most frequently inasmuch as they seem to satisfy the needs of the widest range of users: historians of technology and design, public historians and restorationists, local historians, railroad historians, buffs, and modelers, with additional regular use by historians of business and labor. *Production/operations*, which is closely tied to technology, and *labor* are in a dead heat for second place. Interestingly, labor research has been concentrated in the files of top and middle managers. Hagley's series of grievance case files are seldom, if ever, used, and the VRD case files have not attracted the anticipated interest, which so far has been almost entirely limited to genealogists.[143] Records pertaining to capital have so far been underused, which probably reflects both a general lack of interest in the subject and an ignorance of how files on these facilitative functions can illuminate other areas of activity.

The same parameters may also be used to draw inferences about any missing pieces of the archival puzzle. Of the PRR's two 1968 merger partners, the New York Central Railroad's archives had been reduced almost entirely to corporate records. Comparison with the PRR archives revealed the magnitude of the loss. The archives of the New York, New Haven & Hartford had been placed at the University of Connecticut but was largely limited to corporate records and those from the secretary's office and legal department. Again, analysis using the four parameters confirms that coverage of many of the most important functions and structural elements is missing.

To sum up, we have seen how functions constitute the fundamental framework of business activity; how specific records arise naturally from them; how functional linkages are formed; and how functional analysis enables us to choose among record types. We have seen how functions are articulated in pursuit of strategies and how strategic analysis enables us to assign relative importance among records of a single type or within series. We have seen how certain strategies cause functions to be embodied within certain types of structures and how structural analysis reveals where the records of particular functional clusters will be located. We have seen why and how detail matters. Beyond this, I can give further examples but be no more specific. I do not recommend the employment of elaborate flow charts or protocols.[144] The four parameters, in my view, are fundamentals that need to be grasped to understand the creation and function of business records. This is an attitude to be internalized, not a simple checklist. It comes together, in the words of one symposium participant, in the expertise of the archivist.

Application of the Concepts to Other Classes of Records. It is possible that analogous principles could be considered for the appraisal of other classes of records. All organizations exhibit structural typologies that are closely linked to their activities, norms, and goals. To the extent that organizations have managers who plan and direct flexible, goal-oriented activities similar to those of business, something like the strategic concept, though not the specific strategic goals and options, ought to apply. Certain elements of the military, the space program, or government-sponsored hydroelectric and flood control projects come readily to mind, while the recording, social service, and regulatory agencies that form the basis for much of the writing on public records are clearly the least "businesslike."

What does this exercise suggest about how such appraisal concepts might be constructed in other fields? First, we may begin with a historical treatment of those fields, such as Chandler's, but we should use that only to discover basic concepts underlying both the activity itself and the historian's treatment of it. As we have seen with business, such concepts are just as likely to be laid out in the prescriptive works and socializing institutions through which persons become creators of the class of records in question, in this case the schools of business administration with their associated texts and methods. Latest and best knowledge and practice should rule, although earlier variants can often be obtained from now-obsolete textbooks and training manuals.[145]

Second, a better fit is achieved through using sources internal to the activity under study than through sources that constitute criticism from the outside or are several steps removed (one of the reasons why using Max Weber on bureaucracy may not be very productive). The idea is to inhabit the conceptual framework of the records creator, which means not straying too far above or below it or to either side. By focusing our efforts on the prescriptive and norm-instilling agents, we look at exactly those things that enable persons to perform the specific actions in question to the full level of detail. If we are serious about focusing on the mind of the creator, that means knowing how the creator is trained, works, and thinks, not what others think of the creator.

Third, we should set reasonable limits for ourselves and resist the temptation to universalize. Thinking about documenting all of society is simply too complex a task, but complex tasks can be tackled by breaking them into smaller and smaller pieces. We can do meaningful analysis at the level of business and industry, even more meaningful analysis at the level of railroads or iron and steel or banks, and still more meaningful analysis at the level of the firm.

Fourth, archivists will have to master detail. The great bulk of modern records seem to arise from the need for greater and greater detail on an ever wider range of phenomena, driven by the widespread adoption of the scientific method and the regulatory impulses of the modern state. Some details are critical, much is little more than filler, and a great deal falls somewhere in between. We need better understanding of what constitutes relevant detail for a variety of functions and uses and of what constitutes adequate representative populations.

Business Records and Archival Theory: Some Implications. To attempt to fit the records of modern business into the world of theory as derived from traditional European archives is rather like being asked to shoehorn an automobile assembly line or particle accelerator into the Orangerie at Versailles.[146] The evolution of corporation law shows why this is so. American entrepreneurs successfully freed themselves from the constraints of premodern legal traditions. A legalistic approach cannot capture the intricacies associated with strategy and structure and particularly with innovation; it simply misses the point.

If we agree that to be considered archives, documents must be consciously set aside as memorials, as spurs to memory,[147] we must also realize that widespread societal consensus tends to award full archival status very selectively, usually to records of property rights, formal obligations, and entitlements.[148] Only records of those rights and obligations that must occasionally be traced in an unbroken chain of proof unambiguously demand and receive the full archival treatment. Furthermore, in American society, at least, there is no universal authority that bestows archival status on a consistent basis. Most business records are not so much conscious memorials, strictly speaking, as expendable byproducts of the drive for control and efficiency. Others, following Ferguson, are really nothing more than the necessary intermediate steps between the "mind's eye" of the designer and the realized object. Those business records that are unmistakably archival are those that I have denominated corporate records. They partake of most, if not all, of the standard archival properties: they are fundamentally juridical; they are summary records of actions; most of them are not about anything in particular; they resist subject arrangement.[149] Even the physical treatment is similar, with registry systems prevailing long after they have disappeared from managerial records.

However, the assertion that such circumscribed archives and the winnowing processes to which they are subjected will somehow automatically produce an adequate source for any important class of secondary users is patently false.[150] This is particularly true in modern societies with extreme divisions of labor and in which "scientific" modes of data collection and analysis have taken root. Research strategies may be warped to fit the available sources, but when set side by side, in "taste-test" fashion, it is clear that corporate records are usually passed over, and their static, summary, juridical, traditional archival nature is one of the reasons for the choice.[151]

Three examples may suffice to show why this is so. For a variety of reasons including traditional archival ones, modern records management tends to preserve corporate records and subject managerial records to the shortest possible retention spans. Hagley has acquired the records of two large bituminous coal companies. The records of the Westmoreland Coal Company had been allowed to collect relatively undisturbed and were rich in managerial records. Those of the Consolidation Coal Company, usually the industry leader, were subjected to both records management procedures and decentralized, uncoordinated destruction, so that only the corporate records and current, short-term paper remained. Hagley patrons seeking in-depth understanding of most aspects of the coal industry have been obliged to use the former archive.[152] While the New York Central was as different from the PRR as General Motors from Ford, most of its story has been erased, and its archives has lost most of its explanatory power. It has been purged of too much detail on important functions and thus sees comparatively little use.[153]

To consider the actual specifics of the loss, take the case of the employment of women on the railroads during World War I and World War II. While the PRR managerial records are rich in detail, including policy discussions, statistics, and reports of special female inspectors of working conditions, evidence in the corporate records is limited to the installation of separate toilets, the only point at which the employment of women impinged upon property and capital expenditures.[154]

Managerial records, while richer in research potential, do not entirely conform to the archival nature of traditional theory. Because managers analyze data to inform decisions, the very process mirrors that of many other types of research. Many managerial records are most definitely about something, so that managerial files can be categorized by subject. Indeed, larger firms generally adopted a subject arrangement of correspondence as the only efficient means of data retrieval, often using techniques and equipment developed for library use by the Library Bureau and other purveyors of office equipment.[155] In many ways, managerial files are somewhat analogous to books and might even be given whimsical titles like "The Big Engine that Couldn't" or "How Come our Passengers Are Sweating like Pigs?" Disregard content, and they are practically incomprehensible.[157] It is precisely this analytical/decision-making orientation that renders them superior evidence of mental and physical activity.

Managerial records also fail to conform to archival theory in other ways. They are, after all, not so much about "public faith" as about private interest. Furthermore, "perpetual memory" is not seen as a universal good. Some things need to be forgotten, and not just closeted skeletons. Most business firms are obligated to periodically "reinvent" themselves in response to changing external conditions if they are to survive. There is nothing "perpetual" about them. Memory is often an impediment to change, to new ways of doing and thinking.[158] Conrail, the successor to the PRR, could not succeed without destroying the PRR's ossified corporate culture, and that included destroying or disposing of its memory and records, particularly the managerial ones.

Most records of physical detail of the nonjuridical sort were also excluded from premodern archives. In their earlier forms such records included observations of the natural world, sets of instructions or recipes, maps, engineer's notebooks (of which those of Leonardo da Vinci are best known), and alchemical formulas. Such information tended to circulate in closed communities, often as closely guarded secrets.[159] Once their original efficacy was lost, such records might acquire collectible status as ancient treasures or curiosities. Their present-day counterparts are the ubiquitous and voluminous records of science and technology, our modern arcana and craft "mysteries," rich in jargon and nonverbal thought. These records, too, are about something, usually expressed as "how to" or "do this to obtain this result." Yet the centrality of these activities to modern societies demands that these fundamentally nonjuridical records be brought into archives and understood by archivists.

Appraisal, the Archivist, and the Profession. The model also holds broader implications for archival education and practice. Unlike certain aspects of archival theory, these parameters are not easily reduced to a simple catechism. We may give names to strategy, structure, and function and endlessly subdivide and categorize, but that is not the same thing as being able to recognize them "in the wild" as it were. If the parameters only form a sort of grammar, how do we learn to decipher and interpret the complex documents that are actual archives? I would answer, in the same way that we learn any language or, indeed, any complex human skill, by building vocabulary and experimenting with form and by amassing an ever-greater repertoire of patterns. Again, it all comes together in the expertise and experience of the archivist. This kind of expertise can only be acquired by doing, and experience can only be built through collaborative work, not pedagogy.[160] We need to collaborate in the experience, the actual experience of making actual appraisals. We need to pay more attention both to sharing relevant experience among institutions and building and conserving expertise within our individual institutions.

This may help blunt some of the more obvious criticisms of the approach that I have laid out, namely, that it involves saving everything or that it is too costly and time consuming, the Rolls-Royce of appraisal. All experience is difficult to acquire in some way but, under the right circumstances, acquires its own momentum. The PRR appraisal was certainly expensive, but it was definitely not inefficient, and part of that efficiency was gained through prior experience with similar records. Likewise, the experience was not lost, like a paper read once and cast aside, but made subsequent appraisal (and processing and reference) much easier. The efficiency and efficacy of appraisal rests not in the parameters themselves (they are at best a kind of mental road map), but in the archivist's ability to use them in practice.

We must face the constant quandary of balancing integrity with cost, the documents' ability to speak with the audience's need and disposition to listen. As a professional, the practicing archivist is like the lawyer or engineer,[161] not a scientist who searches for abstract truths or constructs holistic frames of reference (although these may play a large role in the business at hand), but a technologist who must occasionally work in the absence of or in advance of theory and who must use a variety of tools to produce a useful product in response to conflicting and often irreconcilable demands.

Endnotes

1. Ralph M. Hower, "The Preservation of Business Records," *Bulletin of the Business Historical Society* 11 (1937): 37–83; Francis X. Blouin, Jr., "An Agenda for the Appraisal of Business Records," in *Archival Choices: Managing the Historical Record in an Age of Abundance*, ed. Nancy E. Peace (Lexington, Mass.: Lexington Books, 1984); Christopher Densmore, "Understanding and Using Early-Nineteenth-Century Account Books," *Midwestern Archivist* 5 (1980): 5–19; Dennis E. Meissner, "The Evaluation of Modern Business Accounting Records," *Midwestern Archivist* 5 (1981): 75–100.

2. Larry Steck and Francis X. Blouin, Jr., "Hannah Lay & Company: Sampling the Records of a Century of Lumbering in Michigan," *American Archivist* 39, no. 1 (1976): 15–20; Maureen A. Jung, "Documenting Nineteenth-Century Quartz Mining in Northern California," *American Archivist* 53, no. 3 (1990): 406–418; Richard Carter Davis, "Getting the Lead Out: The Appraisal of Silver-Lead Mining at the University of Idaho," *American Archivist* 55, no. 3 (1992): 454–463.

3. Bruce H. Bruemmer and Sheldon Hochheiser, *The High-Technology Company: A Historical and Archival Guide* (Minneapolis: Charles Babbage Institute, 1989).

4. *Directory of Business Archives in the United States and Canada* (Chicago: Society of American Archivists, 1990); Standard and Poor's, *Standard & Poor's Register of Corporations, Directors and Executives* (New York: Standard and Poor's, 1995); corporate archives are most common in entertainment and media, financial services, insurance, and food products.

5. The arguments are most sharply drawn in the debate between Eastwood and John W. Roberts in *Archivaria* 37 (1994): 111–133. See also Luciana Duranti, "The Concept of Appraisal and Archival Theory," *American Archivist* 57, no. 2 (1994): 328–344; Terry Eastwood, "Nailing a Little Jelly to the Wall of Archival Studies," *Archivaria* 35 (1993): 232–252; "How Goes it with Appraisal?" *Archivaria* 36 (1993): 111–121; and "Towards a Social Theory of Appraisal," in *The Archival Imagination: Essays in Honour of Hugh A. Taylor*, ed. Barbara L. Craig (Ottawa: Association of Canadian Archivists, 1992), 71–89; Heather Mac-Neil, "Archival Theory and Practice: Between Two Paradigms," *Archivaria* 37 (1994):6–20.

6. On the difference between protecting archival nature and appraisal see also Terry Cook, "Another Brick in the Wall: Terry Eastwood's Masonry and Archival Walls: History and Archival Appraisal," *Archivaria* 37 (1994): 98.

7. Duranti, "Concept of Appraisal," 336.

8. For appraisal as pure policy decision see Frank Boles, "Mix Two Parts Interest to One Part Information and Appraise Until Done: Understanding Contemporary Record Selection," *American Archivist* 50, no. 3 (1987): 356–369; Frank Boles and Julia Marks Young, "Exploring the Black Box: The Appraisal of University Administrative Records," *American Archivist* 48, no. 1 (1985): 121–140. The following analysis might find a resting place, albeit a Procrustean one, within the first two parts of their "value of information module."

9. On the accumulation of records in dead storage prior to the formation of the National Archives in 1934, see Martin I. Elzy, "Scholarship versus Economy: Records Appraisal at the National Archives," *Prologue* 6 (1974): 183–185. Most of the large corporate archives now at the Hagley Museum and Library originally accumulated under conditions of nonarchival storage.

10. For an example of interest-group pressure that could not be ignored, see Susan Steinwall, "Appraisal and the FBI Case Files: For Whom Do Archivists Retain Records," *American Archivist* 49, no. 1 (1985): 52–63.

11. For example, MacNeil, "Archival Theory and Practice," 9–10; Davis, "Getting the Lead Out," 456–457; Cook, "Another Brick in the Wall," 99–100; Boles and Young, "Exploring the Black Box," 124–125; Bruemmer and Hochheiser, *High Technology Company*, 15–100.

12. Terry Cook, "Mind over Matter: Towards a New Theory of Archival Appraisal," in Craig, ed., *Archival Imagination*, 38–70.

13. See Eastwood's attack on Cook in "Nailing a Little Jelly," 248.

14. *Standard Industrial Classification Manual* (Washington, D.C.: Office of Management and Budget, 1986), 427–443.

15. MacNeil, "Archival Theory and Practice," 9.

16. T. R. Schellenberg, *Modern Archives: Principles and Techniques* (Chicago: University of Chicago Press, 1956), 139–160.

17. Practices that had been devised at the Baker Library of the Harvard Business School on the basis of eighteenth- and nineteenth-century firms quickly proved inadequate when applied to more complex twentieth-century organizational forms. The Baker scheme is described in Arthur H. Cole, "Business Manuscripts: Collection, Handling, and Cataloging," *Library Quarterly* 8 (1938): 93–114. As the title indicates, Cole's model was further compromised by being derived from library practice associated with personal papers.

18. The PRR (1846-1968) was by most measurements the largest and most important United States railroad and usually among the top twenty American corporations. The majority of its archives was acquired by a consortium of nine repositories

from 1985 to 1986 under a grant from the National Historical Publications and Records Commission. As appraisal archivist, the author led the team that appraised the records in the field from 1984 to 1986 and later directed the secondary appraisal, arrangement, and description of that portion of the records deposited at the Hagley Museum and Library. The project is described in Michael Nash and Christopher T. Baer, "Final Report on the Penn Central Railroad Appraisal Project," report, Hagley Museum and Library.

19. Cynthia A. Montgomery and Michael E. Porter, eds., *Strategy: Seeking and Securing Competitive Advantage* (Cambridge: Harvard Business Review, 1991), xii.

20. Alfred D. Chandler, Jr., *Strategy and Structure: Chapters in the History of the American Industrial Enterprise* (Cambridge: MIT Press, 1962), and *The Visible Hand: The Managerial Revolution in American Business* (Cambridge: Belknap Press of Harvard University Press, 1977). The PRR is covered in 105–187 of *The Visible Hand*.

21. Francis X. Blouin, Jr., "A New Perspective on the Appraisal of Business Records: A Review," *American Archivist* 42, no. 3 (1977): 312–320.

22. JoAnne Yates, "Internal Communication Systems in American Business Structures: A Framework to Aid Appraisal," *American Archivist* 48, no. 2 (1985): 141–158.

23. Much of the post-Chandler revisionism in business history nevertheless focuses on matters subsumed under the concepts of "strategy and structure," albeit in different industries and along different paths. For example, Philip Scranton, *Figured Tapestry: Production, Markets, and Power in Phildelphia Textiles, 1885–1941* (Cambridge: Cambridge University Press, 1989).

24. Arthur A. Thompson, Jr. and A. J. Strickland III, *Strategy and Policy: Concepts and Cases* (Dallas: Business Publications, 1978); Jay Galbraith and Daniel A. Nathanson, *Strategy Implementation: The Role of Structure and Process* (St. Paul: West Publishing Company, 1978); Yedzi H. Godiwalla, *Strategic Management: Broadening Business Policy* (New York: Praeger Publishers, 1983); Thompson and Strickland, 84–86, list some typical hybrid strategies. For another variant of Table 2 see, Michael E. Porter, *Competitive Strategy: Techniques for Analyzing Industries and Competitors* (New York: The Free Press, 1980), xviii.

25. Perhaps the best summary of this literature may be found in Montgomery and Porter, eds., *Strategy: Seeking and Securing Competitive Advantage*.

26. See 102–104, below.

27. Louis Galambos, "What Have CEOs Been Doing?" *Journal of Economic History* 48 (1988): 246.

28. Ibid., 248–251. For another perspective on the importance of innovation in American business, see Michael E. Porter, "The Competitive Advantage of Nations," in Montgomery and Porter, eds., *Strategy: Seeking and Securing Competitive Advantage*, 136–138.

29. Thompson and Strickland, *Strategy and Policy*, 45.

30. Henry Mintzberg, "Crafting Strategy," in Montgomery and Porter, eds., *Strategy: Seeking and Securing Competitive Advantage*, 404–407.

31. Compare, for example, the level of evidence of the activities of the early-nineteenth-century Lehigh Coal & Navigation Company contained in its minutes with that contained in letters of its principal officers. Minutes of the Board of Managers, vols. A–G, 1821–1863, Lehigh Coal & Navigation Company Records, MG-311, reel 2293, Pennsylvania Historical & Museum Commission, Harrisburg, Pa.; Superintendent's letterbooks, 1844–1878, Acc. 1293, Hagley Museum and Library, Wilmington, Del.; Josiah White Papers, Coll. 1166, Quaker Collection, Haverford College, Haverford, Pa.

32. Galambos, "What Have CEOs Been Doing," 253, quoting Nathan Rosenberg.

33. Ibid., 253–254. The forms of the records themselves may be evidence of managerial innovation. See Yates, "Internal Communication Systems," 144–154.

34. For example, the Weberian bureaucratic approach put forward by Michael Lutzker, "Max Weber and the Analysis of Modern Bureaucratic Organization: Notes toward a Theory of Appraisal," *American Archivist* 45, no. 2 (1982): 119–129. For a critique of Weber's assumptions regarding business bureaucracy and an alternative sociology of the corporation, see James S. Coleman, "Social Organization of the Corporation," in *The U.S. Business Corporation: An Institution in Transition*, eds. John R. Meyer and James M. Gustafson (Cambridge: American Academy of Arts and Sciences, 1988), 94–111.

35. For some typical examples, see Michael E. Porter, "How Competitive Forces Shape Strategy" and "The Competitive Advantage of Nations," in Montgomery and Porter, eds., *Strategy: Seeking and Securing Competitive Advantage*, 14, 20–23, 137–148.

36. For the well-known differences between General Motors and Ford, see Chandler, *Strategy and Structure*, 46, 143–144, 301, 372–374.

37. F. M. Scherer, "Corporate Ownership and Control," in Meyer and Gustafson, eds., *U.S. Business Corporation*, 43. For a historical overview see Chandler, *The Visible Hand*, 15–49.

38. Carlo Cippola, *Before the Industrial Revolution: European Society and Economy, 1000-1700*, 2d ed. (New York: W. W. Norton & Company, 1980), 194–198; Charles E. Freedeman, *Joint-Stock Enterprise in France, 1807-1867: From Privileged Company to Modern Corporation* (Chapel Hill: University of North Carolina Press, 1979), 3–4; Ronald E. Seavoy, *The Origins of the American Business Corporation, 1784-1855* (Westport, Conn.: Greenwood Press, 1982), 97.

39. James Willard Hurst, *The Legitimacy of the Business Corporation in the Law of the United States, 1780-1970* (Charlottesville: University Press of Virginia, 1970), 1–13, 153–159.

40. For discussion of the various protagonists, their theories, and various corporate reform movements see, John Henry Culley III, "People's Capitalism and Cor-

porate Democracy: An Intellectual History of the Corporation" (Ph.D. diss., University of California, 1986).

41. Thomas K. McCraw, "The Evolution of the Corporation in the U.S.," in Meyer and Gustafson, eds., *U.S. Business Corporation*, 3; Freedeman, *Joint-Stock Enterprise*, 4–7; Culley, "People's Capitalism," 39–42; Hurst, *Legitimacy of the Business Corporation*, 3–6.

42. Joseph S. Davis, *Essays on the Earlier History of American Corporations* (Cambridge: Harvard University Press, 1917), 1:7, 10, 20, 88–103.

43. McCraw, "Evolution of the Corporation," 4; Culley, "People's Capitalism," 89–94.

44. There is no comprehensive treatment of this subject. For some of the major states, see Edwin Merrick Dodd, *American Business Corporations until 1860 with Special Reference to Massachusetts* (Cambridge: Harvard University Press, 1954); John W. Cadman, Jr., *The Corporation in New Jersey: Business and Politics, 1791-1875* (Cambridge: Harvard University Press, 1949); Louis Hartz, *Economic Policy and Democratic Thought: Pennsylvania, 1776-1860* (Cambridge: Harvard University Press, 1948); George W. Kuehnl, *The Wisconsin Business Corporation* (Madison: University of Wisconsin Press, 1959). For New York see Seavoy, *Origins*.

45. Dodd, *American Business Corporations*, 11; McCraw, "Evolution of the Corporation," 4.

46. Seavoy, *Origins*, 65–67, 154–155, 180, 191; McCraw, "Evolution of the Corporation," 5–6; Hurst, *Legitimacy of the Business Corporation*, 132–135.

47. Dodd and Seavoy give detailed descriptions of the powers granted by special and general acts in Massachusetts and New York respectively. The details of relevant partnership and incorporation laws may be found in the annual session laws and compiled civil codes of each of the states.

48. Pennsylvania finally abandoned special incorporation with the adoption of its 1873 constitution. Its *General Incorporation Act* of 1874, among other things, forbade one company from owning the stock of another. Mining and manufacturing companies were forbidden to operate company stores. *Laws of the General Assembly of the State of Pennsylvania . . . 1874* (Harrisburg, 1874), 73–107.

49. *Laws of Pennsylvania, 1874*, 271–273. Note the very size of the act as compared to the corporation law of the same year. For Carnegie's companies, see Joseph Frazier Wall, *Andrew Carnegie* (New York: Oxford University Press, 1970), 471–472, 534–536.

50. Chandler, *Visible Hand*, 319–331, 418–424; *Report on Standard Oil Company and Former Subsidiaries, Revised to May 1st, 1912* (New York: General Services Corporation, 1912), 1–3.

51. James C. Bonbright and Gardiner C. Means, *The Holding Company: Its Public Significance and its Regulation* (New York: McGraw-Hill Book Company, 1932), 59–63. These charters were practically *carte blanche* grants and helped provoke

the more restrictive constitution and laws of 1873–74. The Hagley Museum and Library has the records of two of these companies, the Reading Company (Acc. 1520) and the Pennsylvania Company (Acc. 1807).

52. Bonbright and Means, *Holding Company*, 57; Culley, "People's Capitalism," 83–85; Christopher Grandy, "New Jersey Corporate Chartermongering, 1875-1929," *Journal of Eonomic History* 69 (1989): 677–692.

53. Hurst, *Legitimacy of the Business Corporation*, 147–149; Culley, "People's Capitalism," 84–86; Grandy, "Chartermongering," 685–691. Chartermongering also included tax and legal advantages, such as the jurisdiction of Delaware's Chancery Court. Maine, West Virginia, and Nevada also joined the chartermongering sweepstakes.

54. On Carnegie Steel, see *Moody's Manual of Industrial and Miscellaneous Securities*, (New York: O. C. Lewis, 1900), 400–401; on DuPont, see "E. I. du Pont de Nemours & Company Chronology" in *A Guide to Manuscripts in the Eleutherian Mills Historical Library*, John Beverley Riggs (Greenville, Del.: Eleutherian Mills-Hagley Foundation, 1970), 576–583; on Baldwin, see *Moody's Manual of Railroad and Corporation Securities* (New York: Moody's Publishing Company, 1912), 2919.

55. Scherer, "Corporate Ownership and Control," 43–44.

56. The lives and deaths of representative corporations may be traced in corporate history manuals such as Coverdale and Colpitts, *The Pennsylvania Railroad Company, Corporate, Financial, and Construction History of Lines Owned, Operated, and Controlled To December 31, 1945* (New York: Coverdale and Colpitts, n.d.), 4 vols.; "History of the Origin and Development of the Pennsylvania Power & Light Company," typescript, c. 1964, Hagley Museum and Library. On typical rules governing corporate demise, see *Delaware Code Annotated* (St. Paul: West Publishing Company, 1953), 4:292–434.

57. Michael Nash, John Rumm, and Craig Orr, *Pennsylvania Power & Light Company, A Guide to the Records* (Wilmington: Hagley Museum and Library, 1985); "Penn Central Project Data File, Predecessor and Subsidiary Companies," curator's file, Hagley Museum and Library.

58. Christopher T. Baer, "A Guide to the History and Records of the Bethlehem Steel Corporation," finding aid, Hagley Museum and Library, 1990.

59. For example, a relatively insignificant company formed in 1919 to make ship parts in Pennsylvania was subsequently transformed into the operator of four steel plants on the West Coast and then into the present Bethlehem Steel Corporation, courtesy of a liberal Delaware charter. See Baer, "Bethlehem Steel," 1, 297, 303.

60. McCraw, "Evolution of the Corporation," 6–7; Culley, "People's Capitalism," 56–59; Hurst, *Legitimacy of the Business Corporation*, 65–70, 157–159.

61. Hurst, *Legitimacy of the Business Corporation*, 152–153; Culley, "People's Capitalism," 106–109; Ellis W. Hawley, *The New Deal and the Problem of Monopoly:*

A Study in Economic Ambivalence (Princeton: Princeton University Press, 1966), 240–244, 309–344, 401–419, 472–494.

62. See Coverdale and Colpitts, *Pennsylvania Railroad Company, By Laws and Organization, 1893–1955*, Acc. 1807, Box 1418, Hagley Museum and Library; Thompson and Strickland, *Strategy and Policy*, 126. Legally, managers' power to design their "organizations" rests on the recognized right to adopt bylaws as a sort of internal constitution.

63. Galbraith and Nathanson, *Strategy Implementation*, 114–118.

64. The functions of "management," according to a widely accepted formula of Luther Gulick's, are planning, organizing, staffing, directing, coordinating, reporting, and budgeting. See James P. Baughman, "Management," in *Encyclopedia of American Economic History*, ed. Glenn Porter (New York: Charles Scribner's Sons, 1980), 832–833.

65. Chandler, *Visible Hand*, 94–109; Yates, "Internal Communication Systems," 145–146. In some instances, functional departmentalization was a slow, almost organic process. However, Hoskin and Macve have argued persuasively that in certain pivotal cases the internal control systems that enabled large firms to function effectively were consciously designed by managerial generalists as a "knowledge-power" system based on techniques borrowed from the military and the academy. See Keith W. Hoskin and Richard H. Macve, "The Genesis of Accountability: The West Point Connections," *Accounting Organisations and Society* 13 (1988): 37–73.

66. Thompson and Strickland, *Strategy and Policy*, 127–131.

67. In its simplest formulation, line officers deal with people and staff officers with things; line officers with the primary function and staff officers with ancillary ones. See Chandler, *Visible Hand*, 106–107.

68. Chandler, *Visible Hand*, 106–107; Thompson and Strickland, *Strategy and Policy*, 140–143.

69. For example, on the PRR, the Real Estate Department was created in two steps in 1874 and 1884 by segregating functions previously performed in Engineering (surveys and maps) and Legal (deeds and titles). Examples of new creations include the Signal Department in 1883 and the Electronic Data Processing Division of the Financial Department in 1962. The Public Relations Department grew out of the consultancy of Ivy Lee (1906-34). See "Penn Central Project Data Files, Departments, Regions, and Divisions," Hagley Museum and Library.

70. Galbraith and Nathanson, *Strategy Implementation*, 118–119; Chandler, *Visible Hand*, 151–156, 315–320, 330–334.

71. Galambos, "What Have CEOs Been Doing," 255; Michael E. Porter, "From Competitive Advantages to Corporate Strategy," in Montgomery and Porter, eds., *Strategy: Seeking and Securing Competitive Advantage*, 238–244.

72. Chandler, *Strategy and Structure*, 158–162; *Visible Hand*, 376–483; Galambos, "What Have CEOs Been Doing," 249; Yates, "Internal Communication Systems," 153–154.

73. Chandler, *Strategy and Structure*, 67–113; Christopher T. Baer, "Corporate Structure of E. I. du Pont de Nemours & Co., 1902–1990," curator's file, Hagley Museum and Library. Note that business firms use designations like *department* and *division* with less-than-military precision, often applying the same term to two or more hierarchical levels.

74. For examples, see table "Major Acquisitions of the Du Pont Company, 1910– 33," David A. Hounshell and John Kenly Smith, Jr., *Science and Corporate Strategy: Du Pont R&D, 1902-1980* (Cambridge: Cambridge University Press, 1988), 608–611.

75. Alfred D. Chandler, Jr., "The Enduring Logic of Industrial Success," in Montgomery and Porter, eds., *Strategy: Seeking and Securing Competitive Advantage* 270.

76. McCraw, "Evolution of the Corporation," 11.

77. *Laws of Pennsylvania, 1814*, 154–173; *1815*, 72–83; *1833*, 144–155; *1874*, 73– 107, 271–273; *By-Laws of the Board of Directors together with the Charter of the Pennsylvania Railroad Company and its Supplements* (Philadelphia: Crissy & Markley, 1853).

78. *Revised Statutes of the State of Delaware* (Wilmington: Charles L. Story, 1915), 910–1014.

79. Regulation is generally superimposed on ordinary business activities and often results in the generation of documents that would not otherwise arise in the normal course of business affairs, such as 10-K reports or affidavits of compliance with the Clayton Act in the awarding of contracts. Comparison of pre- and postregulation variants of functionally similar documents in a given industry is instructive. On federal regulation mandating the creation and retention of otherwise unnecessary records by both state governments and the private sector, see Thornton W. Mitchell, "New Viewpoints on Establishing Permanent Value of State Archives," *American Archivist* 33, no. 2 (1970): 172–173.

80. *Regulations to Govern the Destruction of Records of Steam Roads Prescribed by the Interstate Commerce Commission in Accordance with Section 20 of the Act to Regulate Commerce, Issue of 1914* (Washington, D.C.: GPO, 1914).

81. For a good example see the records of the unincorporated Lehigh Coal Mine Company (1792–1829) in Lehigh Coal & Navigation Company Records, MG-311, Pennsylvania Historical & Museum Commission (PH&MC). The records consist of a minute book with records of stock transfers and an account book. They were preserved in the LC&N archives as continuing evidence of purchased property rights. The equivalent of managerial records for this simple firm are scattered among the personal business correspondence of the individual managers.

82. Little Britain (Pa.) general store account book, 1796–1807, Acc. 2018; Manheim, Petersburg and Lancaster Turnpike or Plank Road Company Records, 1850– 1863, Acc. 2047; George Bowen & Company Records, 1829–1898, Acc. 2064;

all Hagley Museum and Library, are records of relatively simple businesses with little differentiation of record types.

83. For example, Samuel G. Wright papers, 1809–1845, Acc. 1665; E. I. du Pont de Nemours & Company Records, Series I, Part I, Correspondence, 1802–1890; Bartley Crucible and Refractories Company Records, 1909–1986, Acc. 1973; all Hagley Museum and Library. Record descriptions available on RLIN data base.

84. Penn Central Project Data Files, Departments, Regions, and Divisions, Hagley Museum and Library; Bruemmer and Hochheiser, *High Technology Company*, 11–12; Yates, "Internal Communication Systems," 152, 156; Boles and Young, "Exploring the Black Box," 125.

85. On the PRR, W. W. Atterbury (president 1925–1935) sought relief from his long tenure as vice president-operations by delegating most of his responsibilities and exploiting his "head of state" role through involvement in politics and international affairs. His successor, M. W. Clement (president 1935-1949), had no such ambitions and closely monitored all company activities. See the differences in their files, PRR Records, Office of the President, MG-286, PH&MC.

86. Bruemmer and Hochheiser, *High Technology Company*, 12; Yates, "Internal Communication Systems," 152.

87. PRR Records, Office of Chief Engineer-Philadelphia Improvements, Acc. 1810/2123, Hagley Museum and Library.

88. See also Yates, "Internal Communication Systems," 152–153.

89. Galbraith and Nathanson, *Strategy Implementation*, 119.

90. Penn Central Project Data Files, Departments, Regions, and Divisions, Hagley Museum and Library; Riggs, "Du Pont Chronology," 576–583; Baer, "Corporate Structure of E. I. du Pont de Nemours & Co."

91. Baer, "Corporate Structure of E. I. du Pont de Nemours & Co."

92. Penn Central Project Data Files, Departments, Regions, and Divisions, Hagley Museum and Library. See also Bruemmer and Hochheiser, *High-Technology Company*, 2, 11.

93. Chandler based his description of the PRR organization entirely upon the manuals of 1858 and 1873 (*Visible Hand*, 533). While certainly the most important for his argument, they nevertheless give a misleading picture of the company over its entire history.

94. The separation of ownership and management is a standard theme in U.S. business history. See, McCraw, "Evolution of the Corporation," 8–11.

95. For example, North Pennsylvania Railroad Company Records, Acc. 1999, Hagley Museum and Library.

96. James A. Ward, *J. Edgar Thomson: Master of the Pennsylvania* (Westport, Conn.: Greenwood Press, 1980), 85–90; Alvin F. Harlow, *The Road of the Century: The Story of the New York Central* (New York: Creative Age Press, 1947), 332, 420.

97. Charles Brelsford McCoy Papers, Acc. 1815, Hagley Museum and Library.

98. Lukens Steel Company Records, Acc. 50; Alan Wood Steel Company Records, Acc. 333; Joseph Bancroft & Sons Company Records, Acc. 736; J. E. Rhoads & Sons, Inc., Records, Acc. 1156; Sun Company Records, Acc. 1317; Westmoreland Coal Company Records, Acc. 1765; Wawa, Inc., Records, Acc. 1772; Strawbridge & Clothier Records, Acc. 2117; Joseph E. Seagram & Son Records, Acc. 2126, all Hagley Museum and Library. For independent confirmation of greater support for archives in family firms, see Christopher L. Hives, "History, Business Records, and Corporate Archives in North America," *Archivaria* 22 (1986): 49.

99. For example, Lukens Steel Company Records, Acc. 50; and Charles L. Huston Papers, Acc. 1174; Sun Company Records, Acc. 1317; and J. Howard Pew Papers, Acc. 1634, all Hagley Museum and Library.

100. For example, the feud between the two branches of the extended Huston family of Lukens Steel. Christopher T. Baer, "A Guide to the History and Records of the Lukens Steel Company," finding aid, Hagley Museum and Library, 88–89. For other examples of discord in family firms see Scherer, "Corporate Ownership and Control," 55–56.

101. McCraw, "Evolution of the Corporation," 8. Recently, the computer has worked to make middle managers an endangered species by assuming many of their networking and coordinating duties.

102. Yates, "Internal Communication Systems," 146–156. Yates, like many business historians, sees such reporting systems as primarily serving an analytical function (146). However, Hoskin and Macve, in "The Genesis of Accountability," see them as a system of discipline via self-discipline, to create the impression that the boss is always watching and of inevitable accountability.

103. This approach is similar to the "cluster concept" developed at the National Archives for appraising related series. See Terry Cook, " 'Many are called, but few are chosen,' Appraisal Guidelines for Sampling and Selecting Case Files," *Archivaria* 32 (1991): 29.

104. Yates, "Internal Communication Systems," 156–158.

105. Michael E. Porter, *Competitive Strategy*, 4–21.

106. Highlighting "externalities" in business records is analogous to Cook's elevating the "citizen" or "client" as a third factor equal to structure and function in the analysis of public records ("Mind over Matter," 54–56). I have chosen not to give externalities that level of importance because they seem to be capable of being subsumed within the idea of strategy, which is not present in Cook's analysis.

107. For example, the PRR Records, Hagley Museum and Library, contain substantial information on General Electric, Westinghouse, and the Baldwin Locomotive Works. Officers of Lukens Steel participated in committees of the National As-

sociation of Manufacturers, and the Lukens Records, Hagley Museum and Library contain reports not preserved in the main NAM archives.

108. For example, Tom Nesmith, "Archives From the Bottom Up: Social History and Archival Scholarship," *Archivaria* 14 (1982): 5–26; Dale C. Mayer, "The New Social History: Implications for Archivists," *American Archivist* 48 (1985): 388–399; John C. Rumm, "Working Through the Records: Using Business Records to Study Workers and the Management of Labour," *Archivaria* 27 (1988/89): 76–88.

109. Eastwood, "Nailing a Little Jelly," 238.

110. I have rejected the records of a number of small firms on such grounds, including those of Limestone Products of America (sandbox sand and chicken feed supplements) and the Merrick Scale Company (weighfeeders), although these played only a minor role in the strategy of their parent, Penn Virginia Corporation. Penn Virginia Corporation Records, Acc. 1764, Hagley Museum and Library.

111. For the importance of detail in technological thinking, see Tom F. Peters, *Transitions in Engineering: Guillaume Henri Dufour and the Early 19th Century Cable Suspension Bridges* (Basel: Birkhäuser Verlag, 1987), 9–10. In architectural design, *detail* refers to the special articulations of surface treatment and the junctions between dissimilar surfaces and materials.

112. John Bartlett, comp., *Familiar Quotations*, 16th ed., Justin Kaplan (Boston: Little, Brown and Company, 1992), 783.

113. For an analysis of engineering disasters as design failures, see Eugene S. Ferguson, *Engineering and the Mind's Eye* (Cambridge: MIT Press, 1992), 169–193.

114. See Rumm, "Working Through the Records," 82–86 for a more complete description of personnel records.

115. For an example of how various mechanical details were recycled in the creation of Thomas Newcomen's 1712 steam engine, see Ferguson, *Engineering and the Mind's Eye*, 13–21.

116. Arnold E. Roos, "A Case Study in Frustration: Archives, the History of Technology, and the Restoration of Yukon Riverboats," *Archivaria* 25 (1988): 51–72.

117. Yates, "Internal Communication Systems," 158.

118. Cook, " 'Many are called,' " 26.

119. Bruemmer and Hochheiser, *High-Technology Company*, 12; Yates, "Internal Communication Systems," 152.

120. For example, bridge plans, Phoenix Bridge Company Records, Acc. 1179; Contract file, Reading Company Records, Acc. 1520; Deposit ledgers, Philadelphia Saving Fund Society Records, Acc. 2062; Package designs, Irv Koons Records, Acc. 2132, all Hagley Museum and Library.

121. For a definition of throughput as an index of efficiency in production, see Chandler, *Visible Hand*, 241.

122. On the richness of detail in case files, see Cook, " 'Many are called,' " 25; Leonard Rapport, "In the Valley of Decision: What to Do about the Multitude of Files of Quasi Cases," *American Archivist* 48 (1985): 173–189.

123. See also Bruemmer and Hochheiser, *High-Technology Company*, 2. A good introduction to nonverbal thinking in engineering may be found in Ferguson, *Engineering and the Mind's Eye*, 41–152.

124. For example, in the PRR Engineering Department, letters and drawings were usually filed separately. Only the letter files survived, rendering references to Plan A or the red versus yellow lines nugatory unless a folded reference print was attached.

125. For example, ship drawings, cost books, and specifications, Harlan Yard, Bethlehem Steel Corporation Records, Acc. 1699; PRR Operating Department, Maryland Division Service Record Cards, Acc. 1807; Research reports, Radio Corporation of America Records, Acc. 2069, all Hagley Museum and Library.

126. The best and most concise treatment of such techniques is, Cook, " 'Many are called.' " My own experience suggests that periodic or random sampling is worth considering for human populations, where the use of such concepts are a well-established form of analysis, but inappropriate for things and complex cyclical phenomena. On the (to my mind inappropriate) sampling of quantitative accounting data for Hannah Lay & Company, see Streck and Blouin, "Hannah Lay & Company," 17–20. For a different view of sampling, see Mayer, 395.

127. On the nature of engineering design, see Ferguson, *Engineering and the Mind's Eye*, 1–40. The axe-head example illustrated on 6–7 shows the particularistic orientation of technology.

128. See Cook, " 'Many are called,' " 42.

129. Earlier writers such as Hower in "The Preservation of Business Records," 44–48 developed a function/genre-based classification. John Armstrong and Stephanie Jones, *Business Documents: Their origins, sources and uses in historical research* (London: Mansell Publishing Limited, 1987) continues this tradition. Davis, "Getting the Lead Out," 457 is an attempt to create a functional typology from a single, incomplete specimen.

130. Joan K. Haas, Helen Willa Samuels, and Barbara Trippel Simmons, *Appraising the Records of Modern Science and Technology: A Guide* (Cambridge: MIT, 1985).

131. My own views on the subject were most influenced by David Bearman, Helen Samuels, and others at the Bentley Historical Library in August 1986. I had been taught a similar style of functional analysis in architectural school 20 years earlier.

132. This first attempt at a comprehensive functional typology for business records was contained in the author's "Coping with Industrial Records: Putting Appraisal

Theory to Work," (paper delivered at the Spring 1988 MARAC meeting, Allentown, Pa.).

133. For example, the business functions described by Bruemmer and Hochheiser, *High-Technology Company*.

134. This summary treatment is based on my training and experience as an architectural and engineering designer. Design education relies more on example and practice than on texts, although there is a large literature on design theory and history. For a perspective on design in engineering see, Ferguson, *Engineering and the Mind's Eye*, 1–40.

135. The scheme puts greatest emphasis on close analysis and understanding of past actions. However, most businesses save their records for what are essentially "maintenance" purposes. In part, this is the functional aspect of the difference between corporate and managerial records.

136. See also Angelika Menne-Haritz, "Appraisal or Documentation: Can We Appraise Archives by Selecting Content," *American Archivist* 47 (1994): 538.

137. A checklist for developing a strategic profile may be found in Thompson and Strickland, *Strategy and Policy*, 92–94.

138. Sources included, George H. Burgess and Miles C. Kennedy, *Centennial History of the Pennsylvania Railroad* (Philadelphia: PRR, 1949); and Stephen Salsbury, *No Way to Run a Railroad: the Untold Story of the Penn Central Crisis* (New York: McGraw-Hill Book Company, 1982).

139. For example, Michael R. Marrus, *Samuel Bronfman: The Life and Times of Seagram's Mr. Sam* (Hanover, N.H.: Brandeis University Press, 1991); George W. Franz, *A Centennial History, Eastern Building Materials Dealers Association, 1892-1992* (Virginia Beach: Downing Company, 1992); Alfred Leif, *Family Business: A Century in the Life and Times of Strawbridge & Clothier* (New York: McGraw-Hill Book Company, 1968).

140. The PRR appraisal was a three-step process. The first selected about 60,000 of a total 400,000 linear feet on the basis of written descriptions. Of the 60,000 linear feet actually appraised, about 10,000 linear feet were retained. The percentage breakdowns given reflect the second step. These numbers exclude the corporate records, which were divided into so many series that it proved impractical to measure them in the "before" state. The VRD and labor totals are warped by the complete preservation of the case files and the Engineering Department by the absence of drawings. Mention has also been made of the absence of most top-level records from the Traffic and Sales Department, rendering any comparison meaningless. These figures are for the preliminary appraisal performed by the project team. Some participating repositories requested some series be shipped without review and selection or be subject to less stringent appraisal criteria. Hagley conducted further fine-grained appraisal and elimination of redundancies during arrangement and description. Some other repositories applied their own standards.

141. James Gregory Bradsher, "When One Percent Means a Lot: The Percentage of Permanent Records in the National Archives," *Organization of American His-*

torians Newsletter (May 1985): 20–21, noted a retention rate of 1.39 percent; Douglas A. Bakker, "Corporate Archives Today," *American Archivist* 45 (1982):285, noted 1 to 3 percent retention in a sample of corporate archives.

142. This researcher nonetheless found much relevant information in the records that were retained.

143. George Brightbill, Temple University Urban Archives, in a personal communication with author, February 8, 1996, notes that the VRD case files receive on average about eight calls per year.

144. For one of Roberts' salvos against the mechanistic use of flow charts and modules see, John W. Roberts, "Practice Makes Perfect, Theory Makes Theorists," *Archivaria* 37 (1994): 114–115.

145. For the PRR we used, among others, L. F. Loree, *Railroad Freight Transportation* (New York: D. Appleton & Company, 1926); Ray Morris and William E. Hooper, *Railroad Administration* (New York: D. Appleton & Company, 1930); William E. Hooper, *Railroad Accounting* (New York: D. Appleton & Company, 1915).

146. This was the basis of Schellenberg's criticism of Jenkinson. See Richard Stapleton, "Jenkinson and Schellenberg: A Comparison," *Archivaria* 17 (1983/84): 75–85. Whatever Schellenberg's shortcomings as a theorist, I believe that his writings constitute an accurate rendition of American social realities.

147. Eastwood, "Towards a Social Theory," 74.

148. See for comparison, Eastwood, "What is Archival Theory and Why is it Important?" *Archivaria* 37 (1994): 126.

149. On these properties, see Eastwood, "How Goes It?" 116–117; Eastwood, "Towards a Social Theory," 81–81; Duranti, "Concept of Appraisal and Archival Theory," 331–334.

150. For such assertions, see Duranti, "Concept of Appraisal and Archival Theory," 337; Hives, "History, Business Records, and Corporate Archives," 46. Terry Eastwood admits ("Towards a Social Theory," 78) that this Jenkinsonian assumption that administrative memory is equivalent to the best societal memory is belied by the actual history of North American archives.

151. At Hagley, this seems to be the case whether the researchers are academics, public historians, antiquarians, business people, engineers, or lawyers.

152. Westmoreland Coal Company Records, Acc. 1765; Consolidation Coal Company Records, Acc. 2030, both at Hagley Museum and Library. The Consol records proved useful to a researcher investigating company formation by members of the Mellon family, one of the questions they are actually capable of answering.

153. The records of the New York Central have been placed at the New York Public Library, Bentley Historical Library, Penn State University, and the Ohio Historical Society. Partial microfilm copies of minutes are available at Hagley

and PH&MC. Other records had been given to Syracuse University before the Penn Central merger.

154. For an article written from these records, see Michael Nash, "Women Workers and the Pennsylvania Railroad: The World War II Years," *Labor History* 30 (1989): 608–621.

155. William Henry Williams, *Railroad Correspondence File* (Boston: Library Bureau, 1902). This version of the Dewey decimal system was first developed on the PRR's Lines West between 1897 and 1902 and was in use as late as 1976. Of course, managers in the public sector also adopted this practice. Subject filing also depended upon a number of innovations including the typewriter, carbon paper, and vertical filing cabinets. For an overview of filing systems, including this one, see Schellenberg, *Modern Archives*, 81–91, and JoAnne Yates, *Control through Communication: The Rise of System in American Management* (Baltimore: Johns Hopkins University Press, 1989), 25–63. On subject arrangement being more comprehensible to outside researchers see Mayer, "New Social History," 397.

156. The actual file titles are: "300.4 Class S2 locomotive – Design & construction," Box 326; and "915 Suburban Station – Ventilation," Box 1488, PRR Records, Acc. 1810, Hagley Museum and Library.

157. Assertions such as Eastwood's ("How Goes It?," 116–117) that pertinence-based selection is too vast an undertaking because it is necessary to make comparisons across a whole universe of documentation can also be called into question. The most meaningful "universe" is not necessarily that broad. All of the PRR departmental central files were shaped by pertinence-based selection after themselves being selected on the combined basis of provenance and pertinence in accordance with the four parameters.

158. The idea of "reinvention" is a staple of business writing. For some successful and failed cases of corporate reinvention drawn from Hagley's holdings see the author's essays in, *Works: Photographs of Enterprise*, ed., Martin W. Kane (Philadelphia: University of Pennsylvania Press, 1992) particularly 92–93. On inertia and ossification in business, see Porter, "The Competitive Advantage of Nations," 139. On archives as the embodiment of "public faith" and "perpetual memory" see Duranti, "Concept of Appraisal and Archival Theory," 331–333.

159. For recipes and formulas, see William Eamon, *Science and the Secrets of Nature: Books of Secrets in Early Modern Culture* (Princeton: Princeton University Press, 1994); for engineers' notebooks, see Ferguson, *Engineering and the Mind's Eye*, 1–152, particularly the illustrations.

160. For a description of practice as collaboration among colleagues in engineering, see Ferguson, *Engineering and the Mind's Eye*, 32–35.

161. For a similar statement of the difference between scientific and technological thinking in an engineering context, see Peters, *Transitions in Engineering*, 9.

6

Avoiding Accidents of Evidence: Functional Analysis in the Appraisal of Business Records

Bruce H. Bruemmer

Whether a lemonade stand or a multinational corporation, business is a process of transactions supported by communication. In a literate society, business is conducted primarily by oral and written communication. The "leavings" of this communication, mostly in the form of paper records and graphic materials, form the foundation for most business histories and historical information.

For historians and other researchers of modern business, the current state of this documentary foundation is meager. Many are exasperated by the lack of records and how little they reflect the real communications and decision making of a modern business. A glance at most published business histories is telling, with a number of authors singing anew the virtues of oral history because of the lack of surviving documents. Records may remain, but often they are not the most appropriate records for historical use. Joseph C. Robert, in writing the preface to his history of the Ethyl Corporation, warned of "the accident of evidence," which tempts a historian "to identify the *available* as the *important*."[1] This is a pitfall for archivists as well. There is no Darwinian law for business documentation; the best historical records do not necessarily survive over the most historically worthless. For that to happen, someone must actively guide the preservation of historical documentation.

The best way for a business to turn accidents of evidence into purposeful documentation is to develop an archival program, but even corporate archivists complain of too few pragmatic tools to aid them in improving historical documentation across a business. Recently archivists have sought to use an analysis of institution's functions as an aid to targeting and selecting historical records. This chapter will look at the discussion of functional analysis and its application to modern business records, primarily by corporate archives.

Selection of Business Records

Even with active guidance, the selection of records in a modern company is a difficult task. The problem is that there is so much data in a corporation, and no formula exists that one can use to determine whether records should be saved or destroyed. There have been many calls by archivists for a list of selection criteria for business records, but these lists are too broad in scope to be of much practical use. While there will always be certain types of records that offer clear historical value, selection by type of record is fraught with problems. A type of record yielding historical information in one business may not be so revealing in another. Most archivists look favorably at saving minutes, but there are certainly minutes created in companies that convey very little information. Personality can affect the value of record type, as in the case with planning documents, which usually are interesting and valuable. Reputedly, the Control Data Corporation once required its executives to submit two planning documents covering a one-year and five-year period. Seymour Cray, noted for his disdain of bureaucracy, wrote a one-sentence annual plan stating that it was one-fifth of his five-year plan.[2] As a planning document, the memo was worthless. As an insight to Control Data's management, it was priceless. In short, a record type alone does not presume historical value; its context must be considered.

Assuming the goal of a business archives is to document the history of the company, how do they typically go about this process? Many rely on acquisition techniques to shape the selection of historical records. That is, they identify noncurrent records and then select from them. There are three categories of techniques typically used to acquire records within a business: unsolicited donations, surveys, and records schedules.

The first, unsolicited donations, occurs when the archives is recognized as the place to send old records. Every time someone cleans out an office and finds aged material, it goes to the archives. The problem with this technique is that there is no control over what comes into the archives, and, consequently, the donor determines the historical value of the record. Such records may focus on the activities of the donor, who, in the overall history of the organization, may play an insignificant role. Such donations may secure immortality for certain employees or help document their favorite project, but they will not necessarily document the most critical products or events of a business.

The second method, the records survey, is an important tool for the archivist. It involves visiting a storage area or office to locate collections of records. The surveyor examines records to determine dates, the content of groupings of records, their provenance, and their extent. Selection occurs as one becomes more familiar with the records and can decide what can be saved or discarded.

The third method, the records schedule, is used if there is a records management system in the corporation. The archivist reviews all records schedules and notes those records series that should eventually come to the archives. This system is most productive when there are specific department records schedules, rather than a company-wide records schedule that describe series of records in general. In theory, the archivist has final review over all company records slated for destruction. In practice, many important groups of records may never find their way into even an excellent records management system. Some systems are solely a service to departments, and it may be politically impossible to give the archivist the last word on the survival of records. Still, if a system is in place, it is a good way to select records.

There are four severe shortcomings to these methods of acquisition. First, the initial selection of records of the first two methods is not made with historical or institutional goals in mind; they are "accidents of evidence." The life cycle of records describes the normal progression of records creation, use, storage, and disposition. As stated before, there is no principle that guides the natural survival of historically valuable records at the end of this cycle. Unless someone intercedes and selects records for preservation, they are likely to be lost. Second, unless records are selected by a consistent authority with a mission to document the institution, the selection of records and their usefulness will be compromised. For example, if each department of a business made their own decisions about records selection, the results would depend on those who have no common interest, knowledge, or goal in documenting the entire institution. Third, a large business is a complex system whose communication may stray considerably from formal, organizational lines. Appraisal of records based on departments may miss important documentation generated by interdepartmental or team projects, or frequent restructuring; it may duplicate unimportant records. Fourth, such methods tend to focus on documenting the highest executive levels of a business on the assumption that all important information will gravitate and be found at the "tip of the iceberg" of the organization chart. This is not the case in a modern, multifunctional corporation, where key decisions are made at lower levels and where information "at the top is only one piece of an organic system of flows that controls and coordinates activities."[3]

Functional Analysis

Archivists unhappy with the state of appraisal in modern bureaucratic institutions have sought to move away from accidents of evidence by basing archival selection on an analysis of institutional functions. An analysis of the basic functions of an institution defines the information necessary to document each function. By using functional analysis as a planning and analytical technique, an archivist can decide which functions are most important to document and how they should be documented. The selection of records, which is the last part of this process, is informed by this analysis.[4]

As an example, the functions of a lemonade stand include product research (What kind of lemonade: fresh or frozen concentrate?), production (How to make it? What sort of inventory?), marketing (Where to sell at what price to which consumer?), advertising (How to motivate auto drivers to stop at the stand?), finance (Will my parents capitalize the raw material? Will there be adequate cash flow?), and administration (Can I trust my brother to help without reducing profit margins?). All of these functions are essential to the mission of the business: to make a profit and sustain the business.

An archivist engaged to document this activity might choose to concentrate on a few critical functions. For a lemonade stand, marketing, advertising, and administration could be considered the most historically interesting functions because they are apt to include the most variables to the success or failure of the lemonade stand. So the archivist will look for the best sources of information that document those functions. Here, the archivist's task would be simple because the organization is simple. He or she would select those records with evidential value relating to marketing, advertising, and administration. But in this case, the lemonade stand is managed by a six-year old who relies heavily on oral communication and leaves a poor written record of transactions. In this over-simplified example, the traditional approach to documenting the business is confounded by a lack of records.

This problem illustrates a major advantage of functional analysis. It defines requirements for adequate documentation without regard to extant written records. In the case of the lemonade stand archives, alternative forms of records (photos, videos, oral histories) would provide the necessary documentation. In more complex situations, functional analysis informs the archivist about critical areas that are not adequately represented by records on hand. This raises the possibility of locating similar information in the records of other departments, in other forms of documentation (audio/visual, publications, data bases), or of creating documentation to fill the void (oral history). The other possibility is to choose not to take further steps to fill gaps in documentation, and hope that adequate records will present themselves in the future.

The lemonade stand is a simple business system with little, if any, organizational structure. It consists of one person interacting with an environment. A typical business is a "system of cooperative activities" involving a number of individuals.[5] While the efforts of these individuals are organized around common functions, the number of formal and informal relationships and of different paths of communication increases with the population of the organization (see Figure 1). The task of documenting the organization obviously becomes more complex as the organization becomes more complex. Businesses use organizational structure to keep these cooperative activities efficient and effective, but structure often is a simplistic model of individual relationships. Modern businesses may still produce organization charts using the military or line model, but no one believes that the charts come close to describing the communication and relationships of managers and employees in a modern corporation.

A major problem in documenting complex organizations is that records management generally is driven by the structure of the organization. Departments are usually charged with the proper disposition of their records. If structure comes close to accurately representing relationships and communication, then the task of adequately documenting a business is straightforward. However, structure is still an ever changing aspect of modern American business. The recent emphasis on teams and the gutting of middle management in an attempt flatten organizational hierachies may be as ephemeral as zoot suits, but it is a good indication that structure is a moving target. Perhaps this is more a problem of high-tech companies, but structural change appears to be a feature of even large, staid companies. The functional elements of a company change less so; someone or some group makes decisions on marketing, production, research. Someone or some group actually develops products and packages them. An archivist who understands what a company is supposed to be doing will be able to better identify who was responsible, what processes were involved, how decisions were made, and, consequently, what records to save.

Figure 1. Map of Increasing Lines of Communication in a Business Setting

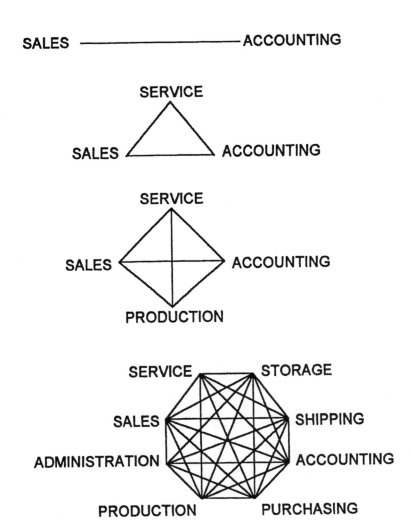

LINES OF COMMUNICATION

SALES ———————— ACCOUNTING

SERVICE

SALES / ACCOUNTING

SERVICE

SALES / ACCOUNTING

PRODUCTION

SERVICE   STORAGE

SALES   SHIPPING

ADMINISTRATION   ACCOUNTING

PRODUCTION   PURCHASING

WHY SYSTEMS ARE NEEDED!

From H. John Ross, *Technique of Systems and Procedures* (New York: Office Research Institute, 1948), 7.

Organizational complexity might be manageable if this did not have a multiplying effect on the volume of business records. The ease in which records are copied means that any one manager's files might consist largely of documents circulated "for your information." As a company matures, record production and maintenance tends to rise with the growing bureaucracy, sometimes dramatically. One study of a high-tech company found direct lines of communication across functions during the firm's entrepreneurial phase, and more longitudinal communication within departments as the firm grew and imposed communication protocols. The escalating lines of communication became almost comical when a piece of correspondence revealed that "informational copies" had been distributed to over thirty individuals![6] While this might be evidence of other problems with a company, it well demonstrates the potential of a copying machine to confound archival appraisal through sheer volume and duplication. Documenting a company by focusing on records that happen to remain is likely to be stymied by the sheer quantity of records, which themselves may poorly represent the history of the firm.

Functional analysis can compensate for these shortcomings by establishing documentary goals for the archives or collecting repository. An analysis of an institution's discrete functions will prompt questions of what should be documented and to what extent. Only after that point should work proceed on what should be preserved. This is not to suggest that one should ignore an organization's structure and remaining records; they are important and obvious sources to a company's history. Nonetheless, to attempt to document a business without understanding its key functions is to fixate on records that may not say much about a firm. Thus, if a software company was famous for custom-made application software, historical documentation should concentrate on the function of product development. The archivist of a company whose primary purpose is the mass sales of consumer goods, like the Veg-a-matic, is probably more interested in marketing than product development, although production and inventory could be critical functional components as well. Given enough time, resources, and importance, one might divide individual functions into separate components to make large functional areas more manageable.

Other less obvious business functions that escape traditional documentation can reveal themselves through functional analysis. Some scholars have written about corporate culture and its importance to motivating, retaining, and inspiring company employees. Moreover, one author has explored the place of storytelling in business and advocates its use as a tool for managing change, indoctrinating new employees, and demonstrating leadership.[7] Storytelling is, after all, just another form of corporate communication that resists textual documentation. A functional analysis of management or the use of human resources is likely to show how this undocumented area might be better preserved.

Recent Models

Although elements of functional analysis were advocated by Theodore Schellenberg and Margaret Cross Norton, archivists have only recently advocated the use of functional analysis in archival appraisal.[8] Beginning in 1986, the American archival profession saw a number of articles and books based wholly or in part on functional analysis. This analysis was aided by a broad ranging discussion of documentation strategies, which sought to better different areas of archival documentation by expanding the scope of collecting beyond traditional archival formats, and simultaneously, expanding the involvement of institutions beyond a single archives. Most important to functional analysis is the emphasis that documentation strategies placed on defining documentation beyond traditional paper records. In describing a hypothetical documentation strategy on the Boston-area high-technology industry, Helen Samuels posed the question to archivists: why are we limiting our view of documentation to traditional archival records when archivists know that better documentation can be found from published sources, oral history, and other nontraditional formats?[9]

While documentation strategies fell out of favor among American archivists, the discussion helped push them to consider expanding their sources beyond traditional paper originals. Even before the advent of documentation strategies, archivists involved with the records of science and technology had set the stage for functional analysis. The 1983 report of the Joint Committee on Archives of Science and Technology outlined a number of strategies aimed at improving the state of documentation in this neglected area. They noted the need to appraise records "by knowing the ways in which and the purposes for which the records were produced."[10] In no other area of archival collecting were archivists more unsure of themselves, owing largely to archivists' unfamiliarity with scientific and technological techniques, the growing volume of postwar science and technology records, and the unusual pattern of communication in scientific endeavors. This prompted those archivists who had to deal with these records to look more expansively and creatively for methods to document science and technology.[11]

Two years later, archivists at the Massachusetts Institute of Technology published an appraisal guide to science and technology records that was the first publication to dissect a specific activity into separate functions. *Appraising the Records of Modern Science and Technology: A Guide* divided the world of science and technology into three areas: personal, professional, and scientific and technological. The latter category was divided into nine functions, such as funding, hypothesizing, thinking, and visualizing. Each function was explained in greater detail, as were the record series usually associated with it. Special appraisal considerations were included, such as documenting instruments of science. Although the work was biased towards the perspective of documenting such activities in an academic setting, it was a good analysis of a specific documentary area.

Those archivists who were looking for a quicker method of dealing with the volume of records or the complexity of record systems found no solace in the *Guide*. While archivists were clamoring for better methods of selection, the functional approach simply expanded the list of items that archivists needed to consider. Instead of reacting to and selecting those records that happened to remain, archivists were told first to define areas that were important to document regardless of what remained. While functional analysis offered greater control over documentation and promised relevant documentation regardless of format, the price was more tasks and decisions for the archivist. For many, this was no solution.

As to the methodology needed to incorporate functional analysis into the routine of an archivist, the *Guide* was silent. The goal of the publication was not to offer "absolute and easy answers in appraisal," but to describe functions and appraisal considerations so they could be "taken and interpreted by individual archivists working in specific institutional settings."[12] While ranked in importance, the appraisal recommendations offered in the *Guide* had to be filtered according to the resources available to each specific institutional archives.

In 1989, the Charles Babbage Institute released *The High-Technology Company: A Historical Research and Archival Guide* , which was the first guide to promote a functional perspective of appraisal in a business setting. It follows a structure similar to the MIT guide by laying out the functions of a company from basic research through marketing and sales. Each function is described, as are records that are commonly associated with it. The publication addressed the tension in asking the archivist to do more while facing ever more preparation by proposing a method of applying a functional model. It advocates the investigation of key products that generate "diverse historical, organizational, and documentary information from all facets of a company in order to aid in the identification of historically valuable records."[13] The study of these products provides the archivist with a snapshot of the type of documentation that might be available for any specific period of time. The study is led by interviews of key personnel, and enables the archivist to get away from relying solely on those records that escaped the trip to the dumpster. Equipped with the insight about what ought to be available, an archivist could make better selection decisions over what records remain. He could compensate for inadequate documentation by looking at alternative sources, or by developing documentation through oral history (see Table 1).

Most business functions are reflected in the development, release, and support of a product. If products are selected from different points in a firm's history, then a study of them can provide a road map through the functions of a business, regardless of changes in managerial theory or style. For example, at one company management began to require project planning reports for new products, distinctly different from production techniques in force when the company was a small, entrepreneurial firm. The records that reflect these two periods were markedly different in character and value.[14] Similarly, if a special task force had been created over a product that did not follow normal organizational line, the product study would have still uncovered the documentation associated with it. Even more important, as today's corporation embraces team management, an analysis of functions through products can uncover information on documentation that would confuse anyone attempting to follow an organization chart. Surprisingly, the method illustrates the importance of documenting certain functions that archivists and historians have typically overlooked or held in low regard. Archivists often pass over documents from the production department, but for some companies production can be critical to their success.

There are limitations to the use of products to provide a core sample of functions in a corporation. First, the technique relies heavily on oral interviews. If the development of the product occurred so long ago that there are few persons left on this earth to describe it, then the product is not a candidate for this method. Second, the method may work less well for service industries. The development of service products may parallel manufactured products, but in many cases a study of products in the service sector would not yield the same information on the functions of a business. Third, products simply may not move serially across all functions. Many manufactured products have no basic research or product research component. The key to overcoming this problem is to choose carefully those products for study. Fourth, the usefulness of the information breaks down in companies with vastly different divisions producing entirely different product lines. The only answer here is to expand the number of product studies.

Shortly after *The High-Technology Company* was published, Helen Samuels published *Varsity Letters: Documenting Modern Colleges and*

Table 1. Stages of a Product Probe

STAGE	ACTION
1	Develop general historical information
2	Identify products for the probe
3	Develop information about the product, historical issues, and records using interviews and other sources
4	Identify and select records
5	Identify gaps in knowledge about products and other historical issues relating to the company

From Bruce H. Bruemmer and Sheldon Hochheiser, *The High-Technology Company: A Historical Research and Archival Guide* (Minneapolis: Charles Babbage Institute, 1989), 102.

Universities. It advocates the same functional approach to appraisal for the documentation of colleges and universities that *The High-Technology Company* does for business. However, instead of a list of functions that follows a serial progression from product development onward, Samuels divides the functions of a university into three missions: teaching, public service, and research. Also covered but not treated as a "mission" is the function of sustaining the institution, which includes the administration of institution (see Figure 2). *Varsity Letters* is significant because it moved the issue of using functional analysis beyond the appraisal of technology-related records. It analyzes in detail the functions of an institution of higher education, and in doing so shows how functional descriptions can aid documenting any institution, whether business, academia, government, or some hybrid.

While most of the book is a generic description of the functions of colleges and universities, it also offers the Institutional Documentation Plan as a methodology to apply functional analysis in the appraisal of records and other documentation. The plan is an alternative to traditional archival collecting policies and its premise is "that the determination of what is to be documented and a knowledge of the documentary issues must be established before collections are sought."[15] Basically, the plan follows six steps that are led by the analysis of an institution's functions, assessment of existing historical information, determination of documentary goals, and comparison of those goals balanced against resources. As with *The High-Technology Company*, Samuels' Institutional Documentation Plan seeks to move the archivist away from records that happen to remain to the compre-

Figure 2. Functional Map of a College or University

From Helen W. Samuels, *Varsity Letters: Documenting Modern Colleges and Universities* (Metuchen, N.J.: Society of American Archivists and Scarecrow Press, Inc., 1992), *20*.

hensive documentation of historical function independent of record type or department.

The 1990s also brought an effort to expand models of functional analysis in two broad areas: the United States Congress and the health care system. Whereas previous works focused on individual institutions and their documentation, these expanded the analysis of functions into areas of interest to many repositories. In some respects they are the pragmatic outcome of the discussion over documentation strategies because they brought together archivists with special expertise to map out interinstitutional functions. Early on this tactic was demonstrated by a project initiated by Joan Warnow of the American Institute of Physics. It sought to improve documentation of "big science" by moving the focus of archivists from individual institutions to multi-institutional collaborations. Warnow felt that the documentation of specific scientific institutions did not reflect the real process of modern science, which can be organized around teams that transcend institutional boundaries.

While *The Documentation of Congress* centers on one institution, the Congress of the United States, it describes historical documentation in a host of settings. Nearly ever state historical society has congressional records, in addition to the National Archives, Library of

Congress, and other repositories. The question posed by the Task Force on Congressional Documentation was, simply, whether or not the critical functions of Congress were adequately documented by all of this records collecting. The project's director, Karen Paul, noted that "although research materials that exist are large in quantity, they are uneven in quality and difficult to work with, and are woefully incomplete in terms of presenting a comprehensive, useful, historical record."[16] The task force divided the functions of Congress into five areas: the legislative process, representation, political activities, external relations (media, lobbyists, think tanks, etc.), and administration and support. From that analysis they made specific recommendations for improving the documentation of Congress by all interested repositories. There is no question that a functional approach gave the task force insight to identify areas in which Congress was poorly documented. This volume is now essential reading for anyone involved in legislative archives.

Documentation Planning for the U.S. Health Care System is not as prescriptive as the work on the records of Congress, and it defines functions more broadly than any of the previous works. The universe of health care in the United States is assigned six functional categories: patient care, health promotion, biomedical research, education, regulation and policy, and the provision of goods and services (see Table 2). These functions are then examined in the context of type of institutions in the system (state government, federal government, professional associations, corporations, etc.). For example, the section on health industries looks at pharmaceutical companies, medical supplies and equipment manufacturers, medical publishing, and insurance companies. These four industries are analyzed according to the six categories listed above. While this approach helps archivists understand some of the shared functions of different health care organizations, it does not go into great detail on the functions of each type of institution and is well removed from the type of institutional functional analysis of previous works.

The last chapter of this work offers a model of "documentation planning," which is likened to "strategic planning for archives."[17] It differs from the other models in two respects. First, it emphasizes the need for institutional archivists to look beyond their own institution to better define the functions that are most historically important. Thus, the documentation of Children's Hospital in Boston is informed by understanding this hospital's relation to others in the area and the country. Second, archivists are urged to define those of the six functional categories (patient care, health promotion, etc.) that are most important to the institution. So, in the case of Children's Hospital, the archivist decided to rank highly any documentation relating to bio-

Table 2. Functional Analysis of an Industry

The U.S. Health Care System: An Archival Perspective

Institutions and Organizations	Functions of the U.S. Health Care System					
	Health Care Delivery				Regulation/ Policy Formulation	Provision of Goods/ Services
	Patient Care	Health Promotion	Biomedical Research	Education		
Delivery facilities	1	2	2	2		
Agencies/foundations	2	1	2	2	1	
Research facilities	2		1	2		
Eduational institutions	2	2	1	1		
Professional/voluntary associations	2	1	2	1	1	
Health industries		2	1			1

1 = primary function, 2 = secondary function.

From Joan D. Krizack, ed., *Documentation Planning for the U.S. Health Care System* (Baltimore: Johns Hopkins University Press, 1994): 3.

medical research because of Children's international reputation in that area.[18] At this point, the plan quickly turns to the structure of the hospital and the identification of records. In this model, the functions being analyzed relate more to the health system than individual institutions. In this way it is very different from *Varsity Letters* or *The High-Technology Company*.

Implications for the Documentation of Business

The contrast in the scope of functions presented by various publications suggests that business archives and repositories engaged in collecting business records (henceforth, *collecting repositories*) would use functional analysis differently. While business archives can adopt a broad-scale functional analysis like *Documentation Planning for the U.S. Health Care System*, collecting repositories clearly are the primary beneficiaries from an industry-wide approach. As illustrated above, those repositories concerned with statewide documentation of health care, as well as the archives of professional organizations with interests beyond their own institution, will find the broader approach in *Documentation Planning* of great use. An institutional archives, however, requires more detail. The functions presented in *The High-Technology Company* is a starting point for them.

The use of institutional functional analysis by a collecting repository is necessarily limited. Pragmatically, collecting repositories rarely win the opportunity to conduct an internal analysis of an ongoing business. In a few cases, this approach might be used if a single business was important enough to merit the attention (and was willing to receive the attention). Unfortunately, projects involving business records over the past 20 years illustrate the unwillingness of management to allow academicians free run of a company's records.[19] And even if CEOs have a moment of weakness, corporate lawyers caution against opening any business records to outsiders.

Conversely, business archives may have limited need for looking at their operations through an industry-wide lens. While a curator of a collecting repository will want to look at an entire industry to avoid documenting similar companies, the archivist of a business archives will not fashion a collecting policy with a competitor's archives in mind. A curator interested in documenting the soft-drink industry may find enormous and unnecessary duplication between the records of Pepsi and Coca-Cola, but that circumstance will hardly matter to the archivist of the Coca-Cola. Precisely this situation exists between state archives. Looked at nationally, the differences between the departments of agriculture of Minnesota and Wisconsin are minor. But the state archivist of Wisconsin is not likely to suspend documentation of the Wisconsin department because Minnesota had fully documented theirs. This is not to say that nothing is gained by a comparison of the two, or that the functions of the agriculture system in the United States is superfluous to the documentation of a single state department. But a state archives, like a business archives, is responsible for documenting its own operations. A business archives does not need to worry about the documentation of a competitor, except as it relates to its parent company.

In both situations, functional analysis equips archivists with information that otherwise would be obtained only through long experience. Someone who has spent years involved in the study of an industry, state, or region, comes equipped with much of the information needed to make decisions about archival documentation. Likewise, a person with a long tenure at a single company who had been involved in many different departments is likely to have an intuitive sense of what is important to document. Often, however, these individuals are not those with archival skills, as in the case of retirees assigned to "do something" with the history of a company. And what of the archivist that comes to a company to develop a new archival program? Functional analysis offers a way to define important historical issues, events, and products in an environment where historical information may not exist.

An approach that aims to document the total company rather than one department (such as legal or communications) may pay long-term dividends in the breadth of services that the archives can offer. Instead of concentrating on product information for the legal department or pictures and video for the communications department (which are the bread and butter of many corporate archives), the corporate archivist who has documented multiple functions stands to hold relevant information on decision making, management, and policy. For example, the Hewlett Packard archives staff scans agendas for corporate board meetings, looking for areas that the archives might provide pertinent institutional memory. Thus a board meeting about compensation might be supplied with a time line of significant compensation decisions in the past. Archival services such as this not only require an entrepreneurial archivist but an archives that contains far more than product information and interesting visuals.

For the curator of a collecting repository, the functional analysis of a specific industry can quickly define the documentary landscape. The added bonus to such an approach is that information can be shared with colleagues. Obviously, the analysis presented in *Documentation Planning for the U.S. Health Care System* shows the importance of industry to anyone involved in documenting health care from the perspective of a state, region, or a professional society. Moreover, for many years archivists have bemoaned the inability to share appraisal information, and some even proposed recording such data on national bibliographic data bases.[20] In some respects, functional analysis makes practical the sharing of information used in appraisal. It is not as detailed as sharing information at the records series level, but such functional descriptions offer enough information to put appraisal decisions in some context.

Weaknesses

Of course, one can overanalyze anything and end with little actual documentation. For any one institution, functions can be broadly construed or they can involve the minutia of functions within other functions. The scope of the functional analysis is not a small matter and will affect the implementation of a documentary plan. The key to applying functional analysis to business documentation is knowing where to stop. At what level should one stop analyzing and start documenting? In a business, one function could be analyzed to a ridiculous level. For example, the production of a mainframe computer is no simple task, involving assembly, inventory, quality assurance, scheduling, packing, transport, cost control, documentation, and field maintenance of the main computer and its peripherals, not to mention relevant software components. At what point in this case do you decide which parts are critical to the historical documentation of the company? Or is everything important?

This complexity increases with the size of a company, particularly if functions are spread over different geographic areas. The system breaks down for certain multidivisional companies and all conglomerates because their functions and lines of communication are so different. For example, analyzing the functions of Litton Industries does not make much sense because Litton is a conglomeration of very diverse businesses. In this case, it would be better "to document a single division and the central office than to cut off a horizontal layer."[21]

The methodology offered by current writings on functional analysis is not objective or precise. Its weakness is similar to that of collection policies; they tend to be too broad in their application and offer too much room for interpretation from various quarters, whether the archives is an institutional archives or a collecting repository. The approach offered by a "documentation plan," as with any strategic plan, is only good if it is approached honestly and informed by accurate information. There are no checks or "trip wires" to indicate a fully or superficially explored function. There is no algorithm to figure if one function is more important than another. Try as we might, appraisal resists attempts to make it a numbers game. The Boles-Young "Black-Box" model illustrates the complexity of appraisal algorithms, and even the "Minnesota Method" proposed in this book requires broad generalization in defining the business areas of a state.[22]

More damning to functional analysis are the time and resources required to do it well. The reality of archives in today's business environment is that a new corporate archives has from three to five years to sell the program to the company by developing services that meet the "bottom line." Archivists quickly learn to provide services to communications, the legal department, and other areas that will quickly recognize their value. More entrepreneurial operations establish profit centers, such as licensing historical products, which assures a greater measure of survivability for the archives. But the game is one of survival, where an academic approach to documenting a company represents a luxury of time and resources.

Collecting repositories, too, can hardly justify the time to analyze the functions of all of the businesses or industries in which it might be interested, whether the analysis focuses on a single business or an industry. Moreover, the circumstance of many business collections precludes all but the most cursory preparation for appraisal decisions. One historian recounts an offer by the president of Varian Associates to take anything he wanted from the company's records warehouse. He drove to the facility in an empty station wagon and confronted hundreds of cubic feet of records. Overwhelmed by the scale of selection required, he drove away empty-handed. Similarly, Michael Nash of the

Hagley Museum and Library described the acquisition of the Sea-
grams' records in 1995, in which he had about two weeks to select
from thousands of records. Needless to say, he did not preface his
work of looking at and appraising the records with an analysis of functions.

The Necessity of Functional Analysis

There is no doubt that many fine business collections will continue
to come to repositories as huge caches of papers. There is no doubt
that business archivists will build fine institutional archives through
the quick identification of core documentation without the need to
analyze the functions of a business or industry. However, if business
is accurately described as transaction and communication, then the
changes that are occurring in communication will soon defy the development of institutional archives through accidents of evidence. The
computer is the main culprit of this change. Through the computer,
information processing has not only altered the definition of a record
but appears to be changing the nature of communication in business
and within a company.

As measured against the rapidity of improvements in computing
technology, the change brought about by the computer on business
documentation has been slower but no less dramatic. In the United
States, the introduction of the UNIVAC in the early 1950s signaled
the adoption of data processing for specific tasks such as payroll, inventory, and amortization tables. Even with the adoption of management information systems in the 1970s, the computer remained expensive, centralized, and on the periphery of business communication.
After 40 years, however, the computer has become portable and a large
portion of business communication is electronic. Oddly enough, the
production of paper records has grown with the rise of machine-readable records. The ability to duplicate documentation, whether through
copying machines or computers, is the major reason for this proliferation of paper. In spite of the growth of paper records, key business
documentation now occurs only in machine-readable form. The concept of the paperless office, once mere fantasy, seems palpable today.

Nothing has stymied archivists more than the changes to documentation brought about by the computer. Techniques developed 15
years ago to cope with the preservation of information in data bases
now seem quaint in their simplicity. Flat-file data bases have been
eclipsed by multifunctional, relational data bases in which information
is lost if the data are stripped from their software. Electronic mail is
not just replacing other forms of business correspondence, but it offers

the qualities of informality and speed never before seen in a business setting. All manner of electronic communication, from faxes to video conferencing, have changed the style of doing business internationally.

While the implications of all of this change is numbing, one thing is clear: the days of finding accidents of evidence in the closets, basements, and vaults of businesses are numbered. Paper is a remarkably stable recording medium; magnetic tape, optical disks, and floppy disks may be somewhat stable, but the technology to read them is not. Magnetic computer tape thrown in a storage area for five years might as well be pitched in a dumpster. Computer records lacking the information to translate them are virtually unreadable.[23] The result is that archivists can no longer linger at the end of the records cycle to recover historical documentation. We will be forced to define such documentation at the middle or even the beginning of the records cycle. As some individuals have speculated, archivists may become custodians of metadata—records that describe records—and our role as custodians of records will shift to locators and preparers of information. For collecting repositories, this implies that there will be vastly fewer relevant records from which to select. If the business archivist does not wish to share the same restriction, he or she will need to be involved in selection of records as they are produced.

The consequence of this statement is enormous because it insists that archivists identify historical documentation before any analysis of records. While the archival professional has relied on records management scheduling to help identify records in advance, this practice has never occurred at or near the creation of records. Functional analysis is one of the few tools at the command of archivists to help guide archival practice in the electronic environment because it dictates documentary requirements before records are analyzed. This nicely matches the urgency that electronic records place on historical appraisal. David Bearman notes, less simply, that "archivists will need to rely more on the empirical analysis of organizations as systems, rather than normative descriptions, since the functional origin of transaction and the links between dispersed agents will be of greater importance as the organizational locus of the document creator becomes less significant in less hierarchical organizations." Bearman's solution to the overwhelming mass of data represented by electronic information processing is the development of "intelligent communications gateways" that will provide automatic document analysis through software. But most important is Bearman's insistence that retention decisions will be based on "functional provenance."[24]

In his analysis of American and European organizational culture, Bearman asserts the power of electronic communication to flatten bureaucratic hierarchies. While this is an arguable point, it is certainly in line with current American thought on restructuring the business organization. Here again, functional analysis becomes an essential approach to documenting modern business. Greater emphasis on interdepartmental teams and fewer levels of management means that those techniques that are based on organizational structure are less useful. If records management systems based on paper tend to be driven by structure, then they are wholly inadequate in an electronic world. Terry Cook best summarizes:

> The implications of information systems and systems re-engineerings, of data interchange and migrations, of corporate data models and system functionality patterns, combined with the previously mentioned weakening of hierarchy, general diminution of the importance of structure, and the complexity and volume of modern records [are] creating a new archival world. In this situation, the archival professional needs to rethink its basic tenets and adopt strategic tools. The institutional functional analysis is a very complementary tool to such information systems realities.[25]

Where, then, does this leave the noninstitutional archivist? The answer is predicated upon the goals of the collecting repository. If the intent is to document the outward profile of business (corresponding to levels B through D of the Minnesota Method proposed by Mark Greene and Todd Daniels-Howell), then curators will find little change in their options. In fact, electronic records may enhance the ability of repositories to collect external information about a company. Consider an annual data base of World Wide Web pages taken from business sites within a state or industry; archivists could harvest this resource with relative ease, and the resulting information would surpass the information content of a collection of annual reports and catalogs.

But if the target is to understand decision making or critical events and activity within a business, it will be exceedingly difficult for outsiders to document a business in an electronic environment. Even if businesses were willing, the economics of working with electronic records would deter most collecting repositories. Along similar lines, the National Archives of Canada established guidelines about when to leave archival electronic records in government institutions rather than transfer them to the National Archives. The major reasons against transfer had to do with the cost of transfer and the cost of duplicating access to the data.[26] However, this action is grounded in a scheme that follows the identification of function and value of governmental information systems, not a scheme that is available to a repository seeking to document a business. Donations of electronic business records may occur if individuals inside the corporation take extraordinary steps to accumulate and preserve the information, just as some individuals take highly unusual steps to preserve some paper corporate records. Yet, if relying on such haphazard efforts to document business activity in our society is not desirable in a world of paper records, it is even less adequate for electronic records. Without the ability to work with a business as these electronic records are produced, outside archival repositories will have few options beyond the superficial documentation of a business enterprise, with or without functional descriptions of industries.

The Documented Life

How far business and our society is from a total embrace of electronic technology is debatable. As we get there, documentation will flourish. Already historians and archivists long for the good old days when the survival of few records, whether the fittest or not, meant that archivists had fewer difficult decisions and that historians had the convenience of fewer contradictory primary sources. In recent years, both professional groups have witnessed the problems inherent in the overabundance of documentation in our society. We may learn that this present difficult state is but a modest preview of coming attractions. Bill Gates, in *The Road Ahead*, states that storage capacity of recording media will continue to grow at an amazing rate while costs similarly decline. He envisions a state of technology not far off in which one could have a completely "documented life." He writes:

> Your wallet PC will be able to keep audio, time, location, and eventually even video records of everything that happens to you. It will be able to record every word you say and every word said to you, as well as the body temperature, blood pressure, barometric pressure, and a variety of other data about you and your surroundings. It will be able to track your interactions with the highway, all the commands you issue, the messages you send, the people you call or who call you. The resulting record will be the ultimate diary and autobiography, if you want one.[27]

For most of us mortals, the implications of a society where everyone could lead a "documented life" are overwhelming, never mind what this would mean for commerce. But Gates' scenario raises some interesting questions for archivists. How would we cope in an environment where potentially everything is documented and preserved, where there are no accidents of evidence to artificially filter the huge volume of records? Would our present experience and knowledge of record systems stand up to such a challenge?

With the possibility of a documented life and a documented business, something close to functional analysis will need to guide all archival appraisal. The job of the archivist will focus on filtering information to make it accessible, not on the custody of that information.

Even with the prospect of the "documented life," the most exasperating part for archivists will be coping with the transition. All of us can recite a progression of obsolete recording media within our lifetime and most of us have remnants of analog or digital technology in our homes for which there are no players or decoders (eight-track tapes, anyone?). The necessity for archivists to move away from a system of selection that is led by a single recording format, such as paper, is obvious. Functional analysis promises to provide archivists with a plan that will allow them to ply limited resources towards a documentary goal in the midst of enormous changes in business organization, communication, and culture. If archivists remain distant from this change and steadfast in their reliance on accidents of evidence, they will not strengthen their role in American business and will fail in their service to society. If we rise to the challenge, we may discover that the archives itself has become an essential business function.

Endnotes

1. Joseph C. Robert, *Ethyl: A History of the Corporation and the People Who Made It* (Charlottesville: University Press of Virginia, 1983), xiii.

2. Bruce H. Bruemmer and Sheldon Hochheiser, *The High-Technology Company: A Historical Research and Archival Guide* (Minneapolis: Charles Babbage Institute, 1989), 17–18.

3. JoAnne Yates, "Internal Communication Systems in American Business Structures: A Framework to Aid Appraisal," *American Archivist* 48 (spring 1985): 156.

4. For those who work in a business environment, I am not discussing the analysis of a functionally divided company, but the analysis of the functions of a company, and the processes and communications that make up those functions—in essence, a study of functions in order to better understand what a company really does regardless of structure or what it says it does. This information is used to lead archivists to decide what is necessary to document in a business, regardless of record types or assumptions about the nature of archival records.

5. Chester I. Barnard, *Functions of the Executive* (Cambridge: Harvard University Press, 1938), 75.

6. Bruemmer and Hochheiser, *The High-Technology Company*, 117.

7. Peg C. Neuhauser, *Corporate Legends and Lore: The Power of Storytelling as a Management Tool* (New York: McGraw-Hill, 1993).

8. Terry Cook, "Taming the Information Behemoth: Institutional Functional Analysis as a Tool for Appraising the Records of Modern Society," draft, November 5,

1993. This work was the result of a meeting in Boston of a group of archivists to study institutional functional analysis from the perspective of churches, cultural organizations, businesses, hospitals, and state and national governments.

9. One of the first writings to state this issue was Philip N. Alexander and Helen W. Samuels, "The Roots of 128: A Hypothetical Documentation Strategy," *American Archivist* 50, no. 4 (1987): 518–531.

10. Joint Committee on Archives of Science and Technology, *Understanding Progress as Process* (Chicago: Society of American Archivists, 1983), 23.

11. Much of the inspiration for attention in the 1980s to the records of science and technology grew out of the Department of Energy study developed by the American Institute of Physics, which was retrospectively used as a case study of documentation strategy. See Joan N. Warnow et al., *A Study of Preservation of Documents at the Department of Energy Laboratories* (New York: American Institute of Physics, 1982).

12. Joan K. Haas, Helen Willa Samuels, and Barbara Trippel Simmons, *Appraising the Records of Modern Science and Technology: A Guide* (Cambridge: Massachusetts Institute of Technology, 1985), 9.

13. Bruemmer and Hochheiser, *The High-Technology Company*, 101.

14. The company was the Control Data Corporation, which was used as a case study to test out the efficacy of a "product probe."

15. Helen Willa Samuels, *Varsity Letters: Documenting Modern Colleges and Universities* (Metuchen, N.J.: Society of American Archivists and Scarecrow Press, Inc., 1992), 254.

16. Society of American Archivists, Congressional Archivists Roundtable Task Force, *The Documentation of Congress: Report of the Congressional Archivists Roundtable Task Force on Congressional Documentation* (Chicago: Society of American Archivists, 1992), vii.

17. Joan D. Krizack, ed., *Documentation Planning for the U.S. Health Care System* (Baltimore: Johns Hopkins University Press, 1994), 228.

18. Ibid., 208.

19. The archival landscape is littered with projects that aimed to improve documentation of business via public archives. The State of Wisconsin exemplifies this effort. It was the site of a business archives survey in the 1950s, a shared archivist promoted by the State Historical Society of Wisconsin to care for the records of Oscar Mayer and Allis Chalmers in the 1960s, and a project grant to the Area Research Center at University of Wisconsin-Parkside to work with businesses around the Kenosha area to preserve records in the 1970s. None of these efforts produced ongoing business archives.

20. See Max J. Evans, "The Visible Hand: Creating a Practical Mechanism for Cooperative Appraisal," *Midwestern Archivist* 11, no. 1 (1986): 3–13.

21. Yates, "Internal Communications Systems," 158.

22. The "Black Box" attempted to chart all factors relating to appraisal. See Frank Boles, *Archival Appraisal* (New York: Neal-Schuman Publishers, 1991). The Minnesota Method, intended for use by collecting repositories, is described in the chapter by Mark Greene and Todd Daniels-Howell.

23. The most compelling example is provided in preserving information in the data libraries of the German Democratic Republic after reunification, as related by Michael Wettengel of the Bundesarchiv in "Archival Preservation of Electronic Records and German Unification" (paper presented at the 59th annual conference of the Society of American Archivists, Washington, D.C., August 1995).

24. David Bearman, "Diplomatics, Weberian Bureaucracy, and the Management of Electronic Records in Europe and America," *American Archivist* 55, no. 1 (1992): 180.

25. Cook, "Taming the Information Behemoth," 9–10.

26. Terry Cook, "Leaving Archival Electronic Records in Institutions: Policy and Monitoring Arrangements at the National Archives of Canada," *Archives and Museum Informatics* 9 (1995): 144.

27. Bill Gates, *The Road Ahead* (New York: Viking, 1995), 267, CD-Rom version.

7

Documentation with an Attitude:
A Pragmatist's Guide to the Selection and
Acquisition of Modern Business Records

Mark A. Greene and Todd J. Daniels-Howell

> No particular results, . . . but only an attitude of orientation, is what
> the pragmatic method means. William James, *Pragmatism*, 1907.[1]

Archival pragmatists have been roundly criticized recently.[2] Yet the
fact remains that the goal for most archivists and curators is to do good
work rather than to create, sustain, or test archival theory. The need
for improved methods of acquisition is particularly acute because of
the conflict between old attitudes and new realities:

> Our instinct is still to see ourselves in the role of a twentieth-century
> Horatius-at-the-Bridge: the last line of defence between preservation
> and oblivion. This causes us to make utterly ludicrous decisions
> regarding acquisition by cloaking ourselves in the virtue of main-
> taining culture: If I don't save it, who will?[3]

As the twentieth century moves to a close, however, there is increasingly intense pressure for repositories to collect less but serve
more. Instead of Roman heroics, archivists need a prosaic, practical
method of selection.

This essay presents a case study of the Minnesota Historical Society's (MHS) multiyear effort to develop a pragmatic approach to the
selection of twentieth-century business records. MHS is one of the two
largest collecting repositories of business records in the nation. Unlike

its peer, the Hagley Museum and Library, the mission of MHS encompasses all aspects of history—political, social, cultural—not simply economic. The choices we face, therefore, are those of most collecting repositories: balancing the documentation of business against all other documentary areas, and then deciding which businesses can/should be documented and to what degree. To be useful, the pragmatic method we developed had to take into account a reasonable amount of real-life complexity but remain simple enough to actually help us make daily work decisions. We wanted the method to provide structure and consistency, specifically setting priorities for identifying Minnesota businesses whose records we would seek and, for each business, what level of documentation to acquire. We hoped to find a way to account for and minimize the inevitable political pressures brought to bear by boards and administrators on archivists, respond to the wide variety of constituencies we serve, and have enough time left over to document the rest of Minnesota history. We have dubbed what resulted (because all the good names were taken) the Minnesota Method.[4]

As a pragmatic method, "no particular results" will be found here, no lists of "what should be kept." What we offer, instead, is "an attitude of orientation," an approach or method for thinking about selection choices. It is important, in this respect, to differentiate between the method as an abstract attitude of orientation and the particular or concrete application of it we adopted for use in our institution—a model, as it were, based on the method. Any use the Minnesota Method may have for other repositories will be based not on the specific decisions we made, or even on the specific criteria upon which we made the decisions, but on the general approach to decision making we adopted. One of the basic premises of the method, in fact, is that all appraisal is local and subjective. Other premises that underlie the method are: the potential universe of twentieth-century documentation will always exceed the resources of any repository; it is impossible to define or achieve "adequate" documentation, but it is possible to make selection more rational and efficient relative to a specific repository's goals and resources; to do this records creators must be appraised long before actual records are appraised; establishing sensible criteria for appraising records creators depends on a certain amount of analysis. Our method borrows important concepts from various selection and appraisal literature, but it grew largely from our lack of success in applying most recent writing on appraisal to our daily work amidst archival reality as we know it.

Even so, the goal of our method is narrow, as archival appraisal writing goes. Our method is not meant to apply to documentation projects generally or to all archival institutions—it was developed for, and may be only applicable to, documentation of business by collecting

repositories. We have a limited hope that the pragmatic method presented here may encourage more collecting of business records by
manuscripts repositories by offering a flexible alternative to the daunting lists of "core" series mandated in some archival writing about
business records. Because the documentation project that gave birth
to the method was not the result of (nor dependent on) any external
funding (nor even of any significant internal funding), we believe that
it is accessible to and will work well for both large and small repositories. Although not designed as an approach for special subject repositories or business archives, the Minnesota Method may prove
useful (or at least thought provoking) in those settings as well.

The Setting

The Minnesota Method derived from the specific problems facing
us as curators at the Minnesota Historical Society and the more general
problems facing any archival professional who grapples with documenting twentieth-century U.S. business records. Timothy L. Ericson
has summed up these general problems succinctly:

> Archivists whose responsibilities include collecting private records
> are struggling at a verge today. It is the place of encounter at which
> our traditional thinking regarding appraisal and acquisition devel-
> opment has confronted the extraordinary volume and increasing
> technological complexity of contemporary records.[5]

To those archivists and curators who appraise and acquire business records, Ericson's verge may look rather more like a precipice.
The widening gulf between the extant record universe and the resources of repositories is so dizzying that we have generally closed our
eyes to it and hoped we would not one day tumble over the edge. The
cliff where modern business records meets repository collecting policies is one of the steepest. Neither repositories whose sole purpose is
to collect business records, nor repositories whose mission is to document business along with other forms of human activity in a particular
geographic region have so far developed successful methods to safely
negotiate the verge.

The Documentary Universe. The most salient issue driving the
need for a new acquisition and appraisal approach to business records
is the vast number and variety of twentieth-century corporations, generating an astounding quantity of paper records[6] and, as the century
draws to a close, an equally astounding quantity of nonpaper records.
The biggest corporations in the United States, after all, have gross
revenues, "populations" (employees), and documentary output larger

than many entire nations. There are a mind numbing number (13,695,500 in the U.S. in 1987)[7] and variety (the Standard Industrial Classification [SIC] alone has over a thousand categories) of business firms. Bulk is not the only issue, however. To some extent, "the fear of being inundated by great masses of paper" has been replaced in the age of electronic records "by the consciousness that nothing will be left for appraisal if we don't formulate fundamental principles . . . that will guide our everyday decisions."[8] Furthermore, the increasing decentralization of large business organizations combined with increased fear of liability grounded on information found in retained documents, plus the vicissitudes of mergers and hostile takeovers, have undermined the best efforts of even the strongest corporate archives to preserve substantial and significant documentation of major corporations, with "archival" control lagging even farther behind records management control.[9]

If purposeful attempts within corporations to manage, appraise, and preserve these records have never approached adequacy, it is no wonder that the size of the problems has led many manuscripts repositories to consciously or unconsciously neglect the collecting of twentieth-century business records. Arthur Cole noted in 1945 the twin problems of "the bulk of physical quantity of recent business records, and the lack of mechanism for equating scholars' demands with librarians' supplies."[10] A half century later the problems are somewhat different but even worse. The small amount of survey work that has been done indicates that repositories that collect business records are not actively grappling with large twentieth-century companies.[11] As Francis X. Blouin, Jr. has noted, "Due partly to the unavailability of modern business records and partly to the bulk of those record groups that are available, research-oriented repositories find that they have neither the budget nor the space to continue to document the workings of U.S. business enterprises in the twentieth-century in the way they documented enterprises in the nineteenth and earlier centuries."[12]

The Minnesota Historical Society. Unlike many historical societies, MHS has traditionally documented business aggressively. Business records constitute the single largest holdings of MHS's manuscripts collections: 21,000 cubic feet, covering 520 separate collections; almost half of the total cubic feet are the records of a single railroad. MHS's first capital campaign in the early 1990s heightened the importance of businesses (and the families who founded them) to MHS's administration. The highly visible new building that resulted from the fundraising tremendously increased the number of unsolicited offers of business records, including three from Fortune 500 companies with potentially staggering quantities of records. In fact, Minnesota boasts more Fortune 500 companies per capita than any state save

Illinois; was the seat of milling, lumber, and railroad empires in the nineteenth century; and is home to major concentrations of banking, super-computing, and medical technology in the twentieth century. Currently, there are 120,000 business establishments in the state,[13] and untold numbers of business leaders and trade associations. To face this onslaught, MHS employs two manuscripts acquisition curators.[14]

Documenting the complete history of business in a single state is an unrealistic enough task for two curators. It is made almost preposterous when seen as part of a larger mandate to "collect and preserve the materials and records of human culture relating to Minnesota and Minnesotans"—politics, culture, society—everything, not just business.[15] Ericson has recently issued a forceful and appropriate jeremiad against overly general collecting policies as major handicaps to curators trying to formulate workable acquisition policies: "How can we even argue that it is possible for a regional archives to 'document' comprehensively a particular geographical area—no matter how small—when one good-sized accession of business records would fill its shelves and occupy the attention of its staff into the next millennium?"[16] He suggests that institutional policies are the point of attack and correction, and while this may be true at some repositories, it is wishful thinking for others. What is unrealistic to archivists is often bread and butter to administrators and resource allocators—not to mention to our public. Mission statements, and even collecting policies, will for many repositories undoubtedly remain unrealistically broad so long as boards rather than archivists have the authority to define them. Certainly it is true in Minnesota that neither the manuscripts curators nor their department head had the authority or ability to change MHS's broad collection policy statement; we could only hope to effect changes in the way that policy was implemented on a day to day basis.

The fundamental commitment to business records, combined with ever-increasing inquiries from corporations and unrelenting demands to grapple with MHS's other collecting areas, reinforced a tendency at MHS to be more reactive than proactive, taking what came (rather than defining priorities) or rushing out to rescue records of folding companies or those whom the newspaper reminds us are celebrating chronological milestones. In addition, there had been a tendency to assume that agreeing to accept records from a company was the same as agreeing to serve as its archives—if it was important enough to document at all, it was important enough to document completely.

This type of holding action largely ignored the question of whether we were (as documentation strategy told us we should be) selecting and acquiring "adequate" documentation of Minnesota business.

While we had no clue what adequate documentation might mean, we were fairly sure that current documentation efforts were not adequate, in large measure because they did not consciously respond to the major changes in the state's economy over the last 40 years. Lumber, mining, and railroads have receded as influential industries, to be replaced by high technology (Cray Research, Control Data, Honeywell, 3M), retailing (Dayton-Hudson, Best Buy, Musicland), health care (Group Health, Medtronic, Mayo Clinic, Hazelden), and airlines (Northwest). With some exceptions, this shift had not been clearly reflected in MHS's acquisition of business records.

In addition to the increased number of donation offers (and suggestions for collecting from our administration and board members) and the need to successfully target those industries dominating Minnesota's modern economy, our collecting rate required a reexamination of our acquisition and appraisal approach. While the new building contained about 50 percent more storage space than our previous facility, our past rate of acquisitions would fill this space in less than half the time it took us to outgrow our previous building. We could not continue to select and appraise business records in the same way we had done in the past. Space and staff limitations compelled a thoughtful discussion of how best to deal (if at all) with targeting, acquiring, and appraising collections that would sensibly document business in Minnesota. A new method was required.

MHS had already confronted the problem of prioritization as part of the project we completed in 1993 to revamp our appraisal of congressional collections. To be sure, there were many differences between congressional records and the business universe.[17] Some aspects of the congressional project were relevant to business, however. First was the recognition that documenting the state's entire delegation meant we could and should approach the records of each congressional office differently than if we appraised them in isolation. A similar orientation would be useful in approaching business sectors. Second was the decision to take more complete records from senate offices than from representative offices. This explicit recognition that some of our delegation were more equal than others was to be expanded many fold when we looked at business.

Finally, we found in the congressional project that archival literature did not address our needs. Many authors had written on collecting and appraising congressional records, but none from the point of view of a repository having to prioritize congressional collections against other demands. We found we faced a similar frustration when we turned to archival appraisal literature hoping for some assistance in setting priorities, allocating resources, and making appraisal decisions for business records.

Archival Literature. F. Gerald Ham's plaintive 1975 query about appraisal, "Why must we do it so badly?"[18] spawned many voices seeking to redress the problem. Writers on appraisal have given us (in rough chronological order) collection policy, collection analysis, the "Black Box," documentation strategy, institutional functional analysis, macroappraisal, social use, and documentation plans, to name only the most prominent. The result has been a stimulating but often confusing cacophony of ideas. As Frank Boles noted in a somewhat more circumscribed context, "Despite important contributions in all of these areas, the relationship of these many subjects to one another has not been discussed."[19]

That there has been little attempt to date to compare, contrast, or reconcile this wide-ranging appraisal literature is regrettable enough; worse is that much of the appraisal literature is not relevant to the working realities of curators in collecting repositories. Most writers on appraisal have been institutional archivists, and "the appraisal theory they developed was conceived within the context of a single institution seeking to preserve its own records."[20] This writing has largely ignored the most fundamental and complex issue facing repository curators: deciding which records creators should be collected and to what degree. True, archival literature on collecting policies has stressed that such prioritization should occur and has even offered some tools— such as collection analyses and user studies—for assisting in the setting of such priorities. However, these writings have suffered from being few, overly broad, and sometimes too beholden to library theory.[21]

To the extent that appraisal literature has depended upon institutional archivists, this slighting of acquisition policy is natural. After all, institutional archives have the outer parameters of their documentary universe pre-defined, though of course questions may remain about priorities within those parameters and the extent to which relevant external documentation (from publications to the personal papers of founders or employees) should be collected. The Boles and Young "Black Box" appraisal taxonomy is an ambitious attempt to explicate how an institution should evaluate records series and folders to determine whether they are worth preserving in the institution's archives.[22] Though developed for university archives, the Boles and Young emphasis on extensive analysis of the records themselves in order to make preliminary appraisal decisions has typically been the approach curators have taken: our broad mandate includes documenting business, so any business that approaches us to donate records is asked "are these particular series any good?" For repositories, at least, we think this is the wrong question. Instead of analyzing record series (or functions, for that matter) first, curators need to prioritize the broad topical areas their repository seeks to document and decide which records creators will be solicited and accepted within each area.[23]

More recently, the black box taxonomy has been replaced, supplemented, modified, or refined (take your pick) by institutional functional analysis.[24] Functional analysis (and its sibling, documentation planning), argues that records be appraised only after the functions of an institution are defined and understood. Record appraisal then becomes a matter of identifying or creating records that best document the institution's functions. Because it is institutionally based, functional analysis implicitly shuns any prioritization among similar institutions and suggests that there is a universal and objective set of records that comprise "adequate" documentation of each and every example of a particular type of institution.[25] Ironically, despite the detailed foray into analyzing and describing functions prior to appraising records, functional analysis produces, in the end, recommendations for the retention of records series very similar to those advanced by more traditional archivists writing decades earlier.[26]

As an institutional appraisal approach, functional analysis skirts the very problem most crucial to repositories: evaluating not the functions of an institution or the quality of its records, but the relative importance of one institution to another within the context of their repository's larger documentary goal. Nor is prioritizing records creators an all or nothing proposition. Agreeing that two businesses should each be documented is not the same as saying they should be documented equally. The decision to document a business exists not as a static point, but as a continuum, ranging from detailed to superficial acquisition of the records. Repositories are not empty vessels into which institutional archives are placed wholesale. Repositories are distinguished from warehouses and records centers by this act of analysis and selection. In the real world, it is not only unavoidable but worthwhile to document different companies to different levels.

The Canadian cousin of functional analysis, macroappraisal, does explicitly shift archivists' focus from appraising actual records to appraising records creators and emphasizes the need to prioritize record-creating entities. Like functional analysis, macroappraisal was developed for institutional (government) records and places exclusive priority on why records were created (function), where they were created (structure), and how they were created rather than on secondary—particularly informational—values.[27] In fact, macroappraisal's leading theorist has called subject or thematic approaches to collecting (what repositories do by definition) "unarchival," apparently because such an approach values the content of records as much as the context of their creation.[28] For a subject or geographically focused repository, therefore, macroappraisal per se is not the answer.

In postulating "A Social Theory of Appraisal," Terry Eastwood rejects both context and content as bases for appraisal and argues instead for "appraisal based ultimately but not exclusively on an assessment of use" by society.[29] He refers to use as a "scientific theory" based on "the objective facts of archives" that derive from the status of archives as evidence of transactions and suggests that the "scientific analysis of the archivist" consists of assembling "evidence that any particular transactions endure in importance in society through continued recourse to evidence in them." Archivists have long called for a better understanding of use,[30] though its exact role in appraisal has been a matter of some debate.[31] However, Eastwood's argument begs the question of how (or indeed whether) to evaluate use: by the number of times a piece of evidence is requested; by the number of times it actually proves "useful" to the user; by the quality *and* quantity of use; by the importance of users.[32] Such questions must have precise answers if current and past use are to provide "us with empirical grounds on which to rest our projections" of future use, and thus provide a basis for appraisal.[33]

Of recent appraisal theory, documentation strategy is the one specifically formulated to apply to manuscripts repositories. Documentation strategy began as an effort to extrapolate a broad model from the specific effort to coordinate documentation of research projects in physics. The prototype effort at the American Institute of Physics, which began in the 1960s, hoped to help the institutions whose scientists were involved in multi-institution projects effectively document the project as a whole.[34] Since the mid-1980s, however, documentation strategy has been represented as a much broader and more ambitious concept.[35] This broader documentation strategy (which is the version most archivists are familiar with today) presents an approach for the "adequate documentation" of a specific geographic area, topic, process, or event, leading to the ultimate goal—"the natural dispersion of the integrated documentation of modern society."[36] This is an ambitious and inspiring but unrealistic vision based on two unworkable assumptions. First, adequacy of documentation implies that there is (or can be) broad consensus on universal appraisal criteria; as Richard Cox has stated clearly, "the criteria that provide the basis for archival appraisal decisions are independent of records creators and their institutions and are generic to recorded information."[37] This is an unsupported—and we believe, insupportable—postulate, and one that unrealistically raises the expectation of our public and resource allocators that there is an objectively definable end point to documentation efforts. Second, documentation strategy argues that single archives or repositories are not the proper locus of documentation and appraisal decisions. After analyzing the interinstitutional nature of scientific research, many documentation strategists have extrapolated a hypothetical world where (1) the records of no institution are usefully complete in themselves and (2) no archives or repository can on its own usefully document any institution, topic, or geographic area.[38] Few would quarrel with the need for greater cooperation among institutions, but documentation strategy posits that independent repositories should become not only partners in but agents of a central documentation plan. For better or worse, however, few repositories have a clientele or resource allocators who see their institution's mission as helping to document all of modern society—the missions are inevitably narrower and more selfish than that.[39] Pragmatically, it seems to make more sense to improve the mechanisms of the archival invisible hand, improving the acquisition policies and methods of individual repositories working independently (but not competitively) to acquire better documentation overall.[40]

So it remains largely true, as Margaret Hedstrom noted several years ago, that "both the theory and methods are inadequate and inflexible for appraising contemporary records."[41] Our survey of archival appraisal literature left us feeling, as Barbara Craig has said with some eloquence, as though we have been chasing a chimera:

> that shining white future, where all problems of acquisition will be solved by the application of the right theory of appraisal. By discussing appraisal and particularly the history of appraisal in a moral discourse, the right decisions taken in the past become accidents, while the wrong are the result of a faulty theory. By looking for What is Right and What is Wrong, we create an artifical dichotomy that is not only useless in a practical sense, but misleading because it blurs the nuances which give reality its unique form and substance.[42]

Craig goes on to ask, "Would we not be better served and satisfied if we separated theory from method?"[43] It may well be that the question is not really one of theory versus method, however; lack of nuance and subjectivity can be errors found in method as well as theory, after all.[44] We seek a method that acknowledges and responds to the "form and substance"—and complexity—of reality.

The Minnesota Method

Though we found most writing on appraisal somewhat wanting as we considered the problems of documenting twentieth-century business, there are conceptual or structural elements in those writings that had immense practical value. Our method borrows freely from recent literature, and we gratefully acknowledge our debt. A kind critic might suggest that we have fashioned a new synthesis—a quilt, if you will—that blends the best pieces from many methods into a new whole. (Of course, even a kind critic, knowing the two present authors, might call it a crazy quilt.) From collection policy literature we took the accepted notions of collection analysis, documentation project definition, and cooperation with other repositories. Documentation strategy lent more form than substance, but the skeleton of many of its procedural steps proved quite utilitarian. Macroappraisal contributed the crucial formulation of prioritizing records creators, though the original formulation seems to have meant it in a different way than we accepted it. Though functional analysis was developed for institutional archives, the idea of making functions (rather than record types) the primary delimiter of the documentation level accorded a specific business made eminent sense. The "Black Box," though created as a static taxonomy for appraising records series, suggested both the concept and content of our fluid decision tree. Less kind critics might suggest that our method is a Frankenstein's monster, a hideous conglomeration of parts sundered from their rightful wholes. (Though fortunately we did not actually have to rob any graves to construct the method, we realize that those from whom we borrowed may consider the way we have used parts of their systems to be a grave offense of another kind.) Like the monster, the method does function (at least, it is functioning at the Minnesota Historical Society), despite its disjunct origins. Whether it will ultimately terrorize the archival village or become a productive and accepted member of archival society will be for others to judge.

The outline in Figure 1 summarizes the basic steps of the Minnesota Method and suggests its main intellectual debts. Essentially, the method suggests that certain steps are necessary for rationalizing the collecting of modern business records. How the steps are carried out and the specific choices made in each step will be unique to each repository; the method suggests only the basic approach or orientation. However, we have chosen to present a narrative and analytical account of how and why the steps in the method were implemented at MHS, in order that the presentation is not so abstract and general as to be meaningless. In order to reinforce the subjectivity of our institution's decisions, though, there are points along the way in which we suggest how other hypothetical repositories might differ in their application of the method. The basic approach consists of defining the institution's mission and goals and analyzing its extant holdings; surveying the broader documentary universe and receiving input and advice from outside the repository; defining—based on the repository's particular mission, resources, and clientele—a broad set of criteria for organizing and prioritizing records creators into broad groups; establishing a range of documentation levels to permit flexibility in accepting collections from creators of different priority status; defining, if neces-

Figure 1. An Outline of the Minnesota Method

I. Define, Analyze, Survey (from Collection Policy)
   A. Define collecting area: geographic, chronological, type of
      business, etc.
   B. Analyze collection
   C. Survey other relevant repository holdings and collection goals

II. Determine Documentary Universe and Consultation (from
   Documentation Strategy)
   A. Research documentary universe
   B. Survey relevant government records, printed and other
      documentary sources.
   C. Consult with selected subject experts, researchers, creators, or
      business archivists

III. Prioritize (from Macroappraisal)
   A. Define criteria for prioritization
   B. Prioritize industrial sectors, individual businesses, geographic
      regions, and/or chronological periods into two to five tiers

IV. Define Functions and Documentary Levels (from Functional
   Analysis)
   A. Define functions and information most appropriate to particular
      collecting area
   B. Define documentary levels relating to these functions

V. Refine Prioritization Test (from "the Black Box")
   A. Refine prioritization within tiers
   B. Connect documentary levels to priority tiers—what will be the
      practical, operational differences in approach to top priority
      companies versus second priority, etc.
   C. Test the model by applying it to real companies, either those
      already accessioned or realistic possibilities

VI. Updating—Collection analysis, research, and consultation should
   be updated every three–seven years

---

sary, further criteria ("decision points") for further refining the
prioritization of creators down to the level of individual businesses;
linking the priority group levels, the decision points, and the documentation levels; using this intellectual framework to guide acquisition decisions and reappraisal decisions; revising the framework
over time to account for changes in the structure of the economy, the
success of past collecting, and the evolution of repository mission
and resources.

One broad point must be addressed at the beginning: the Minnesota Method is meant to be efficient and effective, but it is not meant
to be easy or simple. Applying the method requires time. Most difficult,
applying the method requires taking a certain amount of time away

from the daily duties faced by most curators. Barbara Craig has noted that "All appraisal models, even the most mechanical, imply that the archivist has adequate research time, thinking time, consultation time and sampling/study time. I suspect that, more often than not, such leisure is not available."[45] Craig is correct to the extent that many appraisal methods assume that the archivist has the sort of study time that, for most of us, comes only with grant funds and project archivists—or perhaps with research leaves.

The Minnesota Method presumes that without major infusions of outside funding and extra staff the breadth and depth of analysis will be limited. However, limited analysis is different than no analysis. Though the level of study may vary, it is important to understand that "Appraisal is a work of careful analysis and of archival scholarship, not a mere procedure. Applying guidelines or criteria in the appraisal process, as well as developing broader acquisition strategies, only works if such application is based on a rich understanding by the archivist" of the documentary universe.[46] Whether undertaken by a lone arranger or small repository working group, it is necessary that time be made to analyze what is to be documented and to understand the problems in accomplishing the documentation.

So if it is futile (not to mention unfair) to harangue archivists to do more things in the same 24-hour day, and equally futile to assume that grant money will rain down to give us the extra staff or time we need, is it possible to improve our acquisition efforts? We argue that our appraisal method is pragmatic precisely because it makes better use of archival time and resources, allows archivists to work more efficiently and with more useful results. To be sure, during the defining, consulting, and prioritizing phases of the method something else will not get done that might have been, though exactly what gets sacrificed is one of the many things that will need to be decided at the individual repository level. The staff at MHS did not develop the Minnesota Method by staying late after work, coming in on weekends, or otherwise expanding the number of hours in our day. We did it by deciding that taking staff time away from both reactive appraisal work and solicitation of new collections was a smart investment that would pay dividends in the relatively short term by allowing us to work smarter rather than harder and longer.

Indeed, the very impetus for our internal project was that there was more appraisal and solicitation work to do than we could do, and we needed a way to decide which parts of it would get done and why. After all, whether we are conscious of it or not, we are constantly applying priorities: when we dash off to rescue 100 cubic feet of ledgers and journals from the Sixth National Bank of Podunk even though we have equally large collections from the First, Second, and Fourth

National Banks, we are spending time and valuable shelf space on that collection rather than others; when we spend two days surveying every last nook and cranny of filing space in the Metropolis Insurance Company offices rather than first asking what it is we would like to find there and then stop after we find it we are likewise defining priorities. The method presumes that we would be better off making thoughtful and proactive choices rather than responding reactively and more or less mindlessly. Despite not requiring external funding, implementation of the method will require some reallocation of internal priorities—but any change from the status quo will require the same.

To begin, then, at the beginning: it was in February 1993 (we wish we could report that it was a dark and stormy night, but it was simply a bitter cold day) that the manuscript section of MHS's Acquisition and Curatorial department, along with the department head, met to define a project for analyzing the society's business collecting policy. To ensure that these discussions would not become too insular, five other staff members (all but one from other departments), and one colleague from another institution were invited to become an advisory group.[47] This core team developed the process, raised the questions, and debated the answers that developed into the Minnesota Method. The method itself, however, is not dependent upon an advisory group: all of the collection policy issues and activities described below can be undertaken by a lone arranger as well as by a small team, though of course certain policy decisions will ultimately require the advice and consent of repository or parent institution administrators.

Define, Analyze, Survey

Any collection effort requires a defined topic (twentieth-century business in X region/state/county/city; computer-related businesses in the U.S.), that carries within it some restrictions by geography, chronology, and/or business sector. Policy, tradition, and practical experience told us clearly that the Minnesota Historical Society was committed to documenting the state's twentieth-century businesses as part of our overall goal of collecting "items that bear a relationship to Minnesota, to its peoples, and to their interaction with the larger society, both national and international."[48] While archival literature has urged that collecting goals should be narrow or done collectively as part of documentation strategies, our method presumes that the topic is relatively large and broad and that some effort to document this unrealistically large topic will be made by a single repository. This is, we believe, the reality faced by most curators at most repositories. This situation is not ideal, but it is real.

Still, traditional collecting policy and collection management strategies emphasize the need to avoid direct competition,[49] and this is crucial. While recognizing that political pressure may sometimes override the principle, the Minnesota Method assumes that in areas where two institutions' collecting agendas overlap, enough interinstitutional cooperation and communication will exist to virtually eliminate vying for the same record groups. Such cooperation and communication actually does exist, on the whole, among Minnesota repositories; we assume our archival community is not alone in this.

This includes the assumption that collecting repositories should do nothing to undermine the formation, existence, or strengthening of business archives. Indeed, it has been the policy at the Minnesota Historical Society to actively promote the creation of business archives. This is necessity as the mother of ethics. Having conceded that the task of documenting the state's businesses is beyond the means of a single repository, fostering the creation of business archives both improves overall documentation and makes the repository's documentary universe that much more manageable.[50]

Collecting twentieth-century Minnesota business is still too large a task to accomplish, even if one is willing to cede some collections to other repositories and encourage the formation of corporate archives. If acquisition efforts are going to be narrowed at the operational level, a close understanding of existing collections is needed. Collection analysis is a crucial tool in our method. It is too easy to make erroneous assumptions about the strengths of current holdings.[51] Although MHS had completed a major manuscript collection analysis effort in 1980, its categorization of business sectors, its method of evaluating the strength of holdings in each category, and the changes in both the state's economy and our collections in the intervening years meant that analysis had limited value.[52] We determined that a new survey should focus exclusively on business holdings and find some practical means to evaluate the quality of each collection. To this end, we added an accounting of the major types of material found in each collection. At the very least, an analysis of record types done from extant finding aids would give some indication of which collections were mostly "public relations" (otherwise known as "historical") conglomerations and which likely documented a variety of business functions in some depth.[53] Our analysis, therefore, divided all business collections into 20 categories by industry sector,[54] and for every collection specified title, dates, size (in cubic feet), date first accessioned, and codes representing the predominant record types found in the collection (e.g. minutes and board packets; annual reports and financial statements; daily accounting records such as journals and ledgers; advertising material; employee records; sales or manufacturing data; sound and visual material; correspondence; government regulatory reports; legal files; research and development files).

Upon first glance, the collection analysis indicated that MHS had done a good job of documenting business in Minnesota through the mid part of the twentieth-century. We had the records of 50 lumber-related businesses, 15 mining-related businesses, and 45 transportation-related businesses (including the mammoth Great Northern and Northern Pacific Railroads). Significant numbers of collections existed for utilities, real estate, and agriculture as well. However, a second look at the analysis raised various concerns. First, could one tell whether a sector had been reasonably (let alone adequately) documented? In the case of lumbering, MHS seemed to take care of this question by collecting virtually all of the lumber companies in Minnesota. In the case of manufacturing, though, only 22 collections exist, and they represent very few of the state's best known or major manufacturers. Second, the kinds of records found in most collections were largely incomplete. Fifty-eight percent of the collections had only one or two major series present. Minutes were present in only 26 percent of the collections. The kinds of records most likely to be found in these collections consisted of cash books, monthly accounting statements, and other accounting minutiae.

Collection analysis may be used to develop documentation projects but is hardly sufficient to do so.[55] Knowing that gaps exist does not mean that the gaps are important enough (relative to other priorities) to fill. Knowing that a particular business sector is well documented does not determine whether additional documentation should be sought (which depends, in part, on whether the sector continues to be important, whether it has undergone significant changes not represented in the current documentation, etc.). Knowing that many collections consisted of public relations material or daily accounting records did not answer the question of who might use such limited conglomerations or to what degree. Although we knew where we were in terms of our business holdings, we still had to figure out where we wanted to go and how to get there.

Determine Documentary Universe and Consultation

As imperative as it is to understand one's own institutional priorities and collections, it is equally important to understand the larger documentary universe in which one operates and to seek some perspective from outside the parameters of the repository. These are steps outlined in documentation strategy. "The key elements of documentation strategies are an analysis of the universe to be documented, an understanding of the inherent documentary problems, and the formulation of a plan to ensure the adequate documentation of an ongoing issue or activity or geographic area."[56] Documentation strategy focuses necessary attention on the broader context of documentation, reminding us, for example, to consider documentation contained in government records and nationally published sources when considering the documentation of business. Documentation strategy also insists on a formal process of soliciting opinions from subject experts and records creators during this analysis, understanding, and formulation. Our method embraces all these elements but rejects the multi-institutional context in which documentation strategy sets them. Moreover, our method relied not on a large documentation group but on a small, almost entirely internal team supplemented by catch-as-catch-can meetings with a small group of external (unpaid) consultants. For all intents and purposes, the work of the team could have been done by one person and consultants could have been consulted by phone.[57]

Analysis of the documentary universe consists of several steps. The first consists of research in readily available published sources. Broad trends and the shape of the current economic landscape in the repository's collecting area, documented through the local press or relevant trade publicaitons, should be understood. Federal and state documents, including censuses and regulatory reports, should be consulted. Because we kept this type of analysis to a fairly high level of generality, at MHS we were able to accomplish it in snatches of time over the course of several weeks.

Some attempt must also be made to survey (if only in the most general terms) the type of records held in (or likely to be acquired by) relevant state or federal archives. At the very least, some knowledge must be gained of the relative regulatory environments of different business sectors; it may well be that where more documentation is required by government, less needs to be acquired by manuscripts repositories. We specifically included the deputy state archivist as a member of our project group so that he might keep us informed in this area. For a repository that did not house state or local government records, the alternative would be to add a government records archivist to the telephone consulting team. Similar situations exist in other repositories that should be understood and countered during the primary phase.

Archivists have long preached that "appraisers also should consult with knowledgeable individuals outside the archival profession to ensure that the best possible information is available for their appraisals,"[58] and this is even more true at the level of understanding the documentary universe and formulating broad documentary goals. It makes sense to start by consulting those who do or reasonably would use business records. This user group will vary from repository to repository: for some repositories the academic community is the principal set of researchers whose needs must be met; for others (such as MHS), there is a much broader public that must be considered as well. Generally, archives have done a poor job of documenting how researchers actually use existing collections. In particular, very little work has been done regarding use of business collections.[59] What evidence does exist suggests that academic users, at least, offer little useful guidance, mixing calls for the retention of almost everything with conflicting assessments of what appraisal choices should be made if appraisal is necessary.[60] Local historians, students, and exhibit curators may have radically different needs than business historians (who may have different needs than economic historians). What are these needs and how can they and should they be prioritized against scholarly use?[61] If possible, therefore, a select number of local academics and other users should be sought for advice and consultation, for short meetings or telephone conversations. Generally, such individuals are more than happy to share their expertise so long as no major or long-term commitment of time is required.

It may be possible at this juncture to consult with records creators, but in our experience the average businessperson is not particularly interested in spending time discussing the historical documentation of his or her or other businesses. (If this were not true, there would presumably be many more real corporate archives.) However, corporate archivists, who to some extent represent records creators (that is, corporate archivists generally are concerned with preserving documentation valued by the corporation rather than with broader societal desires for historical information),[62] probably will be willing to discuss documentary problems with a manuscripts curator. Corporate records managers, too, may be able to provide useful information about records being created and records systems. It is even possible that business executives who serve on the repository's board may be willing to discuss their views of records in terms of business utility (and liability). Whatever small group of outside experts and corporate archivists called upon at this stage should be consulted occasionally throughout the rest of the method, particularly if no internal documentation group exists to provide feedback.

The MHS group arranged a series of meetings (usually lasting between one and two hours, with most taking place at professional conferences or locally) with academics, business archivists, and other business collections curators, to broaden further the perspectives brought to bear on some of the questions in our project plan.[63] These meetings provided us with valuable information on the use of records inside and outside of businesses, as well as varying perspectives on which businesses were most important to document and which records within businesses were most important. We were encouraged to look at records for the information they could provide about social history, women's history, and local history. We were encouraged to seek out the records of companies that were innovators in their field. We were urged to document at least a portion of each company from top to bottom so that researchers might fully understand the decision-making and communication processes. We were urged to seek the records of the state's largest and best-known companies because these would attract researchers from around the country. It was even suggested that we should not be selecting businesses or appraising records at all, but rather letting come what may. We learned that some of the best corporate archives in the nation do not hold such core records as board minutes, that at some corporate archives employee publications are the single most heavily consulted source, and that the reporting lines and resources of an archives had at least as much to do with the records it held as did any functional analysis or core collection concept. As we might have predicted, these discussions yielded neither a consensus nor even a common thread that would lead the way in defining for MHS which businesses should be documented and which records should be preserved from those businesses. Nonetheless, pieces of many of these suggestions were woven into the fabric of the Minnesota Method.

These same experts and the documentation analysis can be used to begin defining documentary problems that may be encountered. Problems may range from loss of records due to mergers and acquisitions, to shift from paper to electronic media for many records and much information, to a lack of any consensus among the experts about what should be done.[64] The most basic problem in most instances, however, is the same one that launched the Minnesota documentary project, which is that the documentary universe is too vast for the repository's limited resources, so some substantial prioritization will have to be done. All of our consultants agree on this, though not all academics do.

Prioritize

Appraising and setting priorities among the records creators is the single most important—and probably the single most difficult—step in the process. It is here that all the prior research, consultation, collection analysis, and the like must be brought to bear. These priorities are the crucial step in moving from an unmanageable universe of potential documentation to a manageable one, and from a haphazard accumulation of records to a planned one. It is crucial to understand that priorities exist and choices get made either implicitly or explicitly. Ultimately, the collecting of one business necessarily means that some other one will not be solicited or acquired. If thoughtful, conscious priorities are not set, the priorities dictated by chance (what business went bankrupt this week, which business has its CEO sitting on the repository's board) become completely determinative. Even so, setting priorities is the most difficult step to speak of in general terms, because the criteria for prioritization is completely relative; it can and should vary from repository to repository based on their broader collecting goals and emphases, staff and space resources.

Fundamental to our method of prioritization is to begin far above the level of actual records. Though macroappraisal was developed for government archives, its most general principle—that appraising records is the last thing that happens in appraisal, following an appraisal of the records creators—is applicable to a repository documentation project:

> Evidently, this type of macro-appraisal emphasizes . . . [and] assesses the capacity of institutions to create records of value in a global way rather than dealing directly, one by one, with the tens of thousands of records series, databases, and media collections which any large jurisdiction will contain, let alone with individual records. In ranking records creators, their functions, and their constituent 'parts,' an archives should divide all of the records-creating agencies for which it is responsible into priority categories.[65]

A division of records-creating entities into priority categories is what lies at the heart of our method. At a given repository, prioritization can be based on any one of dozens of combinations of specific criteria, many of which are themselves more subjective than objective. (See Figure 2 for a summary list of possible criteria.) Most of these criteria will be applicable either to individual companies or to industrial sectors (e.g., lumber and paper products, law, services). Because the criteria will often not be amenable to numerical precision, general rankings (high/medium/low) are useful, and thus the final rankings will depend not on an attempt to determine a numerical average but rather on the result of discussion and consensus. Whether sectors or individual businesses are ranked, the prioritization process will end with two to five tiers. (More than five becomes unwieldy and is not likely to provide any benefits).

At MHS our collection analysis had broken businesses down into logical industry groupings. Some of these, however, had little relevance today. For example, the fur trade is no longer a major industry in Minnesota. Other sectors, such as medical technology, did not exist as part of our collection analysis but now play a major role in Minnesota's

Figure 2. Possible Prioritization Criteria

Examples of criteria for first level of prioritization—referred to here as "tiers." Can be used singly or in combination. We would suggest using general rankings (high/medium/low) for those criteria with no adequate numerical basis. Can be applied to individual companies or to industrial sectors (lumber and paper products, law, services). Because these criteria are a mix of objective and subjective, quantitative and qualitative, the "sum" of several criteria cannot usually be derived mechanistically or mathematically.

Gross revenue

Number of employees

Number of firms

Capitalization

Change in any of the above over last 10 or 20 years (may indicate important growth sectors in the economy)

Other rankings (Fortune 500, Fastest Growing Companies, 100 Best Companies to Work For)

Relatively strong identification with region/state/county/city (dairy farming in Wisconsin; lumber in Oregon; snowmobile and hockey stick manufacturing in Minnesota)

Extent of extant documentation in repositories or corporate archives

Level of government regulation (hence likely level of documentation in government records)

Relationship to other important topics of documentation (if documenting labor unions is also an institutional goal, industries or companies with union work forces might receive priority; if environmental history is a collecting strength, priority may be given to natural-resource-intensive industries)

Technological innovation

Age

economy. Therefore, we needed to define sectors that would be most appropriate to the current Minnesota economy and widely understood. We consulted several internal and external sources, including the Standard Industrial Classification (SIC), and finally settled on a hybrid based in large part on the SIC.[66] We could not adopt the SIC sectors directly because many sectors prominent in the Minnesota economy get grouped together in ways that are not meaningful to MHS, such as health care, hospitality/tourism, entertainment, and advertising being grouped under the services sector. Therefore, we chose to break out and rearrange some of these sectors to more appropriately define the Minnesota economy as we understood it from our sources. The final breakdown includes 18 sectors, each one further broken down into its various sub-parts as indicated by the SIC.[67] These decisions were not scientific and made little or no reference to economic theory but were tailored to the practical problems we faced in our state at this time.

Our next step was to prioritize these sectors into one of four groups. In order to do this we looked at three factors for each sector: economic impact (which was broken down into number of employees in the state and revenue), extant documentation, and identification with or uniqueness to Minnesota. There are a number of ways to look at economic impact, including market capitalization, profits, and assets, as well as those mentioned above. After considerable discussion, however, we came to believe that number of employees was the most significant measure of a company's economic impact on its locality, and by extension the most significant measure of a sector's economic impact on the state. Although revenues are an important measure of a business's or sector's health, for large multistate and multinational firms much of their revenue can be derived outside of Minnesota, and much of its profits distributed to shareholders also out of state. Number of employees, on the other hand, translates directly into economic impact in a geographic region. Extant documentation was based in part on our collection analysis, as well as our collective knowledge about the collections in other repositories in the state, the existence of printed materials, and government records. Each sector was ranked in one of four categories from poor to very good. Identification with or uniqueness to Minnesota was the final factor we considered. Here we sought to place a sector within its national context. For instance, the Lumber and Forest Products sector has a strong historical identification with Minnesota. Transportation is a sector that has been and continues to be identified with Minnesota because of the presence of the Great Northern, Northern Pacific, and Soo Line Railroads, and Northwest Airlines. On the other hand, the Real Estate/Land Development and Legal sectors are not particularly unique to, strong in, or identified with Minnesota. Each sector, then, was ranked in one of four categories from limited to very high based on the collective knowledge/judgment of the committee.

The final rankings of the sectors into four tiers from high to low priority was based on the consensus judgement of the committee considering all three factors. No attempt was made to mathematically weight certain factors or to compute the rankings within the factors.

Nor was there any attempt to divide the sectors equally into these tiers. Thus, the top two tiers contain only three sectors each, the third tier contains seven sectors, and the fourth tier contains five sectors. For the Minnesota Historical Society, then, the top priority sectors are Agriculture/Food Products and Services, Health Care, and Medical Technology. (See Figure 3, MHS Sector Ranking Chart.)

Not only the particular results, but the very basis of the prioritization itself was (and should be understood to be) peculiar to MHS. Many different specific approaches to this same goal of prioritization are not only possible but integral to our method. Florence Lathrop, of Harvard's Baker Library, has suggested quite correctly that

> A number of criteria can be used to select industries [as the focus for a repository's collecting]: the centrality of an industry to the local or national economy in a particular time period; the size of an industry, measured in a variety of ways—its contribution to gross national (or regional) product, the number of firms involved, or the number of employees; the significance of an industry with respect to organizational structure, labor relations, technological innovation or transfer; the extent of an industry's impact on other components of American social and political history, such as ethnicity, family structure, or foreign relations.[68]

Two hypothetical examples, to contrast with MHS's choices, should clarify the malleability of the method's approach to prioritization. A small county historical society decides that it will rank as its highest priority the top ten employers in the county because without those employers the economy of the county would disintegrate. (With equal justification, the repository could give top priority to the smallest employers, figuring that these smallest of businesses are the least well documented elsewhere.) A special subject repository documenting the air and space industry nationally simply uses the criteria of gross revenue as a ranking because the repository is less interested in the social impact of the companies or their influence on the economy overall, than in any company's dominance in the industry of which it is a part. The repository can set as its collecting goal the top 25 companies in the industry overall, or the top 5 in each distinct SIC subindustry (aircraft manufacturing, aircraft engines and engine parts manufacturing, search and navigation equipment manufacturing). Ranking by revenue runs the risk of missing important small companies where innovation may thrive, but documenting innovation is not an objective good in documenting business—any more than is gross revenue—and can be ignored in favor of other criteria. There is no objective or universal formula for beginning the process of prioritization.

The ultimate ramifications of this appraisal relativism are significant, to be sure, and perhaps uncomfortable for some. For example, it

Figure 3. Sector Ranking Chart

SECTORS	ECONOMIC IMPACT # of Employees	Revenue[1]	EXTANT DOCUMEN-TATION	IDENTIFICATION/ UNIQUENESS TO MN	PRIORITY TIERS
Agriculture/Food Products & Services	205,998 (4)	19.45 (4)	Very good	Very high	1
Farming	162,741	6.5			
Food Products	40,093	12.2			
Agr. Mfg.	3,164	.75			
Associations	2,346 (18)	.225 (16)	Poor	Limited	2
Entertainment/Sports	34,000 (12)	1.6 (12)	Poor	High	3
For Profit	28,000	1.3			
Not for Profit	6,000	.286			
Financial Products/ Services	126,500 (7)	35.0[2] (2)	Fair	High	3
Banking	35,500	8.5			
Other	71,000	26.5			
Health Care	217,000 (3)	11.2 (6)	Poor	High	1
For Profit	76,000	4.1			
Not for Profit	141,000	7.1			
Hospitality/Tourism	153,000 (6)	4.2 (10)	Poor	Fair	3
Legal	16,000 (15)	1.5 (13)	Good	Limited	4
Lumber/Forest Products	32,000 (13)	5.6 (9)	Very Good	Very High	3
Merchandising	398,600 (1)	104.7 (1)	Fair	High	2
Retail	266,000	32.2			
Wholesale	132,600	72.5			
Manufacturing (nonag.)	187,000 (5)	25.3 (3)	Good	High	3
Media—General	71,000 (10)	5.9[3] (8)	Good	Fair	3
Media	7,300	NA			
Publishing/Printing	46,700	4.5			
Advertising	4,500	.5			
Public Relations	12,500	.9			
Medical Technology	14,400 (16)	1.3 (14)	Poor	Very High	1
Mining	7,100 (17)	1.0 (15)	Very Good	Very High	4
Other Technology	112,000 (8)	11.5[4] (5)	Poor	Very High	4[5]
Manufacturing	80,800	8.4[6]			
Services	31,200	3.1			
Real Estate/Land Development	100,000 (9)	NA	Fair	Limited	4
Service	290,000 (2)	8.0 (7)	Poor	Limited	3
Transportation	72,600 (11)	2.6[7] (11)	Very Good	Very High	2
Air	23,100	NA			
Other	49,500	2.6			
Utilities	28,500 (14)	NA	Good	Fair	4

[1] In billions of dollars.
[2] All revenue figures in this sector are estimates based on a *Corporate Report Minnesota* article.
[3] Revenue for this sector is incomplete due to incomplete data.
[4] Revenue for this sector is incomplete due to incomplete data.
[5] This sector is the documentary focus of the Charles Babbage Institute for the History of Computing, at the University of Minnesota; major companies (IBM, Seagate, etc.) are not Minnesota based.
[6] Revenue figures for ordnance are not available.
[7] Revenue for this sector is incomplete due to incomplete data.

is all well and good to say that the Minnesota economy is not dominated by the real estate industry nor particularly known for its real estate companies, but where in the country will one find a state that would make the real estate industry a priority one sector? Our approach may wind up relegating certain industries and undoubtedly certain subindustries to perpetual underdocumentation because they are not dominant in or identified with any region, state, or city in the nation. The legal industry, the insurance industry, the banking industry, and independent service providers and retailers of all stripes come to mind as other businesses that are so ubiquitous that they could conceivably never make any repository's priority one list. Is this a problem? First, the concern is based on exactly the sort of Horatius-at-the-Bridge mentality that we believe is impossible to sustain. The fact that some other repository might not collect real estate offices is no reason for MHS to do it, and if the end result is that real estate offices do not get collected, it will be too bad but not something the curators at any given repository—nor the archival profession as a whole—should lose sleep over. Some archivists will insist that as a profession we have a responsibility to ensure that somebody is documenting the legal industry; but if there is no repository that sees it as in their self-interest to do so, how can the profession force such documentation to occur? The archival profession might want to lobby the American Bar Association to raise money to support a national law firm records repository at a volunteer university, or it might lobby some of the major law firms to start corporate archives (after all, the insurance industry is well documented not because repositories are eagerly collecting insurance records, but because many of the major firms in the industry have corporate archives), but it cannot expect repositories to collect law firm records out of some abstract concern to ensure that society preserves records of all industries.[69]

Define Functions and Documentary Levels

As fundamental as this macroprioritization is, it means little without at least one further step: defining what the priorities mean in a practical sense. The easiest means of division and definition would be for a repository to say it will seek or accept material from every company in the top tier sector(s) and will seek or accept "everything" from every one of those companies, but will neither seek nor accept any documentation from companies in sectors from the bottom tier. Few repositories are likely to have the luxury of so simple an approach. It is more likely that the tiers will ultimately connect to gradations of documentation. The documentary gradations will fall between active solicitation and passive acceptance of material on the one hand, and between complete documentation and minimal documentation on the other hand. Our method refers to this as defining "documentation levels." The exact definition of each documentation level (and again there probably should not be more than five) like the criteria used for prioritization, is subjective and relative.

To put this more baldly, there is no universal and objective criteria for determining archival (or historical) value: "archivists of different archival institutions may also use different criteria in evaluating records, for what is valuable to one archival institution may be valueless to another."[70] To paraphrase Ericson, curators should not first ask why would I save this, but rather why would I save this? Even if a series seems to have some level of evidential and/or informational value, "we must then pause to ask, 'So what?' "[71] Every document has potential use to someone at some time, but appraisal requires first and foremost a consideration of the costs of acquiring particular documents or records versus the relevance of those records to the goals and clientele of the repository. Implicit in this position is the conviction that repositories are obliged to worry more about the value of particular records to their patrons than to the records creators. Though for the records creators—and therefore for their respective institutional archivists—the records of Kraft Foods and a corner video store are equally important, this probably will not be true for a repository seeking to document the evolution of the Midwest's economy. The repository may well wish to document many more business functions of Kraft, and document them more thoroughly, than for the video store (if any records of the video store are acquired at all). By the same token, a county historical society will likely define documentary levels much differently than a national special subject repository.

Because in most instances there will be insufficient uniformity among the companies under consideration to assume that the same record series will be valuable from all companies, a modified functional analysis approach seems most sensible at this point; that is, instead of linking documentary levels to lists of specific record types, the levels should be linked to broader functional characteristics of business. Thus, a specific documentary level may seek to capture public relations, strategic planning, and marketing functions, while a lesser level may seek to capture only strategic planning (in whatever documentary format). At MHS we created five documentation levels (Do Not Collect, and levels D through A) in ascending order of comprehensiveness. Each level builds upon the documentation that would be accepted at the previous level (see Figure 4).

To some extent, documentation levels can be applied both to sectors and to individual companies. A top priority sector may be one in which the repository solicits material from a large range and number of individual companies; a low priority sector may be one in which minimal documentation of one or two companies will be deemed to suffice. (Such an interconnection between sectors and companies will be more fully explicated in the Further Prioritization step, below.) The references to specific types of records in the documentation levels are meant to apply at the series level only. For example, retaining "product packaging" for documentation level A does not imply keeping *all* product packaging, but that some portion of the series would likely be retained. Further appraisal at the folder level, which might dramatically reduce any series, is expected. In addition, documentation levels can only suggest general examples of specific record series and types that would be included at each level because the types of records generated from one type of business to another, and from one size of business to another, varies greatly. For example, manufacturing, R&D, or engineering studies would have no meaning when looking at a bank's records; employee training videos may have a very different value when documenting a service business than when documenting a manufacturing company.

A few other observations are necessary to further clarify the documentation levels. Behind the documentation levels lies an assumption that, for want of a better name, can be called the "Exception Clause." What this means is that at any level of documentation, the exceptional history, circumstances, or records of a particular company—or the need to support other collections at MHS—may compel the inclusion of a particular record series (or record type, or even set of folders) normally excluded by that documentation level. For example, the acquisition by the Sound and Visual section of the complete newsfilm archives of a local television station may mean that if business records are offered to the Manuscripts section, particular record series that directly support research use of the films might be acquired even if such series would normally not be included in the level C documentation otherwise accorded to a broadcast media company.[72] Another example: summary employee and recruitment records would normally be sought and accepted only for companies documented at level A; for a firm that falls within a level C documentation and that was renowned for its innovative and successful recruitment of minorities, the overall level of documentation would not rise, but summary employee and recruitment records might be added to the other level C documentation.[73]

Just as significantly, oral history's role in documentation is so variable that adding it formally to the documentation levels (or to the flow charts — see Figure 7) is not possible. For companies being documented at level A, oral history may be used to improve already ex-

Figure 4. Documentation Levels for Twentieth-Century Business at the Minnesota Historical Society (from least to most comprehensive)

Do Not Collect

Means just what it says, no records relating to the company would be accepted by the Manuscripts section of MHS. This decision would not necessarily bind other collecting units, such as Sound and Visual, Museum.

Level D

Level D documentation is an attempt to preserve minimal evidence of the existence and purpose of a company. Typically, the only records sought for level D documentation would be annual reports, some product information (such as catalogs), and printed, film, or video company histories (if no such histories exist, one or more photos of the main or best-known company building). Depending upon the quantity of catalogs produced, only a sample may be sought and acquired. *Businesses at level D will not be actively solicited by MHS staff.*

Level C

At level C, minimal documentation is sought relating to the internal facets of corporate history, with relatively more weight given to external documentation. Generally, internal communication, legal, R&D, marketing and production (except as evinced in such external documentation as catalogs), employee training, facilities, and anything but the most summary financial information would be excluded from level C. Other functions, such as planning, decision making, and employee culture will be documented at a much more summary or superficial level than for level B. Most attention will focus on documenting the basic chronology of the company, its products or services, and the way they were presented to the purchasers. *Businesses at level C will not be actively solicited by MHS staff.*

Examples of records series and types that would be sought and retained at level C are board minutes, personnel manuals, broad planning documents (five-year plans), newsletters, miscellaneous historical files (these would include, typically, files with stray clippings and memos relating to the company founder, select photos of early buildings and of founders, and certain paper artifacts as the "first formulary" notebook MHS recently received as part of a small donation of records from Ecolab).

Level B

Level B seeks to document both internal (decision making, planning, internal communication, production, facilities, legal, employee training and culture, R&D, summary accounting, etc.) and external (marketing, community relations, products, stockholders, financing, etc.) facets of a company, but typically this will only be done at the highest administrative rung: CEO and board correspondence and subject/project files of any substance would be sought and retained; however, little if any documentation would be sought below the level of the CEO and board. Moreover, personal and family papers would typically be neither sought nor accepted for purposes of documenting the business (although such papers may warrant preservation as social history). *Businesses at level B normally will not be actively solicited by MHS staff.*

Figure 4. Cont. Documentation Levels for Twentieth-Century Business at the Minnesota Historical Society (from least to most comprehensive)

Such documentation would usually be found in a wide range of documents. Examples of records series and types that would be sought and accepted at this level include articles of incorporation, constitution and bylaws, patents, annual manufacturing/R&D/engineering studies, product and market research materials, annual production reports, sales analyses, video and audio recordings of commercials, stockholders reports, board packets, employee training material, photo files (of, for example, production facilities, products, workers, founders and principle officers, point of sale displays).

Level A

The highest level of documentation, level A seeks to thoroughly document both the internal and external facets of a company. *Businesses at level A will be actively solicited by MHS staff, as resources permit.* It is important to note the fact that in our model, companies in the lowest priority sectors can be level A while those in the top priority sector may be as low as Do Not Collect. This paradox reflects the importance we attached to the size of a company's work force, since generally level A companies will be those that are top 25 employers in the state. (See the discussion connected to Figure 7, below.)

The documentation of internal communication, typically found in such documents as correspondence and memoranda, is one of the most important distinctions between level A and level B. A second major distinction is that level A typically will include documentation of the individuals who most shape the evolution of a company; hence, extensive papers of the founding families would be sought and accepted.

A third distinction is that level A records will be sought further down the organizational ladder of the company than records at other levels. The presumption is that the company is important enough to document at its operational levels, rather than simply at its highest administrative levels. For large decentralized firms, this would probably mean seeking documentation to the division level; at a smaller company it might mean seeking documentation to the department level. Given a functional organization, this presumption would mean seeking documentation at the level of VP for sales, VP for marketing, and so on. Note, however, that no hard and fast rules apply here. Not only business size, but issues of corporate cooperation and records management, repository resources (see discussion of "costs of retention," below), and company organizational structure will have a great deal to say about the hierarchical depth of documentation attempted or accomplished for any firm.

Figure 4. Cont. Documentation Levels for Twentieth-Century Business at the Minnesota Historical Society (from least to most comprehensive)

The potential impact of the size of the company on the functions being documented might be considerable. Rochester Silo, a small company but once one of two major silo manufacturers in the nation, sold its products essentially door-to-door to farmers in the Midwest; level A documentation for Rochester Silo may include documentation of individual customer contacts (or a sampling thereof), especially if such documentation would provide evidence both of what farmers wanted in a silo and how the company built its market. However, individual customer contact would not be included in level A documentation of Northwest Airlines (unless examples of customer letters were included in reading packets prepared for the vice president of customer relations) because of their vast bulk, because of the stronger likelihood that summary data exists, and because the customer service itself is "mass produced" rather than customized. For levels below A, the distinction between large and small companies is less important because no attempt is made to go below the highest rung of the corporate ladder.

Because level A documentation is intended to be both broad and deep, it normally will encompass a wider range of records series and types than other levels. Among records that may well be sought and accepted to document the internal and external facets of a company for level A (but not at any lower levels) are contracts, legal files, accounting records of more detail than presented in annual reports (though this does not mean ledgers, journals, receipts, vouchers, etc., in the late twentieth century it might mean quarterly statements, or annual statements from divisions or departments that are only summarized in the corporate annual statement; it may also include material relating to loans or to stocks), technical notebooks, product and packaging design, technical bulletins, internal photos and videos (training and documentary), architectural and engineering drawings, correspondence and subject files below the CEO, summary employee and recruitment records, minutes below the board.

cellent documentation by filling specific gaps in the written record or analyzing particularly important turning points in the corporate history. For companies being documented at level D, but for which political pressure exists to do something special, a broader oral history approach may offer a means of satisfying political expediency while not adding record bulk. While oral histories can, of course, impose a strain on staff resources, our experience has been that companies are sometimes much more willing to provide a grant to support an oral history when they would be much less interested in supporting appraisal or processing work on their papers. This has to do, presumably, in part with the fact that oral history focuses so much more explicitly on the individuals in the company rather than on what might be perceived as impersonal paper and electronic records. What is true for oral history may be equally true for the role of three-dimensional artifacts. MHS's extensive Museum Collections have acquisition goals and appraisal criteria distinct (though not entirely separate) from those of the Manuscripts section; there have and will continue to be occasions when pressure to document a business can be met by accepting artifacts and not records. Indeed, it is sometimes the case that a business eagerly offers artifacts for donation while at the same time rejecting requests to donate records.

Finally, MHS's documentation levels attempt to strike a balance between the needs of academics for fairly detailed documentation across a broad range of functions at certain companies, amateur historians' more likely need for well-organized summary data, and the more symbolic importance attached to the preservation of "stuff" by many nonresearchers. In particular, documentation levels C and D, by which MHS would only seek and accept fairly minimal levels of documentation from a particular business, may seem contrary to traditional archival assumptions about acquiring the best documentation possible of any entity documented or none at all. Such an attitude is both impractical and foolish for an institution with a broad mandate and a very diverse user base. In our experience, citizen historians working on a history of their town or county seem to make more extensive use of company publications (such as annual reports and employee newsletters) than of most other business records series.[74] Indeed, according to our conversations with our "consultants," the same is often true of academic researchers and of internal clients at corporate archives as well.[75] Conversely, our experience with modern minutes and correspondence (not to mention ledgers and journals) has led us to question the assumption that they are "must haves" for every company or organization. Most minutes provide less information than an annual report; unless the company is one for which a generally detailed and comprehensive set of records is desired, minutes are probably less valuable (per cubic foot) for most researchers than company publications. We also have learned that our exhibit curators are delighted to be able to display a colorful company publication, whereas they blanch (to our dismay) at the idea of showcasing a minute book or letter. Moreover, we have come to recognize (in no small part through the fundraising tours we conducted for MHS's capital campaign) that there is a remarkable value in being able to say our collections hold something from a particular company or family, no matter how small that collection might be. The good will engendered by being able to demonstrate a broad (even if superficial) set of collections for low priority businesses outweighs the relatively slight investment of staff time to acquire and catalog a set of annual reports.

Our documentation level definitions are not meant to be universal; the definition of documentation levels will vary from repository to repository. While three hypothetical repositories may each wind up defining four documentation levels, there need be no correlation of the levels from one repository to another. The definition of the documentation levels will depend on a combination of the following factors: relative importance of business collections to the overall collecting priorities of the repository (which derives from the repository's mission and clientele); and resources such as space, staff, and technical expertise at the repository. The role of business collections in the repository's overall collecting goals is an issue that functional analysis and macroappraisal largely ignore because it was developed for institutional archives. Special subject collecting repositories that define some portion of the business universe as their focus are also immune from this consideration. However, most repositories, whether regional, state, county, or local, need to make this decision. It is, indeed, part of the collection policy issues discussed above, but at the point of defining documentation levels such basic prioritization most directly applies. The level of documentation that the county historical society can manage at best—minutes and advertising material—may be all a state historical society wishes to have even from top tier companies, if business documentation is low on its list of priorities. Conversely, the county historical society may be willing to fill up all of its remaining stack space with relatively complete documentation of the decision making and strategic planning, manufacturing, advertising, and personnel functions of the 10 largest companies in the county to the exclusion of other collections. Thus, the most basic collecting issues will shape the definition of documentation levels.

While repository mission and clientele will obviously loom large in the basic decision about the relative priority of business collections in the overall collecting goals, it will also have subtler effects on the shape of documentation levels. If the special subject repository is located at a university and serves academic researchers almost exclusively, the functions it documents for each company, and the depth to which it documents each function, will largely reflect the needs of its clientele. If the university has a strong management school, management functions may be emphasized in repository documentation of business; if the university is strong in labor-management relations, that aspect of business can and should receive emphasis by the repository. A county historical society with virtually no academic usership will logically tailor its documentation approach to the community historians and high school students that it principally serves. This may well mean focusing on documentation at the highest level of summarization and on public documents such as annual reports, scrapbooks, and product catalogs. It may mean a higher likelihood of acquiring extensive biographical information on individual employees (who would be county residents) than would be true for the state or subject repositories.

In the end, the most concrete delimiter of documentation levels will be the space, staff, and technical resources of the repository. For example, our hypothetical county historical society, which will probably have less than 100 cubic feet of shelf space to devote to documenting business and a single professional staff member to acquire, catalog, and curate all papers and artifacts, will probably set much narrower documentation levels than a state historical society such as MHS with thousands of cubic feet of still empty stack space and multiple staff members devoted specifically to acquisition, processing, and reference. In the former case, the highest level of documentation may consist only of the most basic records of decision making (usually found in board minutes) and end product and service (illustrated by advertising material, perhaps); in the latter case, the same documentation may describe the lowest level. For the special subject repository, it may be possible to solicit extensive documentation of a wide range of business functions from every one of the 25 or so companies in its top tier. For such a repository, it may well be possible to conduct a full-fledged functional analysis for each company under consideration, following the model outlined in *The High Technology Company* (by comparison, at MHS a full functional analysis will be undertaken only for companies we wish to document to level A).

Refine Prioritization and Test

After the initial prioritization, there will often be a need for further prioritization. This will be particularly true if the tiers represent sectors rather than a smaller number of ranked businesses; if a tier represents one or more sectors, then the refinements (we call them "decision points") within the tier will essentially prioritize individual companies. (See Figure 5 for a summary of the decision points we considered; please note, we did not adopt all these decision points for the MHS model.) Some of these decision point criteria can be the same as those used for the creation of tiers. However, when applied within tiers, they relate to individual companies rather than to industrial sectors. In the particular instance illustrated below, these criteria were applied in a simple "true/false" decision point, but they could be employed with high/medium/low ranking. Thus, within each tier, some companies will be ranked higher than others. Moreover, the prioritizing of companies must also be linked directly to the documentation levels. After experimenting with several forms, including a standard matrix, we found the simplest method of expressing the intersection of ranked tiers, decision points, and documentation levels to be a series of flow charts. While fairly easy to construct and follow, such a representation does lack compactness.

To be more concrete, MHS's prioritization of sectors had not really moved us much beyond previous attempts to focus MHS's collecting efforts. In order to parse out the thousands of businesses within each sector more effectively, we had to establish means to prioritize those businesses. We thus began the second round of prioritization by defining 11 factors that reflected a number of institutional concerns and priorities and could have a bearing on a business's ranking within a sector. Some of the decision points are borrowed directly or indirectly from the Boles and Young appraisal taxonomy, although they are used in our method somewhat differently. The factors and their definitions are as follows:

1. **Top 25 Employer**—One of the 25 largest companies by number of employees in the state. (Most of these employers are also the 25 largest companies by revenue as well.)

2. **Top 5 Regional Employer**—One of the five largest companies by number of employees in each of the six non–Twin Cities regions in the state as defined by the Department of Trade and Economic Development. (The Twin Cities have been excluded as a region because the top five employers in this region are also the top five employers for the entire state.) (See Figure 6, a state map from Minnesota's Department of Trade and Economic Development.) This criterion is aimed at ensuring that our collecting efforts are not narrowly focused on the Twin Cities (where most of the state's largest employers are located), but actively target major employers in the state's regional economies as well.

3. **No Other Repository**—No other repository exists that has this business as part of its collecting policy and is capable of preserving that business' records. Normally, if such a repository exists, we would expect to refer the collection there.

4. **Within Costs Of Retention Limits**—This factor looks at an estimate of the potential costs to the repository for storage, processing, conservation, and reference, as defined by Boles and Young[76] and determines whether or not they exceed the repository's financial capabilities. Because of MHS's size, costs of retention are only a consideration if we would normally consider documenting a company at level A. Indeed, because of the possible long-term strain on the institution, our institutional policy requires likely accessions of 500

or more cubic feet be approved by the director, and accessions of 2000 or more cubic feet be approved by our board.

5. **First Offer**—In the case of a Top 5 Regional Employer, this is the first time that a collection from this type of business has been offered to MHS from any region of the state. For example, a bank collection from southwestern Minnesota is offered to us, and we have not received any other regional bank collections. In the case of an industry leader, first offer refers to the first time that a collection from this type of business anywhere in the state has been offered to MHS. Our goal here is to reduce what Ericson has labeled the "cow-shaped milk jugs" syndrome[77] of accepting numerous examples of the same type of company for no better reason than that they are offered. Such redundancy may be defensible for top priority industries (such as, in the past, lumber and the railroads), because multiple examples permit the documentation of the industry—not just specific companies—in depth. For lower priority sectors, "society must regard such broadness of spirit as profligacy, if not outright idiocy."[78]

6. **Minority Business**—A business that is owned wholly or in majority part by a member(s) of a minority group as is commonly determined by race, religion, gender, sexual orientation, or disability. This decision point was included because of MHS's broad commitment to diversify our collections.

7. **Corpus**—An exceptional body of records (in terms of completeness, substantiveness, and long duration) exists for this business, and therefore, its inherent value may somewhat transcend the value of the business itself.

8. **State or Local Identification**—A particular business that is strongly identified with the state, or is unique to the state, and is therefore expected to be part of the repository's collections (e.g. the world's largest hockey stick manufacturer is a small Minnesota company that would not be a priority for MHS if not for its strong state and local identification). This criterion is an attempt to account for the iconographic or symbolic importance of certain businesses above and beyond their actual economic status.

9. **Politically Important**—MHS administration, board members, or influential outside actors request that a particular business be documented. (This obviously comes in subtle and not-so-subtle forms, from direct requests to casual comments from board members about good friends wanting to "do something" about their company's historical records.) This criterion is borrowed from the module "Implications of the Appraisal Recommendation" by Boles and Young. In his book, Boles makes political considerations a "kicker," a factor that in and of itself can override all other components in the

taxonomy.[79] That political considerations can and do override curatorial appraisal decisions is unarguable. However, unlike the
Boles model, which implicitly assumes an all or nothing scenario
(you either take the collection or you do not), our method is based
on a wider range of outcomes and thus political factors need not
have so dramatic an influence. For example, political pressure may
convert a Do Not Collect company into a tier one company at level
A documentation, but circumstances would more likely turn a Do
Not Collect into a level D or C documentation—or a level B documentation into a level A. The method is intended, indeed, to give
curators an additional means of blunting the effect of political pressure, both because a formal priority ranking is somewhat harder
even for board members to override than an informal collecting
policy and because the curator can agree to accept some documentation without agreeing to acquire dozens, hundreds, or thousands
of cubic feet even from a large corporation.

10. **Illustrative Example**—A business that will serve to illustrate all
    businesses within its industry. For instance, one video store is col-
    lected to illustrate the kinds of records generated by all video
    stores. This factor is designed to account for those ubiquitous small
    businesses that are common to almost every community but do not
    individually distinguish themselves in any particular way. Like first
    offer, this criterion is an attempt to preclude accepting numerous
    examples of the same type of business, although its effectiveness
    will depend in part on what level of SIC category the example
    illustrates.

11. **Industry Leader**—Leadership in an industry will be defined by
    size of employment in the state. In the event of similar employment
    figures for more than one company, sales figures, production,
    awards, etc., may be used to distinguish leadership. Sectors some-
    times lump together very disparate industries, some of which might
    be completely ignored if there was not some explicit recognition of
    them.

Having defined priority sectors, documentation levels, and decision points, we linked these three together into a series of flow charts
(see Flow Charts). Since the priority assigned to a sector should have
great influence on the level of documentation of the businesses within
the sector, each priority sector had to have its own set of flow charts.

Although the flow charts for the different priority sectors are similar in the decision points encountered, the outcomes are rather different. Six of the decision points were chosen to be starting points in
the following descending order: Top 25 Employer, Top 5 Regional
Employer, Industry Leader, State or Local Identification, Illustrative

Figure 5. Decision Points

"Decision points," or criteria for refining prioritization within tiers. Some of these criteria are the same as those used for the creation of tiers; however, when applied within tiers, they relate to individual companies rather than to industrial sectors.

Number of employees—overall in region, or within industry

Gross revenue—overall in region, or within industry

Capitalization—overall in region, or within industry

Illustrative example

First offer—whether or not your repository already has a collection from a similar company

Other repository—whether or not an appropriate amount of documentation already exists for a similar company in the repository or in another local repository (including a local corporate archives)

Minority ownership

State or local identification—whether or not the particular company is closely associated in the popular mind with the state or county doing the documenting

Cost of retention—whether or not the repository has the resources to accept a particular level of documentation from the company (the record universe at large corporations may place beyond the resources of a repository to accept the level of documentation the model would otherwise suggest)

Corpus—a set of records so complete and/or substantive that they become more important than the particular status of the company that created them

Missing corpus—if a business has destroyed most or all of its important records, a repository may not wish to take "the leavings"

Political considerations—does the repository director or someone on the board have an active interest in seeing the company documented, or documented to a certain level

Age of company

Example, and Politically Important. Thus, a business under consideration for documentation would first be placed in its appropriate priority sector. Then it would be plugged into the flow chart by going through the above series of starting points. If a particular business were a Top 25 Employer, then one would proceed through a series of decision points to reach an outcome, the documentation level. If the business is not a Top 25 Employer, one would proceed down to the next level (Top 5 Regional Employer) and so on until reaching the appropriate starting point in the flow chart. Each starting point is followed by a unique set of decision points and outcomes. For instance,

**Figure 6. Minnesota Department of Trade and Economic
Development State Map Divided Into Regions**

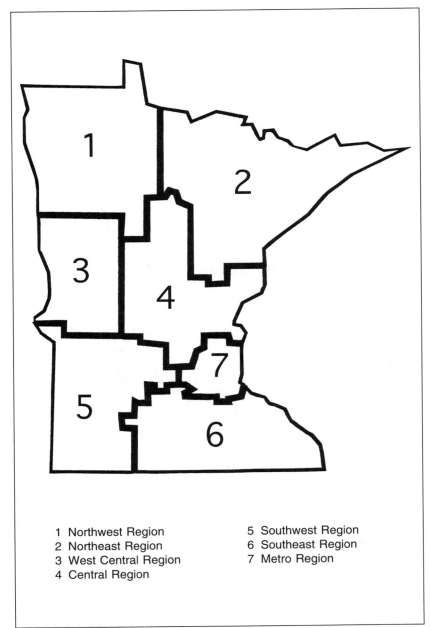

1 Northwest Region   5 Southwest Region
2 Northeast Region   6 Southeast Region
3 West Central Region   7 Metro Region
4 Central Region

if a Priority Sector 1 business is a Top 25 Employer, then the next decision point is No Other Repository. If the answer is false, then the outcome is Do Not Collect. If the answer is true, then the next decision point is Within Costs of Retention Limits. A false answer here results in a level B documentation level. A true answer results in a level A documentation level. A slightly different scenario is played out if the prospective business is from Priority Sector 4. The starting point and the first decision point remain the same. However, the next decision point encountered upon receiving a true answer to No Other Repository is First Offer. A false answer leads to documentation level C, whereas a true answer leads to Within Costs of Retention Limits. A false answer elicits a documentation level B and a true answer, a documentation level A.

Needless to say, not all eventualities can or should be built into these flow charts. Hence, we also articulated some broad assumptions that underlie the use of the method. First, the tension existing when those businesses offering to donate records are not the businesses the society most wants to document is impossible to fully explicate in a model. Generally, within any priority tier, the method suggests that documentation will be fuller for businesses that employ the most people. If a smaller company of the same type offers to donate records, before the records of the largest employer have been acquired, the question becomes, Should MHS document the smaller employer to the higher level simply because the records have been offered? Normally, the answer will be "no," and MHS staff will instead work to acquire the records of the larger employer. However, when it is known that the larger employer has its own archives, has not retained records to support the appropriate level of documentation, or has clearly and unequivocally refused to donate records, then the smaller employer would be documented to the higher level.

Second, the method overall is meant to be a solicitation tool in several ways. It defines those sectors and businesses that should be actively solicited. Of course, prioritizing a company is no guarantee that the company will donate records. However, the method is intended to free staff resources to solicit and follow up with targeted companies (thus increasing the chances of success), by reducing the amount of staff time spent responding to "walk-ins" and to extensive surveys and appraisals of lower priority businesses. Generally, if limited staff resources required delaying or refusing work on one company in favor of another, the company in the higher tier would take precedence. The method should also assist MHS's efforts to convince reluctant but important businesses to donate records, by representing a formal and professional approach to documenting business. In this last regard, the method should help signify in intellectual terms what the Minnesota History Center signifies in physical terms—strength, expertise, stability.

Third, decisions to take records from a business may legitimately be made for reasons other than the desire to document the business itself. For example, a bank that would normally be documented at level D—or not at all—might have commissioned, for a promotion campaign, excellent photos of the business districts of the towns in which it had branches. In this instance documentation of the business itself would not normally include photos (except possibly for one or two of the bank itself), but the promotion photos in this case might be acquired on their own merits as excellent documentation of the community. Another example: the CEO of a firm maintained, as part of the company records, the files of a statewide industry trade group he founded and led for many years; regardless of what—if any—records might be acquired to document the business itself, the trade group files may be acquired. The point at which an awareness of the social history potential of business records gives way to appraising records created by business purely for their social history (or other) value is admittedly a murky one.[80]

Finally, and most importantly, the method is not meant to be mechanistically determinative. That is, it will be rare that a company can be plugged in to the flow chart and the repository's acquisition attitude toward that company determined precisely at the other end. Why, then, go through the motions at all? Following the general premises of pragmatism, the method is meant to define an orientation toward a specific business, not a precise directive. As we have said, many factors can influence the exact functions to be documented or the specific records to be acquired. Two tier 2, level B businesses may not be documented exactly the same; but the approach toward a tier 4, level D business will widely differ from that toward a tier 2, level B business. In addition, the exercise of running a business through the flow chart will often prompt questions the answers to which are not immediately clear—the result will be internal discussion and possibly redefinition or refinement of the model. To take one example, an independent bookstore (merchandising sector, tier 2) closed recently in St. Paul after 18 years in business. The store was owned by a woman, was an anchor for a retail neighborhood and well known in the city. Its documentation level would vary from Do Not Collect to level B, depending upon whether it was defined as a minority business, an industry leader, and/or as having state or local identification. Staff discussion ensued concerning whether the industry we were considering was bookstores or independent bookstores, what constituted "local" identification, should age be a factor in the process, whether women were a minority of independent retail business owners, and how did this bookstore compare (in number of employees, age, and renown) to its major independent competitor. Further research indicated that the closed store was not the oldest, largest, or best known independent bookstore (much less the largest bookstore) in the city. The discussion among the staff about how to apply these categories in this instance likely had as much long-term value as the final decision itself. The goal of the method is to make acquisition more rational and thoughtful, not to give easy answers to difficult questions.

As with every other stage in our approach, the specific decision points adopted by another repository would likely be different, and there is no magic involved in the reduction of the method to a flow chart, either. Our hypothetical special subject repository may not need decision points at all, if it is simply going to make priority rankings based on gross revenue within a single industry. On the other hand, it could decide that below the top ten companies one or two additional measures—minority ownership and evidence of technical innovation—will come into play in prioritization. The county historical society may wish to make the age of the business the only other criteria, in addition to employment size, that it considers when making decisions about solicitation and documentation level. Conversely, its decision tree may be even more complex than ours. Fewer decision points may permit construction of a matrix rather than a flow chart, or obviate the need for any graphic representation of the process. Again, the mission, resources, and environment that define the repository will define this stage of the method.

Crucial to the development of the model was continual testing on existing business collections and on companies from which we had not yet collected records. As noted in the case of the St. Paul bookstore, these real-life examples enabled us to reengineer and fine tune the model to more accurately reflect the collecting reality at MHS. In addition, the process of running a business through the flow charts made us confront the possibilities that certain businesses would be documented to a greater or lesser degree than our more traditional response might have produced. As noted above, it has been an all too common approach for us at MHS to collect some or all of the records of any businesses that were closing. We have been good practioners of the reactive custodial approach to manuscripts and archives, rushing out to appraise the records of virtually any old or reasonably well-known business that closed—or any business (even new and unknown) that approached us with a donation offer. Such firmly grounded tradition and emotional attachment to it will not easily give way to this new method.[81]

That transition is beginning. We have applied the model in several instances, ranging from a small, but fairly old, Minneapolis greenhouse that was going out of business to one of the nation's largest sugar producers and major employer in west central Minnesota. In the former case, the model clearly indicated that we would not collect records from this business, although our past practice and tradition very likely would have led us to just the opposite conclusion. In the case of the sugar producer the model just as clearly indicated that this is a documentation level A company, the same conclusion we reached over 15 years ago when we collected the earliest records of this company. For other companies that have donated records in the past, the model could just as easily lead us to new levels of documentation, either greater or lesser. For instance, a small gear manufacturing company from which we collected virtually all records 20 years ago would not warrant documentation at all in our model today. However, because of our past relationship with this company, our response is likely to be that we will continue to accept records from it if offered, but only at a level D.

We will also use the model to reappraise current holdings of twentieth-century businesses.[82] We believe that our goal of improving documentation of business in Minnesota is just as valid for existing collections—if applied carefully and thoughtfully—as it is for businesses yet to be collected. For example, the further back in time we look at a business, the more we will have to adjust prioritization within the model to reflect the economy, the extant documentation, and its identification with Minnesota during that earlier time period. This will likely mean confronting some hard choices about some of our business collections that are now chiefly made up of detailed accounting records or "historical collections." Yet, a rational documentation process such as the Minnesota Method demands no less of us.

Updating

Since the Minnesota Method is designed to account for a variety of factors in the collection development and appraisal process, including repository mission, existing collections, clientele, and the like, it must be regularly updated to remain viable. We suggest that each of the steps in the model be reviewed at least every three to seven years. While broad institutional mission is not likely to change, surely collections, the economic landscape, and possibly users will have changed enough such that some reorientation of priorities will need to take place. There is obviously a tension here between how often a repository should review this process in order to remain current with the changes and how often it is practical to expect to be able to do it. The manuscripts curators on the MHS advisory committee who will have to carry out such a review pushed for a period of every seven to ten years, while those on the committee concerned with the model's potential lack of flexibility to deal with change pushed for two to three years. In the end we settled for a middle ground of formal review every five years. For a special subject repository collecting businesses in a rapidly changing industrial sector the review of the model may need to take place every other year. For a county historical society whose local economy is fairly stable and unchanging, a review once every 10 years may be often enough. But no matter which end of the spectrum a repository chooses, if it fails to review the steps and structures of the model, a new tradition of collecting will develop that is no better than the traditions of the past the method sought to replace.

Broader Horizons?

In the end, we have some hope that our method will serve the work of most collecting repositories engaged in documenting twentieth-century, U.S. business. The method was developed for collecting repositories rather than corporate archives (although it may have some applicability within an institutional archives). As the hypothetical examples were intended to illustrate, we think that the method will work well for both general and special subject repositories, for both large and small repositories. Obviously, only successful implementation in other settings will demonstrate the worth of this method. Moreover, only the structural outline or skeleton of the method is meant to be transferrable from one repository to another; every repository setting will flesh out the content and practice of the method to suit its peculiar needs.

Notwithstanding the fact that the method has no greater ambition than to assist with acquisition decisions for repositories collecting twentieth-century, U.S. business records, the possibility of broader applications has not entirely escaped us. For collecting repositories the three classes of records creators most analogous to businesses in terms of their variety, number, importance, and capacity to generate large quantities of archival material would be nonprofit organizations, churches, and labor unions.

Technically, nonprofit status characterizes everything from political parties to churches, most hospitals to most cultural institutions (many establishments in the latter two categories are included, however, in the U.S. census bureau's definition of "business"). While a precise definition would be critical, for the moment we are considering nonprofits to encompass such groups as professional organizations and garden clubs, amateur athletic leagues and study clubs, nonpartisan citizen's leagues and fraternal organizations. Even at the state level (leaving aside all the local chapters affiliated with state organizations) there are hundreds of such groups, and their relative priority (either compared amongst themselves or against other genres of records creators) from a historical standpoint is hardly obvious. Churches, a type of nonprofit organization, are so varied and numerous in and of themselves as to warrant their own category. Labor unions, while not so varied and numerous as businesses, are too varied and numerous for most repositories to document all of them in a given locality.

Within each of the three categories there are subdivisions that can be considered analogous to a business sector and could be ranked based on factors such as number of members, rate of growth, identification with the locality, age, and so on. For nonprofits, the sectors might be sets of organizations such as fraternal or athletic. For churches, denominations may make useful sectors, and labor unions are already demarcated by federation and then by work. Within each of these three categories, as with business, there are individual organizations (or, for churches, denominations) that maintain their own archives at the national and/or state level, but to one extent or another all three categories are also collected by manuscript repositories; an approach similar to the Minnesota Method may, therefore, be workable.

It is also possible that the method may have application within an institutional archives setting. It requires some temerity to suggest this, since functional analysis, documentation planning, and macroappraisal have focused so intensely on appraisal in an institution and our method was an attempt to fashion an approach for collecting repositories. Still, in part because the method has borrowed from institutional appraisal literature, it may be relevant as a synthesis if nothing else. The method can be used in addressing, to some extent, two of the principal weaknesses of functional analysis and documentation planning—the absence of prioritizing among functions within an institution, and the assumption that every institution of a particular type should document itself the same way. Macroappraisal confronts the issue of prioritization most clearly but so far seems to suggest that prioritization is more a matter of which records creators are first scheduled rather than the relative level of documentation to be sought.[83] Applied within an institution, our method would encourage ranking functions (or structures) based on criteria peculiar to the archives and its parent institution and using that ranking to make decisions about what will be documented more or less substantially, or not at all. For example, an archives directly subordinate to the marketing department of a consumer products company may (assuming most of its users were from marketing) devote enormous resources to documenting marketing functions, ad campaigns, packaging, trademarks, and the like, and little or no resources to documenting labor-management relations, production, or finance.

In point of fact, this type of prioritization already occurs in corporate archives because corporate archivists (more keenly than many of their colleagues, perhaps) are aware of who butters their bread and on which side it is buttered.[84] Hence, archives lodged in public relations offices may tend to acquire very different sets of records than archives lodged in legal departments. But functional analysis posits a core collection necessary to adequately document a business, whereas our method embraces a much more subjective and relativistic attitude and asks simply that choices be conscious and well considered. Whether this offers any true advantage to corporate archivists is of course for them to judge.

Conclusion

One might argue that our method, applied within an institution, would become merely a rationalization for inadequate archival work. Indeed, the same accusation can—and undoubtedly will—be made of the method as it applies to repositories. Such a criticism would stem from a fundamental disagreement over the nature and goal of archival work. It is a disagreement over whether appraisal criteria can be objective or must be subjective, over whether acquisition strategy should have as its goal some universal, "adequate" documentation of U.S. society or simply the making of relatively rational and efficient choices in the face of overwhelming opportunities.

A decade ago, in a seminal article that introduced documentation strategy to the wider archival community, Helen Samuels wrote:

> Hard questions must be asked about what will and what will not be documented. How many institutions or events must be documented and what will be left undocumented? How much information is enough? . . . [D]ocumentation strategies must help archivists select those institutions and events to be documented and examine the ramifications of leaving others undocumented. . . . Is it necessary to preserve the records of every labor union and every railroad? If not, will any evidence remain of the labor unions and railroads whose records are not preserved? Is it an all-or-nothing question? Twentieth-century institutions are documented in a variety of published sources. . . . Can archivists evaluate these published sources and then recommend a minimum archival record that should be preserved for each union and railroad?[85]

To a very large degree, these are the same questions we asked as the advisory group assembled at MHS to consider the problem of documenting business in Minnesota. But a small, essential difference separates our questions and thus our answers from those Samuels posed. "How much information is enough?," she asks. We believe that is the archival equivalent to the question, How many angels can dance on the head of a pin? Because the answer is subject to no objective parameters, there can be no objective answer. Samuels and others suggest that "adequacy of documentation" (that is, enough information) is not only knowable and definable, but reachable by following documentation strategy; a definition by consensus is presumed to arise out of the documentation group. On the contrary, each constituency represented in that group has a different set of priorities; the sum total of all their definitions of adequacy is guaranteed to be more than the resources available at the repository.[86] We would argue, rather, that adequacy of documentation, like the existence, size, and the terpsichorean preferences of angels, falls in the realm of faith and spirit, not in the realm of logic or even consensus. Worse, as musing on pinheads diverted theologians from grappling with matters of faith more relevant to the daily lives of their parishioners, the shibboleth of adequacy of documentation diverts energy and attention from acquiring better documentation and making better use of repository resources.[87]

As pragmatists, our goal is to improve documentation of twentieth-century business within the constraints of an overwhelming records universe, unrealistically grand repository goals and all too realistically limited resources, and an imperfect but educated understanding of the needs of varied users. To do this we have suggested analyzing extant documentation, considering the documentary universe as a whole before appraising its parts, establishing criteria (not universal, but variable, based on the goals and resources of any given repository) for prioritizing solicitation and accessions, and defining (when necessary) graduated levels of records appraisal to reflect the fact that some individual companies will have to be more thoroughly documented than others. As Edmund Burke said about economy, the true goal of archives "consists not in saving but selection";[88] we have tried to produce a pragmatic method of selection to better document the economy. This may seem a modest goal on paper, but in practice it seems ambitious enough.

Figure 7. Flow Charts

Priority Sector 1

Agriculture/Food Products & Services
Health Care
Medical Technology

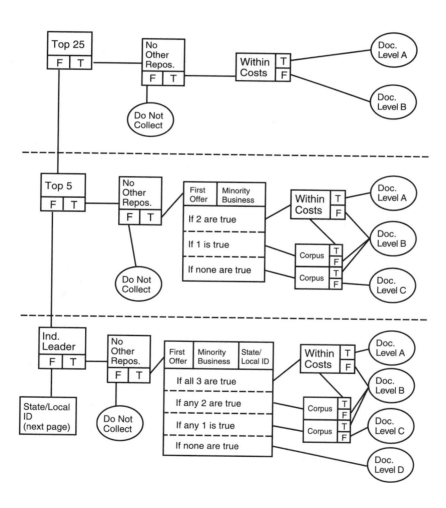

Figure 7. Cont.

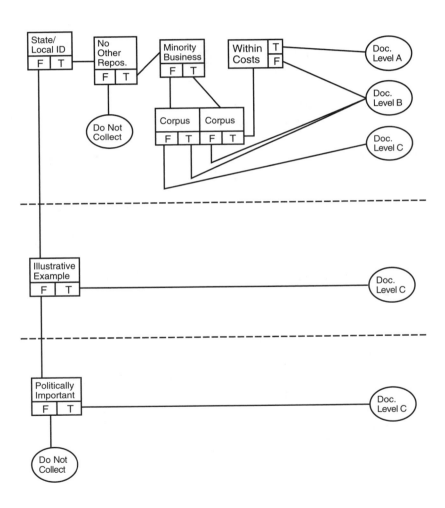

Priority Sector 1

Agriculture/Food Products & Services
Health Care
Medical Technology

Figure 7. Cont.

Priority Sector 2

Associations
Merchandising
Transportation

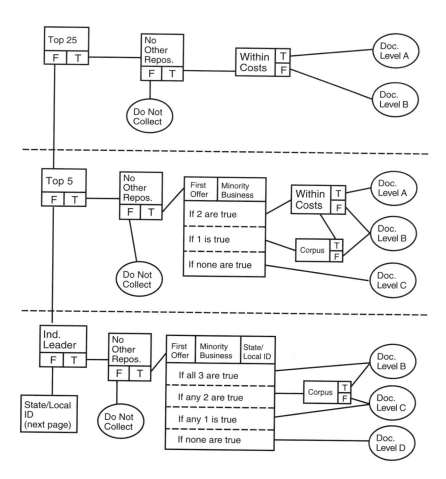

Figure 7. Cont.

Priority Sector 2

Associations
Merchandising
Transportation

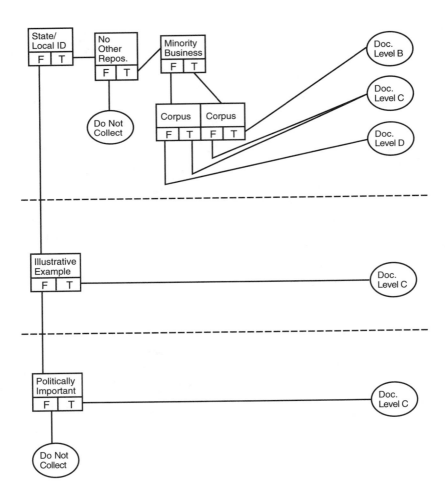

Figure 7. Cont.

Priority Sector 3

Entertainment/Sports   Manufacturing (non-Ag)
Financial Products/Services   Media
Hospitality/Tourism   Service
Lumber/Forest Products

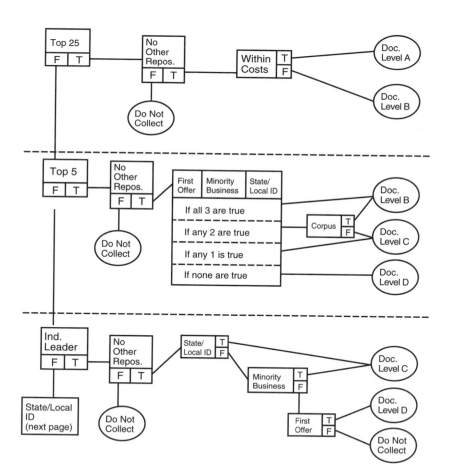

Figure 7. Cont.

Priority Sector 3

Entertainment/Sports   Manufacturing (non-Ag)
Financial Products/Services   Media
Hospitality/Tourism   Service
Lumber/Forest Products

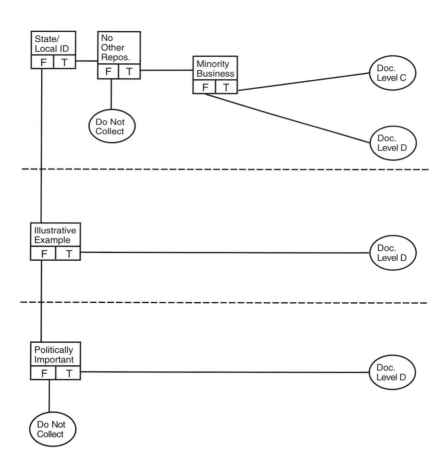

Figure 7. Cont.

Priority Sector 4

Legal   Real Estate/Land Development
Mining   Utilities
Other Technology

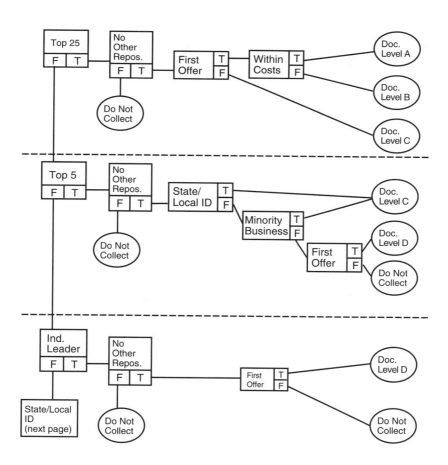

Figure 7. Cont.

Priority Sector 4

Legal   Real Estate/Land Development
Mining   Utilities
Other Technology

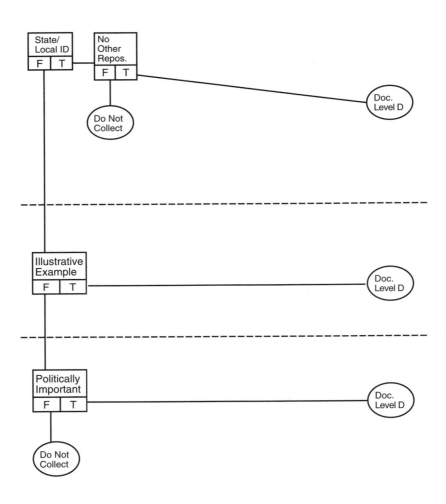

Endnotes

1. William James, "What Pragmatism Means," in *Pragmatism and Four Essays from The Meaning of Truth*, Meridian Edition (1974), 47.

2. See, for example, Luciana Duranti, "The Concept of Appraisal and Archival Theory," *American Archivist* 57, no. 2 (1994): 338–41; Terry Eastwood, "From Practice to Theory: Fundamentals US Style," *Archivaria* 39 (spring 1995): 137–50.

3. Timothy L. Ericson, "At the 'rim of creative dissatisfaction': Archivists and Acquisition Development," *Archivaria* 33 (winter 1991/92): 69. Ericson is here updating Gerald Ham's analysis of the weaknesses of archivists' custodial mindset in, "Archival Strategies for the Post-Custodial Era," *American Archivist* 44, no. 3 (1981): 207, 210. Ericson's assessment—and ours—is that, 15 years after Ham's critique, a custodial mentality still reins.

4. While the method itself is the result of consensus among an advisory group assembled by the Minnesota Historical Society (see note 47, below), only the two authors—not the rest of the advisory group nor the Minnesota Historical Society generally—are responsible for the entirety of the opinions, explications, and interpretations offered in this essay. Even less responsible for any flaws in this essay, but contributing generously and substantially to its merits (if any), are several colleagues who volunteered to read and criticize various early drafts: Bruce Bruemmer, Timothy Ericson, Laura Graedel, Dennis Meissner, Kathryn Neal, James O'Toole, Richard Pifer, Christine Weideman, Joel Wurl. Thanks, too, to Frank Boles who, as formal commentator on our paper at the Records of American Business symposium in April 1996, tried (to no avail) to show us the error of our ways.

5. Ericson, "At the 'rim of creative dissatisfaction,' " 66.

6. Few companies, apparently, bother to keep track of how many records they create in a year. Even those with records management departments actually see only a fraction of the records created, since many records are destroyed on the basis of general schedules. It is instructive to note, however, that the Great Northern and Northern Pacific Railroads, which could afford to store unusually large percentages of their total documentary record, had accumulated roughly 750,000 cubic feet of records in a little less than a century of operation. The quantity judged to have enduring value was a staggering 15,000 cubic feet. The records center at 3M, a Fortune 500 company headquartered in St. Paul, Minnesota, holds 20,000 cubic feet of records, most of which turn over every 3 to 10 years.

7. Bureau of the Census, *Statistical Abstract of the United States, 111th Edition* (Washington, D.C., 1991), 533.

8. Angelika Menne-Haritz, "Appraisal or Documentation: Can we Appraise Archives by Selecting Content?" *American Archivist* 57, no. 3 (1994): 530.

9. Nor are corporate archivists even agreed upon whether their first duty is to assemble generic archives or to focus on the immediate needs of their primary clients in the company. For the situation in corporate archives, see Douglas A.

Bakken, "Corporate Archives Today," *American Archivist* 45, no. 3 (1982): 279–281; Philip F. Mooney, "Commentary I," *American Archivist* 45, no. 3 (1982): 291–293; Eldon Frost, "A Weak Link in the Chain: Records Scheduling as a Source of Archival Acquisition," *Archivaria* 33 (winter 1991/92): 80–83; Duncan McDowall, " 'Wonderful Things': History, Business, and Archives Look to the Future," *American Archivist* 56:2 (1993): 350–54; Elizabeth Adkins, "The Development of Business Archives in the United State," unpublished paper (1996), 10–13.

10. Arthur H. Cole, "Business Manuscripts: A Pressing Problem" *Journal of Economic History* 5 (May 1945): 44.

11. Nicholas Burkel's 1980 survey of university manuscripts repositories discovered that more than half the respondents collected business records, and most of those "indicated that their records reflected small companies—those with fewer than 100 employees. Slightly more reported that most of their records were of privately held companies," rather than publicly held. Burckel, "Business Archives in a University Setting: Status and Prospect," *College and Research Libraries* 41, no. 3 (May 1980), 229.

A much smaller and more random survey of collecting repositories conducted in 1996 tends to confirm this situation. Of the 14 respondents, all collected at least some business records. However, the type of business most represented in the collections was "general stores." Moreover, when asked to compare the evolution of dominant industries in their state or region to the evolution of their collections, virtually all repositories reported that their collections much more accurately reflected the economy of the nineteenth century (and to some extent the early twentieth century) than that of the mid- to late-twentieth century. Finally, only four of the repositories held collections from more than two active firms. The survey, prepared jointly by MHS and the Hagley, was mailed to 33 repositories. As of the end of February 1996, 14 had been returned. Such a small sample group was selected because we were frankly unsure whether the survey instrument was too demanding to elicit any response. It was demanding but apparently considered important. As one repondent noted: "This survey was time consuming but well worth the effort, as it made me think seriously about collection development issues and helped to identify important trends here." If time and funds permit, we will send the same survey to a larger group of respositories this summer. In the meantime, we are grateful to the following individuals and institutions for taking the time to complete the survey: Michael Kohl, Clemson University Libraries Special Collections; Kermit J. Pike, Western Reserve Historical Society Library; Nancy Boothe, Rice University Special Collections; Harold L. Miller, State Historical Society of Wisconsin; Rick Stattler, Rhode Island Historical Society Library; Elizabeth Knowlton, Georgia Department of Archives and History; Rob Spindler, Arizona State University Department of Archives and Manuscripts; William Myers, Ohio Historical Society; Nancy Bartlett, University of Michigan Bentley Historical Library; Karyl Winn, University of Washington Libraries; Peter Blodgett, Huntington Library; Saundra Taylor, Indiana University Lilly Library; Mark Shelstad, University of Wyoming American Heritage Center; Terry Abraham, University of Idaho Special Collections.

12. Francis X. Blouin, Jr., "An Agenda for the Appraisal of Business Records," in *Archival Choices: Managing the Historical Record in an Age of Abundance* , ed. Nancy E. Peace (Lexington, Mass.: Lexington Books, 1984) 69.

13. Bureau of the Census, "Minnesota," in *County Business Patterns* (Washington, D.C., 1992), 3.

14. The two curators are the authors of this essay. They are two of seven professionals who staff the society's Acquisition and Curatorial Department. Of the other five, only the sound and visual curator (Bonnie Wilson) and the department head (James Fogerty) are involved in any way with business records or any other major manuscripts collections. (The other curators are responsible for art, maps, and books.) In addition, the staff of five curators in the society's Museum Collections Department are involved in appraising three-dimensional artifacts of all types, including business products, packaging, and advertising. MHS also employs four manuscripts processors.

15. From the mission statement of Minnesota Historical Society, "Collections Management Policy," 1994.

16. Ericson, " 'At the rim of creative dissatisfaction,' " 72.

17. Minnesota has eight representatives in addition to its two senators, so we were able to define a goal of acquiring papers from all of Minnesota's congressional delegation and concentrate our deliberations largely on what series of papers from a congressional office had the most historical value. In addition, all congressional offices generate essentially the same records (though they do not organize them alike), so we could adopt essentially a single blueprint for appraising records series. But the universe of businesses in Minnesota is far too vast for the society to hope or want to acquire records of all companies, and different types of businesses (not to mention different size businesses) generate very different types and quantities of records. For details of the congressional records project, see Mark A. Greene, "Appraisal of Congressional Records at the Minnesota Historical Society: A Case Study," *Archival Issues* 19, no. 1 (1994): 31–43.

18. F. Gerald Ham, "The Archival Edge," *American Archivist* 38, no. 1 (January 1975): 5.

19. Frank Boles, "Mix Two Parts Interest to One Part Information and Appraise Until Done: Understanding Contemporary Record Selection Processes," *American Archivist* 50 (summer 1987): 357.

20. Ericson, " 'At the rim of creative dissatisfaction,' " 67.

21. See, for example, Linda J. Henry, "Collecting Policies of Special Subject Repositories, *American Archivist* 43, no. 1 (1980): 57–63; Edmund Berkeley, Jr., "Appraisal of Current Private Papers and Collection Development," *Midwestern Archivist* 6, no. 1 (1981): 59–71; Gloria A. Thompson, "From Profile to Policy: A Minnesota Historical Society Case Study in Collection Development," *Midwestern Archivist* 8, no. 2 (1983): 21–39; Faye Phillips, "Developing Collecting Policies for Manuscript Collections," *American Archivist* 47, no. 1 (1984): 30–42; Jutta Reed-Scott, "Collection Management Strategies for Archivists," *American Archivist*

47, no. 1 (1984): 23–29; Judith E. Endelman, "Looking Backward to Plan for the Future: Collection Analysis for Manuscript Repositories," *American Archivist* 50, no. 3 (1987): 340–55; David P. Gray, "A Technique for Manuscript Collection Development Analysis," *Midwestern Archivist* 12, no. 2 (1987): 91–103; Christine Weideman, "A New Map for Field Work: The Impact of Collections Analysis on the Bentley Historical Library," *American Archivist* 54, no. 1 (1991): 54–61.

22. Frank Boles and Julia Marks Young, "Exploring the Black Box: The Appraisal of University Administrative Records," *American Archivist*, 48, no. 2 (1985): 121–40. Of course, Boles and Young were not attempting to define both a documentation approach and a records appraisal approach, only the latter. Also see Frank Boles, *Archival Appraisal* (New York: Neal-Schuman Publishers Inc., 1991), and Robert Sink, "Appraisal: The Process of Choice," *American Archivist* 53, no. 3 (1990), 452–58.

23. Ericson, " 'At the rim of creative dissatisfaction,' " 68.

24. For expositions of functional analysis, see Bruce Bruemmer and Sheldon Hochheiser, *The High-Technology Company: An Historical Research and Archival Guide* (Minneapolis: Charles Babbage Institute, 1989); Helen W. Samuels, "Improving Our Disposition: Documentation Strategy," *Archivaria* 33 (winter 1991/92): 125–40 and *Varsity Letters: Documenting Modern Colleges and Universities* (Metuchen, N.J.: Society of American Archivists and Scarecrow Press, Inc., 1992); Joan D. Krizack, "Hospital Documentation Planning: The Concept and the Context," *American Archivist*, 56, no. 1 (1993): 16–34; Krizack, ed., *Documentation Planning for the U.S. Health Care System* (Baltimore: Johns Hopkins University Press, 1994).

25. Krizack (introduction and "Documentation Planning and Case Study," in *Documentation Planning for the U.S. Health Care System*) coins the phrase "documentation plan" to suggest a middle ground between functional analysis and documentation strategy. She does make an important contribution by insisting that even institutional archivists need to ask hard questions about the context of their institution in the larger universe of similar institutions, and she is cognizant of the fact that the level of resources available will shape the actual size and content of a specific archives (xv). However, Krizack defines extensive "core documentation" for a hospital—we count 61 series in her list (213–14)—and refers to this as "the minimum documentation that should be preserved" (211–218); she thereby connotes a universal objective criteria for defining archival value. Samuels (*Varsity Letters*), too, claims that she is presenting guidelines rather than directives (24) but expects that every function of an institution must be documented (though not to the same level), and her many sections on the "Documentation" of various functions use the adverb *must* with remarkable frequency. Bruemmer and Hochheiser, *The High Technology Company* , does a better job of distinguishing between observations of types of documentation and recommendation for retention and does apply functional analysis in a collection repository setting. However, the underlying assumption in such an application is that the company in question deserves the fullest possible documentation. While in such circumstances functional analysis is of definite benefit to repositories, such circumstances are rare, as we try to suggest more fully below.

26. See Maynard J. Brichford, "Preservation of Business Records," *History News* 2, no. 10 (August 1956): 77; Ralph W. Hidy, "Business Archives: Introductory Remarks," *American Archivist* 29, no. 1 (1966): 33–5; Ralph M. Hower, *The Preservation of Business Records*, (Boston: Business Historical Society, Inc., 1941); Arthur M. Johnson, "Identification of Business Records for Permanent Preservation," *American Archivist* 24, no. 3 (1961): 329–332; Jack King, "Collecting Business Records," *American Archivist* 27 (July 1964): 387–390; David Lewis, "Appraisal Criteria for Retention and Disposal of Business Records," *American Archivist* 32, no. 1 (1960): 21–24; Robert W. Lovett, "Of Manuscripts and Archives," *Special Libraries* (October 1973): 415–418. John C. Rumm, looking at business records from the less traditional perspective of a labor historian, does not so much disagree with the records preservation demands of business historians as wish to add to their list payrolls, discipline records, time and attendance sheets, and other employee records. John C. Rumm, "Working Through the Records: Using Business Records to Study Workers and the Management of Labour," *Archivaria* 27 (winter 1988/89): 67–96.

27. See Richard Brown, "Records Acquisition Strategy and its Theoretical Foundation: The Case for a Concept of Archival Hermeneutics," *Archivaria* 33 (winter 1991/92): 34–56; Terry Cook, "Mind Over Matter: Toward a New Theory of Archival Appraisal," in *The Archival Imagination: Essays in Honour Of Hugh Taylor*, ed. Barbara L. Craig (Ottawa: Association of Canadian Archivists, 1992), 38–70; Bruce Wilson, "Systematic Appraisal of the Records of the Government of Canada at the National Archives of Canada," *Archivaria* 38 (fall 1994): 218–31. Barbara Reed, "Appraisal and Disposal," in *Keeping Archives*, 2d ed., ed. Judith Ellis (Port Melbourne, 1993), 196–98, provides an interesting comparison of functional analysis and macroappraisal as two sides of the same coin, though Terry Cook, "Documentation Strategy," *Archivaria* 34 (summer 1992): 186–88, would seem to disagree.

28. Terry Cook, "Documentation Strategy," 187.

29. Eastwood presents two very similar forms of the same argument in, "Towards a Social Theory of Appraisal," in Craig, ed., *Archival Imagination*, 71–89, and "How Goes it with Appraisal?" *Archivaria* 36 (Autumn 1993): 111–121. The quotes and analysis that follow are drawn equally from the two essays. The argument that use should be a criteria in appraisal has a long history in archival literature, going at least as far back as G. Philip Bauer's writings in the 1940s, up through Maynard Brichford's appraisal manual for SAA in the 1970s, and on through Leonard Rapport's article on reappraisal in the early 1980s. (For summaries of this literature, see Boles, *Archival Appraisal*, 2–10 and F. Gerald Ham, *Selecting and Appraising Archives and Manuscripts* (Chicago: Society of American Archivists, 1993), 7–14, 91–94. Indeed, in "The Role of Use in Defining Archival Practice and Principles: A Research Agenda for the Availability and Use of Records," *American Archivist* 51, nos. 1, 2 (1988): 74–86, Lawrence Dowler argued ahead of Eastwood that "use, rather than the form of the material, is the basis on which archival practice and theory ought to be constructed" (74).

30. In addition to Dowler, "The Role of Use," and the accompanying commentaries by Jacqueline Goggin (87–90) and Anne R. Kenney (91–95), articles that have

called for better understanding of users include Paul Conway, "Research Use in Presidential Libraries: A User Survey," *Midwestern Archivist* 11, no. 1 (1986): 35–56; William J. Maher, "The Use of User Studies," *Midwestern Archivist* 11, no. 1 (1986): 15–26; Jacqueline Goggin, "The Indirect Approach: A Study of Scholarly Users of Black and Women's Organizational Records in the Library of Congress Manuscript Division," *Midwestern Archivist* 11, no. 1 (1986): 57–67; William L. Joyce, "Archivists and Research Use," *American Archivist* 47, no. 2 (1984): 124–33; Elsie T. Freeman, "In the Eye of the Beholder: Archives Administration from the User's Point of View," *American Archivist* 47, no. 2 (1984): 111–23; Bruce W. Dearstyne, "What is the *Use* of Archives? A Challenge for the Profession," *American Archivist* 50, no. 1 (1987): 76–87.

31. Standing with Bauer, Brichford, Rapport, and Dowler in urging that secondary research use be an important criteria in appraisal are Goggin, Freeman, and Joyce; see also Elizabeth Lockwood, " 'Imponderable Matters': The Influence of New Trends in Social History on Appraisal at the National Archives," *American Archivist* 53, no. 3 (1990): 394–405; and Frederic Miller, "Use, Appraisal, and Research: A Case Study of Social History," *American Archivist* 49, no. 4 (1986): 371–92. Largely rejecting the idea that use is important in appraisal, and thus hewing more closely to the European tradition articulated by Hilary Jenkinson in the early part of this century (for a summary of Jenkinson's views, see Duranti, "The Concept of Appraisal and Archival Theory," 334–39) are Roy C. Turnbaugh, "Archival Mission and User Studies," *Midwestern Archivist* 11, no. 1 (1986): 27–33, and "Plowing the Sea: Appraising Public Records in an Ahistorical Culture," *American Archivist* 53, no. 3 (1990): 562–65; Karen Benedict, "Invitation to a Bonfire: Reappraisal and Deaccessioning of Records as Collection Management Tools in an Archives—A Reply to Leonard Rapport," *American Archivist* 47, no. 1 (1984): 43–49.

32. These are hardly hypothetical questions. A few years ago at MHS we confronted a vocal group of amateur railroad history researchers who vigorously petitioned us to acquire the roughly 1,000 cubic feet of Authorization for Expenditures (AFEs) for the Soo Line Railroad as part of the historical records of the company. That these researchers would have used these records (evidence of financial transactions from purchasing shovels to building marshalling yards) there was no doubt (in their minds or ours); the use would have been almost entirely for the purposes of constructing scale models and exhaustive histories of the equipment and supplies used by the Soo Line. In essence we turned our back on this use and suggested to the railroad that the AFEs be destroyed. Did we thus support or undermine the "preservation of a lasting cultural memory" (Eastwood, "A Social Theory of Appraisal," 84)? If we had accessioned the AFEs and thus been forced to turn away (for lack of shelf space, if nothing else) the 50 cubic feet of records from the early venture capital firm First Midwest Capital—use of which was far less certain—would we have been closer or farther from adequately fulfilling Eastwood's charge to be "documentary memory keeper and facilitator" for Minnesota (80)? The request by labor historians (see Rumm, "Working Through the Records") for preservation of detailed employee records poses exactly the same dilemma—accepting such records from the Soo Line (or any other company) de-

creases the records we can accept from other companies or nonbusiness sources. Whose use needs take priority and why?

33. Oddly, having claimed empirical objectivity for his theory, Eastwood rejects the notion of asserting "ideal values, universal values of the preservation of archives" and refuses to permit demonstrable lack of use to validate reappraisal.

34. Larry Hackman and Joan Warnow-Blewett, "The Documentation Strategy Process: A Model and a Case Study," *American Archivist* 50 (winter 1987): 29–47, presents a case study of the American Institute of Physics efforts. Also, e-mail from Joan Warnow-Blewett to the authors, April 16, 1996.

35. The broader documentation strategy appears to begin with Helen Willa Samuels, "Who Controls the Past," *American Archivist* 49 (spring 1986): 109–24. See also Hackman and Blewett, 12–29; Philip N. Alexander and Helen W. Samuels, "The Roots of 128: A Hypothetical Documentation Strategy," *American Archivist* 50 (fall 1987): 518–31; Richard J. Cox and Helen W. Samuels, "The Archivist's First Responsibility: A Research Agenda to Improve the Identification and Retention of Records of Enduring Value," accompanied by Frank Boles and Frank G. Burke, "Commentary," *American Archivist* 51, nos. 1, 2 (1988): 28–51; Karen Dawley Paul, project director, *The Documentation of Congress* (Washington, D.C.: United States Senate Historical Office, 1993); Richard J. Cox, "The Documentation Strategy and Archival Appraisal Principles: A Different Perspective," *Archivaria* 38 (fall 1994): 11–36; see, too, the interesting gloss in Reed, "Appraisal and Disposal," 199. In addition to the critiques offered by Burke and Boles, an excellent analysis of documentation strategy is Terry Abraham, "Collection Policy or Documentation Strategy: Theory and Practice," *American Archivist* 54, no. 1 (1991): 44–53; from an entirely different perspective, attacking documentation strategy for focusing too much on content and not enough on context, see Cook, "Documentation Strategy," 181–89.

36. Samuels, "Improving Our Disposition," 126.

37. Cox, "The Documentation Strategy," 21; emphasis in original. If appraisal criteria is universal, it is curious that proponents of documentation strategy themselves are not agreed whether the documentation plan should focus on functional issues or searches for specific record types. In this regard, contrast Hackman and Warnow-Blewett, "The Documentation Strategy Process," 24, with Alexander and Samuels, "The Roots of 128," 526.

38. In particular, see Samuels, "Who Controls the Past?" 110–13; Hackman and Warnow-Blewett, "The Documentation Strategy Process," 45–46; Cox, "The Documentation Strategy," 21–22.

39. For the best critique to date of the interinstitutional philosophy behind documentation strategy, see Boles "Mix Two Parts," 363–67 and Boles, *Archival Appraisal*, 103. Even Karen Dawly Paul, project director, *The Documentation of Congress*, which has been cited by proponents of documentation strategy as a stellar example, does nothing if not exemplify the limitations of documentation strategy. The project brought a team together to identify a documentation area, the extant

resources, and the documentary needs, but there is no structure (or funding) for implementing the strategy or for measuring or reviewing progress that may occur through the voluntary and uncoordinated efforts of interested repositories. So too the very Records of American Business project, for which this essay was written, substantiates rather than diminishes this criticism of documentation strategy. The RAB is meant to raise awareness among creators, users, and archivists about the importance of business records; the RAB itself is collaborative. But this thin veneer of documentation strategy belies the fact that there is not—there cannot be—the type of ongoing, formal, directive work that is at the heart of documentation strategy. A documentation strategy for American business is flatly impossible without a massive infusion of external resources that would dwarf the generous NEH grant that made the RAB itself possible.

40. Max J. Evans, "The Visible Hand: Creating a Practical Mechanism for Cooperative Appraisal," *Midwestern Archivist* 11, no. 1 (1986): 7–13, called for a concrete system of sharing appraisal decisions among state government archives to promote better informed, and possibly more consistent, appraisal decisions for similar records. This proposal is being put into practice by the Intergovernmental Cooperative Appraisal Program (ICAP), which has already completed a pilot project involving state and federal appraisal and retention of Food Stamp records (*Food Stamp Records Project: Final Report*, March 1995). In some respects, our proposal, too, calls for a more visible hand, in that it requests (though does not require) overt cooperation and sharing of collecting decisions among repositories. Still, our method assumes less formal cooperation than either documentation strategy or the ICAP.

41. Margaret Hedstrom, "New Appraisal Techniques: The Effect of Theory on Practice," *Provenance* 7, no. 2 (fall 1989): 2.

42. Barbara L. Craig, "The Acts of the Appraisers: The Context, the Plan and the Record," *Archivaria* 34 (summer 1992): 176.

43. Ibid, 177.

44. Conversely, as Terry Eastwood has said, "theory in the archivist's hands is only so good as it serves the work." Terry Eastwood, "Towards a Social Theory of Appraisal," 72. This sentiment is pragmatic to the core: "truth in our ideas means their power to 'work'" (James, "What Pragmatism Means," 49). Though the distinction between method and theory may be an important one, the distinction remains blurry (at least to us) within the archival canon. We have avoided attempting to categorize other appraisal writing as "theory" or "method" for this reason, and because the distinction does not seem to have a great deal of pragmatic value for our daily work. For similar reasons we would not embrace John Roberts' iconoclastic rejection of archival theory per se—see his "Archival Theory: Much Ado about Shelving," *American Archivist* 50 (winter 1987): 66–74, and "Archival Theory: Myth or Banality?" *American Archivist* 53 (winter 1990): 110–20—but we agree with his general concern that too much archival writing is distant from the practical reality of working archivists.

45. Craig, "The Acts of the Appraisers," 178.

46. Cook, "Mind Over Matter," 47.

47. The Advisory Group consisted of the following MHS personnel: Todd Daniels-Howell, Acquisitions and Curatorial; Mark Greene, Acquisitions and Curatorial; James Fogerty, Acquisitions and Curatorial (chair); Lydia Lucas, Processing; Dennis Meissner, Processing; Hampton Smith, Reference; Duane Swanson, State Archives; Bonnie Wilson, Acquisitions and Curatorial; and Bruce Bruemmer, of the Charles Babbage Institute, was the "outside" member of the group.

48. Minnesota Historical Society, "Collections Management Policy," September 1994.

49. Phillips, "Developing Collecting Policies," 31–32, 34–35; Reed-Scott, "Collection Management Strategies," 25. Also see Philip P. Mason, "The Ethics of Collecting," *Georgia Archive* 5 (winter 1977): 45–47.

50. The improvement of business documentation overall does not depend solely on expanding quantity of records preserved, and business archives are not necessarily better from the standpoint of documentary quality than business collections in repositories. However, as we argue below, the quality of a collection is very much in the eye of the beholder, and what is certain is that repositories have no realistic expectation of being able to solicit or acquire records from all businesses; therefore there is no objective good to be gained by repositories failing to support the creation of business archives.

51. Endelman, "Collection Analysis," 341; Thompson, "From Profile to Policy," 31, 34.

52. See Thompson, "From Profile to Policy," 21–39, for an overview of the MHS collection analysis. That project compiled a list of collection strengths and weaknesses based on tallies of title, subject orientation, size, and date span. In turn these strengths and weaknesses were used subjectively to establish high, medium, and low priorities for future manuscript collecting. Within these priorities 6 business sectors were included: statewide farmers' organizations (high); twentieth-century transportation (high); nineteenth- and twentieth-century flour milling (high); health maintenance organizations (medium); advertising, printing, and publishing (low); and, twentieth-century merchandising (low). However, the collection analysis had identified 13 more business sectors that were not prioritized at all.

53. Gray reports that the State Archives and Historical Research Library of the State Historical Society of North Dakota did indeed record form of material—along with many other categories—when a collection analysis of its manuscripts holdings was done in 1986. The North Dakota analysis also recorded evaluations of such things as "information level" of each collection, "completeness," and "relationship of the generator" and then derived a "research value rating" for each collection on a scale of one to four (four being strongest). While there were many factors not judged that might have been in determining research value (for example, relationship to published, government, or three-dimensional collections), this analysis is the only one recorded in the archival literature to attempt a systematic (though of course not objective) evaluation of collection quality. The North Dakota manuscripts holdings are relatively small by state historical society standards

(1,700 cu. ft. in 1986), which made this more detailed approach feasible. The analysis falters badly when it attempts to evaluate the overall quality of documentation within 20 topical areas because it takes the highly subjective research value ratings for each collection and uses a complex mathematical formula to derive topical quality in ratios figured to three decimal points. The illusion of precision and objectivity undermines an otherwise laudable effort.

54. The categories were:
- Agriculture Related Businesses
- Associations
- Construction
- Entertainment
- Finance/Banking/Insurance
- Fur Trade
- Health Care
- Hotels/Restaurants
- Legal
- Lumber/Logging
- Merchandising
- Manufacturing (nonagricultural)
- Mining
- Printing/Publishing
- Real Estate
- Service
- Tourism
- Transportation
- Utilities

The complete list of collections, organized by category, is available upon request from: Minnesota Historical Society, 345 Kellogg Blvd. West, St. Paul, MN 55102-1906.

55. Weideman, "A New Map," 54–60; Thompson, "From Profile to Policy," 34–39.

56. Samuels, "Improving Our Disposition," 126.

57. For another, though hypothetical, example of applying the framework of documentation strategy in a single institution and without a documentation group, see Mark A. Greene, "Store Wars: Some Thought on the Strategy and Tactics of Documenting Small Businesses," *Midwestern Archivist* 16, no. 2 (1991): 93–94.

58. Maygene F. Daniels, "Records Appraisal and Disposition," in *Managing Archives and Archival Institutions*, ed. James Gregory Bradsher (Chicago: University of Chicago Press, 1988), 59.

59. As part of the NEH grant that funded this symposium, the Hagley Museum and Library oversaw a citation analysis project to provide substantive information about the type of records used and types of businesses studied in scholarly articles over the past 25 years. The results of that survey are reported in Michael Nash's chapter, "Business History and Archival Practice," elsewhere in this book. In short, the Hagley study found a clear indication that archival sources are not used

very heavily by business historians compared to internal and external publications; the archival source cited far more frequently than any other was executive correspondence. Two studies of other topical research areas provide additional suggestions of the extent to which scholars are likely to make extensive use of available primary sources: Goggin, "The Indirect Approach," provides evidence that even when primary sources are available, scholars prefer to rely on secondary sources; Miller, "Use, Appraisal and Research," provides evidence supporting the opposite conclusion. Miller's study suggests, however, that financial records and executive correspondence are the least utilized series among "organizational records," and that economic and business history articles made among the least use of primary sources of any kind (382–85).

60. Blouin, "An Agenda," 70, points out that "the methodological cleavage between business and economic history" has undermined any former agreement on the relative value of sources. Additional evidence of the diversity of scholarly opinion can be found in the exchange chronicled in Laurence Kipp, ed. *Source Materials for Business History* (Cambridge: Harvard University Press, 1967), 1–39, among historians and archivists during a colloquium at Harvard, and the articles cited in note 26, above. Also, see the summary of views from the society's consultants, below.

61. The survey of manuscripts repositories undertaken by the society and the Hagley (see note 13) reported that scholars were never higher than second in rankings of user groups; genealogists were first at seven institutions and students first at the other seven; scholars ranked from second to fourth (out of seven). None of the repositories had a means of identifying which groups used business records most. MHS is currently undertaking an internal study, based on matching call slips with researcher registration forms, to gain some insight into who is using what records from which business collections. In the end, appraising creators is intertwined with appraising users. While the actual role of use in appraisal remains problematic, all repositories must be sensitive to the priorities of their constituents or face becoming irrelevant or nonexistent. Fortunately, appraising users does not have to be so black and white as appraising creators, because to some extent different users can and do want similar records from similar companies (see below).

62. Clear evidence that this is true can be found in the unpublished results of a survey undertaken by Elizabeth Adkins in 1992, which showed that over a third of corporate archives do not permit outside research access at all, and of those that do permit it the median number of outside researchers they serve annually is nine.

63. During separate meetings in May 1993 the advisory group spoke with George Green, professor of history specializing in business history, at the University of Minnesota, and with business archivists Karen Benedict (a consultant) and Elizabeth Adkins (Kraft General Foods). In June, the advisory group met with JoAnne Yates, an economic historian from MIT who was in the Twin Cities doing research at the Babbage Institute. In September, during the annual meeting of the Society of American Archivists, the advisory group met with: Michael Nash, Hagley Museum; Phil Mooney, Coca-Cola Archives; Claudette John, CIGNA Archives; Jonathan Dembo, Cincinnati Historical Society. Later that month, the group also met

with corporate archivists Jean Toll (General Mills) and Liz Johnson (H. B. Fuller). In November, the advisory group met with Andrew Van de Ven, a professor of organizational dynamics at the Carlson School of Management, University of Minnesota. Notes from all these discussions are in the authors' possession, but we have not ascribed specific opinions to specific individuals here because their conversations with us were in the context of what was then an internal rather than a public process. JoAnne Yates, however, has published "Internal Communication Systems in American Business Structure: A Framework to Aid in Appraisal," *American Archivist* 48, no. 2 (spring 1985): 141–58.

64. Bruemmer and Hochheiser, *The High-Technology Company*, 127–29; Krizack, introduction to *Documentation Planning*, 10–11; Adkins, "The Development of Business Archives," 13; Paul C. Lasewicz, "Strangers in a Strange Land: Archival Opportunities in a Multinational Corporation," *Archival Issues* 19, no. 2 (1994): 131–36; McDowall, " 'Wonderful Things,' " 351–54.

65. Cook, "Mind Over Matter," 53. On the other hand, macroappraisal presumes that a deep analysis of all individual records-creating entities will occur prior to prioritization. In our method such creator-by-creator analysis—of the hundreds, thousands, and tens of thousands of businesses in a county, state, or region— preceding prioritization is impossible. More plausible would be an intense analysis of every business sector or subsector, but this probably is a practical possibility only for special subject repositories. A repository dedicated to documenting the history of computing, for instance, could and probably would be able to insist that its staff develop a formidable understanding of the computer industry. But most regional, state, and local repositories, charged with documenting most or all social, political, economic, and cultural facets of their geographic region will not have staff who are expert on any facet of business history. These are repositories with staff who are jacks of all trades, masters of none. Again, this is not to say that a certain level of research and understanding are not absolutely necessary, only that the level of research and understanding envisioned by macroappraisal is not assumed by our method.

66. The internal sources included the 1980 and 1993 MHS collection analyses and an early 1993 Manuscript section draft list of business collection priorities. External sources included the Pioneer Press Business Twin Cities 100, 1994, and *Corporate Report Minnesota*, 1993, as well as the Standard Industrial Classification in U.S. Dept. of Commerce, Economics and Statistics Administration, Bureau of the Census, *1992 Industry and Product Classification Manual* (Washington, D.C.: GPO, 1992).

67. These are: Agriculture/Food Products & Services (including Farming, Food Products, and Agricultural Manufacturing); Associations; Entertainment/Sports; Financial Products/Services; Health Care; Hospitality/Tourism; Legal; Lumber/Forest Products; Merchandising; Manufacturing (nonagricultural); Media - General (including Media, Publishing/Printing, Advertising, and Public Relations); Medical Technology; Mining; Other Technology; Real Estate/Land Development; Service; Transportation; Utilities.

68. Lathrop, "Toward a National Collecting Policy for Business History: The View From Baker Library," *Business History Review* 62 (spring 1988): 142.

69. Moreover, depending upon the particular application of the method, the sector prioritization is not so draconian—not so black and white—as it may first appear. In the MHS model, for example, large businesses would be solicited for substantial documentation even if the sector in which they fit is a low priority (see Figure 7, below). Thus even though Financial Products is in a priority 3 tier, Norwest is a top-25 employer and would be considered for documentation level A. Similarly, while the MHS model emphasizes large companies, there are decision points (see pages 194–96, below) that turn our attention to representative small businesses, to minority-owned businesses, and similar groups. What remains true, however, is that in the MHS model banks (and real estate companies) will receive much less attention than they have in the past, and more staff time will be directed toward soliciting records of the health care industry.

70. Theodore Schellenberg, *Modern Archives: Principles and Techniques* (Chicago: University of Chicago Press, 1956), 149.

71. Ericson, " 'At the rim of creative dissatisfaction,' " 68.

72. This is, in part, an attempt to mitigate the isolation of our format-specific collecting efforts. See Terry Cook, "The Tyranny of the Medium: A Comment on 'Total Archives,' " in *Canadian Archival Studies and the Rediscovery of Provenance*, ed. Tom Nesmith (Metuchen, N.J.: Society of American Archivists, Association of Canadian Archivists, and Scarecrow Press, Inc., 1993), 403–413.

73. As John Roberts notes, "until there is an Esperanto of bureaucratic organization and an Esperanto of records creation, there cannot be a canon of content-based archival thought that would be an accurate guide to anything" ("Archival Theory: Myth or Banality?" 117). Still, without defining broad orientations ahead of time we would be back to having to appraise every records series of every business; our method is an attempt to mediate between the nuances of record context and the limitations of staff time.

74. Brichford made a similar observation 40 years ago: "In selecting business records for preservation, the potential users should be considered.... In many instances, they are likely to be amateur historians more accustomed to newspaper accounts than piles of correspondence, legalistic documents, books of entry with vague column headings and streamlined forms." "Preservation of Business Records," 77.

75. This was especially true of Van de Ven's research on organizational change in the health care industry. For additional evidence of the extensive use made of annual reports by scholars, see Martha Lightwood, "Corporation Documents - Sources of Business History," *Special Libraries* (May–June 1966): 336–337. Distinguished historian Arthur Cole asked 50 years ago whether it really made sense for the Baker Library to devote 324 feet of stack space to records of the Slater textile company that had been used nine times in 14 years, as opposed to filling that space with books or other types of sources that would undoubtedly be used more frequently ("Business Manuscripts," 50).

76. Boles and Young, "Exploring the Black Box," 127, 133–35.

77. As an example of archivists' tendency to thoughtlessly acquire endless sets of similar but not strictly duplicate records, Ericson quoted a critic of museum collecting policies who referred to an institution with 200 eighteenth-century, cow-shaped milk jugs " 'ranged side by side on a shelf . . . like some huge herd on a farm.' " Ericson, " 'At the rim of creative dissatisfaction,' " 70.

78. Ham, "The Archival Edge," 12.

79. Boles and Young, "Exploring the Black Box," 135, and Boles, *Archival Appraisal*, 77–78.

80. Our consulting expert George Green spoke eloquently of the social history value of certain business records. See also Thomas D. Clark, "Records of Little Businesses as Sources of Social and Economic History," *Bulletin of the Business Historical Society* 19, no. 5 (November 1945): 151–158.

81. There is more than tradition involved in the reactive approach to appraisal taken by many archives. There can be an emotional involvement in appraisal decisions that cannot be taken lightly—as was made clear to us during the MHS committee's discussion of the St. Paul bookstore. As members of society archivists can be touched by issues and events, such as the closing of a favorite business that was important to one's community. In this we fully agree with Terry Cook that "archivists are agents, conscious or unconscious, willing or unwilling, of the historical process in which they find themselves" (" 'Another Brick in the Wall': Terry Eastwood's Masonry and Archival Walls, History, and Archival Appraisal," *Archivaria* 37 [spring 1994]: 102). Nevertheless, we believe that archivists can transcend their emotional attachments at least to some degree and work toward making rational and thoughtful (though not scientific and objective) choices. Although we agree with F. Gerald Ham that appraisal is thus ultimately more an art than a science (*Selecting and Appraising Archives and Manuscripts*, 72), we heartily support Virginia Stewart's statement that, "Even an art form demands rigor, attention to detail, and some rationale for the technique" ("A Primer on Manuscript Field Work," *Midwestern Archivist* 1, no. 2 [1976]: 4).

82. Our experience with the congressional appraisal guidelines as a means to reappraisal of existing congressional collections leads us to believe that the same can be done with business collections. In 1995 MHS worked with an NHPRC/Mellon Fellow (Sushan Chin) to test the use of the congressional appraisal criteria on two collections from the 1970s. While we found that congressional offices in that decade organized and labeled their files rather differently than is usually the case today (and that, therefore, we had to perform detailed analysis of samples of every series to ensure that we knew accurately the function reflected by and the content of each series), the general guidelines proved largely applicable. Indeed, we removed 320 cubic feet from the two collections (roughly 60 percent of the total). Based on our experience last year, further reappraisal is taking place this year.

83. According to a presentation at the 1995 annual SAA meeting in Washington, D.C. by Peter Horsman of the Netherlands National Archives on the PIVOT project, the Dutch are using macroappraisal to encompass prioritization similar to that in our model, to the extent of deciding that certain government agencies will simply

not be documented. There is nothing in macroappraisal writing that rules out such ranking, but our Canadian colleagues have tended to couch prioritization in terms of what would get done later rather than what would not get done. In the real world of archival appraisal, we suggest, there is often no actual difference between putting something off and not doing it at all.

84. Elizabeth Adkins, "Business Is My Bread and Butter: Collecting Business Records Within the Corporation" (paper presented at the fall 1993 Midwest Archives Conference, Davenport, Iowa, October 1993) 2–5. This is not something spoken much about in the literature, but it was the gist of what we learned from our corporate archivist consultants.

85. Samuels, "Who Controls the Past," 120–21.

86. Even Hans Booms, who first argued for an appraisal strategy that relied on a documentation group (he called it an advisory board), has acknowledged that "the experience over twenty years of working with historical advisory boards and commissions convinced me that it is virtually impossible to bring any significant number of academic historians to a consensus.... I also learned to regard with skepticism the advice of the officials who produced the records...." See his "Uberlieferungsbildung: Keeping Archives as a Social and Political Activity," *Archivaria* 33 (winter 1991/92): 29.

87. In 1992, NHPRC director Gerald George asked in an *Annotation* column, "how do we measure progress in documenting history?" (Gerald George, "Maybe the Entire Field is Naked," *Annotation* 20 [March 1992]: 5). We would respond by saying that the extent to which we are "adequately" documenting American history is unfathomable, not simply because we cannot possibly determine how many significant records are being produced and compare that to how many are being preserved, but because we have no reasonable definition of what a "significant" record is. Regarding, for example, the Soo Line records referred to previously, we are prepared to say only that refusing the AFEs, and accessioning the records of First Midwest, made our documentation of Minnesota business more balanced, that it was a more efficient use of limited resources, and that it was, therefore, the better choice in the circumstances. The result will be that those who would have had us save the AFEs will still probably use the Soo Line records we did accession; we will also be able to serve the probably smaller set of researchers who will be interested in studying early venture capital firms. This is one, very imperfect way to measure progress in documenting history: by being able to demonstrate that more and more people are making more and more use of the material we do acquire.

88. Burke, *Letter to a Noble Lord*, 1796, quoted in John Bartlett, comp., *Familiar Quotations*, 16th ed., ed. Justin Kaplan (Boston: Little Brown and Company, 1992).

8

Blown to Bits:
Electronic Records, Archivy,
and the Corporation

Richard J. Cox

Introduction

Archivists concerned about the implications of the increasing reliance upon electronic records by corporations could ask themselves: Will the continued embracing of electronic information technology by American businesses substantially affect an archival mission stressing the acquisition of records that seems to have been less than successful before the serious impact of this technology? In other words, I am doubtful that the archival community has adequately supported the preservation of archival records in corporations, that the profession has not been very successful in convincing American capitalists of why their archival records are important to them and to society.[1] I am also doubtful that archivists have provided a suitable strategy or path to the documentation of American business, the rise of the corporation, the changing nature of corporations in the transition from a national economy to a global economy, or any other aspect of American business we could consider that occurred *before* the shifting from paper to electronic information and recordkeeping systems.

What is my evidence for this? What has any of this to do with electronic records? And, you might ask, why would I start with such a negative perspective?

The evidence is overwhelming that we have not done well with the management of American business archives. While there are only a few essays that suggest the reasons for such problems, most notably JoAnne Yates' exploration of the appraisal of corporate records,[2] we also need to consider the lack of development of business archives, the severance of corporate records management and archives administration, and the paucity of writing about the value of archival records for the American business.[3] These kinds of matters, coupled with the archival profession's seemingly primary interest in collecting business archives rather than nurturing institutional archives in businesses, suggest that the roots of the problems in appraising and managing business electronic records extend back long before the advent of electronic recordkeeping and information systems. An essay by Christopher Hives, now a decade old, suggested that it was in the late 1930s that we discovered that the collecting of business records was not a satisfactory solution;[4] yet, here we are, still primarily focused on collecting.

Consider, for example, what seems to pass for the appraisal of business records in this country. The American archival profession has stressed the acquisition or collecting of business records for historical research purposes rather than the nurturing of institutional archives in American corporations for administrative and other purposes more immediately relevant to the businesses. While the number of corporate archives may have grown, the quantity of business records accessioned into archives has probably increased at a much higher rate (or, at least, the latter seems to be the greater emphasis by the archival profession). Is this due to the focus of the archivist, or the predilection of American businesses not to favor the value of archives? In other words, is it easier to persuade businesses to dump their older records onto repositories rather than to communicate with them why archival records are valuable?

The reason, ultimately, may be academic, but the wisdom of the strategy is not so easily dismissed. This strategy may have worked when the size of American businesses was generally smaller and the quantity of their records substantially less, reducing the strain on the repository wanting to acquire the records. This strategy may have been necessary for companies that were going out of business and inclined to destroy their records, although here the question of the significance of the records and their potential use has often been swept aside by the rush to make sure that the records would not be destroyed, the archivist adopting, as Tim Ericson would say, the role of "Horatius-at-the-Bridge: the last line of defence between preservation and oblivion."[5] This strategy may have been the most utilitarian when there was no need for the archivist to justify to the creator of the records the rationale for expending money on supporting an institutional archives, but in fact could help to rid these organizations of their old stuff.[6]

I am not starting in such a negative fashion in order to present an exposé of the appraisal of American business records; in fact, I am not confident we have done a very good or consistent job in appraisal in any area.[7] Instead, I believe that the increasing dependence on electronic records via information and recordkeeping systems (the focus of my essay) renders many of the standard archival approaches obsolete while providing new opportunities and new insights for the archivist committed to documenting American business. Electronic recordkeeping systems make possible a new approach to business records management from the archival perspective that has a better chance for success because they force an end to the inadequate objective of collecting such records by established archival repositories; such collecting often has risked the integrity of the archival records because of the desire to acquire information for researchers' uses rather than evidence needed to support the corporation or for documenting its evolution and work.[8] In other words, we need to understand that the advent of the new and rapidly changing electronic information and recordkeeping systems provides the incentive for archivists to return to the appropriate mission, helping and encouraging businesses to develop their own institutional archives serving their own needs first and foremost.[9]

As the title of my essay suggests, the game has changed substantially. Our society and its institutions, including its businesses, are well on the way from a dependence on paper-based to electronic-based records systems. While the transformation is not without major organizational and societal problems, it is nonetheless true that the computer is firmly ensconced in the corporate world and that many of the resources of these institutions will be used to improve and refine (not reject) computer-run tools.[10] Archivists will need to become problem-solvers in electronic records management, rather than apologists for the good old days of paper, filing cabinets, and records cartons.

Some realities will need to be faced. It will become increasingly difficult to transfer physically electronic recordkeeping systems to archival repositories. Archivists will have to create virtual repositories through the development of policies, standards, and other gatekeeper (meaning the assumption of broader responsibilities than mere custodial ones) functions.[11] Archivists will need to stop thinking only in terms of custodianship and develop different approaches as appropriate.[12] Archivists will also need to cease thinking of corporate records as grist for the historian's mill and make, instead, new arguments in favor of evidence for the support of the corporation's ongoing work. Research will need to be done to support the development of practical methods to ensure that crucial electronic records of failed companies can be preserved. All of these issues I consider to be positive ones because they force archivists to return to their real business of managing records.

What follows is a description of how American businesses are embracing electronic information technology, then a consideration of what archivists and records managers need to do in regard to the management of electronic recordkeeping systems possessing archival value. As you will see, the considerable hype surrounding the possibilities of the use of computers has far exceeded any serious or sustained analysis of what the technology has actually supported. I begin with a description of the prediction of where American businesses are heading and then describe what seems to be happening in their present use of the technology. While we all must admit that it is difficult to determine what is going to happen with the utilization of the technology, archivists must also accept that the nature of the modern corporation and society is rapidly changing (for better or worse). Archivists will have to change their tactics as well if they really hope to identify, preserve, and make available the archival records of the postmodern corporation.

The Future Corporation

Where is the modern corporation heading in the currents caused by the Information Age? We could contemplate many predictions, but I have selected just one as an example. William J. Mitchell, a professor of architecture and dean of the School of Architecture and Planning at the Massachusetts Institute of Technology, has provided a firm and engaging prediction about technology, culture, and institutions in his recent book, *City of Bits*. Mitchell's tome is a lively discourse on where he sees our notion of community, as well as time and place, moving.

Mitchell writes that the "new virtual city becomes a kind of electronic shadow of the existing physical one. In many (though not all) cases, a citizen can choose between going to an actual public building or to the corresponding virtual one."[13] Mitchell is a determinist in that he writes with a tone of inevitability about technology's impact, or even blindness about the challenges and problems caused by the transformation, and we need to be careful of the problems of technological determinism.[14] Nevertheless, Mitchell has written the most balanced of texts predicting future society. Mitchell, as you might surmise, also has much to say about business and economic life in the new city that is relevant to our purpose at hand.

The dean of architecture chronicles the ongoing change in commerce. Record and bookstores are moving in the direction of a virtual operation through central servers producing books and records on demand or even transporting them over the network. Banking is already largely electronic: "Money is no longer bullion in a strongbox, but bits in an online database."[15] Stock trading is already being planned to be a nearly completely virtual process. Businesses have already been deeply affected by bar codes, credit cards, and cash cards: "Salesperson, customer, and product supplier no longer have to be brought together in the same spot; they just have to establish electronic contact."[16] Personally, this sounds quite a lot like my normal life already, as I increasingly make electronic purchases or shop through catalogs or over the Internet.

The office, a centerpiece of the corporation, is considered by Mitchell. At present, he regards offices as

> sites of information work—specialized places where numbers, words, and sometimes pictures are collected, stored, transformed, and disseminated. So their issue is mostly composed of desks equipped with information-handling devices (telephones, computers, fax machines, printers, file cabinets, inboxes and outboxes, and the like), meeting and conference rooms, copying centers and mailrooms, and receptions and circulation spaces.[17]

We can recognize that this is the office that cultivated the primary principles supporting records management and much of modern archives.[18] As corporations grow larger, and as various technologies and accompanying social changes make it possible for them to expand, the familiar corporate headquarters of the central skyscraper area and then the industrial park will become a part of our cityscape and landscape. Mitchell sees this as changing as well: "We are entering the era of the temporary, recombinant, virtual organization—of business arrangements that demand good computing and telecommunications environments rather than large, permanent home offices."[19] It is easy to perceive that the corporation and smaller businesses will be considerably changed in Mitchell's future world:

> So cyberspace communities—like eighteenth-century seaports, nineteenth-century railroad towns, and mid-twentieth-century motel/fast-food strips—play specialized roles within the complex new economic order that develops as a new kind of infrastructure is deployed. They are stops on the infobahn. The world's apparently insatiable greed for bits will fuel their growth, as demand for manufactured goods drove developments of earlier industrial cities and transportation centers. They will flourish as places to make bucks from bits by producing them, skimming them, stealing them, and inventing new ways to add value to them.[20]

Clearly, archivists will have different issues to contend with as they work with such "stops on the infobahn." Are archives to become such stops as well, as virtual repositories?

My own sense is that much of what Mitchell seems to be predicting is already entrenched and well under development. We are daily reminded of this in the pages of computer trade publications with their articles and advertisements of current products and devices, by the chapters of basic textbooks on business data processing, and from the writings on the technical and applied history of electronic information technology.

Again, while we must be cautious not to believe everything, archivists must also be careful not to dismiss everything, perhaps becoming forgotten or obsolete as a result. Another recent book on the city, in this case "as they are, not as they might be," suggested that our struggles to contend with the challenges of the city emanated at least partly from "our inability to anticipate the new technological and social forces that came to bear on our urban condition: the automobile, air travel, electronic communications."[21] Is there a lesson here for archivists and the users of archives?

The Past Corporation

The historical view is perhaps the most profitable in which to catch a first glimpse of the impact of the computer on the modern corporation. The computer in business has gone from a preoccupation with the most basic number crunching of data and the rawest of information (an objective of technologists for centuries before the electronic computer) to the creation of all sorts of electronic systems to control both information and records. This transition can be chronicled in the change from primitive punch cards to electronic calculating machines to electronic devices with large memories and broad computing capacities. In other words, there was a remarkably rapid change from using these machines to just solve mathematical problems to serving a wide array of business functions, even though in the 1950s many still argued that computers would not be useful to American business interests. However, labor, production, accounting, labor subdivision for control and order, measurements, and paperwork of all sorts have become dependent on the computer. By 1990 over 50 million Americans were using computers in their work, when only 20 years before that there had been 75,000 computers in all of the United States and 20 years before that only 10 computers in the country. While for the longest time, it appeared that these machines would not be supporting record systems, we now see that the advent of dependence on software rather than hardware and the growth of networked organizations has made it possible to conduct business virtually paperfree.[22] From the mainframe to the minicomputer to the personal or microcomputer is a transformation that has literally made every employee a records-gen-erating dynamo within their organizations, as well as in their personal lives and homes, posing in the process significant problems about the nature of work, individual self-worth and identity, and society.[23]

We can readily see the effect of the rapidly changing nature of information technology on the business corporation by examining any basic textbook on data processing. Thirty years ago the evidence was already substantial that computers had had a major impact on the management of organizations in such areas as purchasing, inventory control, accounting, and payroll. The focus for this change was on routine and repetitive work, and, actually, the overall impact of the technology on the organizations was not all that great in comparison to what we have witnessed in the past few years. Even in 1967, how-ever, it was determined that "perhaps the most important characteristic in the present corporate environment is the primacy of information and communication."[24] Basic textbooks were both describing the traditional office equipment, such as typewriters and calculators, and the main-frame computers that would be used for large-scale number crunching in accounting, marketing, and other related functions. Thirty years ago, these volumes were predicting the transition from data processing to information services.[25] As anyone can readily tell, information or data seems to be at the hub of concern of many corporate managers, as witnessed by the proliferation of computer magazines aimed at the business person.

The Current Corporation

Current computer magazines are mirrors for the possible and real uses of electronic information technology in the American corporation. Examining many of these magazines would have proved too daunting a task both in terms of preparation of this essay and in the summation of what this literature suggests about the management of business elec-tronic records management. The March 1996 issue of *WIRED*, a jour-nal written by technological determinists and computer enthusiasts bordering on a religious cult,[26] was a rather funky means by which to view what people were offering in terms of electronic information sys-tems. There were advertisements in *WIRED* for powerful notebooks, new workstations, computer display monitors, software promising to change the world and business, and a variety of on-line services.

The promises were dazzling. From Lotus, "it's possible to deliver information about your company and its products and services directly to millions of prospective customers." Connectix promises a "complete camera and software solution that, for under $200, turns your computer into a desktop videoconferencing workstation. Connectix VideoPhone lets you video conference and share a mark-up board. Attend meetings from home. Make office-wide presentations. Or show your ideas to your co-workers down the hall or across the country." Macromedia offers an interactive multimedia product that states that you can "author once in Macromedia Director, and you can play your productions around the world." While all this can be dismissed as advertising hype or the almost religious zeal by which some describe the information technology widgits,[27] it is obvious that the possibilities for electronic information applications are endless. It should also be obvious that the possibilities for the creation of electronic records are equally immense.

We can also acquire a sense of the modern business by considering its desire to evolve into the paperless office. The paperless office was predicted 20 years ago. Current wisdom suggests that the future office will not be paperless, but the discussion about it generally stresses the current information technology products available to the business. While the simplest view is to state that the paperless office is a myth, that paper continues to increase as a presence in the modern office,[28] it is easy to lose sight of the implications of the use of electronic information technology in the office. Some chroniclers of case studies have noted that the key to developing nearly paperless offices was "document retrieval—how each document would be coded for searches."[29] Archivists and records managers, while recognizing the importance of retrievability, would also stress that the integrity of the record is of equal importance; in other words, you need to know that what you retrieved is genuine. The emergence of a substantial legal literature on electronic recordkeeping is but one indication of the concern for the electronic record.[30] Another commentator has noted that "technology has created a paper paradox: As an explosion of information flows in bits across electronic networks, the Internet and on-line services, the ability to create low-cost, high quality, personalized paper-based documents on demand ramps up paper usage to unprecedented levels."[31] However, this observation does not answer or address the question of what is the official record, the paper or electronic version. It also does not distinguish between what is an actual record—a transaction with structure, content, and context—and what is a nonrecord of data stored together for convenience.

The less than paperless or nearly paperless office seems to suggest that powerful document servers, instead of file cabinets, will store electronically all documents (records and other data entities). Office workers will access these document servers through keyword searches or natural language processing or some other information retrieval technique and pull up all or parts of documents for consultation or reuse.[32] Without question, there is the expectation that the technology will be managed by the development of a variety of search devices; however, it is also clear that these techniques are behind the development of the technology and that they are focused on any information rather than information defined by evidence, legal, administrative, fiscal or other concerns generally most pertinent to archivists and records managers.

The present fixation seems to be on document management systems, defined as "automated systems for scanning, storing, retrieving and managing paper documents." Paper records are inputted into the systems, indexed, stored electronically, retrieved through the keywords and indexes, and outputted by reading on the computer screen, printed, or faxed. Advantages enumerated for such systems include that filing cabinets are eliminated, the documents can be accessed immediately and simultaneously by many people, and the individual documents can be made secure by the addition of passwords.[33]

Whether our corporations achieve the paperless office or not (and I certainly remain skeptical that they will) is not the kind of issue archivists or records managers should focus on. For one thing, there is the tendency to believe that there will always be paper records to manage, ignoring the fact that paper may only be a side issue and not the real concern for these organizations. Rather, archivists and records managers need to understand that the growing dependence on electronic information technology will bring with it many questions about the reliability and nature of the new recordkeeping systems. In these questions there are opportunities for archivists and records managers.

Opportunities and the Cybernetic Corporation

For most of the past 30 years in which archivists have been slowly mulling over the challenge of electronic information technology, they have tended to view the technology and its uses and problems as the primary issue. We need to remove this concern as the primary object of our thinking. Archivists had not been particularly successful with corporations long before the advent of the most complex adaptations of the computer. There were other reasons for the failure, and these reasons must not be forgotten as archivists become more technically proficient.[34]

To a certain extent, it almost seems as if the entire corporate milieu has been unkind to recordkeeping, at least as archivists likely conceive of recordkeeping. Robert Jackall's study of ethics in business corporations is just one example of the walls archivists stand in front of as they contemplate their mission. Jackall paints a portrait of a corporate fealty structure, where personal loyalties and ambitions often override all other concerns. Long-term goals, rational objectives, and even legal and administrative common sense are pushed aside in favor of getting ahead. Personal and corporate success are all that matter. While Jackall does not discuss in great detail the nature of corporate recordkeeping, he does make a passing reference to it that suggests that recordkeeping is not favored because it implies a regularity and strictures that can stand in the way of getting ahead: "even where one can follow a paper trail, most written documents in the corporate world constitute simply official versions of reality that often bear little resemblance to the tangled, ambiguous, and verbally negotiated transactions that they purportedly represent. As a result, whatever meaningful tracking does take place occurs within managers' cognitive maps of their world, which, of course, are constantly changing and subject to retrospective interpretation and reinterpretation."[35] Seen in this light, corporate politics are more important than most other issues that the archivist or records manager might be interested in. John Frohnmayer's memoir of his turbulent tenure as chairman of the National Endowment for the Arts from 1989 to 1992 provides the most fitting summary of this: "I understand but cannot embrace politics. Politics is governed by pragmatism; whatever works is wise and right, and the end of accumulating power justifies the means of getting there. In the world of litigation, from which I had come, the rules of evidence and procedure, as well as some unwritten rules of civility, generally prevail."[36] As archivists should also be concerned with evidence and the orderly nature of records and recordkeeping systems, it is no wonder that they often bristle or weary at the thought of working in corporate and political cultures.

All of this sounds extremely pessimistic. However, there is a bright spot in the transformation of American businesses by the use of electronic recordkeeping and information systems. The American model for the administration of electronic records is that "any business entity may, if it desires, utilize electronic recordkeeping as long as its practices and records meet certain prescribed conditions. . . . All that is required is that a taxpayer be able to demonstrate that its system satisfies certain requirements geared towards assuring the integrity of the system and the reliability of the stored data."[37] These "certain prescribed conditions" are where archivists and records managers meet the real world.

It is relatively easy to describe the array of challenges that American businesses will continually face in their use of technology since we have the recent publication of the final report of the United States Advisory Council on the National Information Infrastructure (NII), the product of a task force asked to investigate how the use of electronic networking needs to be harnessed in order to benefit our society. After a description of all the benefits, the advisory council suggested principles for electronic commerce and issues of concern requiring continuing and future action. It noted that since "workplaces will be transformed," there will be a continuing need for new "worker training, education, and adaptation to mechanisms." Issues of "protection of intellectual property, transaction security, integrity of data, consumer protection, and privacy" will be high on the needs of all organizations and society. Government will have to work to ensure that some of these matters are worked on, by legislation, enabling competition, and research and other funding incentives.[38]

The issues should appear familiar to any professional working in managing records or, more broadly, information. Why? First of all, many of the issues really relate to basic control of information needed for the successful management of any organization, especially businesses, and these control concerns have been endemic in corporate management for generations.[39]

Second, many of these issues have been made more crucial because of the shift to electronic recordkeeping and information systems. H. Jeff Smith's study of privacy in American business, while documenting the less than satisfactory response by corporate leaders to this issue, does demonstrate that the new concern has been driven by the increasing use of the information technology.[40] Other efforts, such as one recently started by a committee of the Association for Information and Image Management International (AIIM), have focused on such matters as the basic reliability of the documents in electronic information systems.[41]

Third, and finally, such concerns as reliability and control have been (or should have been) the hallmark of the mission of both archivists and records managers. Such professionals have always been in the evidence business, although it seems as if there had been a drift by archivists to emphasizing the acquisition of materials for historians[42] and by records managers to stressing the more trendy concept of information at the expense of records.[43] It is this latter concern that returns us to what archivists must do as they manage the electronic records with archival (continuing) value produced by American businesses.

The New Paradigm for American Business Archives

The title of this essay suggests that electronic recordkeeping and information systems have blown apart the old ways of doing things. I always hesitate to suggest this, both because of the overuse of the notion of paradigms and paradigm shifts and the nostalgia that it is easy to conjure up for the old perspective about anything.[44] What follows and what concludes this essay is a description of what I believe the archivist and records manager should have always been doing in regards to the management of American corporate archives. While it is certainly technically feasible to acquire electronic records,[45] there are so many costs and other barriers to doing this as to make it not a good choice for achieving any sort of success. The real issue is related to the reasons why we want to preserve the records of American business in the first place.

Three different scenarios, the first from the perspective of the corporate archivist or records manager, the second from the vantage of the archivist at a regional or national repository with a mandate to document and collect the records of some aspect of American business, and the third reflecting on the need for certain national efforts by the archival profession, reveal something about the primary question of managing business archives. Out of these scenarios comes my suggestion for the new role of the archivist in the long-term management of American business records.[46]

The Corporate View. Inside the walls of the typical business, archivists and records managers must learn that their role is to serve business interests first and foremost. This is not to argue that archivists and their colleagues must jettison broader social objectives, ethical or moral values, or even that many businesses will not understand the value of their archival records to a wide array of scholarly disciplines and publics. However, the archivist, in managing all records, must work to demonstrate that the older records support the ongoing activity and mission of the corporation in order to stress the relevance of the records and the considerable costs in managing these records that need to be justified.

The increasing dependence on electronic recordkeeping systems should provide ample opportunity for the archivist to develop and convey this more focused and coherent message. The reasons have been hinted at already in this essay. Electronic recordkeeping systems (many of them, at least) will need to be maintained by their creators because of the technological considerations but also because many of these records and supporting systems will have ongoing value to the immediate work of the organization. (Better hardware and software, declining costs, increased memory storage and other aspects will make it desirable to maintain many more records in a much more accessible fashion.)

Archivists will need to make these new recordkeeping systems viable through more aggressive participation in their design and in the articulation of the reasons corporations need to manage records in the first place. Through the lens of a research project on recordkeeping functional requirements at my university, we have learned that all organizations are subject to a variety of external regulations and legal concerns, and that this requires many specific records or types of records to be managed in particular ways. Archivists are not antiquarians wandering the halls, probing into closets, or looking in wastecans for the miscellaneous valuable record. Archivists are, then, part of a team of systems designers working with corporate legal counsel and other administrators to facilitate the management of records with continuing value to the organization.

Now, I am not suggesting that archivists are some kind of new corporate technocrat oblivious to the traditional values and purposes of the archival profession. Indeed, in the recent work with archives and records in North America, Europe, and Australia, archivists have seemed to suggest that the value of their role lies in the assurance of accountability, corporate memory, and evidence. To accomplish this, we must be able to influence the design of recordkeeping systems to support these purposes, as well as to transform or refine our traditional functions of appraisal and description and reference as necessary (and a tremendous amount of change is needed).[47] We might need to consider that informational value is a subset of evidence. Archivists might need to embrace such approaches as macroappraisal in order to support issues of compliance as well as to support the corporation's own work.

The Regional View. As I have suggested more than once, archivists need to cease acquiring as many corporate records as possible and instead be far more strategic in their work. Macroappraisal needs to be taken on by regional repositories in order to identify the important corporations for the history of that region or because these corporations have national or international significance. However, such appraisal needs to be done not in order to acquire the actual records but in order to identify corporations that need to be nurtured to develop corporate archives. Again, how can it be otherwise? Electronic recordkeeping systems will make it difficult to acquire electronic records unless we have substantial support from the records creators or unless we want to become the equivalent of pothunters spoiling archaeological sites by taking bits and pieces of the recordkeeping systems through paper printouts and other snapshots. Who wants this stuff?

Regional repositories (all archival repositories) need to serve as repositories of last resort but only when important organizations are involved and when the records are jeopardized. Personally, I believe the great age of collecting really ended sometime before the Second World War, before the proliferation of records and the advent of new recordkeeping technologies fundamentally different from the earlier technologies. This means that we become a sort of gatekeeper to records for researchers, much like the federal and some state government information locator services are intended to be. This shifts the attention of the regional repositories from collecting to appraisal, description and access, and public advocacy.

There still remains a sense of futility in whether or not these electronic records really can be saved, which is why the first scenario is the better one. Still, there are other, broader professional objectives that the archival profession must adopt.

The National View. Archivists have not been the most effective of advocates in national policy issues or in industry and technical standards.[48] Now is the time to change this, and there is evidence that change is afoot. I mentioned the AIIM standards committee looking at the reliability of evidence. There are numerous other standards being considered or that need to be considered. The profession needs to get behind a standard that supports the maintenance of records in an electronic environment. Indeed, there are at least two suggestions on the table for this purpose.

Just as importantly, archivists need to work to achieve greater public and government awareness of the importance of records. Opportunity for this abounds everywhere, from scandals about government recordkeeping to controversy about interpretative exhibits in history museums to genuine concern about the impact of the networked information society on political structures, work, and leisure. Being policy advocates requires archivists to have a clear, understandable message that they understand as well. Instead of lamenting the end of history with some sort of impending records holocaust caused by the use of electronic systems, archivists need to be prepared to demonstrate what these systems can be made to do and to support.

Greater public understanding of the issues and the availability of appropriate national and international standards will make the work of corporate and regional archivists easier and, even, possible.

Conclusion

I started out to write one paper and I proceeded to write another. My purpose was to present my views on electronic records in businesses and the implications of such systems for archivists. I wrote less about the technology and more about attitudes and approaches by archivists and records managers. I believe this is appropriate. Educator Thomas J. Galvin, in a discussion about the impact of technology on the information professions, noted that "to center a professional curriculum on current information technology is truly to build it on sand," paying homage to the rapidity of change.[49] Likewise, describing the current state of business electronic records management would not take us very far; by the time this essay is published, the nature of that records management could have altered so greatly as to make nearly irrelevant any proposals for action based on that technology.

My point is simple. Archivists and records managers need to focus on records and recordkeeping systems. They need to assume that, increasingly, the recordkeeping systems will be electronic. They need to move from paper-based approaches to electronic ones. Furthermore, archivists and records managers need to return to their traditional role as experts on records and recordkeeping systems in order to fulfill their long-standing and important mission. Many of the challenges, then, are not represented by the technology but by ourselves.

Endnotes

1. Please notice the use of *adequately* in my statement. I am not implying that important business records have not been saved, or that there are not times when archivists have to seek to acquire such records. Rather, I am questioning whether we have been consistently successful in identifying and saving the most important records, and whether a strategy of acquisition is still relevant on the eve of the twenty-first century.

2. JoAnne Yates, "Internal Communication Systems in American Business Structures: A Framework to Aid Appraisal," *American Archivist* 48, no. 2 (1985): 141–48.

3. For example, it is difficult to find articles in business publications about archives and their value to businesses for their ongoing work. When articles are discovered, they are often written by freelance writers who stress archival records as curiosities, old stuff, or public relations devices rather than for their use to administration, accountability, evidence, or corporate memory. For some discussion of this, see the author's "What's In A Name? Archives As a Multi-Faceted Term in the Information Professions," *Records & Retrieval Report* 11 (March 1995): 1–16.

4. Christopher L. Hives, "History, Business Records, and Corporate Archives in North America," *Archivaria* 22 (summer 1986): 40–57. I believe the interest in acquisition and physical custody is evident in many of the other essays in this volume, whether written from the vantage of traditional collecting repository or institutional archives. The collecting approach is not a problem in and of itself, assuming that it is appropriate to the protection and use of the archival records in question, but collecting is not always the best or even most practical method.

5. Timothy L. Ericson, "At the 'rim of creative dissatisfaction': Archivists and Acquisition Development," *Archivaria* 33 (winter 1991/92): 68.

6. One example always comes to mind. One of the conclusions of a well-known Midwestern archives repository after completing an analysis of its archival records holdings and its mission was that it should declare that the auto industry located

in Detroit would be a priority for collecting because of the "auto industry's enormous size, its economic importance, the hostility of the industry to outside researchers, and the limited number of significant repository holdings." Judith E. Endelman, "Looking Backward to Plan for the Future: Collection Analysis for Manuscript Repositories," *American Archivist* 50, no. 3 (1987): 348. This reveals the desire to acquire records even in the face of the impossibility of doing this in any meaningful way, or when there are other better strategies.

7. Although the discussion about appraisal has matured considerably in the past decade with the writings on documentation strategies, macroappraisal, neo-Jenkinsonianism, and the recovery of the importance of records for evidence and accountability, the application of appraisal has lagged far behind. For the author's discussion about appraisal theory, see "The Documentation Strategy and Archival Appraisal Principles: A Different Perspective," *Archivaria* 38 (fall 1994): 11–36, and "The Archival Documentation Strategy: A Brief Intellectual History, 1984-1994 and Practical Description," *Janus*, forthcoming.

8. A debate has generated about this matter, emphasizing the act of bringing the records into the custody of the archives. One school of thought, built on the Jenkinsonian tradition and now championed most articulately by Luciana Duranti of the University of British Columbia, stresses that the "moral defence" of archives necessitates that the archivist have physical custody of archival records so that they may not be corrupted by the records creator or anyone else. The other school, led by David Bearman and others, argues that the protection of records can be achieved (and in the case of electronic recordkeeping systems, indeed, must be done) without the physical custody but through a variety of strategies including policies, standards, and systems design. While I have been placed within the postcustodial group, my own preference is to chart a middle ground, whereby the commonality of concern for the record and its integrity can be stressed. Compare Luciana Duranti, "The Concept of Appraisal and Archival Theory," *American Archivist* 57, no. 2 (1994): 328–344 to David Bearman, "Diplomatics, Weberian Bureaucracy, and the Management of Electronic Records in Europe and America," *American Archivist* 55, no. 1 (1992): 168–180.

9. I have described what I believe to be the essential characteristics of a business archives in "Managing Business Archives: Basic Considerations," *Records & Retrieval Report* 7 (November 1991): 1–16.

10. Thomas K. Landauer, *The Trouble with Computers: Usefulness, Usability, and Productivity* (Cambridge: MIT Press, 1995) is required reading about this, especially since many of his examples are related to records and recordkeeping systems.

11. David Bearman and Margaret Hedstrom, "Reinventing Archives for Electronic Records: Alternative Service Delivery Options," in *Electronic Records Management Program Strategies*, ed. Margaret Hedstrom, (Archives and Museum Informatics, Technical Report no. 18, Pittsburgh, 1993), 82–98; and Ann Zimmerman, "Partnerships and Opportunities: The Archival Management of Geographic Information Systems," *Archival Issues* 20, no. 1 (1995): 23–37.

12. The issue of physical custody has a long, complicated history involving ownership of public records, records captured in wartime and repatriation, replevin, legal

ownership, and so forth. While there have been many articles published on various of these topics, more work needs to be devoted to the matter of how essential physical custody is for the effective management of archival and nonarchival records. I am indebted to one of my doctoral students, Jeannette Allis Bastian, for a paper on this topic prepared for one of my spring 1996 courses.

13. William J. Mitchell, *City of Bits: Space, Place, and the Infobahn* (Cambridge: MIT Press, 1995), 126.

14. See, for example, Merritt Roe Smith and Leo Marx, eds., *Does Technology Drive History? The Dilemma of Technological Determinism* (Cambridge: MIT Press, 1994) for writings wrestling with how we need to understand technology.

15. Mitchell, *City of Bits*, 81.

16. Ibid., 89.

17. Ibid., 92.

18. My point is that the industrial age office has been what records professionals have been focused on as they have developed methods and procedures. The industrial age office is disappearing, changing into a form similar to that that predated it and that is like what most technocrats are predicting—less hierarchical, more dispersed and independent, greater reliance on individual initiative, and so forth. Refer to Vincent E. Giuliano, "The Mechanization of Office Work," *Scientific American* 247 (September 1982): 148–52, 154, 158, 160, 162–64.

19. Mitchell, *City of Bits*, 97.

20. Ibid., 138–139.

21. Witold Rybczynski, *City Life: Urban Expectations in a New World* (New York: HarperCollins, 1995), 12.

22. See Steven Lubar, *Infoculture: The Smithsonian Book of Information Age Inventions* (Boston: Houghton Mifflin, 1993), 283–400, for the most accessible account of how American businesses and organizations have used electronic information technology.

23. Such problems range from issues of efficiency and overwork to privacy to morals and ethics. The studies about such concerns could fill a bookstore, and they certainly balance in quantity and occurrence the studies predicting technology, especially the computer, as the answer to societal problems and challenges. While the public debate about these issues has raged for 20 years, archivists have been remarkably silent.

24. The quotation is from Charles R. DeCarlo, "Changes in Management Environment and Their Effect Upon Values," in *The Impact of Computers on Management*, ed. Charles A. Myers (Cambridge: MIT Press, 1967).

25. Carl Heyel, *Computers, Office Machines, and the New Information Technology* (New York: Macmillan, 1969).

26. Perhaps the best insights about this type of journal can be gleaned by reading the recent book of one of its regular columnists, Nicholas Negroponte's *Being Digital* (New York: Alfred A. Knopf, 1995). See also Douglas Rushkoff, *Cyberia: Life in the Trenches of Hyperspace* (San Francisco: HarperSanFrancisco, 1994).

27. I recommend a reading of chapter six of Langdon Winner's *The Whale and the Reactor: A Search for Limits in an Age of High Technology* (Chicago: University of Chicago Press, 1986) for an antidote to this type of thinking. My personal viewpoint is that there will be growing dependence by corporations on electronic information and recordkeeping systems, but that this change will not necessarily make the organizations better or worse (this will depend on many other factors). My perspective is simply that archivists and records managers need to be able to manage electronic recordkeeping systems.

28. See, for example, Nancy Dunn Cosgrove, "The Paperless Office: Still a Myth in the Nineties," *Office* 117 (April 1993): 25–28. The estimates of paper being produced is staggering, extending to a trillion pages a year, Thomas F. Connolly and Brian H. Kleiner, "The Paperless Office of the Future," *Logistics Information Management* 6, no. 5 (1993): 40–43.

29. James E. Hunton, "Setting Up a Paperless Office," *Journal of Accountancy* (November 1994): 78.

30. For example, in 1994 a new journal, *The EDI Law Review: Legal Aspects of Paperless Communication*, commenced publication.

31. Glenn Rifkin, "The Future of the Document," *Forbes ASAP*, October 9, 1995, 46–47.

32. David Beaver, "Pushing Beyond Paper," *MacUser* 9 (January 1993): 215–221.

33. Mitchell Jay Weiss, "The Paperless Office," *Journal of Accountancy* (November 1994): 73–76 (quotation 74).

34. Archivists must also understand that the challenges represent opportunity for new visions, methods, strategies, risk taking, and the like. In this way of thinking, I like what the dean of the University of Michigan School of Information and Library Studies has written: "we need first to remember that the word 'crisis' has its origin in the Greek word meaning decision. Similarly, the Chinese representation of the concept of crisis is a composite of two characters: the top one meaning danger and the other meaning opportunity." Daniel E. Atkins, "The Future of Libraries and Library Schools" (paper presented at the Kanazawa Institute of Technology International Roundtable for Library and Information Science, Japan, November 1995).

35. Robert Jackall, *Moral Mazes: The World of Corporate Managers* (New York: Oxford University Press, 1988), 88.

36. John Frohnmayer, *Leaving Town Alive: Confessions of an Arts Warrior* (Boston: Houghton Mifflin, 1993), 167.

37. Amelia H. Boss and Mario A. Decastro, "The Impact of Fiscal Recordkeeping Requirements on the Migration Towards Electronic Technologies: The United States Experience," *EDI Law Review* 1 (1994): 178.

38. United States Advisory Council on the National Information Infrastructure, *A Nation of Opportunity: Realizing the Promise of the Information Superhighway* (Washington, D.C., January 1996), 17–19.

39. See, for example, James R. Beniger, *The Control Revolution: Technological and Economic Origins of the Information Society* (Cambridge: Harvard University Press, 1986); Alfred Chandler, Jr., *The Visible Hand: The Managerial Revolution in American Business* (Cambridge: Belknap Press of Harvard University Press, 1977); and JoAnne Yates, *Control Through Communication: The Rise of System in American Management* (Baltimore: Johns Hopkins University Press, 1989).

40. H. Jeff Smith, *Managing Privacy: Information Technology and Corporate America* (Chapel Hill: University of North Carolina Press, 1994).

41. The first meeting of the AIIM Standards Committee C22 and its effort to develop a standard for the "Reliability of Electronic Business Information" was held on March 1, 1996. The purpose of this group is to make information maintained in electronic form as reliable as it was in paper.

42. See Terry Cook, "Electronic Records, Paper Minds: The Revolution in Information Management and Archives in the Post-Custodial and Post-Modernist Era," *Archives and Manuscripts* 22 (November 1994): 300–328.

43. Discussed in the author's "The Record: Is It Evolving?" *Records & Retrieval Report* 10 (March 1994). For a classic example of the records manager's view, see John T. Philips, "Virtual Records and Virtual Archives," *Records Management Quarterly* 28 (January 1994): 42, 44, 45, 60 in which he argues that "it is presently very difficult to describe a 'record' in many automation systems as anything other than 'an information view at a particular time' " (44).

44. For an analysis of the many differing perceptions of paradigm, refer to Paul Hoyningen-Huene, *Reconstructing Scientific Revolutions: Thomas S. Kuhn's Philosophy of Science*, trans. Alexander T. Levine (Chicago: University of Chicago, 1993). For an example of the kind of old thinking, consider Jonathan Hale's reflection on modern architecture: "The difference between our age and the past is in our way of seeing. Everywhere in the buildings of the past is relationship among parts: contrast, tension, balance. Compare the buildings of today and we see no such patterns. We see fragmentation, mismatched systems, uncertainty. This disintegration tends to produce not ugliness so much as dullness, and an impression of unreality." *The Old Way of Seeing: How Architecture Lost Its Magic (And How to Get It Back)* (Boston: Houghton Mifflin, 1994), 2. While Hale wants new architecture with traditional values and sensibilities, archivists must strive forth in a different way; archivists must seek to design approaches that protect the archival record in the midst of modern organizations that seem fragmented and uncertain.

45. See, for example, the essays by Kenneth Thibodeau describing the approach of the U.S. National Archives Center for Electronic Records in *Playing for Keeps: The Proceedings of an Electronic Records Management Conference Hosted by the Australian Archives Canberra, Australia, 8-10 November 1994*, ed. Stephen Yorke (Canberra: Australian Archives, 1995), 34–51. A close reading of the essays suggest problems with the focus of appraisal (on informational, not evidential value)

and the emphasis on data bases rather than recordkeeping systems. I think the slant is due to the emphasis on doing what is technically feasible in a traditional custodial model.

46. Most of the foundation for my thinking on this matter stems from my involvement in the project at the University of Pittsburgh to develop recordkeeping functional requirements. For information about this project, including citations to its various publications and reports and related work, visit the project's home page at http://www.lis.pitt.edu/~nhprc. Included with this web site are references to many of the recent writings on electronic records management.

47. Some critics of experts, management, and technology do as David Ehrenfeld does, worry about the "increasing habit of documenting everything." Ehrenfeld has looked at such things as the "barrage of paperwork which everyone knows is worthless; the deluge of conflicting, often arbitrary, memoranda; the insistence on accountability without any standards of reference for performance; the requirement of doing more things than are possible, some of which are in conflict with each other; and other forms of control practiced by management—create numerous double binds in the daily lives of the producer." Ehrenfeld, *Beginning Again: People and Nature in the New Millennium* (New York: Oxford University Press, 1993), 53, 58. However, the archivist and records manager should be involved in assisting the organization to be accountable through its recordkeeping without handicapping the organization with excessive rules and regulations. Being involved in the appropriate design of electronic recordkeeping systems may be one way of accomplishing this.

48. That archivists need to become active in other professional organizations is clear when examining the program of the 1996 AIIM annual meeting. Of 112 sessions, none relate to the preservation of archival records. Yet, there are sessions on "managing documents across the organization," "legal requirements for optical disk records and electronic imaging systems," "life cycle management of document-based information," the "use of electronic evidence in litigation," and "laying the foundation for the comprehensive electronic medical record."

49. Thomas J. Galvin, "Convergence or Divergence in Education for the Information Professions: An Opinion Paper," *Bulletin of the American Society for Information Science* (August–September 1995): 11.

9

Facing Reality: Oral History, Corporate Culture, and the Documentation of Business

James E. Fogerty

Preserving the history of business has always been a dicey proposition. Whether one is speaking of groups of businesses comprising an industry, a subgroup of companies within an industry, or an individual corporation, the task is not an easy one. Businesses are, by their very nature, organizations that frequently defy many of the laws of organizational structure. They range from the relatively simply (a local food store) to the immensely complex (a multibusiness multinational conglomerate). They are competitive, often secretive, and devoted (again, by their very nature) to the single-minded goal of making money. They are as well or as poorly organized as those who run them, and those individuals who do run them are seldom interested in history as such.

All of this makes the documentation of business challenging work for archivists and their clients. The comments I will make here deal primarily with American business, but in this increasingly global econ-

This article was written as a product of the author's participation in the Research Fellowship Program for the Study of Modern Archives administered by the Bentley Historical Library, University of Michigan, and funded by the Andrew W. Mellon Foundation, the Preservation and Access Program of the National Endowment for the Humanities, and the University of Michigan.

omy, the realities of documenting business are increasingly global as well. The work of documenting business has been complicated by a number of factors that go beyond the proclivities of the business people who control the corporations and the records. That work has been colored for many years by the feelings so often engendered by business—and especially by big business. The industrial age, and the consequent growth of very large business entities, led to the development of conflicting emotions about business and its place in the larger society.

On the one hand, big business successfully raised the general standard of living for vast numbers of people (in the industrialized world) by creating an increasingly mechanized production of consumer goods—thus expanding the ability of ordinary people to afford such items as automobiles, homes, and luxury goods. At the same time, the practices of business in the pursuit of profit have not always met with universal approval, and the rise of labor unions and government regulation has often pitted corporate management against popular opinion. People like the things business brings—jobs, consumer goods, and services—but also have a well-developed sense of skepticism about the motives of business people, often honed by politicians and labor leaders whose own agendas have often depended on lines drawn between their own interests and those of business.

Documenting business has thus not always proved especially rewarding to those who would practice it. Despite the cachet and legitimacy bestowed upon business history by such practitioners as Allan Nevins, Alfred Chandler, and Ralph Hidy, its practice has often received scant approval in academic circles outside major schools of business administration. Considerably greater cachet has been afforded to labor, social, and public historians who have preferred to view business as lacking in social conscience and business people as predatory. Even the decline in both the power of and public sympathy for labor unions has not greatly altered the public perception of corporations as necessary, but not trustworthy agents of private profit. That corporations have sometimes contributed to this image is indisputable, but subscription to that view by a wide majority of academics and other educators has perpetuated and enlarged that image in the public consciousness.

Documentation of business has also suffered from the dual realities of size and secrecy. Most businesses beyond the smallest generate large quantities of records, and for the very largest—and most potentially influential and interesting—companies the quantity of records generated over a single decade can be vast indeed. Furthermore, the propensity of most business people to protect their proprietary interests has led to disinterest and even hostility to the goals of archivists, historians, and their colleagues with interest in business history. Of the two issues, however, size has undoubtedly proven the most challenging.

To preserve the history of a business, someone must take responsibility for selecting, keeping, and making available the permanent records of that company. Either the company itself must form an archives to perform those functions, or an outside repository must perform them for the company. Neither option has been well used by business leaders over time. Corporations have all too often considered archives to be expensive and nonessential frills, when they have thought of them at all. Archival repositories have all too often been disconcerted by the sheer size and complexity of corporate records, and have by and large refused to venture into an activity for which they feel unprepared. Also, those repositories have often been staffed by professionals whose priorities do not always run to work with corporate records and business people.

While the 1970s and early 1980s did see growth in the number of corporate archives established or enlarged, the reality is that only a fraction of American corporations have active, professionally managed archival operations. Despite the publicity given to the best of them—such as the archives at Wells Fargo, Coca-Cola, Kraft Foods, Chase Manhattan, CIGNA, Aetna, AT&T, and others—most major corporations have not chosen to establish any sort of archives at all. Most, unfortunately, do not even have credible records management programs.

The same has, sadly, proved true for major archival repositories. Apparently fearing to tie up space with business records and undoubtedly concerned about how to select records in the first place, few historical societies or universities—the major homes of most nongovernment archives—have evidenced any interest in large-scale documentation of business. Many have a static historical business collection or two, but few have dealt in the documentation of business in any sustained and organized manner. Only the Minnesota Historical Society and the Hagley Museum and Library have built major archives around the records of corporate America. Harvard's Baker Library holds important business collections but has not added to them in years, preferring to leave documentation of later-twentieth-century business to others. Institutions such as the Walter Reuther Library, the George Meany Archives of the AFL-CIO, and the Southern Labor Archives have not been replicated in the field of business history.

Despite the inadequate representation of business in American archival institutions, documentation of business is unarguably important. The United States is built upon a solid foundation of capitalist business practice, and its major corporations have a global reach and influence that often rivals that of government. Few would argue that in the areas of medicine, food and consumer products, and entertainment American businesses are powerful participants in international popular culture and, indeed, help to shape it on a global scale. Documenting this reality is critical.

Corporations are often taken to be a subset of organizations in general, and thus their documentation has been compared to that of entities such as large federal and state government agencies. While there are similarities in the organization of any entity that is inherently bureaucratic, the superficial similarities to government can be overplayed. Some corporate structures resemble and function like government agencies more than others, but all share characteristics that are quite unlike government operations. In particular, corporations respond to their environments in ways distinctly unlike any government. Their executives can hire and fire employees on a grand scale with little hindrance and can rapidly change the direction of their operations if they wish to. Corporations acquire and divest operations with regularity and discard and add product lines at will.

That change will occur is an accepted fact of life in most corporations. Even in those businesses that have changed slowly, change is accepted as inevitable and, increasingly, as necessary and good. In recent decades, corporations have, in general, become places in which job tenure is unknown, seniority is a liability, and outsourcing is a way of life. Uncertainty—whatever its side effects—is present in corporate life in ways unknown to government bureaucrats and their functionaries, with the result that decision making is driven by considerations that are peculiar to business. Always, the bottom line is paramount, for business is indeed run for profit and the diminution or lack of profit signals the need for change throughout the world of business.

All of these factors affect the documentation of corporate history and the ways in which those who would document business must go about their work. Such factors similarly affect the ways in which the business people who create and control the records of their operations perceive and respond to calls to document their activities.

The records of business have been used variously for years, most notably by historians such as Allan Nevins and Ralph Hidy to prepare studies of businesses and the people who run them, and to deal with the place that business has come to occupy in American social, commercial, and political life. Alfred Chandler's pioneering studies have used business records to document the evolution of corporate structure. More recently, work in such emerging fields as management psychology, organizational dynamics, corporate communication, and studies of corporate culture have included the use of some business records. The question of which corporate records have been appraised as having historical value and retained is a major issue here, since corporate records have tended to be appraised by archivists on their utility in the preparation of the histories of business enterprises. However, those involved in such areas as organizational dynamics, management psychology, and corporate communication, for instance, while they may make use of historical data, certainly do not consider themselves business historians. Moreover, their research may require the use of records that would not survive an appraisal based solely on the needs of business history. By and large, traditional business history has not provided a secure base of use or support for the retention of corporate records, and new fields of inquiry relating to specific business activities have ignored the records in favor of other sources of information. While frequently cited as the primary clientele for whom corporate records are assembled, business historians have often proven uncertain allies and infrequent users.

It might be assumed that the differences between repositories holding corporate records and the in-house archives of corporations would be especially notable in considering issues of appraisal. The archives of a corporation, after all, would seem to have a vastly different mission and clientele than a repository designed to serve a wide research public. Corporate archives are creatures of their corporate masters, designed (one would assume) to serve the needs of the corporation's own marketing, research, administrative, legal, and other staff. The needs of outside users, including business historians, would be irrelevant, since the archives exists only to serve the corporation and not the public.

In fact, this has not always been the case, for while many of the most successful corporate archives have clearly identified the special needs of in-house clients and tailored services for them, many others have not risen to that challenge. This may, in part, reflect the slower-than-necessary pace at which archivists have adapted to the changing needs of existing clients and to the need to develop new clienteles. "While many of us have welcomed the transition from academic convocation to business suit, we have unwittingly participated in the planning of our own demise with our scholarly approach to selling archives," writes Gordon Rabchuk of his colleagues in corporate archives. "We [must] de-emphasize the myth that archives serve a one-dimensional purpose as the gatekeeper of the organization's history."[1] Archivists working with business records in corporations and repositories alike need to adopt a considerably wider focus for the work they do and the clients they serve.

For those who would preserve corporate records, in whatever form, the question of use quickly becomes primary. Without use, the expense of keeping the records cannot be justified either within or outside of the corporation. The question of expense—the bottom line again— underlies many of the considerations involved in preserving corporate records. Size and complexity are critical and are linked directly to the ability of archivists to appraise business records with the same confidence they do personal papers, and, as importantly, to understand the real and potential uses for the records available to them.

In this regard the touchstone of business history, narrowly defined and bounded by generally understood products such as narrative corporate histories, has often formed the basis for appraisal decisions. But even those boundaries have failed to make most archivists comfortable about the process. Records that serve the purpose of business history are saved, and that process is informed by the same tenets that inform the documentation of other organizations, such as government agencies. If other users can find information in the records retained, that is well and good, but those other uses are secondary (if that) to such an appraisal process. Nothing is resolved. The volume is still overwhelming, the complexities remain, and only the rationale is simplified.

The real question is whether traditional business history as such should even be the dominant rationale for retaining corporate records. What is one documenting, when all is said and done? The chronological progression of a business's growth and development? The dry and often barely informative record of formal board meetings? The voluminous and barely usable ledgers of daily financial transactions? Photographs of every trifling change to each of a thousand separate products? There will be a chorus of emphatic "yesses" to all of the above, for each of those items has a constituency, however small, and is further surrounded by the comfortable aura of accepted practice. Nevertheless, to accept such norms is to condemn the documentation of business to the dustbins and to ensure that new and far more enthusiastic users will seldom have their needs fulfilled by current documentary practice. The truth is that even the concept of history as a determinant of business records appraisal needs to be reexamined.

Corporate Culture and Business Records

Few successful corporate archives or successful business records repositories have sold their services to business based upon the appeal of history. That may appear unfortunate, but it is also reality. History does not sell when its goal is simply documenting the past, without apparent utility in the present and to the future. "Lamenting about inherent corporate hostility towards history is certainly not the solution. Instead, [archivists] should look inward and be more critical of our marketing campaigns which have unwisely presented archives as the undisputed foundation for higher learning." One must "recognize that the intrinsic value of business archives can only be appreciated by focusing on its ability to support the larger corporate mission."[2]

Let us instead look at history as a component of other studies, such as those centering on the documentation of corporate culture as a major factor in the success of everything from management style to product development to the effective selling of products to consumers. "Historical forces also shape the ecological context of a work organization. Current practice reflects not only the weight of a firm's past policies and strategies but also the dynamics of regulation, competition, and market structure that mark the organization's external environment during particular eras."[3] Even a relatively traditional corporate history—if it is cast in terms of the developments and philosophies that drove innovation and produced the corporation of the present—can be made relevant to bottom-line concerns with such a focus.

Studies of corporate culture in various guises undergird a considerable amount of work in such areas as business structure, product development, and strategic management. The importance of corporate culture can be seen in the attention paid to its presumed effects on the success or lack of success in shaping some of the largest U.S. corporations. Why has General Motors moved so slowly to meet changing consumer expectations and design demands? Why has General Electric proven so adept at managing a bewildering mix of businesses that range from light bulbs to jet engines? Why has a company with a marvelous consumer franchise such as IBM failed to adapt readily to changing times, while another such company, Coca-Cola, has made successful adaptation a way of life?

The case of history is strengthened when it is equated with learning within a corporate environment. It can, in fact, be dealt with in the context of the myopia that can occur when strategy is not formed with reference to actual history and its lessons. One "form of myopia is the tendency to ignore the long run. . .as a result, long run survival is sometimes endangered." Another "form of myopia is the tendency to overlook failures. . . .As a result, the risks of failure are likely to be underestimated."[4] Historical experience can be used to undercut myopia and its effects on the bottom line. "Designing organizations to learn from experience and to exploit the knowledge of others is possible, and such designs are major contributions to organizational intelligence."[5] History broadly defined thus contributes to that intelligence and to the net results for the organization.

A corporation is a dynamic entity, and if they are appraised and retained with an eye to documenting the evolution of corporate culture, its records can yield uses of considerable benefit to the organization itself. Mergers and acquisitions have become a part of the American business landscape, and properly understood, they offer enormous scope to the enterprising archivist in search of a rationale for the retention of business records. "According to a number of academic institutions which have investigated the phenomenon over the years—the London Business School, Insead, and Harvard Business School included—the most frequent cause of failure among acquisitions generally is the ethereal culture clash between the parties, masking what is little more than mutual organizational misunderstanding. More specifically, LBS research points to an inability to bridge the gap between contrasting values and beliefs."[6] A whole component of the study of mergers and acquisitions includes the assessment of the role of corporate culture in determining the ultimate success or failure of business combinations.

If values and beliefs are a cause for concern in corporate mergers, however, how can one turn that reality to the advantage of archives? "One answer is to use a medium that can successfully transmit 'identity' and 'culture.' The logic is that, if each party is made familiar with the other, and knows how each other operates, the process of union will be that much quicker and easier."[7] History then, carefully applied, can serve a vital corporate purpose. "If identity and culture are the lifeblood of a company, then its history is the artery through which employees can be informed quickly and comprehensively about inherited values, norms, beliefs, systems, and the company's individual way of doing business. [A particularly] efficient way to transmit such information is through a readable and credible corporate history. . . . Unlike the company newsletter, pamphlet or corporate video, no other document or medium can impart the type and range of information that a new entrant otherwise takes years to learn, assimilate, and apply effectively."[8]

There is more than information at stake as well, as critical as that is. There is the indefinable factor of loyalty, or at least acceptance of a company's way of doing business. "Alluding to the 50 per cent failure rate of acquisitions and mergers," John Hunt of the London Business School has noted that "there are compelling financial reasons for assisting in the integration process and transferring the acquired people's commitment to the new owner: 'Winning the hearts and minds is an immediate necessity. Without their commitment it is difficult to achieve the operational and strategic objectives of the acquisition.'"[9]

The value of such assimilation to the corporation is potentially enormous, particularly in those instances where the acquiring company wishes to affect efficiencies by combining its own products with those of an acquired competitor. In such a case it is imperative to achieve an understanding and sharing of a single corporate culture. Without understanding, however, the sharing is nearly impossible to achieve. "Acquisitions and mergers are obvious examples where the creation of subcultures is sudden and swift. Of course, tasks, roles, and inter-action patterns often change with such expansions so that old loyalties vanish and new patterns of commitment and obligation appear as merged and acquired groups reposition themselves vis-a-vis others. But to the degree that an acquisition or merger leaves intact the pre-vious order with its more or less established intergroup structure, new subcultures will be simply added to the now enlarged organization, a process that appears similar to colonization. The power of the colonized to maintain a separate sense of identity within a more heterogeneous environment may actually be bolstered, since a background of foreign normative orders is likely to enhance consciousness of difference."[10] In such circumstances, efficiencies of combination are difficult to at-tain, and the full benefits of the merger may never appear.

Linking Corporate Culture, the Bottom Line, and History

The real, bottom-line value of corporate history—insofar as it doc-uments the development of corporate culture—is clear. This does not mean that every corporation will subscribe to investment in archives or history, but merely that the opportunity to sell such an investment to management is considerably greater when such links can be made. The linkage, of course, must be supported by more than words and promises; the documentation itself must support such uses. It can, if an archive of business records is built with imagination and attention to the real needs of both corporate personnel and a wider audience than that provided by traditional business history.

That such opportunities exist is supported by many real world examples. Lance Ealey and Leif Soderberg have noted the innovative use of corporate memory at such companies as Honda. They find that "Companies without practical mechanisms to 'remember' what worked and what didn't in the past are doomed to repeat failure and rediscover success time and time again,"[11] with consequent costs to the entire operation. Their work is important not only for corporate management but also for the archivists who would serve management. They note that "at one automotive supplier, for example, over 40 percent of the troublesome design issues that plagued a recent new product program had already been resolved in prior programs. Because the engineers didn't review work previously done by others within the company, they wasted about 30 percent of their design time solving problems that had been solved before." They go on to comment that "our experience with other large organizations leads us to believe that such 'design amnesia' is a much more common drain of cash and creativity than most managers imagine."[12] In order to be useful to the engineers, of course, the information must be organized, easily located, and available when needed. That should be the archivist's cue to enter the action.

The belief that corporate amnesia and myopia are major economic factors receives further support from Arnold Kransdorff who comments that "low awareness of the history of business in general and companies in particular makes British industry vulnerable to a form of 'corporate amnesia', which means companies are prone to repeating their mistakes." Noting a reality that affects American companies as well (and a growing number of international businesses by implication), he points out that this "means that in 1995, for example, a large proportion of a company's employees—including managers—will be personally unaware of what happened and how their companies operated in the later 1980s. . . .Given the direct relationship between staff turnover and productivity, the implications for bottom-line output are significant. In effect, discontinuity means lost momentum. With every company distinctly different, increased job mobility means more periods of adaptation for employees to new environments, new cultures and new ways of working."[13]

Information of value to the company and to other clientele frequently does not fall into any easily identified category of record, regardless of format. "Early on, Honda employees were, for example, encouraged to keep notebooks in which they recorded their work progress, highlighting their own creative ideas. These notebooks served two crucial purposes. First, they were a personal documentation of previous work experience, which accompanied an individual to each new assignment and thus helped ensure that precious ideas and solutions were not lost. Second, the notebooks served as a recognized form of copyright protection for ideas the individual might have come up with so that credit for any particular breakthrough could be given to its originator. This simple documentation of individual effort was a first step in the process of cultivating experts. It also served as an effective way to maintain design memory within the organization."[14] The notebooks thus have an importance that may dwarf that of more readily identified records, but their existence and their uses would remain hidden within the technical workings of the corporation without extensive probing by the archivist.

The archives at Coca-Cola have also proven that corporate memory is an asset with bottom-line value. Serving as the repository for everything from early Coke formulas to a remarkable set of advertising materials (objects, paper, and more recently, film, video, and laser-disc), the Coke archives has provided major impetus for the development of the company's brilliant branded merchandise program—one of the first, largest and most successful such programs. The archives thus serves corporate memory by maintaining links to its past, while providing leadership and material support to the development of products that not only provide revenue but also help cement the company's identity, its culture, and its relationship to the larger national culture as well.

Archives, History, and Oral History

Much of the above makes a compelling case for corporate history, but not so much for traditional chronological history of a company's growth as for history that gives precedence to the values and beliefs that have shaped the organization and its work. The value of such history can be readily appreciated by both company personnel and by those studying such fields as corporate culture, management dynamics, and strategic management. Will reliance on traditional archival appraisal net these users the information they need? How much will journals and ledgers reveal about corporate culture? Will any of the records series traditionally regarded as permanent deal with the dynamics of organizational structure and adaptation in human terms? Will they even capture the most salient realities of corporate culture and decision making as they evolve in the present and the future? I believe that they will not be adequate without judicious use of the tool of oral history.

Regardless of whether one believes that many of the business records traditionally regarded as permanent are increasingly expensive and difficult to appraise and maintain and are unlikely to be used by more than a few clients, the fact of their volume and complexity can scarcely be questioned. Neither the advent of electronic data and information systems nor the heralded arrival of the "paperless office" has diminished the volume of information available to document corporate activity. Both the detail and extent have greatly increased along with the complexities of appraisal, storage, and use. Whether archivists are inside or outside a corporation, they cannot hope to master changing management structures or technical networks without guidance from within the company. This is as necessary for corporate archivists as it is for archivists documenting companies from outside. Corporate archivists will seldom be part of the creation of products upon which a business is based, nor are they perceived to be by other employees. The archives cannot be perceived as a special place unconnected to daily activity, though it often is. "Unfortunately this dangerous pursuit of special status has isolated business archives from the daily ongoings of corporate life and has estranged its archivists from their corporate hosts."[15] As individuals standing outside the main corporate processes, corporate archivists need insider information and guidance as surely as do their colleagues outside the company.

Oral history becomes a necessary tool as well as a catalyst in the creation of a corporate archives and information service, when one looks at its role in two areas of primary importance to this process. The first is its potential to capture information on actual process within the corporation and in identifying the special importance of specific series of records and the gaps in what the records cover. In this guise, oral history may provide a road map of sorts through the uncharted territory of corporate activity. Because the map is drawn by knowledgeable insiders, it can greatly aid in the appraisal of records with a view to their actual, as opposed to traditional and assumed values.

The second area in which oral history becomes a critical element in documenting corporate history is that of information creation. The corporate records, in whatever form, do not always provide adequate insight into the actual workings of a business. In particular, they very seldom provide information on motivation and on informal process. What really lies behind decisions made, and how are corporate strategies actually implemented? Documents such as organization charts, for example, are useful in explaining intended operations and information flows. But, as with water when it meets an obstacle that impedes its progress, real operations may well follow different courses than those outlined on a chart. Those informal ways of getting things done will be well known to those who follow them but will be screened from the understanding of those not involved in the process.

Called into question here is the issue of the documentation itself. How do we document organizations such as businesses? Who are the target clients for the information contained in whatever documentation is assembled? Do we follow precedent without relation to the present and the future? Or do we define the reasons for documenting business as the need to record what it does, and how, and through whom? If we believe the latter, then we will define corporate documentation in dynamic terms, using tradition as a reference but guided by reality. Records will not be preserved because tradition has established their permanence but because of their actual utility to both researchers and corporate users. Information on corporate operations will be created when it does not exist as part of a record (again based on the belief that one is engaged in documenting how a business really works, rather than how it appears to work). The advance of technological innovation and the speed with which corporations adapt to changing environments drives these decisions, despite the momentum of tradition and the comfort of familiarity that makes it difficult for many to deal with that speed. "While it is a human characteristic to try to keep things the same, technology is immune to sentimental familiarity."[16]

These considerations are especially important in capturing information that will allow the tracking of information flow within a business and the points at which information is extracted and refined for use in decision making. Data on the generation and uses of information in decision making is especially critical to an understanding of corporate culture and the larger corporate history. Defining the levels at which information is captured, ratified, and the forms in which it is passed on for further use and decision making has major import for many potential users of corporate archives.

Technology, of course, remains both the bogeyman and the heralded savior of archives, depending on whom one talks to. It will either complicate appraisal and long-term use and retention past any possibility of coping, or it will make the archives the center of the information world by its capacity to sort, organize, and store data efficiently. In fact, it is neither an absolute impediment nor a vehicle of rescue. "Technology can help, of course. There is no question that such things as expert systems, design databases, and design networking can help maintain a vital design memory [for instance]. But without the appropriate "humanware" systems to tap this knowledge hardware, nothing much will happen."[17] The same is true for business records appraisal. The existence of records in electronic format may add to their potential value but does not in itself make them valuable. The ability to retrieve information from records easily and in some depth offers major hope to archivists and their clients, while the costs of developing and maintaining the storage and retrieval systems is a major roadblock to such work. In fact, the impenetrability of electronic records by normal archival appraisal methods makes oral history of increased value. Through its mechanism, one can more efficiently determine which electronic data bases yield information of greatest decision-making value and reach a determination on which of those offer the greatest long-term uses and thus rewards for investment.

Documenting the Real Corporation

Implicit in all this is the need to discover and document the real corporation, beyond its traditional records and with an eye to the actual value of information. To successfully track the real corporation, one must look beyond the obvious and the familiar to discover the elements that best describe its culture, work processes, and decision-making structures. Acceptance of these facts of life involves facing the reality that the real corporation cannot be documented solely through retention of traditional records, and that even the appraisal of those records is impossible without an understanding of business culture that can only come through the aid of oral history.

An understanding of the importance of corporate culture and its role in determining much of what and how a business operates is based upon the reality that "An organization is fundamentally a social structure. Even though actions of and within organizations may be motivated by a variety of economic and other objectives, they emerge through processes of social interactions that are shaped by the social structure."[18] Even though the products and services created by corporations are regarded as their primary contributions, the ways in which those end results are created vary as widely as do the cultures within which they come to be. "Machines cannot yet invent themselves. Nonetheless, the objects created are often attributed more value in a business organization than the people and processes that created them. The artifact is asset; the creator a cost. [Despite this] people, individually and collectively, are an organization's most important asset."[19]

Any attempt to understand corporate history without reference to corporate culture will ultimately be unsuccessful. It will never capture the essential reality that corporations are not creatures in and of themselves, as popularly portrayed. Instead, they are dynamic associations of people who change over time, making both individual and collective decisions that determine the course of each corporation's development. How those individuals initiate and react to events is the stuff of real corporate history.

These realities greatly influence both the need for oral history and the ways in which it can best be used. The creation of documentation is at the center of it all, driven by the reality that the records generated by the company contain only part of the story. "Even if time were available, managers are typically 'doers,' not record keepers; their natural inclination is to act, not to write things down. Some are not at ease with the written word in any case. . . .Given these considerations and more, documenting [in written form] is seen intuitively as an unproductive way to use scarce time."[20]

The reality that is the human element in business is best captured by the archivist through structured oral history that allows the creation of documents that cut through the formal record of organization to the informal and dynamic record of everyday operation. It permits definition of the structure of a company, "not in terms of how subunits are composed and decomposed, but as a cluster of statuses and associated roles that collectively define the social structure of a company within which its core management processes are embedded."[21]

Emphasis on the involvement of people—individually or in collaboration—in the development of corporations and their culture is
critical to the work of documenting corporate history. The view of
corporations as monoliths resistant to change may capture the reality
of normal human attachment to the known as opposed to the unknown,
but it ignores the concomitant reality that corporations are predisposed
to change as a requirement of survival in the marketplace. Failure to
capture a record of the human mechanisms that both create and adjust
to change within the corporate environment will result in a highly
inadequate record of corporate history.

Recognition of the human element as central to business operations is underlined in such broadly conceived projects as that undertaken by the editors of *Institutional Investor* in the late 1980s.
Reflecting on the cataclysmic changes in investment banking during
the preceding two decades, Gilbert Kaplan wrote, "To recount what
happened during two tempestuous decades and to dramatize those
events, we have produced an 'oral history' of the period. This approach,
telling the story entirely in the words of the key players, has . . . never,
to the best of our knowledge . . . been applied to the world of finance
or, for that matter, to the business world in general. We found this
approach compelling for a number of reasons, not the least of which
is its reaffirmation of *Institutional Investor's* long-standing conviction
that the essence of high finance is the human element." He concludes
that all of those interviewed for the project "provide an inside view of
the world of high finance that few people ever get to see, and an
introduction to the powerful personalities who have shaped—and are
still shaping—that world."[22]

This project included interviews with more than 30 people who
commented candidly on the personal reflexes that often determined
the course of rapid evolution in investment banking. Those interviews
illustrate the value of oral history as a tool, and, more particularly, the
importance of such a tool in understanding the people and the corporate cultures they create.

This focus on the human element recognizes a key element in
information building within corporations. "With fewer people remaining with any one company for long, there are correspondingly
fewer veterans left to pass down first-hand the longer-term experiences, knowledge, and the accumulated wisdom of a company...Without anyone to pass on the components of a company's
experience to the newer generation, the organization's long-standing
cultural and belief systems—and sense of identity—become dis-
rupted and risk breaking down. It also becomes more difficult for
people to feel part of a wider team. As a result loyalty—and productivity—becomes elusive."[23]

While team building has enjoyed intermittent popularity as a corporate strategy and currently appears under siege as part of the "downsizing and restructuring at any price" mentality, it will always have value in the operation of a successful business. No product or service can create satisfaction for customers for long if it is provided by a disaffected and dysfunctional work force. Even fast-food industry employers—long noted for high turnover and low employee morale—have found that profits increase with the successful introduction of team spirit among their workers. Sooner or later successful enterprises discover that "members of robust organizations share a sense that their group is special and that a definite loyalty and spark unite people. Such unique spirit makes groups fun, and offers people a workplace with which they can identify and from which they can draw both personal security and occupational challenge."[24]

Archivists and the Real Corporation

Emphasis on the human element and on the central role of human systems in the operation of the real corporation poses many problems for archivists tied to reliance on traditional records. They must go further and involve themselves in the creation of information that supplements, provides guidance for the use of, and in some cases supplants the archival records traditionally relied on by both archivists and their clients. Oral history is a useful tool in the creation of information that can both highlight the existence of new patterns of communication and operation within the real corporation and provide the details that explain their emergence and modification.

Tracking evolution and decision-making structures within the real corporation opens the way to the discovery and documentation of such new instruments of corporate culture as the television and the computer. Both have become major factors in the formulation and distribution of elements in corporate culture—and in the modification of those elements by reaction—and are thus key candidates for evaluation when assembling a record of corporate development.

For instance, "more than 90 major companies in North America have their own TV satellite or cable networks, according to a survey from KJH Communications, an Atlanta consulting firm. The companies use TV for rumor control, to boost worker's involvement, to smooth operations in emergencies and to cut millions of dollars in travel costs for training and new product briefings." This is not to say that corporate TV is used only for major events. "Much of what occurs on corporate TV is mundane business. J. C. Penney Co. used to fly hundreds of buyers to district headquarters when it brought out a new line of women's dresses. Now the company puts the garments on television, showing up to 1,500 dresses using 24 different live models." The same is true in the far different world of auto mechanics. "Rudy Sandoval, who owns a small Dodge dealership in Las Cruces, N.M., says his mechanics receive much of their training from television courses broadcast by Chrysler. 'It's quite handy,' says Mr. Sandoval. 'We don't have to travel.' "[25] The use of television has thus radically changed the way in which some businesses do business, and the changes have very human consequences, with face to face meetings and travel replaced by satellite communication.

In a similar fashion, computers have led to even more dramatic changes within business. In-house networks with their bulletin boards may replace newsletters and company meetings; informal networks of employees may disseminate their own information and reaction in ways that have profound implication for the concepts of team building and management control of information. An especially pertinent example of the latter concerns IBM, where, during the height of its recent troubled times, thousands of remarks by employees throughout the company were recorded on "an electronic bulletin board that two low-level managers, acting on their own, set up . . . to give everyone at IBM a chance to sound off. After about a week the managers decided that this Democracy Wall had gone far enough and closed it down, erasing the file from the central computer. But several employees have helped piece together a nearly complete copy, providing a rare unfiltered glimpse at the internal discourse of this troubled behemoth." The importance of such an electronic document to corporate history is obvious. And it gains added importance from the fact that "The irony of IBM employees attempting spontaneous bulletin-board group therapy wasn't lost on the participants. As one of them observed, IBM is a bureaucracy trying to tear down a bureaucracy."[26] The importance of such an informal, nontraditional document to understanding a corporate culture in transition is clear. But its existence could easily escape notice by an archivist unmindful of the realities of doing business in the real corporation. That such realities provide remarkable opportunity to document activities that create few records is not the least of their attraction.

The record of change and frustration in turbulent times is hardly the only example of corporate behavior that has long-term implications for the organization. Even formal or semiformal strategies may be poorly documented. Kransdorff cites such a case in "Delta Airlines, an American company which commands a high degree of corporate loyalty, [and] uses what it calls 'buddy teams'—a technique it developed when it acquired Western Airlines in the mid-1980s. When it picked up many of Pan Am's 7,000 employees in 1990, it appointed groups of Delta and Pan Am employees to specifically familiarize former Pan Am staff with the Delta philosophy."[27] Even when the fact of such a strategy is recorded, information on its operation and success or failure will seldom be part of the record. Archivists must be aware of this reality and be prepared to deal with it.

Reality, Legality, and the Real Corporation

It is in documenting these informal tracks through which information is exchanged, decisions are made, and culture is formed that oral history becomes indispensable. The formal records contain important information on operations and their results but seldom document control—of information, decision making, or process—at any level. This does not mean that the control is not there, or that it is not perhaps more important to reality than what appears in the formal record. Writing again of Honda, Ealey and Soderberg note that "The control is there, only it is maintained through a subtle, finely tuned series of checks and balances."[28] There is little record of those checks and balances, or of the adjustments they undergo as they are applied. Yet, the work of the real corporation is accomplished through just such mechanisms.

Oral history is also critical in documenting such issues as the cult of personality that develops around the founders or key builders of many businesses. In some cases the cult may become quite public, with specific use made of the founder or builder in corporate literature and advertising. In many instances, however, that influence will be felt in subtle ways and interpreted variously by customers, employees, and investors. Providing such information as part of the archives package creates much wider opportunities for use by clienteles that have not often given much attention to corporate records. And they have value within companies themselves insofar as they contain data for marketing and image management, and insight into the process of culture creation and maintenance.

"Organizational studies of the culture creation process offer a seductive promise to entrepreneurs: namely that a founder can create a culture, cast in the founder's own image and reflecting the founder's own values, priorities, and vision of the future. Thus a founder's personal perspective can be transformed into a shared legacy that will survive death or departure from the institution—a personal form of organizational immortality."[29] The promise and the reality of its execution may only be implied in the formal record. Yet, it is an integral component of evolution in the real corporation.

The realities of global expansion for many companies create other opportunities—and indeed necessities—for the use of oral history as a documentary tool. The legal status of many foreign subsidiaries owned by American corporations is one of incorporation in the countries in which they do business in order to recognize the benefits of local operation. Foreign incorporation, however, will usually mean that the records of the non-U.S. company will not be available for recall to an archives in the United States. Even when recall is an option, it will often not be either possible or efficient to move large quantities of records overseas. Those realities certainly do not preclude the gathering of information about the non-U.S. companies and their operations. An excellent example of the use of oral history in such a situation is presented by Susan Box of Phillips Petroleum. Faced with documenting a corporation with diverse foreign operations, she developed an oral history program to document the growth of Phillips' operations in Norway and in particular "to discover if there were differences of opinion on the licensing and construction negotiations between the Norwegians and their American counterparts." Backed by senior management, that project led to a similar effort, initiated by another senior manager, to do similar work with the company's Belgian division. As Box notes, there "were several winners here . . . because we [learned] that there really is a difference between employee perspectives on the same company issues, based upon nationality, [and] the archives . . . gained increased exposure and credibility on both a corporate and international level."[30]

Similarly, oral history has been used in such corporations as CIGNA, Kraft Foods, and H. B. Fuller to document elements of corporate history that have escaped the records. Archives staff at CIGNA have used it to detail events surrounding the merger of INA and Connecticut General that created the corporation; at Kraft Foods, to deal with the acquisition of General Foods, Oscar Meyer and other companies; and at H. B. Fuller, to provide assessment of many of the managerial motivations involved in the company's growth and diversification.

These are only a few examples of the use of oral history to document the operations of complex and multinational businesses in ways that may not be possible through paper or even electronic records. Facing reality is, again, critical. To imagine that a corporation will maintain archives in each of the countries in which it does business is to indulge in illusion. A central archives will have to do the work, and oral history is clearly necessary to document such key factors as the ways in which information and decisions flow between the corporate headquarters and far-flung operations.

The legal considerations noted above, while they pertain to foreign corporations, are the harbinger of larger legal issues that frequently beset the archivist who would document American business. Fear of the "smoking gun" that might lie in corporate records remains quite real, although litigation constantly proves that for every potential problem averted by destroying information, others are created; for each lawyer who would destroy every bit of documentation in sight, there are others who understand that the lack of documentation may be an even greater liability. "In self defense, wise managers at all levels and in all functional areas think it prudent to document every action that conceivably could be challenged later."[31] Protecting the corporation from litigation will always be a key concern, and counsel on self-protection often mirrors this amusingly worded but quite straightforward advice: "The more professional and knowledgeable you are, the less likely you are to make a mistake and the less likely it is that an attorney will want to pursue a questionable or nonmeritorious claim against you. Like big cats of prey, who cut from the herd the weak, the young, and the infirm, plaintiffs' attorneys prefer to pursue the sloppy, the disorganized, and the lazy. If you can document that you did your job, you might be able to convince attorneys that their time is better spent pursuing someone else."[32] There are even more pragmatic views than that: "Even when the shredder wins, the corporation in a legal action may find that the court insists that the missing documents be recreated regardless of cost."[33]

Oral History, Business Archives, and Reality

If tracking the relationship of information creation and use, decision making, and the effects of corporate culture on everything from product development to successful adaptation in the marketplace is important, then the appraisal of corporate records for permanent value must change. Archivists must recognize that the cost of maintaining and servicing corporate archives must be spread over a much wider base of users, and thus appraisal must serve those new clienteles. The reality of serving new clienteles means that one must work with them to understand their work rather than proceeding on the assumption that they must understand archives. The first question archivists should ask prospective clients is, "What do you do, and how?" rather than the all too frequent, "Here's what we have, we hope you can use it." Indeed, the most "appropriate response would [be to] canvass the opinions of others . . . whose particular needs and expectations would serve as the foundation for the development of meaningful products and services."[34]

Increasing access in archives has too often come to mean more and better description, rather than interaction with current and prospective communities of clients. While better and more complete information on what archives hold is certainly important, those holdings need to be better tailored to the needs of users. Work with multiple user communities makes possible a reconciliation and blending of uses that ensures the greatest possible use for the smallest possible quantity of records. This is especially important in the case of business, where poorly targeted holdings create huge investment without a suitable payoff.

If use must be built upon a broader and firmer base of clienteles, then the appraisal of business records must be based upon the workings of the real corporation. Oral history will help identify the ways in which the real corporation functions and the points at which information is created, captured, used, and decisions made. In doing so, the oral history will create documentary evidence that would not otherwise exist.

The careful use of oral history has a subsidiary but not unimportant benefit; it creates documentation that is immediately available in electronic format. Transcripts of interviews, for example, can be made available in either paper or electronic form and combined with images from the archives into products with greatly expanded access and use possibilities.

Facing reality while documenting business involves the admission that business at all levels is a critical component of American society. In the case of large firms, documentation is often unwieldy and complex; in small firms little documentation may exist; in both instances much that is important to the documentation of the ways in which business really works does not exist in any prepared document, regardless of format. Also, it involves the realization that permanent documents do not self-select. Appraisal must be done in concert with potential users, and, most importantly, with those who use the information generated within corporations to make the decisions that guide their operations.

The aggressive use of oral history as a documentary tool as part of an archives-building process may not win many converts among archivists at first. Although the use of oral history by archivists has greatly increased, it continues to occupy a minor place in archives work and to remain suspect by those who truly view themselves as passive recipients of records. I trust that the discussion will help to focus attention on the realities of documenting business in America (and globally) by raising questions of what is being done, and why, and for whom. If documentation is the goal, then a focused, aggressive use of oral history is imperative.

Endnotes

1. Gordon Rabchuk, "Reaching Out for Survival: The Royal Bank Experience," Society of American Archivists *Business Archives Newsletter* (winter 1994): 1, 9.

2. Ibid., 1.

3. John Van Maanen and Stephen R. Barley, "Cultural Organization: Fragments of a Theory," in *Organizational Culture* (Beverly Hills: Sage Publications, 1985), 36.

4. Daniel A. Levinthal and James G. March, "The Myopia of Learning," *Strategic Management Journal* 14 (1993): 101.

5. Ibid.

6. Arnold Kransdorff, "Making Acquisitions Work by the Book," *Personnel Management* (May 1993): 40.

7. Ibid., 42.

8. Ibid., 42.

9. Ibid., 43.

10. Van Maanen and Barley, "Cultural Organization," 41.

11. Lance Ealey and Leif G. Soderberg, "How Honda Cures 'Design Amnesia,'" *McKinsey Quarterly* (spring 1990): 3.

12. Ibid., 3–4.

13. Kransdorff, "Making Acquisitions Work by the Book," 43.

14. Ealey and Soderberg, "How Honda Cures 'Design Amnesia,'" 12–13.

15. Rabchuk, "Reaching Out for Survival," 1.

16. Leonard Tiger, "When 'Corporate' and 'Culture' Clash," *Wall Street Journal*, April 9, 1990, A12.

17. Ealey and Soderberg, "How Honda Cures 'Design Amnesia,'" 4.

18. Christopher A. Bartlett and Sumantra Ghoshal, "Beyond the M-Form: Toward a Managerial Theory of the Firm," *Strategic Management Journal* 14 (1993): 43.

19. Daniel R. Denison, *Corporate Culture and Organizational Effectiveness* (New York: John Wiley & Sons, 1990), 197.

20. J. H. Foegen, "A New Management Paranoia: Documentation," *Management Review* (May 1991): 55.

21. Bartlett and Ghoshal, "Beyond the M-Form," 44.

22. Gilbert E. Kaplan, Foreword to *The Way it Was* (New York: William Morrow and Company, 1988), 12–13.

23. Kransdorff, "Making Acquisitions Work by the Book," 43.

24. Tiger, "When 'Corporate' and 'Culture' Clash," A12.

25. Neal Templin, "Companies Use TV to Reach Their Workers," *Wall Street Journal*, December 7, 1993, B1.

26. Paul B. Carroll, "Computers Indicate Mood at Big Blue is Practically Indigo," *Wall Street Journal*, August 7, 1991, A1.

27. Kransdorff, "Making Acquisitions Work by the Book," 42.

28. Ealey and Soderberg, "How Honda Cures 'Design Amnesia,' " 13.

29. Joanne Martin, Sim B. Sitkin, and Michael Boehm, "Founders and the Elusiveness of a Cultural Legacy," in *Organizational Culture*, 99.

30. Susan C. Box, "Taking Advantage of Serendipity: The Importance of Being Quick, Flexible, and Proactive," Society of American Archivists *Business Archives Newsletter* (Winter 1995): 6–7.

31. Foegen, "A New Management Paranoia," 54.

32. Richard B. Waite, "Lawsuit Craze," *Real Estate Today* (September 1993): 42.

33. John Thackray, "Where Memory Serves," *Across The Board* (July–August 1991): 45.

34. Rabchuk, "Reaching Out for Survival," 1.

10

Corporate Memory in Sound and Visual Records

Ernest J. Dick

Introduction

All manner of businesses in the United States, and all over the world for that matter, are using more sound and visual technologies than ever before. Business has been quick to grasp the practical and creative applications of still photography, sound recording, and moving images. Indeed, business has been adept at inventing a wide array of new markets and new opportunities as the sound and visual technologies evolved. Consequently, sound and visual materials are proliferating and accumulating faster than anyone can imagine.

Despite this inventiveness and the considerable investments in the creation of sound and visual materials, businesses do not necessarily understand and appreciate the corporate asset or cultural value of their creations. The archivist must help the corporation value the sound and visual records that they were responsible for bringing into being. The archivist brings essential expertise to the business "retooling" for the information economy of the twenty-first century or to the business closing its doors and disposing of its assets. No one else has our experience

The author wishes to acknowledge the invaluable assistance of Bonnie Wilson of the Minnesota Historical Society in developing and improving this article.

in selecting, organizing, and accessing huge quantities of unique collections of information.

Even companies directly responsible for the making of sound and visual products do not necessarily understand that they were potentially creating something of ongoing value. Record manufacturers, for example, have often been notoriously delinquent in protecting the master recordings required to reissue classic recordings on new formats. Walt Disney was the exception rather than norm, when in the mid-1930s, a full 40 years after the invention of film, it became the first company to begin actively and self-consciously to protect, safeguard, and reuse its titles.

Sound and visual materials have usually been considered disposable, similar to the products that the company manufactured and sold or the services that the company provided. Sound and visual materials are somewhat cumbersome because they often require complicated playback equipment to be seen and heard. They admittedly cannot be comprehended instantaneously and take time to be played back. As such they have been easily dismissed as transitory and ephemeral, and not warranting an ongoing investment.

This neglect is beginning to change, at least for the businesses whose products are sound and visual materials. In the past couple of decades, many television networks and production agencies have come to see their news libraries and program libraries as potential profit centers. In the 1990s, the purchase of sound and visual archives has become an appropriate investment in the information economy. Microsoft, for example, has been systematically purchasing still photo archives through an agency created for this purpose called Corbis. Also, the growing range of nostalgic, retrospective, and educational audiovisual productions and multimedia "publishing" being conceived these days creates a great need of more and more sound and visual archival materials.

Nonetheless, the businesses who generate sound and visual materials as ancillary to their principal product or services have only rarely begun to understand the potential value of such materials. Sound and visual records have value as corporate assets, as evidence of the corporation's activities, and as cultural evidence. The archivist must be at the leading edge of recognizing and understanding these values and making them manifest to the business that generated the materials and/or the archives inheriting such materials.

Archivists are beginning to appreciate that sound and visual records can constitute the most reliable and authentic documentation of the twentieth-century. These sound and visual records will often have value and meaning in surprising ways, activating emotions and memories with persuasive power. Anyone who values a particular family photograph or a sound recording of a friend who has passed on; anyone who has smiled with delight and recognition at seeing an old television commercial, familiar television serial or classic feature film; or anyone who remembers vividly the ambiance of their highschool gym when particular songs of their youth are now played will begin to understand the power and poignancy of sound and visual materials.

Nonetheless, not all of the sound and visual materials generated by business will have this evidential or cultural potential. Substantial portions of sound and visual materials will deserve to be jettisoned, just as with conventional archival records. The archivist must develop the expertise to ascertain which records have merit and then apply the appropriate conservation, intellectual control, and access processes to ensure that the sound and visual heritage is preserved and available.

Challenges of the Sound and Visual Archivist. The archivist, charged with the responsibility of the records of a business, must become adept at a formidable array of different tasks. Whether faced with overwhelming accumulations of sound and visual material or a conspicuous lack thereof (where the company is known to have been active in generating such materials), the archivist cannot neglect sound and visual materials.

Conventional archival education has not focused on sound and visual records and all their particular challenges. Specialized associations have evolved to meet these needs, and most of the larger public archives have also developed appropriate expertise in sound and visual records. Understanding of how these media were generated and can deteriorate, how they are being appraised and organized, how they should be preserved, and how they can be made accessible is changing so quickly that there exist few publications or periodicals from which to learn. It is recommended to contact the appropriate specialized association[1] or sound and visual archival expert to work through the challenges of your particular collection.

The archivist must become a technical expert in the sound and visual technologies that generated these formats or rely on someone with this expertise. These technologies have gone through an amazing variety of incarnations in a few short decades. Even the most successful of sound and visual technologies have only had a life span of some 20 to 40 years with most technologies remaining current for less than a decade.

The archivist must be able to assess the physical condition of the sound and visual formats and take appropriate measures to arrest their state of deterioration. To simply "read" the sound and visual record, the appropriate playback technology must be searched out, and this can be a challenge, given the rapid obsolescence of many audio-visual technologies. Then such equipment must be operated with great care so as not to further damage or deteriorate the sound and visual records.

At the same time, the archivist must be familiar with the potential of current sound and visual technologies, as well as their limitations, so as to assess their compatibility with the original material and ascertain the most appropriate conservation, restoration, and copying procedures. For example, copying a dirty and scratched 35 mm film to a VHS cassette compromises the original visual quality needlessly. Such a transfer may serve an immediate reference purpose, as will a photocopy of a photograph, and may save wear and tear on the original, but such a copy will not have ensured the archival survival of the original quality of the images.

The archivist must become familiar with the voices, faces, locations, buildings, logos, products, and other details of their company to recognize them and correctly identify them on the sound and visual materials. Given the costs of cataloging, let alone restoring and copying sound and visual formats, the archivist must become familiar with similar collections already held in other archives and perhaps already cataloged and preserved.

The archivist must become a shrewd entrepreneur in recognizing the business opportunities represented by the sound and visual records. The enormous appetite of the electronic information highway for archival sounds and images is real, and those collections and strategic partnerships that can respond to these initial opportunities will reap substantial benefits. However, this is such a new frontier of technological and economic development that no one can know which ventures will succeed and which will fall by the wayside.

The sound and visual materials archivist performs the conventional archival functions of appraisal and selection, organization and cataloging, and providing access. Indeed, classical archival theory is useful and should be called upon in dealing with sound and moving image materials. However, applying such theory and performing such functions with sound and visual materials requires sensitivity to, and appreciation of the unique features and challenges of such records.

The corporate in-house archivist working for the institution that generated the records will naturally have a different mandate and perspective than the archivist working within a government institution, university, or historical society with a wide archival mandate. The corporate archivist has to protect the institutional and business interests of their institution and will, therefore, often have to argue for a comprehensive approach for particular series of records.

The archivist working within the public institution is always stretching scarce public resources to document as wide a cross section of societal activities as possible and, therefore, will be more selective in what can be accepted. At the same time, this archivist will sometimes want to preserve records with no apparent business or institutional value that the corporate archivist is quite prepared to jettison.

Still, the differences between the corporate archivist and the archivist working for the public institution may be greater in theory than they are in practice. When the National Archives of Canada selected television news film for permanent preservation from the French network of the Canadian Broadcasting Corporation, so little had survived from the early years that everyone easily agreed on what should be kept. For television news programming of more recent years, where an abundance of material had survived, the broadcaster did want to retain more than did the archives. However, their differences were not as large as originally imagined and further discussion narrowed their differences further.

Ideally, the corporate archivist and the archivist working within the public institution have lots to learn from each other and will find it instructive and beneficial to listen to each other's rationale and perspective. Listening to the archivist working within the public institution will certainly inform and rationalize the records management strategy of any business institution. Similarly, hearing out the corporate archivist will alert all archives to new and heretofore unimagined uses for archival records. Both institutions will benefit from the process.

Unfortunately, archives are sometimes only called on to deal with business records when companies have collapsed or merged, are moving or downsizing, or are facing some other overwhelming crisis. At this point, the company's archival sense of responsibility is invariably not high, and the public archives have to salvage what they can with minimal corporate assistance.

Our discussion on corporate visual and sound records will recognize the difference of the corporate and public archival perspectives. We will offer recommendations for each archivist dealing with sound and visual materials as well as suggesting how these approaches can sometimes be reconciled.

Appraisal[2]

Appraisal of sound and visual materials has to be a reactive exercise, responding to accumulations that are found. At the same time, appraisal has to be an outreach activity locating sound and visual materials that have gone astray and also proactive in determining what to retain of current sound and visual material being created. Somewhat different selection criteria will be developed, depending on whether a reactive, outreach, or proactive strategy is required, but appraisal should always proceed from the context of the business functions within which sound and visual materials were generated.

Usually, the archivist has to remind the corporation that their sound and visual materials should be considered part of their archival record. Businesses may consider the sound and visual documentation of the corporation's ceremonial events of historic value, but, often, all the other products of sound and visual technologies were jettisoned when they were no longer current.

If sound and visual materials were retained at all, it would normally be within an audiovisual department rather than the records management division of the corporation. At the same time, sound and visual records inadvertently accumulated in neglected corners of warehouses, attics, garages, and basements because no one wanted to throw them out. Such creations were usually expensive, often someone's labor of love, and therefore not always disposed of systematically. Indeed, in such cases all elements of the production process, or of a particular project, may have survived. Time has rarely winnowed sound and visual materials very helpfully, so that the archivist can, indeed, face a glut and a dearth of sound and visual materials at the same time. Neither extreme is desirable, and one has to judiciously develop a course of action somewhere between these two.

Both these reactive and outreach archival strategies are time consuming and ultimately not very satisfactory. Therefore, the archivist will want to recommend a proactive information and records management strategy that will determine what visual and sound records are to be retained before they ever come into being. The efficacy of this proactive information management strategy has become conventional wisdom for textual records but will be even more compelling for sound and visual materials.

Generation of sound and visual materials generally followed two different paths. For some purposes, business developed the in-house expertise and capacity and for others they commissioned outside companies to generate their promotional, training, and other sound and visual products. Most companies used both strategies at various times for various purposes and, most recently, have tended toward using outside production facilities. Ironically, outside production agencies may have developed slightly better archival practices, particularly for still or moving images on film, because such companies more clearly understood the profits to be made from striking additional prints from the original negatives or remastering original recordings for secondary purposes. However, when outside production agencies have produced the sound and visual products, the question of ownership and clearance of further uses invariably becomes more confused. Moreover, the outside production companies may themselves go out of business and then dispose of such materials with little thought of their value to the company for whom they did the work.

Appraising the Record. The archivist must understand and, to some extent, recreate the production process for the moving image and sound materials that they are working with. Virtually all audiovisual productions are the results of editing processes whereby more original footage is shot than is ever used for the final product. The original master materials may or may not have archival value, as will be discussed below, but needs to be identified for what it is. Proofs, work prints, rough edits, mixing tracks, and so on are intermediate stages in preparing the final product and rarely have archival value in themselves. Outs and trims are the material not used in the final productions.

To begin with, the archivist must be able to identify the content of the sound and visual materials at hand and determine of what they consist in order to appraise them. Sound and visual materials are virtually useless without dates, locations, personalities, and events clearly identified. Preferably, this information is clearly indicated on the back of the photographs, on the recordings themselves, on labels, and on the containers. Some playback will be required to verify the reliability of such supplied identification and to complete selection and organization. This involves locating and operating appropriate playback equipment and handling original formats with great care. Sometimes this also means finding the people who created the materials, as sound and visual materials have rarely come under the purview of conventional records management departments.

As with all archival records, visual and sound materials need to be appraised within the context that they were created. Understanding how and why materials were created is fundamental to determining what needs to be retained for archival purposes. We will, therefore, look at sound and visual materials, first, as products for those businesses who generate such products; second, as documentation of business activities; third, as promotion of business; fourth, as internal communications tools; and finally, as they are used in the operations of a business.

Sound and Visual Materials as the Products of Business. Long-standing companies generating sound and visual products for their own sake have recently become aware of the business asset represented by such productions. Many such companies are making substantial investments in state-of-the-art conservation facilities, visually based cataloging, robotic retrieval, and remote access. Some are even purchasing available sound and visual archives to consolidate their investment.

This development will ensure the best preservation and commercial development of sound and visual archives but may, in fact, restrict public research access. Such corporate archives should be encouraged to also develop an open and equitable public access policy. Another approach is for such corporate archives to enter into a partnership with an appropriate archival institution whereby the various archival functions are divided according to the resources and expertise of each institution.

Sometimes sound and visual production companies last only for the purpose of a single production, either intentionally or inadvertently, and the archival disposition of such creations is invariably particularly hazardous. Archives should be encouraged to be alert to the comings and goings of such enterprises and may well need to be particularly proactive in acquiring their sound and visual productions.

Sound and visual productions invariably generate much superfluous sound and visual material that is usually carefully logged and monitored for the purpose of making the production. While there is any possibility of "recutting" or reediting the production for another market, all such material is invariably retained. Thereafter, all such material, including the master copies, can be ignored and neglected. This production rhythm constitutes a formidable appraisal and selection challenge for the archivist inheriting such materials. Initially, the creating team controls all elements of their production, sometimes resisting any involvement of the archivist. However, once the creators have moved on to their next project, it may become difficult to reconstruct the production process and sort out the production masters and negatives from the outs, work prints, test tapes, and proofs that deserve to be jettisoned.

The copyrights and further use rights in sound and visual productions are invariably complicated and difficult to sort out. Often the agencies commissioning such productions purchased limited rights to cover only their foreseeable uses. The corporate archives might be expected to research and clarify such rights confusions and could well justify its added value to the corporation by so doing. Archives are advised to be aware of what rights they are, or are not, acquiring with sound and visual collections. Beyond this, however, archives generally should require their users to assume all responsibility for rights clearances.

Sound and Visual Materials Documenting Business Activities. Business has long used sound and visual technologies to document ceremonial and important events. Such finished productions should undoubtedly be retained for archival purposes. Such footage, particularly when assembled and edited for presentation, admittedly may camouflage rather than reveal the true nature of personalities, locations, and events of the business. Nonetheless, such productions document how the company understood itself and wanted to be understood. The corporate archives should retain all such sound and visual finished productions, whereas the other archives will want to be more selective, selecting only those which document a new range of company personalities, new locations, or a remade image for the company.

Historical and special commemorative sound and visual productions should certainly be retained as examples of how the company understands itself and its evolution. Nonetheless, such productions will be essentially public relations exercises and should not be considered as the definitive sound and visual archival record of the corporation. Corporate and public archivists will treat such historical productions similarly.

Occasionally companies may have also consciously documented a manufacturing process or a building project because it was particularly innovative, complicated, or expensive. Corporate archives will want to retain both the finished products and all the original footage of the sound and visual documentation of such conscious efforts. Other archives may need to be more selective but probably should be comprehensive for those projects selected for documentation.

Departments or outside agencies making commissioned productions often shoot more material than they make use of for the finished productions. Arrangements should ideally be completed before the production is begun to determine the ownership and disposition of such footage. The archival value of such recordings has to be determined on a case by case basis. All archivists can use very similar criteria to retain or jettison this footage. The rarity of recordings of the personalities, event, location, or period, together with the quality of the material are usually sufficient criteria to determine whether they should be retained for archival purposes.

Amateur film and video of company picnics, parties, processes, and meetings are invariably unauthorized, poorly identified, and haphazardly accumulated. Nonetheless, their idiosyncratic and unauthorized perspective may make them valuable if they can be reliably identified and brought under archival protection before they are abused or neglected beyond repair. These will, of course, not usually be found with the company records and, in most cases, should not be considered part of the company collection. Yet, such footage may be irreplaceable and invaluable in documenting company personalities and activities and should be considered for its archival potential. Both corporate archives and other archives should be open to such footage, but neither will likely be able to allocate many resources to searching it out.

Newsreel companies and broadcasters have covered notable events or personalities of businesses for news or documentary purposes since the beginning of these media. Copies of their finished stories can often be supplied to the business if such arrangements are negotiated when the collaboration of the business is being sought. Invariably, more footage is recorded for such productions than they used for their report, and sometimes such footage is still retained in these libraries. However, such footage will be owned by the media that originated the story and may be junked or sold according to their whim. On occasion, the corporate archivist may want to search out such original footage from the news media that originated the coverage. Archivists working within public institutions will undoubtedly prefer to acquire such new footage directly from the newsreel or broadcasters that originated the coverage.

Media-monitoring companies have included radio and television news coverage in recent years and an increasing number of businesses have standing contracts to acquire material relating to their company and areas of interest. Such sound and visual material is invariably very poor quality and usually not legally procured material. Therefore, it is not recommended to retain such material for archival purposes. Such media coverage will occasionally reflect how particular events or controversies relating to a business were treated and thus particular, notable coverage might be considered for archival retention by the corporate archives.

Sound and Visual Materials Promoting Business Activities. Sound and visual productions generated for the purpose of promoting a business's products or activities clearly have archival potential. Virtually all corporations had their products or services photographed at one point or another for promotional purposes. Such material quickly becomes voluminous and even the corporate archives will have to be selective about how much can be retained. Different views of the same product, for example, do not all need to be retained. For images that are retained, the corporate archives should hold the original negatives and high-quality prints. Certainly the corporate archives should retain a comprehensive set of company promotional publications. Other archives may determine that product catalogs, brochures, and advertisements are sufficient visual documentation for archival purposes, although such materials will be limited in the quality of reproduction that they allow.

The visual artwork generated in its various stages by a business, or an outside agency commissioned to develop a promotional campaign, may include works of exceptional distinction and merit. Notable visual artists have worked for such projects, and all archivists should always be alert to such material easily being buried and forgotten. Moreover, one generation's advertising becomes another's art, and decisions about what to keep and what to jettison are invariably subjective. Archives with broad mandates would undoubtedly be looking for more unique and exceptional art work, whereas the corporate archivist might well be prepared to retain more repetitive material. Both, however, should be open to artwork that may become very popular and exceedingly commercial for succeeding generations.

Sound and visual promotional material, over time, will reflect so much more about the image of the company than can ever be understood when they were produced. What personalities and styles were used for their promotions, how they expected their product or service to be used, and even societal values of the time that the company was trying to identify with will be powerfully revealed in sound and visual promotional productions. Nonetheless, from season to season or year to year, such productions may sometimes change very little and, even within a season, many different versions of different lengths might be prepared. The corporate archives might want to be comprehensive in retaining such productions but would certainly not need all the versions that may ever have been generated. Other archives would only consider such productions that reflect substantial changes in the company products or image. Original recordings shot for such productions will usually simply reflect redundant images and sound and thus need not be considered for archival purposes.

Radio and television advertising has almost always been created and distributed by outside agencies. During the advertising campaign itself, copies are prolific but then are often summarily disposed of when no longer required. Such commercials will speak volumes about the company, its products and services, its relationship to the consumer as well as reflecting the social and cultural values of the day. Ideally, companies should include the deposit of high-quality copies of all such advertising as a condition of the contract to make such commercials. This has rarely been done, and thus the corporate archivist will have to search out such commercials in the storerooms of the creating agencies and in the basements of the radio and television stations that aired them. Other archives may prefer to acquire such collections directly from the companies that produced the commercials.

Companies that were innovative in their promotional campaigns, set examples followed by others, or had particularly long-standing campaigns should have a comprehensive range of their sound and visual records maintained. Both Kraft Foods and Coca-Cola, for example, acknowledge that their radio and television advertising are their most frequently requested items from their corporate archives.

Sound and Visual Materials Communicating Business Activities. Film and video has long been used for the training of staff in all aspects of a business's functions. Invariably, such productions are disposed of when new and updated versions are produced. A wide selection of productions actually generated by a business should be retained for their archival value. Here the corporate archives will undoubtedly retain a good deal more than will other archives. Such productions will often document precisely how the company product or service was assembled or prepared—knowledge that is easily lost over the course of time. Moreover, such training films will document tools and techniques that may well have become obsolete. They will reflect how careful or careless, and indeed how dangerous, recommended operating procedures may have been. Training films and videos purchased by a business from others have very little value as records of the business that purchased them.

Similarly, films, videos, or more recently, multimedia productions are being generated for customers to install and maintain the products and services purchased from businesses. These will not only document how the company products and services functioned but how they were expected to be used. Again, all such productions should be considered of potential archival value, and the corporate archives will retain a good deal more than other archives will be able to.

Businesses have long used still photographs in company newsletters and, in recent years, have sometimes instituted video productions as internal communications vehicles. All archives should consider retaining a comprehensive set of such company communications. They provide excellent sources for tracing company developments exactly because they are dated and intended to communicate news of internal interest. The corporate archives may also consider acquiring the original negatives (and good quality prints) and original moving image footage accumulated for such purposes. The actual newsletters or video releases might well be sufficient for other archives.

Sound and Visual Materials as Business Tools. Sound recording for office dictation and transcription was one of the earliest uses of this technology. When the purpose of such recordings was to generate correspondence or a written record of a meeting, then the original recording may have little archival value. In such cases, the manuscript or typed record will invariably be the version that has been authenticated by company usage. In more recent years, such sound and video recordings may never have been transcribed. Then the sound and visual record may indeed become the most reliable documentation of the meeting. Such sound and visual records will need to be retained by the corporate archives, depending on the nature of the meeting. Moreover, if any such recordings happen to include a rare example of a personality important to the company, or a controversial point in the company's history, then the sound and visual recording should also be retained by any archives documenting the business' role in the community. Every company will have legendary figures or events that are frequently referred to in company lore. The sound and visual evidence of such legends may not always support the myths held within an institution, but these records are all the more important as evidence exactly for that reason.

Emerging sound technologies such as answering machines, voice mail, and voice annotation can be similarly understood as office tools and, generally, of minimal archival value. Moreover, such technologies are invariably designed to generate only momentary recordings and are so pervasive that an archival strategy would have to be exceedingly sophisticated and ambitious to select and capture them. The cost and effort of such an archival program could rarely be justified for any archives.

Surveillance video systems have been available for some years and recently have become an effective and efficient component of the security system for many businesses. Recordings generated by such systems are invariably of low quality and designed to be recyclable. When a notable incident is captured on such cameras a proactive strategy is required to very quickly determine whether such recordings are of potential archival value. Copying to conventional video formats would be recommended for any recordings to be retained since security surveillance video systems are invariably idiosyncratic and not designed for longevity. However, such copying must be scrupulously documented to demonstrate the continuous custody necessary for evidence to be accepted in court. The corporate archives might well have to retain more of such material, for potential legal reasons, whereas other archives would be highly selective.

Photographs of employees are another common component of security systems in recent years. The technology employed for such purposes usually generates no negatives and the photographs are not of high visual quality. Such photographs will rarely have any archival value.

Appraising the Medium. As with any archival medium, or type of archival record, the archivist must have a good understanding of the evolution of the use of the particular records being handled. The sound and visual archivist must have a good understanding of the technological evolution of the media and formats that they are dealing with. Each medium and format has its particular time line and technological evolution that must be known to assess the relative importance of visual and sound materials and to develop the appropriate conservation measures.

Still photography was invented in 1839 but was not extensively used by business until the 1890s. From that point until the present, photographers have employed a wide variety of negative formats, including 4 × 5 inch, 7 × 10 inch, and 8 × 10 inch. Color photography became widely available in the 1930s, but black and white negatives and prints will always be much more permanent. Beginning in 1935, Kodachrome color transparency film, with beautiful and somewhat more stable color, was available to commercial photographers. Unfortunately, most color film invented and sold to the present day have much less image stability.[3]

Sound recording was invented in 1877, but for the first 50 years it was a mechanical-acoustical process that made recordings of this period extremely fragile and relatively rare. Thereafter, from the 1920s until the 1950s, most sound recordings were made in recording studios or on relatively cumbersome and expensive equipment. The advent of magnetic tape in the 1950s allowed virtually anyone to make their own recordings for a great variety of serious and frivolous purposes. Mass-consumer sound recording technologies since the 1960s have wide variations in the quality of sound being recorded as well as considerable differences in the longevity of particular formats.[4]

Film technology was invented in 1895 and was combined with sound recording and playback in the 1920s. The 35 and 16 mm formats have always required considerable skill and investments and therefore remained primarily professional formats. The 16 and 35 mm moving image film formats have not been much tampered with over the years, and current playback technology can be used on older film if it remains in good condition. Early moving image film can produce a very high quality reproduction if the film medium has survived without damage over the years.[5]

Video technology was invented in the late 1950s and has gone through some 40 professional and amateur formats in less than 40 years. The most common open reel formats are in the 2 inch and 1 inch widths and for cassettes the 3/4 inch U-matic and 1/2 inch VHS formats. Amateur video formats began to be available in the 1970s and in the 1990s began to approach professional quality. The sound and video technologies have improved dramatically over this time but have not yet reached the visual qualities of film, despite all the promotional enthusiasm surrounding each innovation.[6]

The medium of film for either still images or moving images is a relatively stable archival medium although it will inevitably become brittle and shrink over time. Proper storage and careful handling of still photographs and negatives goes a long way towards their preservation. However, even a small degree of shrinkage for moving image film can impede its smooth movement through sprocket-driven equipment. Moreover, any projection or printing of moving image film is inherently damaging to moving image film and therefore rarely projected prints or master printing material are preferable for preserving the original quality of moving images. Cellulose nitrate was the common base for both still and moving images from the medium's beginning until the early 1950s and has received lots of attention for its highly flammable nature. Nonetheless, it does not necessarily self-destruct and, with appropriate monitoring and storage, may preserve its original images for a good long time. Color dyes for both still and moving image film tend to fade and distort, although film manufacturers have produced some film stocks that are noticeably more stable than others. Cold storage dramatically enhances the life expectancy of film and is strongly recommended for all film stocks.[7]

Magnetic tape was invented in the late 1940s and almost immediately in the 1950s became the preferred sound recording medium for both professional and home recording. The rapid evolution of sound and video technologies, and the consequent varieties of magnetic tape developed for each format, make it difficult to anticipate how long particular sound or video magnetic tapes will survive. Controlled environments with minimal temperature and humidity fluctuations is recommended for all magnetic tape. Also, virtually all magnetic tape will benefit from regular rewinding, as long as the rewinding itself does not further damage the tape. Appropriate cleaning and playback equipment can sometimes yield surprisingly good results as the quality of the sound and image recorded may be better than what past amplifiers, speakers and monitors allowed one to hear and see.

Conservation Implications

The conservation of sound and visual materials tends to be more expensive and difficult than for conventional archival records. Therefore, the conservation implications for taking in such records has to be considered in appraising a collection.

Finding the most appropriate storage environment that an archives or a business can afford is one of the most immediate priorities for sound and visual materials. Often such materials have accumulated in damp and dirty environments with wildly fluctuating temperature and humidity and no supervision or security. Improving this storage environment will do more to preserve the material than any other single measure.

Sound and visual materials are the products of chemical processes that tend to undo themselves over time. Fluctuating temperature and humidity will accelerate this auto-destruction. Cooler temperatures for still and moving image film are known to improve the preservation of these materials, with a doubling of the life expectancy for film with each 10 degrees Fahrenheit that the temperature is lowered. We expect the same result for magnetic tape, but we do not yet have conclusive results. Also, as sound and visual materials age they give off minute quantities of gases that can themselves further accelerate their deterioration. Therefore, good ventilation to disperse such gases is essential in storage areas for sound and visual materials.

Storage containers can often contribute to the further deterioration of sound and visual materials. Tightly sealed containers do not allow for the required ventilation and should be opened. Broken, dented or inappropriate containers can further damage sound and visual materials. For example, acid-laden envelopes for still photo prints and negatives or oxidized (rusted) metal cans for film actually accelerate the deterioration of these media. Appropriate archival containers have been developed for sound and visual material and should be a high priority after improving the storage environment.

Cleaning sound and visual materials prevents contaminants from becoming further embedded and damaging the original media. However, this must be done with considerable care as inappropriate equipment, cleaning materials, and procedures can easily exacerbate their deterioration. Simple cleaning of these media invariably yields surprising improvements in the visual and sound quality of these materials and can be a good deal more effective (and less expensive) than high-tech and electronic enhancement techniques.

Appropriate conservation measures for sound and visual materials can be expensive and difficult to justify relative to other archival media. Archivists have to be judicious in determining which conservation measures are most urgent in their circumstances and which are most likely to be funded by their parent bodies. Periodic monitoring of sound and visual archives is essential to spot materials in the early stages of deterioration. Also, because deterioration and damage to sound and visual materials can be more dramatic than for conventional archival records, sometimes it may be easier to gain resources for remedial conservation for sound and visual records, despite the substantial outlays required.

Copying. Copying obsolete sound and visual formats to contemporary formats is a necessary step to ensure their access and survival. Copying allows such materials to be handled and played back without damage to fragile originals, and it salvages whatever information can be gleaned from deteriorating originals. Such copying, or migration, for either reference or conservation purposes is invariably expensive and labor intensive and, therefore, can rarely be applied comprehensively as archivists and conservators would prefer. Few institutions holding sound and visual materials will be able to afford a proactive conservation strategy, taking all the appropriate measures to protect all records in their custody.

Archives will have to develop a strategy for migrating their sound and visual materials to contemporary formats that will acknowledge the ongoing deterioration of their collection. Criteria for what gets copied first must balance among the stage of deterioration or likely deterioration, high-profile items that are clear priorities for everyone, and immediate access requests. The archivist must always make the case for more proactive and comprehensive copying but often accept that copying will only be funded in response to particular demands. When users require sound and visual materials, they should then cover copying costs, and this can be a perfectly responsible archival strategy for sound and visual materials.

Appropriate preparation of original sound and visual materials must be undertaken before copying. This will require assembling the best possible master material and determining the appropriate original sequence and version of the sound and visual productions. Preparation may also require manually repairing splices, sprocket holes, and tears and undertaking other tedious and time-consuming tasks. There are a great variety of temporary restoration techniques that have been used with some success, including the controlled heating or "baking" of magnetic tape under carefully monitored conditions. All preparation has to proceed with considerable caution and should be tested on samples before comprehensive application. Modern electronic techniques promise much in the "restoration" of sound and visual materials but cannot be relied upon to accurately recover information that has been lost or obscured. Before even considering such electronic enhancement techniques the original materials must be repaired and restored as much as possible.

The archivist must be aware of the distinction between copying for reference purposes and copying for preservation purposes and make difficult choices about which formats and media are to be used for each. Occasionally reference and preservation purposes can be served by making duplicate copies via the same process. However, the archivist must become knowledgeable about the limitations and capacities of a considerable variety of copying technologies. Archival sound and visual materials are often expected to be inferior to contemporary audio-visual technologies and, therefore, can sometimes be copied very poorly. Invariably the original equipment that the media were recorded on, rather than the most contemporary format available, will allow for the best reproduction. Similarly, technicians and operators who are knowledgeable and responsive to the original potential quality should be found. The importance of monitoring this copying process must be stressed. If sound or visual information is lost or obscured through copying it can rarely be reliably recovered by subsequent enhancements.

Successful copying of sound and visual materials should not automatically allow one to dispose of the original materials. Copying processes have improved substantially over the years and thus it may often be possible to go back to original materials and obtain better copies. Also the evolving appreciation of archival materials over the years will provide many reasons to return to original materials to obtain the best and most complete information that they can yield. Therefore, the disposition of original visual and sound materials can only be justified if they deteriorated beyond further use, or if they represent a hazard to the rest of the archival collection.

Intellectual Control

The description and cataloging of sound and visual materials should not proceed in isolation from other archives holding similar materials. Following similar cataloging rules will facilitate the sharing of information about holdings and avoid duplication of effort. Cataloging of sound and visual materials is so labor intensive that no archives can afford to repeat work already done elsewhere.

Collection level and series level description of sound and visual materials will not be sufficient or particularly useful for any subsequent research or further use. Item level description with the title, where one was assigned, as the principal entry is the standard approach for sound and visual materials. Indeed, shot-listing of sound and visual materials is invariably the preferred descriptive strategy. Such detailed levels of description are recommended to avoid having researchers handle original materials and operate the specialized playback equipment that many visual and sound media require. Also, sound and visual archives soon discover that researchers most often request very specific individual items rather than a complete series of records as is more common with conventional textual records.

Such labor-intensive cataloging approaches are never inexpensive, and, therefore, the archivist responsible for sound and visual materials must make very astute judgments about which portions of the collection warrant this treatment. Areas where a collection is strongest and most unique will warrant this investment in time and effort. Also, cataloging of sound and visual materials, more than that of conventional archival records, is driven by anticipated research needs. This can be both an opportunity and a liability for sound and visual materials. The archivist must be adroit in turning research requests into opportunities. Archives with broad mandates may sometimes feel compelled to carefully consider acquisitions according to their cataloging resources and expertise.

Providing Access

Providing immediate and satisfactory access to archival collections for the business that generated the records has to be the first priority for any archival program. Sound and visual materials are often particularly attractive, and, therefore, providing access to them becomes all the more important. The corporate archives will invariably be expected to supply answers to queries or furnish copies and must be equipped to do so. Broadcasters will demand immediate access to visual and sound materials as they work on notoriously short deadlines. If the archives want to work with them such demands should be anticipated and satisfied. Similar requests will be made of all archives holding sound and visual materials. Users of sound and visual materials often do not want to visit the archives as they might with conventional archival records. Archives other than corporate archives rarely hold the rights to sound and visual materials and, therefore, must develop a careful strategy to respond to this expectation.

Anniversaries provide a flurry of requests for access to all sorts of archival records, particularly photographs for various displays and publications. Anniversaries can, therefore, represent a wonderful opportunity for recognizing the value of the archival records, and the archivist must fully exploit these opportunities. However, this flurry of interest can also destroy the original context and provenance of the material by reorganizing materials for the current needs. Such reorganizing of archival materials should be resisted even if such projects are favorite projects for special funding.

Providing access to archival records to exploit them as a corporate asset is of growing interest everywhere. Multimedia publishing, information highway opportunities, and specialty television channels are generating tremendous appetites for archival records, particularly visual and sound materials. Businesses can both be blind to these opportunities or overly optimistic in expecting immediate and dramatic returns from investments in the exploiting of their archives as corporate assets. The archivist must be very shrewd in making use of these opportunities to preserve, catalog, and make accessible archival visual and sound materials without distorting an archival program in pursuit of these opportunities.

It is virtually impossible to imagine all the future uses for visual and sound materials that a business may have generated. To estimate the further-use value of these materials is even more hazardous. Therefore, it is recommended that rights and potential profits be appropriately shared between the business generating the materials, the archives now holding and protecting the material, and the publisher selling the material. In this way, every partner has a stake in making such ventures work.

Conclusion

Sound and visual archival records present a considerable range of challenges and opportunities. The purpose of this chapter has been to provide an archival strategy for dealing with sound and visual records, so archivists will not be intimidated and overwhelmed by them. Yes, they require more time, money, and expertise than conventional archival materials, but they also represent bold new opportunities never heretofore imagined by archivists.

Sound and visual materials are an integral component of the heritage that business leaves for posterity. They represent exceptional business and information value that we have not yet begun to understand. They may well document the enthusiasms, the expectations, and the energy of business better than any other type of archival record. Sound and visual archives may also represent new opportunities for business to become part of the information economy.

Endnotes

1. The Association of Recorded Sound Collections is the North American archival association that deals with all aspects of sound recording in its publications and annual conferences, whereas the International Association of Sound Archives does the same on the international level. The Visual Materials Section of the Society of American Archivists incorporates many of the photographic archives and issues in North America. For film and television, the Association of Moving Image Archivists, with its secretariat at the National Centre for Film and Video Preservation at the American Film Institute in Los Angeles, is the best forum for keeping abreast of all issues relating to film and video archiving. At the international level, one can refer to the publications of the International Federation of Film Archives and the International Federation of Television Archives for discussion of film and television archiving.

2. Sam Kula, *The Archival Appraisal of Moving Images: A RAMP Study with Guidelines* (Paris: UNESCO, Records and Archives Management Program, 1983); Helen Harrison, *The Archival Appraisal of Sound Recordings and Related Materials: A RAMP Study with Guidelines* (Paris: UNESCO, Records and Archives Management Pro-

gram, 1987); William H. Leary, *The Archival Appraisal of Photographs: A RAMP Study with Guidelines* (Paris: UNESCO, Records and Archives Management Program, 1985) are the standard reference works on appraisal of sound and moving image materials. These UNESCO publications can be difficult to obtain but most larger archive libraries should have copies.

3. Mary Lynn Ritzenthaler, Gerald J. Munoff and Margery S. Long, *Archives & Manuscripts: Administration of Photographic Collections* (Chicago: Society of American Archivists, 1984) is a good general introduction to preserving still photographs. A more sophisticated discussion of the evolution of photography can be found in the essays published in Richard Bolton, ed., *The Contest of Meaning, Critical Histories of Photography* (Cambridge, Mass.: MIT Press, 1989).

4. Jerry McWilliams, *The Preservation and Restoration of Sound Recordings* (Nashville, Tenn.: American Association for State and Local History, 1979) is a good general introduction to all archival aspects of sound recordings. Oliver Read and Walter W. Welch, *From Tin Foil to Stereo: Evolution of the Phonograph* (Indianapolis: Howard W. Sams, 1976), is a wide ranging and comprehensive history of the technology of published recordings. The development of sound magnetic recording has been well documented in the journals of the Audio Engineering Society.

5. Eastmak Kodak, *The Book of Film Care* (Rochester, N.Y.: Eastman Kodak, 1983), often available from them free of charge, is a good introduction to all archival questions of dealing with film. Ralph N. Sargent's *Preserving the Moving Image* (Washington, D.C.: Corporation for Public Broadcasting in Washington, 1974) is a more extensive discussion of moving image technological development. The journals of the Society of Motion Picture and Television Engineers have documented many aspects of film and television technology over the years.

6. John W. C. Bogart, *Magnetic Tape Storage and Handling: A Guide for Libraries and Archives* (Washington, D.C.: Commission on Preservation and Access, 1995) is a good introduction to all aspects of video tape archiving. For more sophisticated and current discussions on emerging issues see the newsletter and Internet listserve AMIA-L@lsv.uky.edu of the Association of Moving Image Archivists.

7. Henry Wilhelm and Carol Brower, *The Permanence and Care of Color Photographs: Traditional Color Prints, Color Negatives, Slides and Motion Pictures* (Grinnell, Iowa: Preservation Publishing Company, 1993) is a good discussion of all aspects of film conservation. Also, the Image Permanence Institute at the Rochester Institute of Technology is constantly undertaking research, publishing reports, and offering guidelines for the best archival storage environments and procedures for film.

11

Beyond Business:
External Documentation and
Corporate Records

Timothy L. Ericson

Documenting business, whether individual corporations or the broader business community, has always posed a dilemma for American archivists. We have a love-hate relationship with business records. On the one hand, it is impossible to deny that business is the life's blood of the individual communities, states, or other geographical regions that we seek to document. In certain respects it is the glue that holds society together. The wages paid by businesses are the foundation on which either prosperity or ruin rest. The fluctuation of business cycles has an immediate impact on individuals, families, and civic improvements that depend on tax-based financing. Corporate philanthropy makes possible cultural attractions such as symphonies, orchestras, theaters, and museums that otherwise could not exist. The activity of businesses may have an impact on public health. In other words, documenting business is a responsibility that is far too important for archivists and historians to ignore.

On the other hand, business records present a difficult quandary. Of the thousands of businesses that exist even in a small geographic area, how many collections of records do we really need to preserve? Business records, particularly those of large corporations, have the justifiable reputation of being so voluminous as to defy the best efforts of most archival repositories to preserve and make them available for research. These and other concerns make the questions of appraisal particularly important, but we inevitably have difficulty answering the questions associated with "research for what?" and "research by whom?" Business records frequently are inaccessible for research by historians or others outside of the corporation, or the records come with restrictions that make them less useful as sources of information. Finally, decisions about what records merit long-term preservation frequently differ, depending upon whether they are based upon corporate needs or upon broader historical or cultural criteria.

Because of such factors as these, archivists and historians are wise to consider employing alternate strategies to achieve their documentary goals. The overall purpose of this chapter is to consider one of these: the use of external documentation, to achieve balanced and adequate documentation of a particular business, the business community generally, or of a selected industry. The term *external documentation* generally includes a broad array of sources that contain information about a business concern but which, unlike corporate records, were created by an individual or agency outside the company. Specific categories, discussed later in this chapter, may include state or federal records, newspaper or other published sources, and organizational records and personal papers.

However, before considering in greater detail either the specific forms of external documentation or the instances in which they may be usefully employed, it is necessary to lay some groundwork that will provide a more realistic context to the discussion. The use of external documentation is only one option among several that are available to archivists and historians. This approach has advantages and disadvantages that must be weighed carefully against one another before one decides on external documentation as a viable strategy. Specifically, we need to consider five key questions and issues:

1. **What exactly are the dimensions of the impediments associated with documenting business?** Why can't we just collect and save business records and be done with it? Knowing the nature of the problem will help us to more clearly understand how we can best overcome it.

2. **What are some of the strategies other than external documentation that archivists and historians might employ in order to achieve the goal of better documentation?** Considering these is necessary in order to determine whether using external documentation is the most effective means available to us, or if it is a strategy that might best be used in conjunction with other actions. A knowledge of other options will inform our

decision making about information that may either substitute for business records or fill gaps that otherwise would exist in the documentary record.

3. **What are the benefits and the possible drawbacks of using external documentation as a strategy to achieve better documentation?** Are there limitations to what we can expect to achieve through the use of external documentary sources? Can external documentation be misused? In reality, it probably is only through the selective and informed use of a number of different strategies that the ultimate goal of preserving adequate and balanced documentation can be achieved.

4. **What is the range of external sources at our disposal?** What types of information can external documentation provide for us? What are some of the limitations that are inherent in the use of external documentation?

5. **Based upon the above questions, are there generalizations we can make concerning the use of external documentation?** This question is particularly important because, in many respects, business records are simply a portion of the broader field of institutional records. The use of external sources may have application with respect to documentary concerns of other types of organizations and topics as well.

The Nature of the Problem with Documenting Business

One of the primary problems with documenting business is that the term *business* itself can have many different meanings, depending on the size, organizational complexity, and other factors of the organization it describes.[1] A business can be a single proprietorship or partnership with one or two employees; or it can define a large corporation with 10,000 or more workers. The entire operation and market of a small business can be located geographically within a single community; a larger corporation may be spread out over a far-flung region, including other states and even other countries. The distinction is important because records reflect activities and the information needs of the organization that created them. It is no surprise, then, that the challenges archivists face when preserving the records of American business will differ considerably depending upon the type of business to which we are referring.

Furthermore, any given company may be publicly or privately held, and it can be organized in any way that seemed to make sense to its founders at the time. Business executives have a good deal of leeway in how their companies are organized. Likewise, the records they create will frequently vary enormously in their organization and content, unlike, for example, local, state, and federal public records.

Another dimension to the problem concerns the potential quantity of corporate documentation that is available to preserve. This concern has at least three facets. First, there is an enormous number of corporations in the United States, and neither archivists nor historians can realistically hope to preserve records—even only records with archival value—from all of them. In a similar way, a single corporation may generate an impossible quantity of records that defies preservation in its entirety. Much has been written about the problems associated with the excessive quantity of business records from large corporations, but probably no writer has expressed the situation nationally in a more dramatic fashion than David Bearman in his "Selection and Appraisal" chapter in *Archival Methods:*

> Even if we assume . . . that there might be as many as 10,000 archives in the United States, we must be struck by the disparity between this figure and the over 3 million corporations (over 500,000 of which report incomes [of more than] $1 million per annum) . . . The organizations which could have archives and which archivists would normally wish to document include over 50,000 banks, 20,000 radio, television, and cable stations, 6800 hospitals, . . . 3300 universities and colleges[, and] 25,000 associations.[2]

Although his focus is wider than the business community per se, Bearman's examples clearly show the problems associated with acquiring contemporary records of American business; there are simply too many of them, not only with respect to numbers of corporations, but also to the enormous quantity of records each produces.

The third facet of our concern with quantity is less frequently considered but equally important. How does one approach the goal of documenting the myriad of small businesses whose documentary records may be too sparse rather than too plentiful? Although archivists and historians frequently focus their attention on the "paper mountain," numerically most businesses are not large, multinational corporations; they are small "mom and pop" concerns whose impact is purely local. Collectively, however, the impact of these small businesses is at least as important as that of the large corporations. Unfortunately, those seeking to preserve or use for research purposes historical records from small businesses often discover that there is precious little documentary evidence from which to glean information.

Both situations—either too much or too little—compel archivists and historians to consider other strategies in their quest to collect, preserve, and make available for research purposes an adequate documentary record of the business community.

Perhaps the most difficult dimension of the problem of business records can be described as a "culture clash," or what some would describe as the incompatible missions that businesses and historical agencies seem to have. Corporations exist to make a profit for their owners, not to preserve history or to facilitate historical research in the way that scholars or archivists outside of the business community would like them to do. As the extremely low number of American corporate archives attests, few have been convinced that it is in their economic best interests to do so. The attitude was recently described bluntly by one corporate archivist as an "inherent corporate hostility toward history."[3] The only arguments that will convince many business executives otherwise are those that link preserving history with core corporate functions such as marketing, public relations, or preparing for litigation.

This need, or mission, influences both what records a business may save and what it will make available for research. Like any archival repository, a business archives must define itself according to the mission and priorities of its parent organization and its mandate within the company.[4] This is a necessary part of effectively running any archival operation, but in this case, the mission of the company and the goals of historical agencies and outside researchers are frequently incompatible with one another.

However, many nonbusiness archivists cling to a traditional view of their work that emphasizes cultural, humanistic goals rather than the profit motive. Such people have been slow to accept the fact that scholarship is a tough sell in the business community. Those outside of the corporate world have been slow to embrace or understand the perspective of company executives. They doggedly search for new and better ways to inculcate business executives with their own values, taking comfort in the belief that an appreciation for preserving history will come as the business community becomes more "mature."[5]

The other dimension of the "mission problem" is evident within the community of historical records repositories themselves. Stated simply, there is a considerable difference in perspective between a repository whose primary interest is to preserve records that will support an intensive study of business practice, or of a specific industry, and a repository such as a historical society whose mission is generally focused on documenting a community or a state and of which business is only a "piece of the puzzle." The latter repositories frequently find it difficult to deal with large quantities of corporate records or to satisfy the needs of researchers with varying interests.

The result is that, at least from the scholar's perspective, the "wrong" documentation is preserved. Business records, whether from a corporate archives or those that were later turned over to a historical agency, reflect corporate interests rather than a broader historical perspective. Because corporate archives exist to serve the informational needs of the company, the business records they save are subject to a closer cost-benefit scrutiny.[6] In this context, valuable information is that which serves current business needs and contributes to the company's profit. In the same way, collections containing records that reflect poorly on a company, or that may constitute a liability in possible future litigation, will almost certainly be "sanitized"—with no regard to their value as historical treasures that some future scholar may need—once the records are no longer needed. Archivists and historians need to accept the fact that retention of records purely because of their historical value is a less compelling incentive to save records in the corporate world than in academia.

Consider the possible variations on a single set of corporate records generated by Company X that might be available to scholars for research: (1) a "documentary reminiscence" collected by a good and faithful employee of long-standing; (2) records preserved by a corporate executive interested primarily in self-aggrandizement; (3) documentation collected by the public relations or marketing department in order to "provide products that are wanted and enhance the company's image in some way"; (4) records retained by the office of legal affairs as a resource to help in prosecuting copyright or patent infringement cases. Such motivations, or missions, would yield four very different archival collections. The result of having access to and using only one of the above would result, inevitably, in a skewed and incomplete picture of the Company X's history.[7]

A final dimension to the problem of business records concerns access by outside historians or other scholars. Even when corporate records are preserved, frequently they are not available for use by outside historians and other scholars. In the same way that corporations frequently base decisions on what records will be saved, they are also free to decide who will be able to use them for research. As the result of one survey concluded, "the business is free to organize and *control* [emphasis added] its archives as it wishes, within the guidelines of company policy." Restrictions may be imposed for a variety of reasons, such as to safeguard company secrets or to avoid bad publicity or litigation caused by "muckrakers." When access is given, it frequently is limited in scope and is contingent upon the company retaining the right to review and approve the eventual product of a researcher's work. Even some in-house corporate archivists and historians themselves prefer to limit access to records by researchers in an effort to avoid the inevitable contact with buffs and collectors that results from opening a collection to research.[8]

Possible Strategies

Although the focus of this paper is using external documentation to help achieve an adequate and balanced historical record of business, the improved documentation of business (or any aspect of society for that matter) may possibly be facilitated by employing any one of a number of other strategies. In order to assess whether using external sources of documentation constitutes the most practical and effective approach, it is necessary first to briefly consider several other approaches as a basis for comparison. Having considered the broad range of options, it becomes easier to make decisions based upon one's institutional mission as it relates to the type and extent of information needed. It is also well to remember that the strategies that follow need not be exclusive options. They also may be employed in conjunction with one another depending on the particular circumstances.

Increased selectivity of business records through increasingly rigorous appraisal techniques and collection development policies can help to alleviate many of the problems associated with acquiring and administering voluminous collections of records. The development of formal appraisal guidelines and criteria is not new. The idea has been a prominent weapon in the archival arsenal since at least the time of the First World War. Its earliest stage of formal development in the United States took place at the National Archives and resulted in the articulation of core archival appraisal theory and the definition of archival values to assist archivists in the decision-making process.

More recently, the need to make better decisions has been addressed at the institutional level through the drafting and adoption of more precisely worded and discriminating acquisition development policies. Originally, such policies were almost always done from an institutional perspective, more in an effort to "stake out" territory and without much consideration of what other archival repositories were doing. Traditionally, they were designed to address institutional concerns and articulate internal priorities and goals. Gradually, however, they have proven useful at reducing the size of the "harvest" by narrowing a repository's collecting focus and taking advantage of cooperative approaches when it is feasible to do so.

This approach still has its limitations. Although most archivists and historians would agree to the idea of a national strategy of some sort for business or, for that matter, any other sort of documentation, in reality few do more than pay lip service to the goal. Like world peace, when the time comes to make difficult decisions, the result will almost always be based on a local or institutional self-interest rather than "the greater good."

Newly developed appraisal frameworks build upon previous appraisal theory and acquisition development policy thinking to formulate additional options for archivists and historians to consider. One of the most prominent of recent years has been the documentation strategy that proposed: "An ongoing, analytic, cooperative approach designed, promoted, and implemented by creators, administrators (including archivists) and users to ensure the retention of appropriate documentation of some area of human endeavor."[9] This conceptual framework acknowledges the interrelatedness of modern documentation and incorporates a close "analysis of the universe to be documented" and refined institutional acquisition policies. It encourages the establishment of institutional archives to share in the responsibility for preserving the documentation with historical value that they produce.[10]

Other conceptual frameworks include what has become known as the "Black Box" approach and the use of "documentary probes" to better determine the value of records in an institutional context. The former makes use of a series of "modules" ("Value of Information," "Costs of Retention," and "Policy Implications") as the basis for making decisions.[11] The latter is "a product study [using research, interviews, records surveying, and the description of industrial activity] that generates diverse historical, organizational, and documentary information from all facets of a company in order to aid in the selection of historically valuable records."[12]

More recently, others have advocated a functional approach to selecting records for preservation. For example, in her groundbreaking study *Varsity Letters: Documenting Modern Colleges and Universities*, Helen Willa Samuels "suggests starting the selection process with a different set of questions: focusing first not on the specific history, people, events, structure, or records of an institution, but an understanding of what an institution does—what are its functions." Although her case study uses the university as a context for discussion, a number of the steps Samuels outlines can be applied generically, and she rightly advocates the methodology for use by other institutions, including business concerns.[13]

Another strategy, now more than 30 years old although not widely employed, involves cooperation between historical records repositories to permit the temporary interinstitutional loans for research purposes of original archival collections. The idea is still controversial within the archival community for reasons that are increasingly unclear in an age when museums willingly transport paintings and other works of art worth millions of dollars across the globe for exhibitions in distant lands. Where such interinstitutional archival loans have been implemented, primarily in Wisconsin, they have had a number of notable benefits. Historical records repositories of varying sizes share the cost and the responsibility of preserving records. The ability to temporarily transfer records enables archivists to better serve the needs of researchers. Loans have increased access to records, facilitated research, and reduced competition in collecting. In particular, they have reduced the need to collect so exhaustively while still enabling researchers to bring together a large corpus of documentation that meets their particular needs. In the context of business records, it has served the needs of smaller repositories with a purely local interest in a particular firm and larger research collections that attract researchers with a broader set of interests. It has helped to preclude the problems that inevitably result when small local repositories take on large corporate collections and then find it difficult to maintain the records and make them available.[14]

Another strategy that has found favor in recent years involves archivists contracting with individual businesses to provide fee-based archival services, wherein the business pays for all or a portion of the expenses associated with preserving and making corporate records available. Such fees enhance the amount of resources available for preserving archival records. Although not yet widely used in the archival community at this time, the strategy is gaining in acceptance as archivists find that they can no longer take on the expense of acquiring and maintaining large quantities of records from an ongoing business concern.[15] In a similar development, individual businesses have found that outsourcing archival services is more cost effective than establishing and staffing an in-house archives. Another variation of this strategy is for archives to negotiate a onetime corporate donation to help with the initial acquisition and processing of corporate records.

External Documentation

The final strategy, the subject of this chapter, is employing the use of external documentation to meet documentary needs. This strategy frequently draws upon ideas such as interinstitutional cooperation that are integral to a number of the approaches just discussed above. It has the potential to help obtain information not otherwise available from businesses records for whatever reason. As such, external documentation has the potential to help us to achieve our documentary goals efficiently and more effectively.

However, in order to employ this strategy effectively, we must first examine it critically, looking at possible sources and the advantages and disadvantages of each. At first glance external documentation seems such a logical solution that it has the unfortunate potential to seem a panacea. If not considered carefully it can become an excuse to absolve us from our responsibility to preserve corporate records. External documentation can provide an easy way out that seemingly excuses us from seeking better solutions and making difficult decisions. Failure to look critically at the sources, the advantages, and the disadvantages of using external documentation may result in relying too much on a single option to the exclusion of others.

Sources of External Documentation

Listing and describing in detail the sources of external documentation and the information such sources may contain is far beyond the scope of this chapter. There are too many variations in records, such as those generated by state and local government agencies, and too many information needs to consider to evaluate adequately the quality of each resource as possible external documentation. Even so, a brief overview will suggest some of the common resources that are available and thus help to inform any conclusions concerning the relative merit of this particular strategy. The list that follows is not entirely consistent intellectually in its categorization of records, but it reflects the way that archivists discuss records. Hopefully, the mix of record types and forms will be useful as a way to consider different forms of external documentation and the information they may contain. For the sake of continuity, the specific examples and illustrations that follow are largely drawn from the Milwaukee, Wisconsin region that is served by the author's archival repository.

Published Sources. Monographs or pamphlets, trade catalogs, articles in scholarly or popular journals, and trade and professional journals are probably the external sources that come most quickly to mind. Company histories frequently are the product of the research use of business records, and as such they need only brief mention to remind us that they are a possible source of external documentation. Published sources may vary in quality and extent from well-documented scholarly studies, to coffee-table picture books written as a public relations effort, to highly technical monographs written by and for hobbyists. Included are formal business histories, more general histories of industries, biographies, studies of business practice that use as a case study a particular corporation, and even some community histories that contain a large number of short histories or biographies of significant local business concerns, industries, or leaders.

The number of such sources can sometime be extensive. For example, Milwaukee's Harley-Davidson Motor Company has been the subject of no fewer than 26 full-length books that aptly illustrate the range of documentation that is possible. Included are heavily illustrated volumes written specifically for Harley collectors, more traditional histories, and even two volumes of Harley-Davidson poetry by Martin Jack Rosenblum, the company's current historian, known by his pen name, the "Holy Ranger."

Reference works such as the Moody's and the Standard & Poor's manuals, Dun & Bradstreet reports, the Facts on File series on the automobile and banking industries, and the multivolume *International Directory of Company Histories* are significant sources for understanding American business history. As with other types of sources, published materials must be used cautiously because they were created with a specific purpose in mind. One must ascertain, in archival terms, how published sources are "impartial," or what purposes they were created to serve.[16] The perspective they reflect may not be a reliable indicator of historical truth or fact.

Newspapers. This commonly used source of external documentation, in many respects, could have been included within the category of published sources. Their ongoing nature is sufficiently different from that of a published monograph to warrant highlighting them specifically. In a cumulative sense, the daily or weekly chronicle of major or minor news items and advertisements, as well as the occasional feature articles associated with anniversaries or other events result in a substantial body of potentially useful documentation. Newspapers, particularly those of the previous century, may contain extremely detailed descriptions of industrial activity ranging from brick making and ice harvesting to cheese making and the commercial manufacture of illuminating gas for street lights, businesses, and residences. In very recent years, the advent of on-line, full-text retrieval for many daily newspapers from major cities gives researchers the ability to identify literally hundreds of news features involving individual corporations and industries.

Many large daily newspapers have both on-line editions and also a full-text data base retrieval capability. Using Harley-Davidson again as an example, the *Milwaukee Journal-Sentinel* has a full-text searchable data base dating back to 1990. Even these limited parameters include more than a thousand articles containing external documentation relating to one of the community's most prominent businesses. To this total a researcher would be able to add still other information from commercial newspaper indexes and full-text data bases from daily newspapers in other American cities.

State and Federal Government Records. Such sources hold a wealth of specific documentation relating to individual business concerns and about entire industries, economic conditions, and issues that affect the health and well-being of workers and the business community. Although state and federal census records, especially schedules with manufacturing and agricultural statistics, are probably the most well known of these, other records generated at the federal, state, and local level are frequently even more useful.

Such records are particularly useful in instances when the government exercises its regulatory authority within the business community, such as in the cases of agriculture, transportation, consumer protection, the environment, and finance. They cover a wide range of business-related topics including incorporation, production, licensure, and bankruptcy. Other topics frequently documented in government records, especially in recent years, include issues of employee safety and environmental concerns.

Published government documents and reports from state and local agencies vary from state to state, but the potential for finding extensive and useful documentation is enormous. For example, annual "factory" inspections from the late nineteenth and early twentieth centuries by Wisconsin's Bureau of Labor Statistics frequently contain specific and detailed information on individual businesses ranging from bakeries to stave factories. The published tables summarizing such inspections include the date a business was founded, the size and composition of its work force, the number and type of buildings, and even the type of power that was used to operate machinery. In addition to factory inspections, the bureau also undertook regular initiatives to gather information about workers and conditions in the business community. For example, in 1887 and 1888, agency pollsters surveyed workers from throughout the state, asking such questions as, Does immigration injure your trade? If so, in what manner, and to what extent? Does the town where you live offer any inducements for men of your trade to acquire homes; or is employment so uncertain as to make owning a home undesirable? Responses include the profession of the respondent and the community of residence. In other years the bureau conducted similar surveys focusing on apprenticeship, child labor, and trade unionism. Specific questions explored the opinions from workers in particular industries concerning their pay, level of job satisfaction, vocational education, and work schedule. Much of the information documents the existence of single proprietorships and small, family-owned businesses that would likely not have created or preserved records useful for later scholarly study.

When the records and published reports of this single agency are combined with those of others that oversee business concerns such as banks, railroads, doctors, dentists, creameries, and cheese factories, the end result is a formidable body of external, primary documentation that can be used either in lieu of, or in addition to existing business records that have been preserved for use by researchers.

Archival and Manuscript Resources. Outside of a business that is the focus of attention for preservation or research exists a large, diverse, and potentially valuable category of external source material—one that defies detailed description in an overview such as this. Perhaps one can generalize by including within this category those individuals and organizations with which a particular business may have had dealings over time. Among the most obvious examples are records of labor unions, competitors, and businesses or organizations with which a corporation may have had dealings as a supplier or customer. Neither should archivists and researchers overlook organizations such as better business bureaus and trade associations for external source material. There are other examples as well. The papers of public officials can tell us a good deal about the environment in which business operates and the political pressures that may have prompted particular decisions. For example, a collection of mayoral records from the City of Milwaukee contains extensive files on individual businesses, neighborhood revitalization programs, and downtown redevelopment programs.[17] The papers of a former Milwaukee congressman contain similar files that are regional in nature, as well as others dealing with mass transit, railroads, airport construction, business development, congressional bailout programs and lobbying efforts by business or industrial concerns.[18]

Personal papers of business founders or former employees are another obvious resource, sometimes shedding light on activities, events, and decisions that are not documented in other sources. Such papers frequently contain records of family-owned businesses or of business interests and investments that were part of the family financial portfolio. In the same way, records of organizations that may have benefitted from corporate giving may contain extensive information pertaining to their relationship to various business concerns.

Photographic Records. In certain respects, these records may be included within the above categories, although they are sufficiently important to highlight separately. Such records may be incidental and included as illustrations to some event or condition. Frequently, their collective importance increases as records accumulate over the course of time. Photographic "morgues" maintained by newspapers are an invaluable visual resource—even though they may frequently be as inaccessible as corporate records themselves! Other businesses such

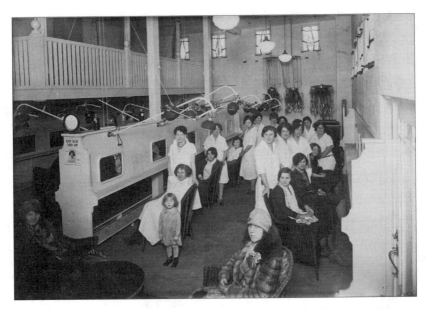

The Kwasniewski Photographic Studio that operated in Milwaukee, Wisconsin, from approximately 1915 to 1940 contains images from dozens of small businesses no longer in existence and for which no records have been preserved. The view shown here from a Milwaukee beauty shop is one of a series that provides unique visual information and also documents an ongoing advertising relationship between the studio and the beauty shop. Customers with new hair styles could receive a discounted portrait from the studio. *(Milwaukee Urban Archives, Kwasniewski Collection UWMAC-19)*

as builders or real estate companies also generate significant quantities of photographic documentation during the course of their business. A collection of more than 30,000 prints and negatives from a former Milwaukee photographic studio provides some of the only remaining documentation of a host of small neighborhood businesses such as furniture and grocery stores, taverns, and manufacturing plants. These and similar examples can provide a type of documentation containing information contained nowhere in business records.

Cartographic Resources. Although they also are frequently contained within those categories of records already discussed above, cartographic resources also merit being highlighted specifically because of the nature of the information they may contain. Sanborn Insurance maps are doubtless the most well known cartographic resource known to business historians. Founded in 1867, the company produced large-scale, extremely detailed maps of business districts and industrial sites

COMMISSIONER OF LABOR STATISTICS. 147a

*Report of Insyection—*Continued.

ESTABLISHMENTS INSPECTED.	NUMBER OF EMPLOYES.			Cost of new building improvements.	Cost of new machinery.
	Male.	Fem.	Total		
RIVER FALLS—PIERCE CO.					
Inspected May, 1893, *by Van Etten.* FORTUNE & ARMSTONG, mfrs. flour aud feed. Two building—one 8-st frame one 2-st. frame; 25 horse power. (water). Estab. 1858........ .... Ordered a railing placed at head of stairway and covers placed over three gears on purifiers on first floor.	6	......	6	....	......
GOSS J. B. & Co., mfrs. flour and feed. Four buildings—one 8-st. and three 2 st, frame; 65 horse power (water). Estab. 1853.....................	7	.....	7	$2,000	$8,0C0
LUND A. W., mfr. carrages, wagons, harness, etc. Three buildings—one 1-st. stone; two 1-st. frame; one boiler; one engine, 12 horse power. Estab. 1881... *Note.—*A fire Jan. 24, 1893 destroyed plant, loss $10,000. *Accident.—*A workman had all the fingers of his left hand cut off on shaper.	15	....	15	4,500	....
MEALEY S. J., mfr. potato starch. One 2-st. and two 1-st. frame buildings, one boiler; one engine, 80 horse power. Estab. 1888 .... *Note—*Closed at time of visit; will start about Sept. 15th. and run three months.	15	.....	15	300	2,200
RIVER FALLS STARCH FACTORY, mfrs. potato starch. Two buildings—one 2-st. frame; one 1-st. brick; one boiler; one engine, 40 horse power. Estab. 1890. .... *Note.—*Factory closed will start up in fall and run about 60 days.	11	......	11	300	....

Published government reports frequently contain surprisingly detailed information, particularly for small businesses whose corporate records may not be available. The example shown here is from the Sixth Biennial Report of the Commissioner of Labor, Census, and Industrial Statistics of Wisconsin, 1893–1894. Included are dates of founding, numbers of employees, types of power used, and even information on accidents during the past year.

across the country. The primary purpose of the maps was to assist insurance underwriters in assessing the relative risk of fire in any given downtown area. Beginning dates vary from state to state, and in rapidly expanding commercial districts the maps were updated as frequently as every second year. On some maps there are updates as recent as 1970.

Unlike many external sources that are found primarily in large urban areas, the size of a community is not a predictor of whether Sanborn maps exist. In Wisconsin, for example, there are maps for communities as large as Milwaukee, and as small as Wilson, Wisconsin, population 155.[19] Although maps for large and small communities alike focus on business districts, adjacent residential areas are also included. Where Sanborn maps of a given community exist for a number of years, it is possible to trace, in surprising detail, the growth of individual businesses over time and to document the growth of business districts as they expanded into areas that were formerly residential.

Atlases of cadastral maps, or "plat books" as they are frequently called, have been published widely for more than a century and are commonly found in archival repositories. Many of those from the late nineteenth and early twentieth century in particular contain locations of businesses such as sawmills, gristmills, or other businesses that lay along rivers. Other atlases include local business or "patron" directories, advertisements, and occasionally, detailed drawings of an individual business concern.

Maps from the decennial census and cartographic resources from agencies of state government, such as railroad maps, also contain a good deal of business-related information, particularly industry-level data. Regional planning commissions exist in most parts of the country, and they produce a variety of very detailed, large-scale maps that contain useful business documentation. There is similar information contained in the other atlases, guides, and gazetteers that were created as an aid to immigrants and for a variety of other purposes.

Oral History. This category and its more broadly considered counterpart, "aural" history (that is heard rather than read or viewed), hold the potential both to fill gaps in the documentary record and to add a different dimension to the documentation of American business. While the former category is widely defined to mean "the product of planned [formal] . . . interviews" that are "intended for research use"[20] relating to a particular topic, the latter can include such sources as the sound and visual archives of radio or television stations that were created to report a "breaking" newsworthy event, or as a part of a public affairs program dealing with a subject quite tangential to the business itself. Either of the two types may be useful by dealing with issues that are not, for whatever reason, contained in corporate records or accessible to researchers.

Unlike other categories of external documentation, oral history in particular may be created either by archivists or researchers and thus tailored to suit their particular needs. In this sense, it is particularly useful for answering very specific questions that have arisen during the course of research or for attempting to fill obvious gaps left in the corporate record. As such, oral history may provide a different perspective on a question or issue associated with a business or fill a gap left in the wake of other corporate and external sources.

However, it is also well to remember that the same versatility that makes either oral history useful in this way also may call into question the accuracy of the information it provides. Because it is seldom "created or received and maintained by an agency, organization, or individual in pursuance of legal obligations or in the transaction of business"[21] in the same way as, for example, the telephone company's record of long distance phone calls, the motives of the person providing the information may legitimately be suspect. As with published sources, archivists and historians should be mindful of the impartiality of oral history sources.

World Wide Web. This most dramatic of recent developments of electronic sources has an ultimate potential that is as yet unknown. What is certain is that resources available via the Internet and by means of other electronic data bases constitute an area of documentation that is going through a phenomenal period of growth! Although these electronic resources frequently overlap categories described later in this section, it is useful to consider them separately, both because of their enormous potential for growth and because of their easy access from remote locations. They may provide both information about particular businesses and information about where business records and sources may be found.

Thousands of publicly and privately owned companies already have created home pages that serve a variety of business needs. At this time, the rate of growth is so rapid that it makes little sense to represent information about Web sites as being current other than in the most general of terms. Typically, Web sites may contain historical information, biographies of executive officers, product information, financial data, annual reports, descriptions of programs, public statements or press releases, position papers on public issues, and other documents or data. In many instances it is possible to find a surprising array of corporate-related information that adds a unique dimension not found in corporate records—even if such records were available for research. For example, a quick search of the World Wide Web for information pertaining to Milwaukee's Harley-Davidson Motor Company reveals the company's own home page, complete with a historical time line outlining important dates from the corporation's founding in 1903. In addition, one finds a remarkable mix, including dozens of other Web sites relating to Harley. Included are the Harley-Davidson Club Netherlands with 1,300 members (where membership requires cycle owners to be "mature"); the Flaming Pig Cycle Shop in Rochester, New York; and the "Official Harley-Davidson Art Collection."

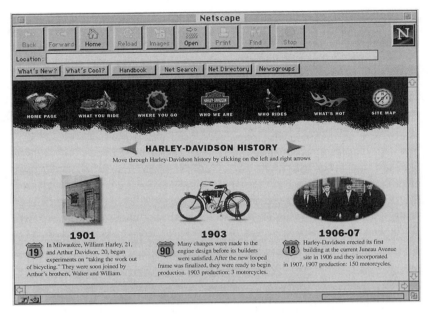

Electronic documentation available via the Internet is a rapidly growing source of information for archivists and historians. Corporate home pages may contain financial and product information, biographies of executives, press releases or position papers on issues of public interest. The example shown here, from the Harley-Davidson Motor Company, even contains a timeline that highlights important milestones in the company's history.

Each of these sites includes an email address that a researcher may contact for further information.

Another category of Web sites worthy of consideration are those created by archival repositories to publicize their programs and holdings. While most of these initially evolved from Gopher sites and contained little more than information concerning hours of operation and telephone numbers, with advances in technology they increasingly contain finding aids to collections of business and other types of records. A number also create periodic exhibits that may be of interest to researchers interested in business history. A recent such exhibit at the University of Delaware, for example, highlights that institution's extensive collection of trade catalogs. An exhibit at the University of Wisconsin-Milwaukee features a history of the Phoenix Hosiery Company, a local business whose records were donated to the university after the company was sold and closed.

Electronic Data Bases. Another category of external resource that has, likewise, undergone a period of dramatic growth, the value of electronic data bases to researchers will doubtless continue to grow over time. Although the level of coverage they provide may be limited, and data may be updated without regard for retaining the older historical information, such data bases may be a valuable source of external documentation when actual business records are not available.

Any attempt to make an overview of available resources in this category is doomed to almost instant obsolescence. Nevertheless, several current examples may be useful to suggest the types of sources that are available and to suggest directions that future projects may take.

There is neither time nor need to review in detail the value of such massive data bases as the *National Union Catalog of Manuscript Collections (NUCMC), the Online Computer Library Center (OCLC)*, and the *Research Library Information Network (RLIN)*, which include extensive information about both primary and secondary business information. It is sufficient to say that they are extremely valuable resources for researchers who want to know where to find information about the location and extent of business-related documentation.

Individual libraries and archival repositories have created their own data bases in the form of on-line public access catalogs that make available information concerning their holdings. An increasing number of these are available through the World Wide Web. Although as a resource for those seeking business-related information, such catalogs are more useful for finding secondary external resources, an increasing number of archives are now making information about their collections available as a part of their host library's on-line catalog, or as a special on-line index.

An increasing number of specialized on-line data bases like *SEC Online* collect information about companies that are publicly held. They may contain information such as financial tables, lists of officers and directors, government reports, notices pertaining to meetings and legal proceedings, annual reports to shareholders, and company resumes. In a similar way, the *ABI/INFORM* data base is a periodical index that includes business-related publications worldwide ranging from *Fortune* and *Forbes* to the *Japan Weekly Times International Edition*. It is searchable using the names of individual businesses and broader subject terms. The list of such data bases grows almost daily. Significant business-related documentation may be found in data bases as diverse as *Business Newsbank, Applied Science and Technology, Government Documents Index, America History and Life, Smithsonian, The Journal of American Culture, FINWEB,* and *Street Link*, all of which contain information ranging from feature articles to health hazard eval-

River Falls, 1884

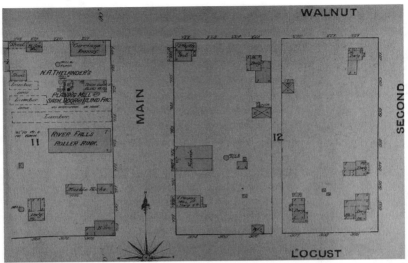

The story of two businesses is documented on this inset from three Sanborn Insurance maps of River Falls, Wisconsin. They document significant growth and change in Andrew W. Lund's carriage and harness business. The 1884 map (above) shows only one small wooden building—a "carriage repository." By 1891 (opposite page, top) the "carriage works" have expanded significantly, employing more than fifty workers. At the bottom of the inset, note the saga of the River Falls Roller Rink. It was physically moved back from the street and converted into a theater or "opera hall" with a boarding house in front. By 1912 (opposite page, bottom) the business had expanded further, although the auditorium was still the roller rink building from the 1884 map.

uation reports from the Institute for Occupational Safety and official corporate and financial reports.

Collectively, data bases such as these contain a significant amount of business-related documentation. Information contained in them includes specific facts about individual business concerns, general information documenting selected industries, and information about where other external sources may be found. Both archivists and researchers would be well advised to stay abreast of their potential to support serious research, particularly when there is need of contemporary information.

River Falls, 1891

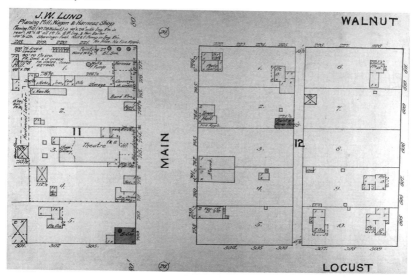

River Falls, 1912

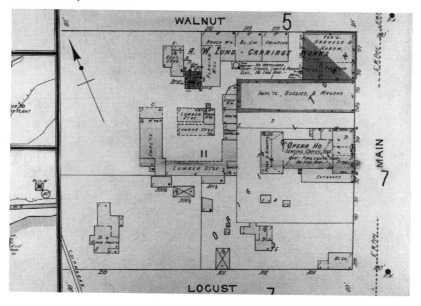

Possible Advantages of External Documentation

External documentation does have the potential to meet a variety of different needs. Perhaps most obvious, it may provide the only source for information when business records from Company X are unavailable. The absence of business records for research may result from a variety of different circumstances. In certain instances Company X may be long defunct and no records were preserved when it ceased operations. It may have been so small that few permanent records were created in the first place, and those that were may have consisted only of a few routine documents that do not meet research needs. Even if Company X is still in operation, executives may have destroyed noncurrent records of historical interest in a cost-cutting initiative or for fear that they might be used against the company in future court actions. The corporation may have been bought up by a larger firm and had its records moved to the new corporate headquarters in a far distant location. Finally, historical records may still exist and be readily at hand, but company policy has placed an absolute restriction on their use by outside historians and other researchers. This situation is one that confounds not only outside researchers; even some corporate historians need to deal with situations in which they need to write "a whitewashed puff piece for a company history" or "never lay eyes on any sensitive company materials."[22] In certain instances, actual corporate documents such as certificates or articles of incorporation and amendments, statements of dissolution, annual reports, income tax returns, financial statements, lists naming corporate officers and directors, property inventories and valuations, and production reports may be retrieved through external sources such as government records in the form of court case files or records from the secretary of state's office. Corporate documents are increasingly available through the World Wide Web as well. In other cases, any of the sources described briefly above may contain useful information in lieu of actual corporate records.

In a similar way, external documentation may make possible a fuller, more accurate account by providing another side to the story. This may be accomplished because external sources frequently offer information that has not been captured in any existing corporate records, or that is not available to researchers. For example, labor and management will invariably have different versions of why a strike occurred, and the former perspective will likely be articulated differently in labor union records than in the minutes of a corporate board of directors. Oral history interviews can sometimes provide a clearer reason for business decisions than memos or sanitized minutes of meetings that are designed to explain an official reason; oral history also may amplify or explain information that is contained in reports or other corporate records.

Depending on the level of interest of a researcher or an archival repository, external documentation may provide a more appropriate level of information by avoiding the need to retain records that document in excruciating detail every action taken in a corporation. In some cases, for example, a few good photographs, a newspaper account written at the time of the company's centennial, and a few reports from state inspections—or even a published account—may be more appropriate for a small repository than volumes of production records, trial balances, cash journals in a small local history repository. The result can be reduced bulk, which can free up archival resources for more pressing needs.

External resources may provide information more efficiently. Information in business records is frequently "repetitive and standardized" and "unlikely to have long term importance other than as samples of working methods employed at a given time."[23] In summarizing this type of raw data, external documentation such as government reports may present the material in a form that is more quickly collected, analyzed, and understood. This is particularly true for statistical data such as that related to production, finances, or certain categories on information related to the work force.

Finally, in certain cases external sources may have a credibility that business records themselves do not. The question of authenticity and impartiality cuts two ways: records are used as frequently to expose actions as they are to cover up actions, but historians and other researchers looking for reasons or motives may justifiably be reluctant to accept at face value "inside" accounts that seem to have been created for public consumption or to support a particular point of view. When records are still in the control of a business, or even after they have been turned over to a historical records repository, they may be suspect. Is this all there is? Or is there something that they are not allowing me to see?

Possible Disadvantages of External Documentation

Notwithstanding the above, there are disadvantages as well. Using external documentation as a strategy is fraught with potential problems that may work against achieving the goal of balanced and adequate documentation rather than helping us to work toward it.

First, archivists and historians have agreed for decades that it is not possible to preserve all primary historical records that might some day have some value for someone. Likewise, the strategy of bringing together under a single roof all significant primary source documentation pertaining to a single topic is also coming under scrutiny as the quantity of records increases and the resources to care for them decreases. The clear implication is that we must increasingly depend on others to share the responsibility. It is no more logical to think that we can either collect or bring together all sources of external documentation than it was to do so for all primary sources.

To share responsibility is to lose control. When one depends on cooperation as a strategy for collecting, it is well to remember that some decisions that influence our own documentary priorities and goals will be made by others in different institutions and with different missions and perspectives. For example, anyone in the state of Wisconsin who had previously deemphasized certain aspects of business collecting, in part because of such rich external sources as corporate income tax returns, would be distressed to discover that the State Historical Society of Wisconsin had reappraised this series of records and sent all 2,739 cubic feet to the paper recycler.[24]

Second, despite the seeming abundance of external sources that exists in some cases, frequently the level of information may be superficial and redundant when compared to actual business records. Relying on such summary information may be a vice as well as a virtue. The temptation may be to rely on external sources too much—as an easy way around a difficult problem. If the strategy is employed in this way, without sufficient critical analysis, archivists may not acquire records needed for in-depth studies requiring detailed information, for such topics as communication systems within corporations, or studies of the evolution of corporate organizational structure.

Third, with some external resources, notably those in electronic form, there is justifiable concern over how valuable such information really is, and even if it is valuable, how well it can be captured and preserved for future research. Many of the electronic resources are oriented to current information; the data bases or Web sites are updated frequently with little regard for preserving "outdated" information. What is available today may not be available in coming years.

Conclusion

So where does this leave archivists and historians? Hopefully with many questions that need to be answered before decisions regarding external documentation are made. Are there generalizations that we can make, or guidelines that may aid in the decision-making process? These final thoughts may provide useful points of departure.

- Whatever decision archivists make about employing external documentation as a strategy to preserve the history of American business, a knowledge of such external sources adds to our ability either to solve research problems we encounter or help others make their way around gaps in the documentary record.

- Before any decisions are made regarding the use of external documentation, archivists and historians should study more closely the nature of the documentary problem we propose to solve in relation to our goals or institutional mission. Too often in the past we have tried to shortcut the process of critical analysis by looking for a "one-size-fits-all" solution. There are so many dimensions to the question of what it means to document business that we need to spend more time analyzing before doing. We need to be precise and critical and not satisfied with the hypothetical benefit of external sources as justification for an easy way out. Such over-simplification has undercut our past efforts; critical analysis is a short-term investment that will result in long-term benefits. Techniques such as documentary probes, functional analysis, or a number of the individual steps that comprise part of the documentation strategy or the Minnesota Method are useful techniques to employ for this purpose.

- Generally, using external documentation to achieve documentary goals is better undertaken in conjunction with other strategies than alone. Knowledge about external documentary sources is useful in making decisions concerning the continuing value of corporate records. Determining the extent to which employing external documentation may be useful should be measured against other options. Undertaking one alternative may mean not having the time or resources to undertake another. Cooperative approaches that include elements of frameworks such as the documentation strategy and similar means may provide better solutions to the problems associated with documenting business.

- Decisions to employ external documentation should be made with the knowledge that the success of the strategy will be based, in part, on the mission of other repositories and will be influenced by decisions over which we have little or no control. With this decision comes the responsibility to guard against changing priorities of other repositories that may influence our decisions and the level of activity that we expend to document business.

- When compared to corporate records, the usefulness of external documentation is limited. In most cases—even though there are apparently a large number of sources—external documentation constitutes a meager substitute for the richness of detail and breadth of information that is available in corporate records. Most external sources are quite general in nature. For in-depth research needs they are probably insufficient to provide adequate documentation.

- Archivists and researchers may wish to consider using external documentation less to provide facts and figures about a particular business directly than to lead them to other sources (internal or external) that will aid in research. Published sources, electronic indexes, and Web sites are good examples of this. The ease with which the existence of external primary sources can be learned alleviates the need to collect and makes the needed information more easily accessible to researchers.

- In certain cases external documentation may be the most efficient means to provide reference assistance for general or frequently asked questions. Examples include records in electronic form such as in Web sites or commercial data bases, and published information.

- External documentation is likely best considered in several specific instances. The first is for small or defunct businesses where records were either not created or destroyed already. Many such business concerns were still the subject of attention by government inspectors, regulations, or local newspapers. The second case is of publicly held businesses or those subject to extensive government regulations. The external sources created because of this are generally predictable, extensive, accessible, and relatively easy to locate. The third instance is when there is a clear need to fill identifiable gaps in the documentary record. Such gaps may result because (1) critical corporate records are missing, (2) the reliability of available internal documentation is suspect, or (3) another perspective is needed in order to complete research satisfactorily. The fourth instance occurs when only general or summary information is required due to the mission of the repository or the research need. The final instance is in order to document the external relationships (as opposed to internal operations) that a business maintains with community organizations such as "charitable and philanthropic activities that businesses support, the informal influence they exert on community politics, the impact that the expansion and contraction of their built environments exercise for good or ill upon the development of the communities in which they reside."[25]

- External sources themselves should be thoroughly examined and used with caution. The documentary record conveyed by a newspaper was created to serve specific needs that may distort as easily as they amplify. The purpose for which records have been created should be carefully considered.

Ultimately, the question of using external documentation is one that needs more investigation, analysis, and discussion. We need to know more about the nature of the documentary problems associated with the business community, the research needs of various constituencies, the effectiveness of alternative strategies, and the range, value, and reliability of available external documentary sources. Hopefully, this chapter will provide a beginning to such discussion and the result will benefit business historians and archivists alike.

Endnotes

1. For an interesting set of variables one should consider when assessing the "representativeness" of business records, see Florence Bartoshesky Lathrop, "Toward a National collecting Policy for Business History: The View from Baker Library," *Business History News* 62 (spring 1988): 134–143.

2. David Bearman, *Archival Methods*, Archives and Museum Informatics Technical Report, no. 9 (Pittsburgh: Archives & Museum Informatics, 1989), 7. The number of archives he "allowed" (10,000) is more than double the number that had been reported in the recently published *Directory of Archives and Manuscript Repositories in the United States* (Phoenix: Oryx Press, 1988).

3. Gordon Rabchuk, "Reaching Out for Survival: The Royal Bank Experience," *Society of American Archivists Business Archives Newsletter* (winter 1994), 1.

4. "Business Archives in North America Understanding the Past, Investing in the Future," brochure produced by the Society of American Archivists, 1991.

5. Robert A. Shiff, "The Archivist's Role in Records Management," *American Archivist* 19, no. 2 (1956): 111–120. A very good article that focuses on the business community and outlines the respective perspectives and arguments nicely. It is particularly interesting to note how little has changed in 40 years!

6. Ibid.

7. Ken Wirth, "Advocating Business Archives" (paper written for Seminar in Modern Archives Administration, University of Wisconsin-Milwaukee, 1994), 10–18.

8. Robert Levy, "Inside Industry's Archives," *Dun's Review* (May 1981): 76, emphasis added.

9. Lewis J. Bellardo and Lynn Lady Bellardo, *A Glossary for Archivists, Manuscript Curators, and Records Managers,* (Chicago: Society of American Archivists, 1992), 12.

10. Ibid., 12.

11. Frank Boles, *Archival Appraisal* (New York: Neal-Schuman Publishers, 1991).

12. For a more complete explanation and case study, see Bruce H. Bruemmer and Sheldon Hochheiser, *The High-Technology Company: A Historical Research and Archival Guide* (Minneapolis: Charles Babbage Institute, 1989).

13. Helen Willa Samuels, *Varsity Letters: Documenting Modern Colleges and Universities* (Metuchen, N.J.: Scarecrow Press, copublished and distributed by the Society of American Archivists, 1992), 1–2.

14. Timothy L. Ericson, " 'This is definitely the future...' Or Is It: Loaning Archival Collections" (paper delivered at the annual meeting of the Association of Canadian Archivists, Ottawa, Ontario, May 26, 1994); "Sharing the Wealth," *MRRC News* 2 (1980).

15. See William J. Maher, "Ensuring Continuity and Preservation Through Archival Service Agreements," *Archival Issues* 19, no. 1 (1994): 5–18. This was the topic of a study/discussion group session by Society of American Archivists' College and University Archives Section at its September 1995 annual meeting. A summary of the session was reported in "The Cuckoo's Nest: Corporate Archives in an Academic Archives," *The Academic Archivist* 14, no. 1 (winter 1996): 4–5.

16. The concept of impartiality in the archival sense is similar to but not synonymous with unbiased. The idea was articulated originally in Hilary Jenkinson, *A Manual of Archive Administration* (London: Percy, Lund, Humphries & Co., 1922). More recently the concept, along with other elements of archival theory, has been articulated by Terry Eastwood in his article "What is Archival Theory and Why is it Important?" *Archivaria* 37 (spring 1994): 122–130.

17. The example cited here is the Records of the Henry W. Maier Administration, 1960–1988, Milwaukee Series 44, Archives and Special Collections, Golda Meir Library, University of Wisconsin-Milwaukee. The collection includes almost 250 cubic feet of textual records, audiovisual records, and microfilm. It is fairly typical of the records of contemporary political figures.

18. The example cited here is the Henry S. Reuss Papers, 1839–1982, Milwaukee Manuscript Collection 112, Archives and Special Collections, Golda Meir Library. The collection consists of 87 cubic feet of textual and audiovisual records from the former congressman's Washington, D.C. and Milwaukee offices. As with the Maier records, it is fairly typical of the type and range of records that one might find in the papers of a contemporary congressional representative.

19. Timothy L. Ericson, "Sanborn Fire Insurance Maps Preserve Historical Data," *FOCUS on the Center for Research Libraries* 7, nos. 4/5 (1987).

20. Lewis J. Bellardo and Lynn Lady Bellardo, *A Glossary for Archivists, Manuscript Curators, and Records Managers* (Chicago: Society of American Archivists, 1992), 24.

21. Ibid, 28.

22. Margaret Price, "Corporate Historians: A Rare but Growing Breed," *Industry Week*, March 23, 1981, 87–89.

23. Tony Cole, "The Nature of Business Records," in *Business Archives Council Record Aids #4* (London: Business Archives Council, n.d.), 2.

24. The quantity is approximate, based upon the most recent entry in the *Guide to the Wisconsin State Archives* (Madison: State Historical Society of Wisconsin, 1984). This example is not intended to suggest that the state historical society erred in its decision. The society's decision was carefully considered and based on sound reasoning. The example simply suggests one of the possible pitfalls in relying on documentation that is controlled by another repository or agency. The same case could be made with regard to the World Wide Web and other electronic resources. Historians and archivists might prefer that those who create such data bases retain noncurrent information, but the creators probably will not do so because they do not share our priorities or mission.

25. Peter J. Blodgett, "Blind Men and Elephants: External Documentation and American Business History" (commentary on "Beyond Business: External Documentation and Corporate Records" session at the Records of American Business Symposium, Minnesota Historical Society, April 12, 1996).

12

Reaching the Mass Audience:
Business History as Popular History

John A. Fleckner

Practitioners of American history are well aware of the paradox of the American public's dislike of history as an academic subject and the public's fascination with it outside schools and universities. Popular history, including popular business history, is a thriving part of the illustrated book and magazine trade, museum exhibitions, theme parks, and television documentaries. Americans also consume popular history in many other, less didactic roles, for example as collectors, hobbyists, and viewers of advertisements and commercials built on historical themes and images.

This essay offers examples of American business history in its many forms of popular presentation. The purpose here is to suggest to archivists that the records of American business history have a wide and growing range of potential uses in addition to their value to scholarship and the conduct of internal corporate business. This overview of popular business history may be useful to archivists in selecting records for long-term retention and in planning strategies for describing records, developing outreach programs, and providing services to current and potential users. Because the circumstance of each archives varies so greatly depending on mission, scope of collections, scale of operations, and range of user base, this essay is generally descriptive rather than prescriptive.

Finally, this essay is neither a full catalog of popular business history forms nor a cultural critique of those forms.[1] Particular attention is given here to popular history produced by history museums (and historical sites) and by corporations. In addition to archival programs operating within museums, many other archives have close administrative or geographic ties to history museums. Archival programs also frequently have exhibition activities of their own as a means of public history education and bringing their collections and activities to wider public attention. To the degree corporate archives are a locus for history making by their firms, the archives are likely to be more successful and the history of better quality.

History Museums and Historical Sites

The United States is a nation of avid museum visitors. In 1975, the nation's 5,000 (approximately) history museums counted some 86 million visitors annually and the number of visitors and museums seems only to grow.[2] These museums are extraordinarily diverse, ranging from tiny sites operated entirely by volunteers and visited by only a handful of local residents to places like the National Museum of American History and the Henry Ford Museum and Greenfield Village with hundreds of staff and millions of annual visitors. Virtually all these museums have in common a commitment to educating a general public audience about the past through exhibitions built upon historical artifact collections.

The business history presented in American museums is as diverse as the museums themselves, but recent examples reflect the influence of academic trends toward social history approaches. In November 1995, the American Advertising Museum of Portland, Oregon, opened *Dream Girls: Images of Women in Advertising, 1890s–1990s*, in New York City as the first stop on a three-year national tour. Using more than 500 examples of advertising (primarily from the museum's permanent collections) and a few household artifacts, the exhibit demonstrates how "advertising's imperfect mirror has refracted the feminine images for one hundred years, displaying women we want to know, women we want to become, women we want to come home to, and women others want us to be."[3]

The emergence of America as a consumer society was also the focus of *Packaging the New: Design and the American Consumer 1925–1975* at the Cooper-Hewitt Museum, the Smithsonian Institution's National Museum of Design in New York City. The exhibit argued that "stylistic change [was] the driving force behind design, manufacturing and consumerism during that half century." The exhibit used "more than 200 objects, including furniture, appliances, original drawings, packaging and advertising." It drew expecially heavily on the museum's holdings of the papers of designer Donald Desky, using examples of his work from the 1920s through the 1950s, ranging from household furniture, to a Saks & Co. window display, to package designs for Procter & Gamble's Crest, Joy, Prell, and Jif.

Exhibits about advertising and design inevitably widen the scope of business history by incorporating consumers as key participants. Similarly, some recent exhibits on industrial history have expanded to include workers as well as owners, executives, and engineers as active parties in their historical narratives. *Who's in Charge: Workers and Managers in the United States* opened at the National Museum of American History and is currently available as a traveling exhibition from the Smithsonian Institution Traveling Exhibition Services (SITES). The exhibit uses artifacts (like the stopwatch Frank Gilbreth used in his early-twentieth-century factory efficiency studies), photographs of workers and workplaces, and workplace ephemera to demonstrate the evolving, and contested, nature of work relationships since the onset of the Industrial Revolution.[4]

For all this diversity of topics, there are some common threads. First, not-for-profit history museums, unlike their corporate counterparts, rarely present the history of a single business firm, focusing instead on historical themes (gender, work relationships, technology), on business personalities, and on aspects of business history with which viewers are likely to be familiar, for example the marketing of consumer products. (An exception here may be the history of a local business that is of central importance to the audience of a local history museum.) Indeed, a hallmark of popular history, in all its forms, is its attention to its audiences and its strategy of connecting with their existing knowledge and experiences.

A second distinguishing feature of museum exhibitions is their reliance on visual content—in the form of artifacts and graphic imagery such as photographs and drawings—to convey information and interpretation. In some instances this visual content may be merely illustrative, in much the way that scholarly publications may be enlivened with a sprinkling of photographs. The more interesting, and often the more successful, museum exhibition will use objects (and other nontextual materials) in more creative ways, taking them as unique forms of evidence in their own right. At the same time, these exhibitions use the very physical being of objects to convey meaning that goes beyond the text of labels.

While acknowledging the informational and expressive qualities of objects, most museum curators today also recognize that understanding these qualities may be greatly enhanced by the associated archival record. Although there is no single definition of the term *material culture*, and no systematic exposition on the relationships of things to the documentary record, archival materials do provide crucial information about the creation, purpose, use, and meaning of objects.[5] The Tupper collection at the National Museum of American History illustrates this point. The collection consists not only of extensive examples of manufactured Tupperware products—readily identifiable by their trademarks and patent information—but of one-of-a-kind items produced by Earl Tupper in his early years as an unsuccessful inventor and Tupperware items designed for very limited circulation. Tupper's papers and oral history interviews with his sons identified these items and placed them in the conext of Tupper's life history. Tupper's papers, including laboratory notebooks, diaries, and business records, added further context to this remarkable business history.

Historical sites, like museums, interpret history to a broad public using artifacts and other historical evidence. To this mix they add the dimension of historic structures and spaces that have great public appeal and can have great educational impact. Today's historic preservation movement has its roots in nineteenth-century efforts to protect such national "shrines" as Mount Vernon and in twentieth-century efforts, like the restoration and re-creation of Colonial Williamsburg. While most of these efforts focused on symbols of national political identity and the homes of the wealthy, Henry Ford took on the task of preserving his notion of America's business and technological history, now embodied in the Henry Ford Museum and Greenfield Village. Today, local and state historical societies and other state historical agencies as well as the National Park Service care for thousands of historical properties.[6]

Business-related sites operated by state historical societies in Minnesota and Wisconsin are typical of those in many other localities. Most focus on small businesses in an earlier, small enterprise period. For example, Wisconsin's sites include Circus World Museum (on the grounds of the Ringling Bros. winter headquarters in Baraboo), Wade House (an inn serving the stagecoach trade), and Old World Wisconsin and Stonefield Village (recreating life in rural and very small town Wisconsin before World War I). National Park Service sites dealing with similar eras of business history include Bent's Old Fort (a commercial trading post on the Sante Fe Trail), Allegheny Portage Railroad National Historic Site (an antebellum canal and railroad connection to the West), Grand Portage National Monument (fur-trading site in northern Minnesota), and the Grant-Kohrs Ranch (Montana cattle raising).

The modern history of American business, especially the industrial era, has received far less attention from historical agencies. In addition to very real problems of scale and technological complexity, there are questions about potential audience interest in a history that seems to lack nostalgic value and that has the potential for political conflicts over interpretive content. Still, the success of industrial history complexes in England and to a more limited degree in this country, suggest that this area may continue to develop, especially as the era of heavy industry rapidly recedes from popular memory and its physical sites become available for historical uses. Additionally, many politicians, planners, and ordinary citizens hope that tourism developed around historical sites—sometimes termed "heritage tourism"—will contribute to economic recovery in Rust Belt areas.

The best known American industrial history site is Lowell National Historical Park, established in 1978. The park is not a landmass owned by the Park Service, but a set of interpretive activities—exhibits, tours, performances, multimedia programs, and the like—developed around a visitor center and Boott Cotton Mills Museum, both operated by the Park Service, and a number of other publicly and privately held local historical sites and agencies. The Boott Mills contain nearly 100 operating power looms as well as "modern exhibits about the people who made the Lowell factory system work." The Park Service interpretation at Lowell is developed around the themes of labor, machines, capital, power, and the industrial city. Historical intepretation at Lowell is supported by collections of the New England Folklife Center, the Lowell Historical Society, and the Center for Lowell History of the University of Massachusetts Lowell, all located in the historic area.[7]

Another model for popular industrial history, and one that is being actively pursued in other regions, is the Blackstone River Valley National Heritage Corridor shared by Massachusetts and Rhode Island. The corridor, as described in a Park Service brochure, "is a special type of national park" that recognizes the "birthplace of the American industrial revolution." The park is not based on federal government land ownership or management but on "people, businesses, nonprofit historic and environmental organizations, 20 local and 2 state governments, the National Park Service, and a unifying commission work[ing] together to protect [the 250,000-acre region's] special identity and prepare for the valley's future." Park literature encourages visitors to "read the landscape," both natural and cultural, and to seek additional information from historical agencies identified on the accompanying map.

History museums and historical sites bring history—including the history of American business—to millions of Americans. Capitalizing on the evocative power of things and places, museums and sites appeal to audiences with histories featuring people and connecting with what the visitor already knows. The archival record enables things and places to "speak" with greater authenticity, specificity, and richer context. These observations contain several implications for archivists who manage business records and who wish to reach broader audiences. First, don't ignore the customer. Marketing materials, especially packaging and advertising, are the familiar public identifiers for most firms. By virtue of their original purpose they are visually inviting and they contain visible expressions of corporate intentions and presumptions. Second, look for human interest items. These may range from a humorous photograph or cartoon doodle, to an oral history reminiscence, to a poignant memo in a personnel file. Third, consider the value of very specific details that, perhaps insignificant in themselves, might connect to a locality or object in ways significant to a popular audience.[8]

The Corporation as Historian

The paradox of the American public's disdain for history as an abstract notion, and its fascination with the popular historical presentations, has a parallel in the corporate world. While corporate rhetoric focuses on bottom-line profits, increased productivity, global competition, and next quarter's balance sheet, American corporations also are producing a steady stream of popular business history. Corporations frequently present their histories in formats common to non-profit history work, including museums, historical sites, and books. But corporations, enjoying far deeper pockets, also reach a far larger and more diverse audience by utilizing advertising and public relations media too costly for other history producers. Indeed, several small business firms have emerged to capitalize on the opportunities presented by corporate demand for history-making services.

Corporate museums have long been a staple of American business history making. A 1943 study, published by the American Association of Museums, reported some 80 company museums in an era during which there were few, if any, corporate archives.[9] The number today is undoubtedly larger, although difficult to determine accurately. Nonetheless, as Philip Mooney has written, corporations recognize that "as an instrument for informal education, exhibits can both inform and entertain the viewer as they allow the corporation to place its marketing, advertising, and technological achievements in the public spotlight."[10]

Today the World of Coca-Cola and the museums of the Wells Fargo Bank in California are the nation's best-known corporate museums and the products of two of the most effective corporate history programs. Housed in its own architecturally distinctive building in Atlanta, the World of Coca-Cola opened in 1990 and soon garnered more than one million visitors annually. The museum is a mixture of commercial dazzle (an overhead "Bottling Fantasy" carrying "apparently endless lines of Coca-Cola bottles" and giant soda fountain shooting twenty foot streams of the soft drink) and historical interpretation. The latter includes brief audiovisual segments on historical events since 1886 as well as the firm's own history, with special emphasis on Coke advertising and the firm's worldwide presence. The museum is an opportunity to display some of the vast contents of the Coca-Cola archives in a setting that harks back to the corporate pavilions of world's fairs.[11]

Wells Fargo's History Department includes an archives and research operation, the stagecoach program (a fleet of 11 vehicles exhibited and operated in some 150 events each year), and the museum group (with more than 100,000 annual visitors). The latter includes the History Room in the San Francisco headquarters building (originally established in the 1930s), and museums in Los Angeles and Sacramento. Each operation "supports the public relations and business goals of the company through exhibits and programs designed to show Wells Fargo's history in the context of California and Western American history." The emphasis is on the period of the Gold Rush through the early twentieth century, and the business purpose of the corporate history is explicitly acknowledged.[12]

Of course most corporate museums operate on a far more modest scale. Outside Seattle, Washington, the Nestle Museum educates the visiting public and employees attending programs at the Nestle Training Center. Both the museum and the center are located on the historic Carnation farm. In addition to a "Founder's Room" featuring portraits of "prominent individuals in company history," the museum has re-creations of a 1950s sweet shop, a general store, a 1915 chuck wagon scene, and a milking barn. Each location displays original and replicated product packaging and point of purchase advertising for the range of brands—including Hills Bros., Carnation, and Nescafe—now owned by Nestle. The museum places Nestle brands in the visual context of a replicated historical space and in a narrative context. This post card caption is an example: "The original Ford Model T Nestle's sales car parked outside the General Store . . . represents the role of the sales 'rep' in expanding distribution of product lines."[13]

The Crayola Factory, a new museum in Easton, Pennsylvania, opened in 1996. It combines hands-on activities for children, re-creations of two small sections of an assembly line, an introduction to Crayola history (which dates from 1903), and a Crayola superstore. Binney & Smith, makers of Crayola crayons and a part of the Hallmark

Cards firm, had been unable to meet the demand for public tours of its nearby factory. The new venue shares a former department store with a regional information center, and the National Canal Museum, all part of a public and private effort to attract tourists and spur economic development in this rust-belt city.[14]

Corporate museums, like corporate archives, do not have assured futures. A recent American Association for State and Local History planning meeting drew representatives from 15 of these organizations, including the Hershey Museum, the Museum of Tobacco Art and History, and the Dr. Pepper Museum and Free Enterprise Institute, the Wells Fargo Museum, and the World of Coca-Cola, to discuss common interests. The group found that simply gathering information about the current number and nature of corporate history museums is difficult, and many participants felt themselves isolated from the museum field and lacking sufficient resources for their programs. They also acknowledged that "the tension between interpreting accurate history and a corporation's view of history can be very dicey."[15]

Corporate history exhibitions of two- and three-dimensional materials are not limited to formal corporate museums. Many corporate archives use exhibition cases and display areas to gain exposure for items of special interest from their holdings. Archives also create portable displays for special occasion use. For example, the Kraft archives has created exhibits to recognize anniversaries of brands such as Breyers' ice cream.

Corporations also continue to produce printed versions of their histories. The anniversary publication, a favorite corporate historical product, and in some instances the inspiration for creation of a corporate archives, can vary from a research-based monograph produced by a professional historian to a customer-oriented marketing tool. Historical consultant Kathi Ann Brown produced *Critical Connection: The Motorola Service Station Story* (1992), based on documentary research and oral histories with local technicians whose businesses provide customer service for Motorola. Among the publications done by the Winthrop Group, a history consulting firm, for a broader audience are *Waste Management: An American Corporate Success Story* (1993), and two illustrated books, *Centennial in Cement: A History of Medusa Corporation* (1992) and *Retail Revolutionary: Kinney Shoe Corporation's First Century in Footwear* (1994). While most corporate histories are written and designed to appeal to a general public audience, only a few have sufficient popular appeal for a commercial publisher. Many are self-published and thus their distribution is limited.[16]

The marketing of replicas of historic products and, especially, the licensing of trademarked historical items appear to be rapidly expanding forms of corporate history making. Unlike a museum visit or a newspaper story, the replicated product or image has a lasting physical presence. In addition, licensing of replicas and reproductions can generate a revenue stream for an entrepreneurial corporate archives.

The Coca-Cola Company undoubtedly has the most extensive licensing program of any corporation. Products carrying the historical Coke imagery include T-shirts and other apparel and a wide range of other items, many of them available at Coca-Cola retail stores like the one on Fifth Avenue in fashionable midtown Manhattan. The possibilities for such promotions seem unlimited. A June 1996 *Life* magazine advertisement by the Danbury Mint offered a replica of a 1927 Coca-Cola delivery truck, "a sunny yellow truck that became a familiar sight to the townspeople" of Chattanooga, Tennessee, location of "the company's first bottler." The truck, emblazoned with the trademarked Coca-Cola name in familiar script lettering, has been assembled from "over 150 parts," and is offered at $129.[17]

Coca-Cola is not alone in seeing the possibilities for extending and reinforcing recognition of its brand identity, and producing additional revenue, through licensing. The 24-page "Spamtastic" catalog enables aficionados of the canned meat product to acquire scores of products bearing Spam's identity. The offerings include replica trucks, Spam can banks, neckties, and *100 Years of Quality*, a corporate history with "hundreds of photographs from the company's archives." The catalog also reminds readers that "The world's infatuation with Spam luncheon meat is chronicled at a unique museum in Austin, Minnesota . . . [where] thousands of museum items and related photos prove one thing: Spam is for keeps."[18]

Product licensing as a revenue generating activity is not confined to the corporate world. Museums, large and small, have added this technique to their business strategies for financial survival. Museum licensing includes both rights to reproduce images of items within the collections—from historical photographs to fine arts pieces—and to reproduce three-dimensional objects. In typical publishing licensing arrangements, publishers pay a one-time royalty fee for use of an image. In a product licensing arrangement, the licensor receives a royalty—perhaps 5 to 10 percent of product sales. Licensed products may be sold on-site in museum shops, through museum catalogs, or distributed more widely in national distribution networks. As revenue needs increase and marketing opportunities grow, museums are pursuing new approaches.

The Smithsonian Institution, following in the footsteps of the Boston, Philadelphia, and Metropolitan (New York) art museums, made its debut on the QVC cable shopping network in September 1996. "What we're here for is not only revenue-generating but information sharing," stressed one spokesperson, pointing to the brief features on

Smithsonian museums incorporated into the QVC program along with product pitches. The Smithsonian Institution licenses its name for use on more than 2,000 products from 60 companies—ranging from brass candlesticks to greeting cards. The Smithsonian also publishes four catalogs annually that reach 15 million households and has extensive gift shops in all its museums. The various archives and libraries within the Smithsonian—especially those with historical photographs, commercial ephemera, and other visual collections—are significant sources for the product licensing efforts and recipients of substantial returns from them.[19]

At the end of the twentieth century, the future role of the Internet as a means of mass communications is a subject of great speculation and uncertainty. Because providing information through the World Wide Web is relatively easy and inexpensive, organizations of all types, including businesses, are experimenting with this fledgling medium. In June 1996, the Ohio State University Business History Page had links to 16 American corporations that include history in their Web offerings. The Chevron link connected with the firm's museum featuring a history of the service station and "a gallery of photos of Chevron tankers from 1903 to the present." Rival Mobil offers an extended corporate history including the evolution of its trademark "from 'mobilis' to Pegasus." (The compilation missed the on-line presence of Spam, which offers its catalog, and of Chantelle Lingerie, Inc., a "120 year old French manufacturer of very high quality lingerie," which provides a company history along with its full catalog.)

As we have seen, corporations have at their disposal a remarkable range of formats to produce and disseminate history for popular audiences. While the illustrated book remains a mainstay, displays and exhibits—within or outside a formal museum setting—offer on-site learning experiences. Use of the corporate past in advertising and the licensing of historical imagery for use in (or on) consumer products enables corporations to reach even wider audiences.

History produced by corporations often is entertaining and educational, but its first purpose is to further corporate objectives. These are likely to include promoting corporate and brand identity and disseminating a business perspective on the corporation and issues important to it. A recent survey of chief executives from the Fortune 500 list made clear just how important brand and corporate identity are to major corporations. Two-thirds of these CEOs saw themselves—not traditional brand managers—as custodians of key brands "with primary responsibility for the management of the brand." These CEOs cited weak and inconsistent communications about the brand as two of the top three common mistakes companies make in managing brands.[20]

Flyer promoting business history exhibit.
Courtesy of the National Museum of American History, Smithsonian Institution, Washington, D.C.

Publishing Popular Business History: Old and New Media

Popular history, including business history, has long had a significant niche in the print, electronic, and film media.

Of the print media, the magazine *American Heritage* has been perhaps the most influential. First published in 1949 by the American Association for State and Local History, it was reborn five years later

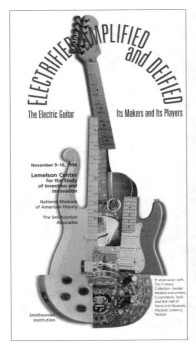

Flyers promoting business history exhibits. *Courtesy of the National Museum of American History, Smithsonian Institution, Washington, D.C.*

under the control of a group of journalistically trained editors with extensive experience in the Time-Life publishing empire. The new *American Heritage* was an immediate success with upper-middle-class readers attracted by its hard covers, lack of advertising, full-color illustrations, and noncontroversial approach to the past. Indeed, as Roy Rosenzweig wrote in 1986, "as the most influential and successful post-World War II historical publication, *American Heritage* has shaped the historical consciousness of a large and crucial segment of the American public; it has given the public its *definition* as well as its *interpretation* of history."[21]

American Heritage, now a division of Forbes, Inc., is brimming with advertising today and printed with soft cover, but it remains visually lavish and wide ranging in its choice of historical subjects. It also contends with a host of other magazines and other media for a popular history audience and it no longer retains its preeminent position in that field.

The success of *American Heritage* contributed, in part, to the emergence of new, special-audience, glossy magazines that have appeared since the 1970s and to the revitalization of older competitors. *Smithsonian* magazine also drew on Time-Life veterans to launch its venture into the mass media and its history articles are very much in the mold of *American Heritage*. *Arizona Highways*, reaching well beyond its immediate region, includes a mix of historical articles such as a March 1995 story entitled "Remember Burma-Shave? It Covered a Lot of Chins and Even More Miles."

Magazines with a business focus also carry occasional popular history articles. For example, in March 1994, *Forbes* reported efforts by the descendants of Campbell Soup founder, inventor John Dorrance, to regain control of the firm from outside management. The same year, *Fortune* portrayed the most recent laureates inducted into the National Business Hall of Fame and described how they "achieved their place in history." Even *Sports Illustrated* dips into business history. "Triumph of the Swoosh," in August 1993, traced the story of "the sneaker giant [from its] humble beginnings" to its international prominence.

The proliferation of specialized magazines has been a dramatic feature of recent publishing history, and at least one focuses directly on business history. *Audacity: The Magazine of Business Experience* is "published quarterly by Forbes and American Heritage" for "today's leadership generation." International Paper is *Audacity's* exclusive advertiser, and recent issues I have received were sent with the compliments of International Paper. Stories in *Audacity* cover a wide range of topics from a history of the *Encyclopaedia Britannica* to the contributions of Frederick W. Taylor, pioneer in the development of "scientific management." Many articles focus on stories about individual firms, for example, the failure of Xerox to capitalize on its early developments in the personal computer industry and 3M's success in continuously introducing new products. *Audacity* stories are well written and illustrated although they perhaps do not achieve the advertising copywriter's promise of "an astonishingly fresh and imaginative approach to understanding money, power, and business."

Popular history also continues to flourish for book publishers. Biographies of all sorts, military history, popular culture (including sports), and politics regularly appear on the best-sellers lists. The History Book Club (an off-shoot of the Book of the Month Club) offers members a choice of 150 titles every three weeks, selected by a "board of historian-advisors . . . [to be] not only intellectually stimulating, but entertaining, as well." Business history, however, is strikingly absent from the lists and the club offerings, except indirectly in treatments of popular culture topics and in the management advice genre.

Motion picture films and, subsequently, television have shaped popular notions of history to a far greater extent than any other media. Dramatic films using the past as a setting were among the first motion picture genres but for the most part they reflected little reliance on written history or on historical source materials. These films might be revealing of the social and political concerns of their times, but they were of little value in understanding the past they depicted.[22]

Today filmmaking is no longer the exclusive province of Hollywood. The rise of television, especially the public broadcasting and cable networks, and the development of the video casette recorder/player make every home, office, and school room a viewing studio. Of particular importance to archivists is the emergence of the modern historical documentary utilizing both familiar archival materials like letters and photographs as well as moving image and sound recordings, a rapidly expanding form of the historical record.

Ken Burns' productions, most notably the series on the Civil War, baseball, and the West, have been extraordinarily successful. These epics are known—if not viewed in their entirety—by vast audiences through repeated public television airings (often during fund-raising drives) and cassette sales. Like most such productions, Burns' early work was supported by the National Endowment for the Humanities, which also supported such noteworthy productions as Connie Field's "The Life and Times of Rosie the Riveter" and many of the independently produced episodes of the PBS series *The American Experience*.

Today, budgets at both national endowments have been slashed, but other opportunities for documentary production have appeared with the growing offerings of television on cable channels such as Arts and Entertainment, Discovery, Disney, and, especially, The History Channel (THC). In late September 1996, THC ("where the past comes alive") listed two current business history offerings, "The Edison Effect: Thomas Edison: The Phonograph/Motion Pictures" and "Ferrari." Like other popular business histories, both take a biographical approach to a legendary figure. THC also sells, through its Web site, cassettes of some of its programs including "Henry Ford: Tin Lizzy Tycoon" and "Drive for the American Dream," a history of automobile commercials.

Production of historical documentaries for television—broadcast or cable—remains enormously expensive, costing hundreds of thousands of dollars. However, new video equipment and technologies now permit productions nearly as polished as these but at costs in the tens of thousands of dollars range. Documentaries on this scale may

be produced in conjunction with a museum exhibition or for use in
classrooms. Museum shops, specialized education publishers, and out-
lets market these videos.[23] The growing demand for such documentaries even spurred the creation in 1990 of the Center for History in the
Media at George Washington University. The center, "the only institute
in historical documentary production in the nation," offers instruction
in historiography, scripting, visualization, and directing.

The research needs of documentary makers—whether outside, independent producers or the creators of in-house presentations—present
special challenges to archival repositories. Frequently, researchers for
these projects are inexperienced and unclear about the scope and direction of the documentary. Often, they are working on tight schedules
and budgets. Because documentaries are, at heart, visual and because
archival materials rarely are organized around their visual content, re-
sesarchers typically will want to see very large numbers of images, to
make frequent copies, and—often much later—to return to retrieve
items to copy or to film. Lastly, documentary producers are seeking fresh
materials. They recognize that their medium is a voracious consumer of
historical materials, rapidly transforming the new and visually arresting
image into the tired cliche through repetition.

Moving images—from historic film and video footage—are especially prized by documentary producers. Here businesess may be an
especially rich source. By the early twentieth century they were commissioning filmmakers to produce public relations films, to document
industrial operations, to create advertisements, and to use their cameras for a host of purposes. Among the film footage in the Hills Bros.
Coffee Company Records in the Archives Center at the National Museum of American History are images of coffee growing in Central
America, coffee roasting and packing in Hills' plants, red-coated company representatives delivering sample packages door-to-door in Detroit in 1941, and construction of the Bay Bridge in San Francisco
(immediately adjacent to the company headquarters). Although assisting researchers in locating film and video footage is time consuming,
archivists may be able to recover some of the costs of managing audiovisual collections. Documentary projects often will pay copying and
reproduction fees and many archives will produce (and charge for) a
master video copy for their own use when previously uncopied footage
is requested by a documentary producer.

Popular Business History as Personal Pursuit

Millions of Americans connect most directly with their nation's
past not by reading or viewing history but as hobbyists and as collec-

tors of the physical remains of that past. Business history, in various guises, is the concern of many of these history practitioners, for example collectors of antique advertising, historical farm machinery, railroad objects, patent medicine-related materials, and automobiles.[24] These history practitioners cover the entire spectrum in terms of levels of commitment, knowledge, and historical skills that they bring to their pursuits. For those whose personal enjoyment is tied to concerns for authenticity and for broader historical context, archival records may have unanticipated utility.

Collecting the artifacts produced in the American past has a long, well-documented history. By the 1920s, American furniture and decorative arts had won their places in such privileged repositories as the Metropolitan Museum of Art and Colonial Williamsburg. In the following decade, Henry Ford's museum and Greenfield Village included these objects and an extraordinary range (and number) of other items including machine-made and every day items that both evoked a nostalgic past and a lesson of technological progress.[25]

The post–World War II period witnessed a dramatic democratization of collecting of all sorts. As a result, prices skyrocketed, and the scope of what was considered "collectible" expanded until there was a recognized specialization (and market) for virtually every object more than a few years old, regardless of how commercially available the object once was. Even professional archivists are not immune to private collecting passions; three leaders in the field—left unidentified here—collect beer bottle caps, plastic swizzle sticks, and mesh caps.

For some large and expensive objects, most collectors and hobbyists must content themselves with photographic images and other surrogates for the item itself. This drawback need not diminish the collector's enthusiasm. For example, railroad hobbyists are a small but regular user group of the extensive collections of railroad company records at the National Museum of American History. Their use of the collection includes ordering reproductions of photographs of railroad cars to use as a basis for model building and tracing the output of locomotive factories to understand the types of engines built and the customers for these engines. The latter records also may contribute to the compilation of genealogies for extant engines. The Minnesota Historical Society reports similar uses of its vast railroad business records collections. At the Smithsonian's National Air and Space Museum, builders of replica airplanes and owners of historic aircraft are the largest users of the drawings and other technical records in the museum's archives.

Like all researchers, collectors seek useful information regardless of its source. For many collectors, print materials scattered in corporate records, libraries, special collections, and museums are especially valuable. Corporate trade literature and marketing materials—including descriptive catalogs, price lists, service manuals, and advertisements—can provide invaluable information. The Archives Center of the National Museum of American History receives frequent requests for information about individual pianos and other musical instruments whose manufacturers' records are now in our custody. Other researchers in the center have included collectors of stoves, glassware, and children's toys.

While some collectors and hobbyists turn to the published corporate ephemera as research resources, others are rapidly acquiring it as a "collectible." The Antique Advertising Association of America is just one organized group of collectors and dealers in the field. *Past Times,* the association's eight-page, four-color newsletter, features examples from members' collections and news of forthcoming shows, sales, and meetings. Recent issues focused on advertising ephemeera for lawnmowers and firearms. The growing collector interest in business ephemera has helped to focus the attention of archivists on this often neglected form of corporate record and to increase their sensitivity to its historical value. Private collectors, motivated by the same sense of historical value and reluctant to disperse the results of their labors, also can become donors (and vendors) to archival repositories. At the same time, the rising value of ephemeral items, their small size, and the lack of item-level controls all heighten security concerns for archivists.

In the post-*Roots* era, archivists came to recognize a vast, often under-appreciated audience of vocational researchers in the areas of family history and genealogy. The ranks of Americans pursuing their interest in the past from personal rather than vocational motivations also includes a substantial number of collectors and hobbyists with interests in business history. Like genealogists, these researchers may focus on the minutely specific—construction details of a single airplane, for example—or range more widely over a time period, industry, or form of material culture. The scope of their work efforts may be limited to their personal satisfaction, or it may extend to wider audiences of colleagues who share their avocational interests. Archivists who seek wider uses for their business records holdings may find new audiences in these collectors and hobbyists.

Conclusion

Popular business history is produced by a wide range of practitioners for a broad public audience. In this regard, and in the diverse forms in which it is embodied and disseminated, it may be distinguished from academic historical scholarship published in scholarly books and journals and intended for an audience with professional historical training. The popular history of American business abounds in a host of print publications, museum exhibits, historical sites, historical documentaries, and commercial products.

One useful way to think of these great outpourings is to distinguish between three distinct purposes or objectives for which they are created. First, nonprofit museums and other historical agencies, historical writers, media producers, and the like create histories intended, above all, to educate their audiences. Second, corporations, trade associatons, and other business agencies produce popular history in every form with the primary intention of contributing to business objectives. These may be as immediate as selling a specific product but, more likely, are intended to enhance a brand identity, shape a corporate image, or promote a corporate point of view. Third, businesses, private organizations, and individuals produce history intended primarily to entertain. This entertainment may be in the form of mass leisure (for example, history by Disney), or it may inspire personal and esoteric activities as among collectors of Pepsi Cola ephemera.

Archivists who seek new uses and users for their business records holdings, new ways to publicize their archives to new audiences, ways to increase the visibility of their archives, and potential ways to generate revenues should consider the many forms of popular business history for possible answers. The needs and interests of producers of this history are not fundamentally different from those of other history creators, especially more recent social and cultural scholarly historians, but there are differences of degree and emphasis. Understanding and responding to these interests will greatly aid in expanding the use of the archives.

Popular history in all its varieties makes particular use of still and moving image visual materials. At best these images do not merely illustrate ideas but serve as sources of historical questions and as historical evidence. In exhibitions, photographs and other graphics, together with artifacts, must initially compete with other distractions for viewers' attention. Typically, these visual materials convey messages so powerfully that narrative captions and texts are, at best, complementary additions. Documentary film/video is above all a visual medium and a filmmaker essentially carries the historical story with images.

In addition to strong visual content, popular history is distinguished by a distinct topical emphasis. Stories about people are a maintstay of popular history. In business history this often means a focus on a small handful of entrepreneurial celebrities—especially

Ford and Edison—but other stories are possible and business records can reveal them. Audiences for popular history respond not only to familiar names but to products and advertisements, the side of business history that, as consumers, they experience firsthand. Thus an *Audacity* story on 3M's history that focused on management methods used as a graphic design element replicas of 3M's Post-It Notes to link the seven pages of the article visually.[26]

Beyond an appreciation for the topical concerns of popular history, archivists seeking to serve this clientele more effectively may need to reconsider some aspects of professional practice and operations. Many of these new users will not be familiar with archival research and techniques. Initial orientation and periodic coaching will help to assure the fragile balance of preservation and access that archivists are bound to maintain. Popular history practitioners will require more copies—low resolution xerographic as well as high-quality reproductions—than other researchers. Sometimes these researchers will be operating with short deadlines and tight budgets. Sometimes they will want to borrow original materials for exhibition or reproduction. With policies and procedures in place, archivists will be able to respond thoughtfully, not simply react.

Scholars value the historical records of American businesses as primary sources for their research monographs. Business executives use these records for corporate legal, fiscal, and adminstrative purposes. These uses largely justify the expenses of preserving these records. There is, however, broader potential for some records of American business. They can become the grist for journalists, public affairs staff, and other popular writers who unlock the history of business to much wider audiences. These records—in their original form, or more often in reproduction—can become part of the history-telling process themselves. Skillfully integrated into exhibitions, licensed reproductions, and documentary films, they can contribute to the sense of wonder, excitement, and learning that accompanies history at its best.

Endnotes

1. Michael Wallace is one scholar who has thought seriously about this topic. See, for example, "The Future of History Museums," *History News* 44, no. 4 (July–August 1989) and "Visiting the Past: History Museums in the United States," in *Presenting the Past: Essays on History and the Public*, Susan Porter Benson, et al. (Philadelphia: Temple University Press, 1986). There are several useful essays in Jo Blatti, ed., *Past Meets Present: Essays About Historic Interpretation and Public Audiences* (Washington, D.C.: Smithsonian Institution Press, 1987). See also other sources cited hereafter.

2. Warren Leon and Roy Rosenzweig, *History Museums in the United States: A Critical Assessment* (Urbana and Chicago: University of Illinois Press, 1989), xvi.

3. The exhibition is described in the museum's newsletter, *Update* (fall, 1995).

4. *Who's In Charge* is described in *Update 1995–96*, the catalog of the Smithsonian Institution Travelling Exhibition Service. Harry R. Rubenstein, curator of this exhibition, discusses the inclusion of workers in museum exhibitions and cites three examples of museum exhibitions that have focused on working people in "Welcoming Workers," *Museum News* 69, no. 6 (November–December 1990): 39–42. He also offers a telling critique of "typical industrial history exhibits."

5. Two widely read overviews of material culture studies are E. McClung Fleming, "Artifact Study, A Proposed Model," *Winterthur Portfolio* 9 (1974): 153–173 and Jules David Prown, "Mind in Matter: An Introduction to Material Culture Theory and Method," *Winterthur Portfolio*, 17, no. 1 (spring 1982): 1–20.

6. This story is told in detail in Michael Kammen, *Mystic Chords of Memory: The Transformation of Tradition in American Culture* (New York: Alfred A. Knopf, 1991).

7. Division of Publications, National Park Service, *Lowell: The Story of an Industrial City: A Guide to Lowell National Historical Park and Lowell Heritage State Park* (Washington D.C.: Superintendent of Documents, 1991). This is the official national park handbook.

8. An example from the National Museum of American History's Archives Center comes to mind. The records of the Apollo Theater in Harlem include several drawers of card files kept as a record of the appearance of each performer. The informal notes include the amount paid and an assessment of the performance. The record not only documents broad shifts in popular tastes but the lives of individuals. Thus, entries for the great singer Billie Holiday document in terse business prose her tragic struggles with drug addiction.

9. Lawrence Vail Coleman, *Company Museums* (Washington, D.C.: American Association of Museums, 1943) cited in David R. Smith, "An Historical Look at Business Archives," in *Corporate Archives and History: Making the Past Work*, eds. Arnita A. Jones and Philip L. Cantelon (Melbourne, Fla.: Krieger Publishing Company, 1993), 127–133.

10. Philip F. Mooney, "The Practice of History in Corporate America: Business Archives in the United States," reprinted in Jones and Cantelon, eds., *Corporate Archives and History*, 15.

11. Neil Harris, review of the World of Coca-Cola Museum, *Journal of American History* (June 1995): 154–158.

12. Harold P. Anderson, "Banking on The Past: Wells Fargo & Company," in Jones and Cantelon, eds., *Corporate Archives and History*, 37–42. Anderson offers this explanation of the role of history in his firm: "In a relatively undifferentiated market like financial services, in which most institutions have similar products and services, marketing and advertising are key competitive elements. When a

vast majority of an institution's customers are retail, with a strong notion of loyalty to a stable and reliable repository for their money, then history is an important corporate asset."

13. Set of eight color post cards and additional information about the Nestle Museum courtesy of David Owens, General Manager, Nestle Training Center at Carnation Farm.

14. Andrew Ratner, "Crayola's New Tourist Attraction Draws on History," *Sun* (Baltimore), September 22, 1996.

15. "Abraham Lincoln and Jack Daniel's Whiskey (or, Discussing Corporate History Issues in Nashville Tennessee)" *Dispatch* (May 1996): 1.

16. By comparison, see George David Smith, "Why Companies Can't Afford to Ignore The Past," in Jones and Cantelon, eds., *Corporate Archives and History*, 183 ff. for a discussion of producing company histories of use to corporate executives following standards of historical scholarship.

17. Philip F. Mooney, "Practice," 9, describes Coke's licensing and similar efforts by archivists at Sears and Anheuser-Busch. See also *Advertising in America: Using its Past, Enriching Its Future*, (Durham, N.C.: Duke University, 1994), a report of a national conference cosponsored by the Center for Sales, Advertising, and Marketing History, Duke University, and the Center for Advertising History, National Museum of American History, Smithsonian Institution, for uses of historical advertising materials by archivists at Coca-Cola, Kraft General Foods, and the Leo Burnett advertising agency.

18. Other examples of licensing recently spotted include a Zippo "salute" to pinup girls, recalling the lighter's use, sixty years ago, of "a beautiful young woman" to introduce its windproof lighter (*Life* [June 1996]). The summer 1996 Hammacher Schlemmer catalog offers the "1955 Schwinn Cruiser Deluxe Bicycle" that "lets baby boomers take a nostalgic ride back in time aboard the classic one-speed bicycle that epitomized the 'cool' 1950s era. Recently reintroduced by Schwinn, this 'malt-shop-style' coaster is fully equipped."

19. *Washington Post*, September 23, 1996, Style section. The report suggested the scale of museum retail operations, citing a record $7.1 million worth of products sold by the Philadelphia Museum of Art during its three-month Cezanne exhibition. The museum earned less than $500,000 of that amount during the museum's two-hour QVC program.

20. John Adams, "Brands at the Crossroads," *American Advertising* 2, no. 3, 18–21.

21. Roy Rosenzweig, "Marketing the Past: *American Heritage* and Popular History in the United States," in *Presenting the Past: Essays on History and the Public*, eds. Susan Porter Benson, Stephen Brier, and Roy Rosenzweig (Philadelphia: Temple University Press, 1986), 22. See also Kammen, *Mystic Chords of Memory*.

22. These distinctions are discussed in Robert A. Rosenstone, "The Historical Film: Looking at the Past in a Postliterate Age," in *Learning History in America: Schools,*

Cultures, and Politics, eds. Lloyd Kramer, Donald Reid, and William L. Barney (Minneapolis: University of Minnesota Press, 1994), 141–160.

23. Northeast Historic Film, Bucksport, Maine, is a unique institution dedicated to preserving historic film, documenting northern New England. In addition to collecting and preserving film, it offers screenings and a video lending library that includes student-made documentaries, original footage of logging and whaling, and home movies.

24. Other Americans make this connection through direct participation in its re-creation as reenactors, living history guides, and the like. Their use of archival sources is more likely to resemble other researchers without formal training in historical research methods, for example genealogists.

25. Kammen, "Authentic Museums to Educate the People About the History of the United States," chapter 11 in *Mystic Chords of Memory*.

26. James C. Collins and Jerry I. Porra, "A Theory of Evolution," *Audacity* 4, no. 2 (winter 1996): 4–10.

13

Collecting Repositories and Corporate Archives: Variations on a Theme?

Karen Benedict

Once a corporation has decided to manage its permanent records, it must determine the most efficient and effective system to employ in order to meet its legal, fiscal, and regulatory recordkeeping requirements, as well as its information needs. Since the 1940s, American businesses have created internal corporate archives programs to administer their permanently valuable records and to provide company personnel with the required access to needed facts, figures, and corporate data.

The Firestone Tire & Rubber Company of Akron, Ohio, is credited with creating the first U.S. business archives in March 1943. AT&T earlier had created a Corporate History Program with an archival records component, but according to the literature, Firestone had the first operation referred to as a business archives. It was established under the supervision of Dr. William D. Overman, who was formerly the curator of history and state archivist at the Ohio State Archaeological and Historical Society. His title was corporate historian and archivist.

The Firestone Archives was created because Harvey S. Firestone, Jr. wanted a corporate history to be written as part of the company's 50th anniversary celebration. He also believed that the records of American industry were a vital part of the documentation of the nation's involvement in World War II.[1]

Firestone had instituted a records management program in 1920 to grapple with the ever-growing volume of company records. However, the records management system had not been set up to preserve permanently valuable or historically important documents. Consequently, when Harvey Firestone wanted the company's history written, it was necessary to establish the corporate archives to identify and locate the records of historical value.[2]

In a 1953 discussion of the Firestone Archives, Overman said, "Based on [the company's business library reference] collection and the contents of the archives, two books have already been written—a biography of the founder and a historical account of the growth and development of the business." However, the archives' contribution went beyond documenting company history, Overman reported. "Experience has also shown that this ever-growing collection is an aid in forming company-wide policy and in solving the day-to-day problems of managing the business."[3]

Through the 1940s and early 1950s, historians and librarians continued to discuss how to best preserve valuable business records. The consensus was that noncurrent business records and the records of defunct businesses should be placed in repositories like the Baker Library at the Harvard School of Business.[4] However, as early as 1945, Arthur H. Cole, the librarian at the Baker Library, concluded that this approach was not the best answer. He believed that collections of business records were typically so large and so seldom used that it was not justifiable, in terms of space and costs, for Baker Library and similar institutions to house them. He suggested that business firms should create and maintain their own archival programs.[5]

Cole's viewpoint prevailed, but the growth of business archives was relatively slow. From the mid-1940s through the 1960s programs were established at such major corporations as the Insurance Company of North America; Time, Inc.; Armstrong Cork; Alcoa; Lever Brothers; Eastman Kodak; Ford Motor Company; Sears Roebuck; New York Life Insurance; Eli Lilly; Proctor & Gamble; Bank of America; Coca-Cola; IBM; Gulf Oil; the Chicago Board of Trade; and Educational Testing Service.[6]

By 1968, when the Business Archives Committee of the Society of American Archivists (SAA) first surveyed companies, 138 responded that they had an "archives." However, this survey did not attempt to separate companies that simply indicated that they were keeping some of their older records from those that had established formal archives programs. Only approximately 10 percent of the 138 companies responding employed a full-time archivist.[7]

Growth in business archives continued through the mid-1980s. During this period, historical societies, state archives, and other re-

positories seeking to preserve regional business history usually confined themselves to collecting the records of defunct businesses. That
practice has been changing since the early 1990s. There is a growing
trend toward repositories collecting the older records of existing businesses. In a few cases, repositories have been willing to act as the
business's archives and to accept more contemporary records.

The various editions of the *Directory of Business Archives in the
United States and Canada*, compiled by the Business Archives Committee and later the Business Archives Section, and published by the
Society of American Archivists, illustrate the fluctuations in the development of business archives.[8] In 1969, the first *Directory* listed 138
business archives programs. By 1975, that number had grown to 195.
In 1980, the listing of business archives reached a high of 210. But in
1990, when the most recent SAA Business Archives Section *Directory*
was compiled, the number of business archives listed had declined to
158. At the same time, there has been an increase in Business Archives
Section membership by archivists affiliated with institutions collecting
business records. During the period of the late 1960s to 1980, the
majority of the members of SAA's Business Archives Section were from
business archives, but by the 1990s between 5 percent and 10 percent
of the members were from repositories collecting business records.
While the *Directory* is not a comprehensive guide to all of the business
archives in North America, I think that it accurately reflects a downward
trend in the creation of business archives programs in corporations.

It is also a sad fact that a number of well-established business
archives programs have been dismantled over the past few years. The
list of closures of corporate archives over the past decade includes
Bank of America, Citicorp Bank, Domino Pizza, International Harvester, OCLC, Sears, Standard Oil of Ohio (SOHIO), J. Walter Thompson Advertising Agency, and United Technologies.

The fate of the records in these closures has varied. In some cases
records were disbursed or discarded. However, after three years, the
Bank of America reconsidered its decision and rehired a professional
archivist. Following a corporate restructuring, the International Harvester program reemerged as part of the Navistar Corporation's archives. The Sears Roebuck archives remained closed from 1989 to
1996, at which time they contracted with an outside firm to provide
archival services. J. Walter Thompson, with the assistance of the de-
parting archivist, Cynthia Swank, arranged to deposit their records at
Duke University. The company has an ongoing agreement with Duke
to continue to deposit records in its archives. In other instances, companies like Kodak, Lever Brothers, Texaco, IBM, Gulf Oil, and Education Testing Service have eliminated the archivist and placed other
company personnel in charge of the records.

The decline in the number of business archives is reflective of events in the 1980s and 1990s that affected the economic well-being of American business. These events included the proliferation of corporate mergers and takeovers, the major recession of the 1980s, and corporate restructuring, or reengineering, with its significant reductions in the work force. Staff and resources for existing business archives programs have been reduced. Companies are less willing to invest in the creation of new corporate archives.

At the same time, the need for the services of corporate archivists has increased. The substantial reduction in the work force makes the archives an even more valuable corporate asset. The elimination of positions and the people to fill them leads to large gaps in the corporate memory. When there are no safeguards or rules in place to protect and preserve corporate records, the employees who retire or are let go often either destroy their records or take their files with them when they leave.

Archives and records management programs are essential to preserve the corporate memory. They establish a systematic approach to identifying and preserving the records that the company must maintain to provide for continuity in ongoing operations, and to protect corporate security and proprietary information. Without a records program in place to govern how the company's records are handled, when employees leave they take with them not only their knowledge of the company's activities, but also the knowledge of how and where that documentation is maintained. Failure to produce required records can cost a company enormous sums in litigation, governmental fines, added licensing or regulatory fees, or environmental cleanup costs.

The nature of business archives has changed over the years. The early literature was filled with articles about business history and the need to preserve records in order to support scholarly research. The focus of contemporary business archives is not on providing resources for business historians. Instead, contemporary business archives emphasize serving the corporate need for access to vital and valuable information.[9] Business archives provide sophisticated information services and add value to the information resources in corporate records by identifying, preserving, and providing company personnel with ready access to needed information about corporate operations. The function of business archives not only is to preserve the records, but also to provide research and reference services by skilled staff familiar with the depth and breadth of the evidence available in the records. Modern business archives furnish crucial litigation support services; they supply supporting documentation for trademark and patent protection; and they are an important link in providing the type of consumer information services that deepen customer loyalty and satisfaction.

Observation of the operation of business archives in the United States over the past 20 years suggests that there are several factors in addition to the external forces already mentioned that can affect the success or failure of programs. One is the depth of the commitment of top corporate management to the establishment of an archives. They must understand that the company is making a long-term commitment to the program. They must be prepared to budget for the necessary initial and ongoing costs for space, equipment and supplies, and professional personnel. Moreover, top management must be willing to secure cooperation for the archives throughout all levels of the company. The archivist needs to have the authority to determine which records are to be permanently maintained, along with the authority to acquire the records at the point when the creating office no longer needs to refer to them for daily operations.

A second key issue is the placement of the archival program within the organizational structure. The common wisdom is that the most effective organizational placement is at the executive level, possibly within the office of the corporate secretary. Placement within the top echelon of management ensures an ability to promote company-wide support and cooperation for the business archives. Generally, corporate secretaries are responsible for maintaining the records of the board of directors and the minutes of executive committees that report to the board, and are responsible for vital records protection for the corporation. Thus, the corporate secretary's office can provide a natural home for the archives because of its already existing records responsibilities.

However, the most typical organizational placement for business archives is at the director's level, or middle level of management, within the offices of communications, public relations, or marketing. This is not an ideal arrangement because the archivist has to work through several layers of management in order to reach the ears of top executives regarding important policy and procedural decisions for the archives. This placement also appears to affect the focus of the business archives program. These programs often concentrate on more publicly accessible information such as annual reports, company publications, records relating to public relations and marketing, consumer-related product information, and artifacts rather than on other facets of corporate operations. While this is important documentation to retain, it does not equip the archives to serve all of the internal corporate information needs that would broaden support for the program.

It is clear that there are significant advantages to a business archives in organizational placement at the corporate secretary or vice presidential level. It is easier at that level to establish appropriate policies and procedures for appraisal and accessioning of records for the program and to secure cooperation for the regular transfer of records to the archives. Regardless of placement, the business archives should attempt to serve the interests of top management. The business archives has a duty to promote the corporate interest through providing the type of information services that the particular company needs and values.

While there is still a clear preference for companies to create their own archives, the recent closings of several corporate archives programs have renewed interest in the placement of corporate records in historical societies and other types of archival repositories. The archival profession has encouraged businesses to seek out suitable repositories to accept their collections when the business archives programs have failed or been abolished, as in the case of the J. Walter Thompson Advertising Agency archives. In addition, more repositories, such as the Hagley Museum and Library, the Cincinnati Historical Society, the Minnesota Historical Society, and the Duke University Archives have aggressively begun to collect the corporate records of both defunct and active businesses in their regions.

This trend has been furthered by the desire of some companies to find ways to deal with records problems without adding full-time personnel to the payroll. In the past, a major obstacle to relinquishing control over their records has been corporate concern for protecting all proprietary, confidential, personnel, private, and privileged information as well as information regarding manufacturing and trade secrets. Also, older records may contain information essential for supporting trademark, licensing, and law suits against the corporation that the company must have at hand when needed.

Some repositories have come up with innovative solutions to these problems. The Cincinnati Historical Society has developed a program to encourage businesses in Cincinnati, Hamilton County, and the surrounding region to utilize its services to preserve and provide access to the businesses' records. The Business Archives Program at the society offers records management assistance, archival administration, and storage services to companies. It charges the donors or depositors of records a fee to cover a portion of the society's cost in providing these services. To allay corporate fears about privacy and access to proprietary information, the Cincinnati Historical Society allows businesses to retain ownership of their records for the period during which they fear that relinquishing such control would compromise their competitive position. At the same time, the society creates a relationship with the corporation that promotes the eventual donation of these records to the society in order to assure their permanent preservation.

It is unusual for archival repositories to accept collections without securing ownership of the records because the institution incurs substantial costs in maintaining the records and making them available for research. Also, it is unusual for repositories to charge donors, or those loaning them collections, for the processing, storage, and access to their records. However, private historical societies, state archives, and other cultural institutions like the Cincinnati Historical Society are being challenged to come up with new revenue sources and new programs to stimulate public and private interest and support. The focus of the Cincinnati Historical Society program is to provide innovative services and to preserve business records that might otherwise be lost or destroyed. Moreover, for-profit corporations are able to afford to pay for these services; and so tax-supported and nonprofit institutions should not be obliged to provide them free of charge.

The Minnesota Historical Society also has established a significant program for the collection of business records. Along with the Hagley Library and Museum in Delaware, it has one of the largest holdings of business records in the United States. Minnesota Historical Society has 517 collections of the records of Minnesota businesses, comprising approximately 20,764 cubic feet of documents. These extensive holdings include the records of agriculture-related businesses; business associations; the construction industry; the entertainment industry; finance; banking; insurance; the fur trade; health care; hotels and restaurants; law firms and lawyers; lumber and logging; and others. The majority of these collections are from defunct companies, but the Minnesota Historical Society aggressively seeks records from active Minnesota corporations if the society feels that the records should be preserved, and if the company is unwilling to establish an in-house archival program—or if the archives program is being abolished.

When a company seeks advice about its historical records from the Minnesota Historical Society, the first suggestion it receives is to consider creating an in-house archives program. The Minnesota Historical Society has helped to create archival programs at Control Data, General Mills, H. B. Fuller Company, Pillsbury, St. Paul Insurance Companies, and 3M Corporation, among others.

Public access to the records of active corporations deposited at the Minnesota Historical Society is negotiated by contract. In general, business records are closed to the public for 10 to 25 years from the date the record was created.

The Minnesota Historical Society presently does not charge corporations for processing, storing, or providing reference services to their records. Yet, the staff does find itself called upon to provide reference services for active corporate records beyond those requested for other collections. Although the Minnesota Historical Society requires ownership of the corporate records deposited there, under certain circumstances the society will formally loan back records that a company needs for an extended, but specified, period of time. Because they have discovered that active businesses produce a larger volume of records than other types of collections and require more demanding reference services, the Minnesota Historical Society is exploring the possibility of adding fees for the processing, storing, and reference services provided for the records of active corporations.

The Hagley Museum and Library in Greenville, Delaware, was established in 1961. It is devoted to the preservation of the records of American businesses and the entrepreneurs that created them. The Hagley has over 20,000 cubic feet of records of more than 1,000 firms. The holdings range from records of the mercantile houses of the late eighteenth century, through the artisan workshops of the nineteenth century, to the multinational corporations of the twentieth century. The museum holds records of northeastern railways, iron and steel industries, banking and insurance, textiles, electric utilities, petroleum and coal industries, high-technology firms, and the early computer industry. The Hagley has the business and personal papers of the Du Pont Company and family, as well as the archives of the Conference Board, the National Association of Manufacturers, and the Seagram Corporation. Like the Minnesota Historical Society and the Cincinnati Historical Society, the Hagley solicits records of active businesses. The museum does not impose charges for the services provided, but it tries to negotiate a fee to cover some of the processing costs when it accepts a collection. The Hagley allows businesses to borrow records if they are required for a project, but tries to provide photocopies rather than the original documents in such cases. Since, occasionally in the past a corporation has borrowed records and not returned them to the collection, the Hagley now asks the companies borrowing original documents to sign a loan agreement akin to those that other museums use when lending materials from their collections.

What are the questions that a corporation should consider when deciding to "do something" with its records—whether it is to have a corporate history written; to celebrate a major anniversary; to locate records to support ongoing litigation; to gain control over the ever-burgeoning volume of records being created; or to use the records for internal purposes such as employee orientation, marketing, promotion, and public relations activities? What factors should a corporation weigh in deciding whether or not to establish an archives program or to place its records in a repository?

First and foremost, corporate executives should have a clear understanding of what they hope to accomplish through the establishment

of an archives or the placement of their archival records in a repository. They need well-defined goals and objectives in order to evaluate
their options. An archival program must encompass more than the
usual accumulation of old correspondence, scrapbooks, and ancient
ledgers that are treasured by some executive and employees as artifacts
and dismissed by others as meaningless "old junk." The program
needs to enable the company to identify, preserve, and make accessible information from all of the corporate records that it must maintain
permanently because of their legal, fiscal, regulatory, evidential, and
informational value to the institution.

Corporate executives realize that there are legal, fiscal, and regulatory requirements for recordkeeping with which they are obligated
to comply that are issued by federal, state and local governments, and
the Internal Revenue Service. In addition, every company generates
records that are essential to support operations, to maintain control
over budget, to document profits and losses, and to protect the firm
from litigation. Without an archival program, corporations do not have
a systematic way to identify the records that should be permanently
maintained to fulfill all legal, fiscal, evidential and informational
needs. Even when a company has a records management program,
usually it does not address the important evidential and informational
needs of the corporation. A business archives can create a cost-effective and efficient system to maintain records and to provide access to
necessary information from them when it is required.

However, establishing an internal business archives is expensive,
and it requires a long term commitment from the company. The costs
of a business archives program include the salary and benefits for
professional staff (the minimum staff being one full-time professional
archivist, and, ideally, at least one full-time clerical assistant); the
space for records storage (which should be secure and climate-con-
trolled); and the proper professional equipment and supplies to protect,
preserve, store, and make accessible records in all formats—hard
copy, microforms, electronic and digital media, photographs, film, audio and videotapes. Also, it is essential to provide adequate office and
work space for the staff and for researchers, either as part of the storage facility or in its immediate vicinity. The archives should be
equipped with computer facilities and software for both archival and
office applications. It should have e-mail, Internet, fax, and photocopying capabilities.

What benefits to a company can justify such costs? The archives
will guarantee the preservation of all of the permanently valuable records of the company. It will provide immediate, on-site access to information from the records and to the actual records themselves when
needed. An in-house archives will allow the company to set and ad-

minister the policy controlling access to all corporate records. It will enable the company to protect sensitive and proprietary information from anyone outside of the organization. Lastly, an in-house program will have a staff devoted to providing reference and research services for company personnel needing data or information.

Since an in-house archives program will provide a company with the highest level of information preservation and retrieval services that it needs, what are the reasons for any company to consider placing its records in an outside repository? First, the company does not take on the obligation of additional personnel to administer the archives; it does not need to incur the total expense for space, supplies, and equipment. While some repositories may charge businesses for services, those charges usually do not represent the full costs incurred by the repository in the processing, storage, and providing reference services for the collection.

Although costs are likely to be less if a company chooses to place its records in a repository, there are a number of other considerations that should be weighed in determining whether an in-house business archives or a repository is the appropriate choice for a company to deal with its archival records. Let us examine these considerations and compare the approaches that are likely to be taken by business archives versus by repositories.

The first consideration is the selection process for the records to be kept permanently, which archivists call "appraisal." Outside repositories will appraise business records in light of the research needs of their public. They will take into account the institution's mission statement and established collection policies. In-house business archives will apply very different appraisal criteria to determine the type and volume of records to retain because their fundamental mission is to serve and to protect the interests of the corporation. Business archives evaluate the company's information needs rather than those of a general research public. Business archives maintain records that are required for legal and regulatory purposes, and those records that document all aspects of corporate operations, regardless of their outside research potential.

Repositories will be constrained by the limits of their stack space available for the storage of any single collection of records. They must evaluate the research potential of records for a large and more diverse public since they are mandated to acquire collections that serve the research needs of all of their constituents. Thus, outside repositories will necessarily stress acquiring those business records that have a broad research interest, that can become the property of the repository, that will be available for public access within a reasonable length of time, and that will not have arbitrary or burdensome restrictions on use placed on the materials in the collection. These requirements may put the mandate of some repositories in conflict with the corporation's need to protect its confidential and proprietary interests.

The second consideration involves the processing of the records and the creation of finding aids to provide access to information that they contain. In-house business archives may not adhere strictly to the accepted standards of the profession. Rules will be bent to make the level and type of information available in a format that better suits the business's needs. It is not as important to create a professionally acceptable finding aid as it is to make the information clearly accessible to company personnel. An advantage for business archives is that they can utilize the corporation's electronic information system to make information available to company personnel. This means that executives and staff can retrieve data or information about records in the archives from their personal computers or terminals at their desks. Since information is at the staffs' fingertips, it increases the use of the data, information, and records that the company has compiled.

Repositories process records and create their finding aids in accordance with accepted professional standards. The guides or finding aids to the collections are designed for a general research public. Although they try to provide detailed information about collections that attract heavy research use, typically, repositories will not describe records beyond the folder level. The volume of records with which they deal precludes item-level description. Since they deal with a much smaller and more focused volume of records, business archives have the advantage of being able to provide item-level description if it is warranted by the significance of the material or the needs of the users.

Third is the matter of physical access to the records. Companies justifiably are nervous about giving people outside of the organization access to privileged information. This concern may include the outside repository staff working with corporate records. Some measure of security may be established through requiring the repository staff involved with a business collection to sign corporate conflict-of-interest and confidentiality statements. A business archives program poses fewer risks for protecting corporate information. As an employee of the company, the in-house archivist's first allegiance is to the company. Also, the company's legal staff is likely to play an active role in designating confidential records and in restricting access to the records in the manner that best serves the company's interests.

Business archives often restrict access to the records to company personnel. In some cases, these limitations are fixed. In other cases, outside researchers are required to submit a written request for access to corporate records. These requests, usually, are reviewed by the archivist, often in conjunction with an executive committee that makes decisions on a case-by-case basis. Only a few business archives, such as that of the Coca-Cola Company, welcome outside researchers.

Repositories, eventually, will provide public access to corporate records because that is what they are mandated to do. The majority of repositories will be willing to work with a corporation to establish a reasonable policy to limit access to recent records until such time as they no longer are considered sensitive or proprietary. It would not be unusual for repositories only to allow public access to business records that were, at minimum, 25 years old.

The fourth area to be evaluated is the provision of reference and research services. Traditionally, legal, marketing, and public relations departments are heavy users of business archives. Usually, there is an immediate need for information, particularly on the part of legal staff. Often, lawyers will need to have original documents rather than photocopies to present as evidence in court. Therefore, having the records on-site is preferable to having to send a staff member out to a repository to do research and retrieve documents.

Moreover, business people frequently are unfamiliar with the setup of repositories and archival research techniques. They may find archival finding aids confusing or inadequate for their purposes. They may be dissatisfied by the regulations governing the use of records imposed by repositories—such as having to leave all belongings outside the research room or only being allowed to use a pencil to take notes. Also, they may be reluctant to take the time to travel to a repository, go through the registration process, wait for the requested records to be delivered to them—sometimes one box at a time—and then to be obliged to conduct all of their research there with limited access to photo-reproduction. In addition to wanting immediate access to information, many corporate researchers prefer to get answers to their questions over the telephone, without having to leave their desks. Business archives provide these research services as a matter of course. It is a part of the justification for maintaining an in-house archival program. For business archives, providing access does not simply mean providing the records, it means providing the information that is being sought by the researcher. Business people are accustomed to the service areas within a corporation providing them with a high level of personalized service. For instance, corporate library staff typically conduct the research on business questions, searching hard copy and data bases for users and furnishing them with the results. Corporate archives are expected to function in the same way.

This is the greatest area of difference between business archives and repositories. Unlike business archives, repositories serve a large and broad-based clientele. The code of ethics of the profession stresses that repositories must treat all users equally. It is not advisable for a repository to promise to provide special services for one group of users that it is not willing to provide to all of its researchers. Therefore, businesses, especially those that are not paying for the services that they receive, should not expect to be treated with special consideration. If a business is placing its records in an outside repository, it must give a great deal of thought to how those records will be used by researchers within and outside of the corporation, both in the short and the long term. The company will need to negotiate with the repository to see that it is being adequately protected against potential litigation, invasion of proprietary information, and untrue or unflattering representations of its actions. It will need to make certain that the repository staff and the company personnel have a clear, mutual understanding of the kinds of services that will be provided and the level of research assistance that company researchers can expect when they need to have access to the business's records.

Given these potential problems, why should a corporation even consider placing archival records in an outside repository? Corporate America plays a significant role in shaping the policies of our country's local, state, and federal government and its political parties and affects the nature of our society. The impact on the operations of government, the economy, and the life of all of our citizens is so great that it is impossible to discuss America and its development without analyzing the impact of business and business policies. The needs of researchers and the general public seeking access to information about American business are best served by the corporate records in repositories, while the needs of active businesses can be better served by in-house archival programs. There is not only a place but a crucial need for both types of collections of business records in our society.

If an active corporation decides to place its records in a repository rather than create a business archives program, the success of the relationship with the repository will depend upon negotiating a donor agreement that serves the best interests of both institutions and is mutually satisfactory in its terms. The following set of questions is intended to help repositories and businesses to negotiate such a contract. It outlines the areas that need to be addressed by both parties. These questions are intended to help to promote discussion, to avoid misunderstandings, and to establish a fruitful working relationship between business and repository.

The questions fall into three categories, although there is some overlap among them. They are (1) the contract or written donor agreement for deposit of corporate records; (2) policies on access to records; and (3) reference and research services required by corporate users of company records.

Contracts or Donor Agreements

1. Will the repository accept collections of business records on loan, or must they become the property of the repository?

2. If a collection of business records is on loan, is there a minimum length of time that they must remain at the repository?

3. Will the repository accept current records?

4. If the repository does not accept current records, how many years must pass after the date of creation of the records before they will be taken?

5. If the records are on loan, does the contract specify causes for abrogation?
   a. Can the company remove the collection if it is dissatisfied with the speed of processing the records?
   b. Can the company remove the collection if it is dissatisfied with the type and specificity of the finding aids created?
   c. Can the company remove the collection if it is dissatisfied with the reference services provided by the repository?
   d. Can the repository return the records if the collection becomes too large for them to house in their storage facilities?
   e. Can the repository return the records if access policies become a problem for the institution?
   f. Can the repository return the records if the level of reference services required by the company exceeds the repository staff's expectations and capacity?
   g. Can the repository return the records if there are budget cuts and it is unable to continue to fulfill the agreement because of staffing shortages or other difficulties?

6. Does the contract set any limits on the size of the collection?

7. Does the contract provide a timetable for the processing and creating of finding aids?

8. Does the contract provide a timetable for making the records available to researchers?

9. Does the repository have set qualifications for project management staff and processors?
   a. What are the qualifications?
   b. Can they be specified in the contract?

10. Does the repository use interns, volunteers, or other temporary employees to process collections?

    a. If so, can the company request only using permanent, professionally trained staff on the project?

11. Does the repository have a conflict of interest or confidentiality statement that staff are required to sign?

    a. If not, will the contract allow the company to impose such agreements on staff working with their records?

Policies on Access to Records

1. Will the repository accept collections of records that will be permanently closed to the public?

2. Will the repository allow some of the records within a collection to be permanently closed to the public?

3. Will the repository accept records if access to the public is restricted for a number of years, such as 25 to 30 years?

4. Will the repository accept records with confidentiality restrictions that will allow access only to designated individuals?

5. Will the repository accept records with access restrictions that require users to request permission from the donor?

6. Does the repository close its stack area to all researchers?

7. Does the repository control staff access to restricted and confidential records?

8. Will the repository allow the corporation to restrict staff access to its confidential records?

9. Will the repository allow company personnel to have access to records prior to or during their processing, arrangement, and description?

10. Will the repository loan back records to the company for special projects for a specified period of time?

11. Will the repository allow the company to take back any records from the collection if the company determines that it needs to retake possession of them for corporate purposes?

12. Will the repository allow corporate counsel to remove original documents from the collection for unspecified periods of time if the records are needed for litigation?

Reference and Research Services Required by Corporate Users of Company Records

1. Will the repository staff perform research for company executives and company personnel working on special projects?

2. Are there limits to the amount of time repository staff will spend on corporate research requests?

3. Will the repository answer telephone requests from company personnel for information or fill telephone requests for photocopies or faxes of documents from the files?

4. Are there limits on the amount of time to be spent on such requests?

5. Will the repository do extensive photocopying of records for the company if needed?

6. Are there limits on the number of copies to be provided for the company in a single request or annually?

7. Will the company pay the standard fees imposed by the repository for duplication services?

8. Will the repository allow company personnel to have unlimited access to photocopiers for their research if access is restricted for other patrons?

9. Will the repository make any priority provisions for company personnel to use photocopiers or microfilm readers/printers?

10. Will the repository make any special provisions for company personnel doing "rush" project work in the corporate records?
    a. If parking is restricted, will company personnel have parking reserved for their use?
    b. If researcher space is limited, will company personnel have priority?
    c. If there are restrictions on the use of personal computers, portable microfilm cameras, scanners, etc., will exceptions be made for company personnel?
    d. If there is an important corporate project, will the repository make provisions for extended hours for research for company personnel?

11. Will the repository perform "rush" photographic, film, or video duplication work for the company, if needed?

12. Will this work take priority over other projects?

The final area of potential negotiation is the imposition of fees for services. In the past, repositories did not charge donors of records fees for storage, processing, or reference services. However, state archives, historical societies, libraries, and other cultural institutions are facing severe cuts in their budgets. Archivists are being challenged by their administrators to find alternative ways to fund some or all of their activities. In the future, it may be customary for fees to be imposed for many of the services that repositories used to provide gratis. The experiment has begun.

Some repositories accepting business records are imposing fees for certain archival services provided to the corporations. They believe that these fees are justified when the size of the business record collection is larger than the typical collection or when the level of reference services required by the company exceeds the expectations of other patrons.

Companies should expect to be called upon to negotiate fees for records storage, processing of the records, reference services in excess of the standard services, and reproduction services. They should request that the repository provide them with an itemized statement of charges for specific services. At present, even those institutions charging fees present a bargain because they are not attempting to recoup their total costs.

Both the repository and the business archives offer a corporation skilled, professional staff trained to provide guidance in the management of permanent records and information services that meet the standards set by the archival profession. These skills and services are valuable and warrant consideration as an investment in today's competitive marketplace. All corporations can benefit, in terms of efficiency and productivity, from the services of a skilled professional archivist guiding the company through the complex laws and regulations that govern recordkeeping in our technologically dynamic society. Establishing a business archives is a sound financial investment for the present and the future. Placing business records in an outside repository assures that those records will be available for research now and for future generations.

Since not all businesses are willing to establish their own archival programs, it is my view that repositories need to be encouraged to actively collect business records that otherwise would be destroyed or lost over time. The programs at the Hagley Museum and Library and the Minnesota Historical Society serve as excellent models for what can be accomplished in this area. With the current economic uncertainties, and a relatively short and unproven track record for the longevity of most business archives, I believe that these repository programs represent a viable, professionally managed alternative for the preservation of business records.

More American businesses need to be brought to the realization that it is important both to the business community and to society in general to preserve and to provide access to their records. The placement of some collections of business records in repositories offers a balance. Repositories provide scholars and other researchers with access to business records, while business archives naturally must focus on providing protection for corporate records and serving the needs of the corporate users of those records.

There is a critical need within corporations for business archives. Businesses need to professionally manage their records in order to make use of them as a permanently valuable resource. Corporations waste hundreds of thousands to millions of dollars annually in redundant studies and projects within their organization due to a lack of control of their records, poor channels of internal communication, and lack of a system to provide access to the information they have generated. A business archives makes it possible for a company to identify, keep, and utilize the significant information and data it has created. However, because of the proprietary and competitive nature of much of this information, it cannot be made available for public research until enough years have passed for it to be considered "history."

I want to suggest that one method for handling the competing information needs of the corporation versus outside researchers may be for a company to create a business archives to meet its internal needs and to donate older records that pose no threat of revelations of private or proprietary information to an archival repository for permanent preservation. During the 50 some years we have devoted attention to business records in this country, there has been an either/or argument about business archives versus collecting repositories providing the best means for maintaining and providing access to business records. Perhaps the time has come to consider a collaborative approach that can balance the corporate interests of the business community with the research interests of society.

The archival profession needs to track the success of programs like those at the Hagley, the Minnesota Historical Society, Cincinnati Historical Society, and Duke University as they aggressively collect the records of twentieth-century American business. It will be interesting to discover whether these collections become too large and burdensome to process and store, and too little used by researchers, as was earlier charged.

It also will be interesting to track the experience at Duke University as they attempt to assume the role of archives for J. Walter Thompson since the demise of the company's archival program. It is an ambitious experiment that will reveal whether this type of collaborative arrangement can survive over a long period of time with mutually satisfactory results.

Endnotes

1. For a full description of the establishment and functioning of the Firestone records management program and archives see William D. Overman, "The Firestone Archives and Library," *American Archivist* 16, no. 3 (1953): 305–309, and "The Pendulum Swings," *American Archivist* 22, no. 1 (1959): 3–10.

2. Overman, "The Firestone Archives and Library," 307.

3. Overman, "The Firestone Archives and Library," 309.

4. See for example: Thomas C. Cochran, "New York City Business Records: A Plan for Their Preservation," *Bulletin of the Business Historical Society* 18 (June 1944): 59–62; Arthur H. Cole, "Business Manuscripts: Collection, Handling, and Cataloging," *Library Quarterly* 8 (January 1938): 93–114; Arthur H. Cole and Thomas C. Cochran, "Business Manuscripts: A Pressing Problem," *Journal of Economic History* 5 (May 1945): 43–64; F. G. Emmison, "Business Archives I—The Selection of Records for Retention," *Aslib Proceedings* (November 1949): 195–201; Oliver W. Holmes, "The Evaluation and Preservation of Business Archives," *American Archivist* 1, no. 3 (1938): 171–185, and "Some Reflections on Business Archives in the United States," *American Archivist* 17, no. 3 (1954): 291–304.

5. See Cole and Cochran, "Business Manuscripts: A Pressing Problem," 43–59.

6. Elizabeth Adkins, unpublished English-language version of an article entitled, "The Development of Business Archives in the United States," 31. This article was published in the summer of 1996 in Italian in the journal *Archivi e Impresse*, published in Milan, Italy.

7. Society of American Archivists, Business Archives Committee, *Directory of Business Archives in the United States and Canada* (Chicago, 1969).

8. The 1969 and 1975 editions of the *SAA Directory of Business Archives in the United States and Canada* were issued by the Society of American Archivists' Business Archives Committee. The 1980 and 1990 editions were compiled by the Business Archives Section and published by the Society of American Archivists. It should be noted that these directories were compiled through distribution of questionnaires. No attempt was made to set standards for what qualified as an "archives." Therefore, many of the listings reflect accumulations of older business records that were not organized or administered by a full-time professional archivist. The directories do not list repositories that collect business records, only companies holding their own records are included.

9. See, for example, Maynard Brichford, "Business Use of Business History," *ARMA Quarterly* 4 (October 1970): 14–16; Robert E. Cole, "Target Information for Competitive Performance," *Harvard Business Review* 63, no. 3 (May–June 1985): 100–

109; "Companies Digging Up Their Past," *Management Review* 71, no. 1 (January 1982): 32–33; Helen L. Davidson, "The Indispensability of Business Archives," *American Archivist* 30, no. 3 (1967): 593–597; Julia Niebuhr Eulenberg, "The Corporate Archives: Management Tool and Historical Resource," *The Public Historian* 6, no. 1 (winter 1984): 20–37; Holmes, "The Evaluation and Preservation of Business Archives," 171–185; Ralph M. Hower, *The Preservation of Business Records* (Boston: Business Historical Society, 1941), 55; Rupert C. Jarvis, "Business Records and the Archivist," *Aslib Proceedings* 9 (1957): 164–176; Paul C. Lasewiscz, "Strangers in a Strange Land: Archival Opportunities in a Multinational Corporation," *Archival Issues* 19, no. 2 (1994): 131–141; Robert A. Shiff, "The Archivist's Role in Records Management," *American Archivist* 19, no. 2 (1956): 111–120; George David Smith and Laurence E. Steadman, "Present Value of Corporate History," *Harvard Business Review* 59 (November–December 1981): 164–173; Gilbert Tauber, "Making Corporate History a Planning Resource," *Planning Review* (September 1983): 14–19; and John Teresko, "Should You Keep an Archives?" *Industry Week* 188, March 15, 1976, 36–39.

14

Business Records: The Prospect from the Global Village

Michael S. Moss and Lesley M. Richmond

A glance at the business pages of any major newspaper reminds readers that commerce and industry work in an increasingly global marketplace, where decisions taken by a company in one country will have ramifications throughout the world. Until this chapter, this book has been largely about American business; but reference has been made to companies, such as Coca-Cola and 3M, that have ramifications throughout the world and use their archives to protect patents and trading rights in almost every country of the world. All historians and archivists know that the internationalisation of business has long antecedents stretching back almost to the earliest surviving business records in the late medieval period. However, it is only recently, with the advent of rapid telecommunications, that markets and consequently economies and even political and legal systems have converged. This convergence demands that those entrusted with the care of business records must be aware of practice and procedure in the major economies in which their clients do business. In addition, these fundamental changes have stimulated research into the comparative advantages of economies over time through the use of collections held in different countries. There is now a strong imperative for business archivists to share experience internationally and learn from each other's methodologies. This essay seeks to set North American experience within the context of the United Kingdom, particularly, and Europe, more generally.

In the United Kingdom, arguably the cradle of modern industrialisation, classical approaches to the past tended to give prominence to "great figures" in the early history of this process, like James Watt, Robert Owen, Sir Richard Arkwright. This concern was not translated into any great interest in their papers, despite the publication from the mid-nineteenth century of glowing hagiographies. However, their papers were often cherished by members of their families and by the firms they had founded, whose wealth and fortune derived from their innovative skill and entrepreneurial flair. In this way, the remarkably complete archives of James Watt and Matthew Boltoun survived in the possession of the families and is now preserved in Birmingham Public Library. Similarly, the extensive papers of the Carron Company was retained by the firm, which continued in family ownership, and is now preserved in the Scottish Record Office. These are just two examples of many such holdings often dating back well into the eighteenth century. These substantial collections of the pioneers of industrialisation were among the first collections of business records to find their way into the public domain in the United Kingdom (other than those retained by the courts as a result of legal proceedings).

There was, until recently, relatively little interest amongst historians in mature economies, let alone those in decline. In Europe all this has changed, stimulated by a growth of concern with the preservation of heritage in the aftermath of the destruction caused by the Second World War, which led to the burgeoning in the 1960s of so-called "industrial archaeology" almost as a separate discipline straddling archaeology and economic history. In a sense, the preoccupation with industrial buildings and landscape was misplaced; but it did have the important consequence of stimulating the search for papers that might provide an explanation for the origins and stages of development of a particular site. As a result, business collections, particularly from manufacturing firms, began to be deposited in record offices throughout the country. Simultaneously, academic economic historians were reminded from a number of different directions that there was more to their discipline than simply providing a macroeconomic context for the more popular political history and that new interpretations depended crucially on access to the records of enterprise of all shapes and sizes, from all sectors and from different parts of the country. Influenced by the work of Alfred D. Chandler on American large-scale corporations, efforts were made to gain access to the archives of Britain's largest companies and to encourage those enterprises to make proper provision for their long-term preservation.

Although the Business Archives Council had been established in England as early as 1934 as the Society for the Preservation of Business Archives, there were no coordinated efforts to locate and list the records of enterprise until the early 1960s, by which time a number of pioneering academic studies had shown that there were large accumulations of records, often dating back to the mid-eighteenth century, still in private hands. The most influential of these studies were L. S. Pressnell, *Country Banking in the Industrial Revolution* (1956) and P. Mathias *The Brewing Industry in England 1700–1830* (1959), both of which relied heavily on the use of this wealth of sources. Both authors became committed to promoting the location and preservation of business records through industry-wide surveys. Unlike much of the rest of Europe but like the United States, historians of enterprise in the United Kingdom could not turn for their sources to the records of either government or the courts, as even after the introduction of limited liability legislation in 1844, business remained largely unregulated, and, with the exception of Scotland, formal failure of a partnership was dealt with outside the courts. At the same time, a number of Britain's traditional commercial and industrial regions were in the final stages of long-term secular decline. Many companies, which 70 years earlier had dominated world markets, were ceasing to trade or being swallowed up by large conglomerates. In many British universities, economic history had been taught since the beginning of the century as part of economics, and it was fortuitous that as this fundamental restructuring of business was taking place, economic history was emerging as a separate, departmentally based discipline. Many of the new departments looked to their regional economies as an early subject of study. After all, the concept of industrial regions had a respected place in classical economic literature,[1] and many of the "heroes" of traditional explanations of Britain's industrial revolution were to be found in the regions rather than in the financial centres of either London or Edinburgh. Crucially, with university expansion there were now more economic historians in post to explore local resources. At the University of Liverpool, Frances Hyde, the first professor, focused his new department on the interpretation of the city's commercial success in the eighteenth and nineteenth century, writing, himself, a magisterial study, *Cunard and the North Atlantic 1840– 1933, A History of Shipping Management* (1975), and fostering a number of others, including Sheila Marriner's *The Rathbones*,[2] and Peter Davies' *The Trade Makers*.[3] These investigations encouraged the deposit of large accumulations of records, notably those of Cunard, with the Archives Department at the University of Liverpool. Likewise, Eric Sigsworth, professor of economic history at the University of Leeds, encouraged many local textile firms that were closing to deposit their records with the university's Brotherton Library. In many cases, at the outset, new departments of economic history also embraced industrial archaeology.

By the 1960s, throughout the United Kingdom, business records had started to flow piecemeal into local record offices and university archives and libraries. Although some of these archives were well established, none had any experience in either appraising or listing business records. To most archivists, one accounting record looked much like another, and in many record offices that were just establishing themselves, particularly those in manufacturing cities, there was an eagerness to take anything that was offered. In the circumstances, it is not surprising that much of this early rescue work was a haphazard response to crisis. The first systematic survey of business records was launched in the west of Scotland, in 1960, by Sydney Checkland (the first professor of economic history at the University of Glasgow), Roy Campbell (also at Glasgow and author of the archivally based and authoritative history of the Carron Company[4]), and John Imrie (then curator at the Scottish Record Office and later keeper). Like other traditional industrial regions of Britain, Glasgow and the west of Scotland were in the grip of relentless secular decline, and some of the leading enterprises had either ceased trading or were threatened with closure. For want of an alternative home, the new department of Economic History had already provided room for the records of William Denny & Bros., shipbuilders of Dumbarton—the world pioneers of steel shipbuilding and marine turbines, and of the North British Locomotive Co., which was at one time larger than Baldwins, its American competitor. Funds were raised from local businesses to establish the Colquhoun Lecturer in Business History at the university and Peter Payne was appointed first lecturer, charged with creating a meaningful collection of business archives to form the basis for a proper understanding of the local business community and economy. Any attempt at a structured survey was soon overwhelmed by the pace of closures in the early 1960s. However, the results of the project published in *Studies in Scottish Business History*[5] was an important milestone. In the first section, summary information was provided about collections by sector and included records of large, small, successful and unsuccessful enterprise. The unique holdings (at least in the United Kingdom) of business papers in the proceedings of the Court of Session held at the Scottish Record Office were also described. The second section contained essays based on the exploration of collections of business archives. This attempted to achieve a similar balance of sector, size, and performance. In Scotland, the surveying work initiated by the Colquhoun Lectureship has continued uninterrupted ever since.

The Scottish survey provided both the impetus and the model for both regional and national surveys elsewhere in the United Kingdom. In the West Riding of Yorkshire a thorough investigation was conducted of the archives of the woollen and worsted textile industries, then in the throws of extinction. Also included was a review of records that had already been transferred to libraries, museums, archives, and local history societies. At a national (United Kingdom) level, as the focus of research shifted from regions to sectors, industry-specific surveys were initiated, of shipping (Mathias and Pearsall, 1972), of insurance (Cockerell and Green, 1976, revised 1994), of shipbuilding (Ritchie 1980, revised 1992), and of banking (Pressnell and Orbell, 1985, revised 1997). Sector surveys continue to be compiled and published, now under the auspices of the Business Archives Council in the series *Studies in British Business Archives*, edited by Lesley Richmond and Alison Turton. The series covers the brewing industry (Richmond and Turton, 1990), shipbuilding (Ritchie, 1992), chartered accountants (Habgood, 1994), banking (Orbell and Turton, 1997), and pharmaceuticals (1997/8). Although undoubtedly useful, the sector approach is self-evidently not representative of the economy as a whole. An ambitious solution to this problem was the Company Archive Survey[6] undertaken by the Business Archives Council between 1980 and 1984 with the objective of surveying the records of the oldest thousand registered companies in England and Wales.

Armed with a list supplied by the Registrar of Companies of the Department of Trade and Industry of the 1200 oldest English and Welsh companies on the 1980 Register of Companies (the span covered the period 1856 to 1889 although the majority of companies were registered in the 1870s and 1880s), the professional archival surveyors undertook 674 surveys of companies within the list. These core surveys produced another 1000 surveys of companies, institutions, and partnerships associated with or subsidiary to the registered companies. The 1200 companies represented four percent of the original population of companies registered between 1856 and 1889 and were still not representative of the companies formed at the time as they had survived when the vast majority had failed. However, it was because they had survived and that there was therefore a greater chance that their records had survived that the survey was undertaken. Business archives were located in 900 different locations covering 8,000 metres of shelf space. The companies varied greatly in size and business, covering the complete range from small, independent family companies to multinationals. Their age and origin also varied from partnerships founded centuries before their registration as companies to those that were formed as legislation was passed in the nineteenth century that permitted joint-stock companies. The published survey produced an extraordinary array of archives covering financial, commercial, manufacturing companies, transport, utilities and mining concerns, and fine arts, sports, political, and other cultural activities, which was a comprehensive representation of British business in the nineteenth and twentieth century. The work of the survey was very successful in drawing attention to business archives, not just to potential users of the collections but also to their owners and prospective custodians. It increased the awareness, value, and potential of business archives to business managers, which led to the establishment of several in-house archives and many corporate archival programmes. At the same time, archivists in local and national repositories were made aware of the collections of business archives in their locality, and a large number of these collections are now permanently preserved in local archival repositories.

The first in-house company archives were established in Germany[7] at the beginning of this century (Krupp in Essen in 1905 and Siemens in Berlin in 1907). During the 1930s, others, especially in the coal and steel sector, were established in Germany while the Bank of England in the United Kingdom made provision for its archives. Some American corporations established archival programmes during the 1940s and 1950s, such as Kodak, Coca-Cola, Firestone, and Sears, but it was not until the 1960s that the number of business archivists within business grew in both the United Kingdom and the United States. Throughout the rest of Europe, the phenomena began in the 1970s with the financial sector and has spread into the commercial, service, and manufacturing sectors.

The reason for establishing an in-house archives, the purpose of a corporate archives programme, and the function of a corporate archivist are diverse and have varied greatly over the last 30 years. The reasons for appointing an archivist to a business vary: identifying and safeguarding a collection as a historical asset; exploiting the public relations potential of the archives; helping in the preparation work for the compilation of a company history or some other anniversary celebration or as the result of such a celebration; aiding brand or patent protection; contributing or controlling the management of all the company's records. The first in-house corporate archives in France was established in 1974, at Compagnie de Saint-Gobain Pont-à-Mousson as a joint archives and records management programme. In the 1960s, many of the appointments in the United Kingdom were part-time or combined with other duties in public relations or some other area. In 1996, most of the hundred-plus business archivists in the United Kingdom are full-time professionals with archives diploma training or other relevant qualifications. Some of the in-house archives of the largest businesses consist of a team of archivists and records managers, but the typical business archives unit in Europe consists of a single archivist with one or more archives and clerical assistants.

Many of the original corporate archives programmes in the United States were set up with the aim of promoting the archives for use by the academic community. Several of the early British corporate archives were, and many have been subsequently, established to help with the preparations of an anniversary (for example the centenary of the John Lewis Partnership in 1964) or the writing of a company history (as with the Times Newspapers, BP, and Burmah Oil Co. Ltd.). However, although this has often been the major spur to the establishment of an in-house archives and a corporate archives policy, it has been for other reasons, such as a service for the administration, public relations, or the legal department, that the archives has usually been sustained and developed. Certainly in the United Kingdom it has been the contribution or control of the management of a company's records by the archivist that has led to the further development of most in-house company archives. In all countries in the Western world, an in-house business archivist must be seen to be contributing to a company's profitability and public profile in a cost-effective manner.

The core objectives of the German in-house archives in the 1930s were to keep incontestable records of all types of legal titles and to prevent or restrict state intervention. More than in North America, where the function of archives and records management are more usually found in separate units, in Europe they are more usually combined within one unit. In the late twentieth century, the function of a business archivist within a business is many faceted; duties include the physical care of the archives to the management of the current and noncurrent records; legal and management information retrieval for various internal departments from the highest level down; cooperation with the public relations and marketing projects from publications to brand names to exhibitions; involvement with staff training (especially induction training) to demonstrate the development of the business; and participation in procedures to ensure compliance with external regulatory authorities. Even the single archivist in a medium-size business often combines records management duties or the maintenance of the company's museum or historical artifact collection with those of archives administration.

Throughout the world, in-house company archives can never provide more than a partial solution to the preservation of the records of enterprise. They are, anyway, fragile and understandably tend to be located in companies or sectors where the exploitation of heritage is a key element in promotion and marketing. Collections continue to be deposited with public archives and libraries at an increasing rate. Throughout Europe there is an emerging pattern of repositories that cater principally to business collections. One of the largest, which collects nationwide, is the Erhvervsarkivet in Århus in Denmark, established in the 1940s. It now houses a formidable number of collections of corporate archives, covering all sectors and every size of enterprise. A constituent part of the Danish State Archives since 1963, the Erhvervsarkivet publishes a guide to its holdings and collaborates with business historians to produce a business history year book. Likewise, in France, the Centre des Archives du Monde du Travail (CAMT) acts as a national repository, although the intention is to set up a regional network if funds permit. The Swiss Business Archives, founded in 1910 and now part of the University of Basel, has about 450 collections; while the Netherlands Economic History Archives (NEHA), founded in 1914, holds about 100 large business history collections extending to over 15,000 shelf metres. Since 1983, the NEHA has maintained the Business Archives Register (BARN) in collaboration with the Central Register of Private Archives and the Dutch Association of Business Archivists, which has details of almost 6,000 collections. ELKA, the Central Archives for Finnish Business Records, set up in 1981, maintains a similar data set of business collections. In other countries there are regional repositories of business archives. In Germany there are business archives associated with chambers of commerce in Rhineland-Westphalia, Saarland, Baden-Württemberg, Munich, and Upper Bavaria. There are four regional business repositories in Sweden, and others are being developed. The Business Records Centre at the University of Glasgow and the Modern Records Centre at the University of Warwick fulfill a similar role for the United Kingdom. In Australia, the archives at Australian National University has similar holdings of regional business records. In some cases firms collaborate to support the archives of their main sector of activity. For example, in Germany the mining industry supports an archives within the national mining museum at Bochum; while in Scotland the brewing industry funds such an archives within the Archives and Business Record Centre at the University of Glasgow.

Nevertheless, throughout Europe the principal custodians of business records are national and local repositories. In many countries whose legal systems have origins in Roman law and later followed the Napoleonic Code, there is an abundance of reference to even very small business in the records of the courts. Under Roman law, all proceedings must take place before the court and cannot simply be reported to the court by an officer acting as the court's representative. As a result, all bankruptcy proceedings were conducted directly through the courts and, as in Scotland, both the case papers and the records of the business, itself, used to investigate and wind up its affairs, are preserved. The recently reopened records of the Reichkammericht at Lübbecke contain huge collections of business papers from all over northern Europe dating back well into the sixteenth century. The Erhvervsarkivet has a large collection of such material. Although bankruptcy, even with the associated risk of imprisonment for debt, lacked the stigma of modern personal financial failure, records of bankrupt enterprise are self-evidently unrepresentative, not just because the business failed but also because, increasingly, there were ways of avoiding the costly legal process. Much more representative are the records of registration to be found in commercial courts that followed French practice. From the introduction of the *Code de Commerce* in 1808, all partnerships (*société de personnes*) in France had to be registered with and make reports to the *tribunaux de commerce*. The records of these courts are voluminous and provide a wealth of detail about the whole population of enterprise unavailable in the United Kingdom or the United States, which were opposed to the bureaucracy of *ancien regime* countries. However, even in the United Kingdom, where registration as a limited liability company has always been optional, the bulk of records is still formidable, and various strategies have been adopted to select records relating to enterprises that have ceased trading for permanent preservation within the national archives.

In the twentieth century, all national archives in Europe have become responsible for large collections of business records from sectors of the economy that have been nationalised. The most extreme examples are the former eastern block countries where the concept of the command economy demanded the extinction of private enterprise. Remarkably, enormous collections of papers of pre-Communist private companies survive. The Hungarian National Archives in Budapest holds miles of records of firms, many of them foreign-owned, that operated in the country before the Second World War. In western Europe, nationalisation was less extensive but included important sectors, notably public utilities (like water supply, gas, electricity, telecommunications, and railways) but also other areas of the economy such as steel, coal, and oil. Most nationalised firms had long histories and considerable market penetration and, therefore, large accumulations of records.

The majority of the records of enterprise that find their way into national or local archives are deposited by firms themselves, like those held by specialist business repositories. Probably the majority of business records in the public domain throughout Europe are now held in regional and local archives along with other collections as in other parts of the world. In some cases, the records are directed to local archives as part of an overall national strategy; for example, the Erhversarkivet places collections of business papers with provincial or city archives if they are deemed to be principally of local importance. However, in most cases deposits of business records are accepted by regional archives like deposits of any other private papers. In fact, in many cases business records come as part and parcel of other collections. Throughout Europe many archives from landed proprietors will contain both estate and business papers. Examples include records of investment in mineral workings, colonial properties, and even substantial holdings relating to family interests in commerce and industry. Lawyers' papers, which have interested archivists and historians for a long time because they contain much material of medieval origin, also include a great many records relating to business. Many lawyers acted effectively as agents or secretaries to firms and therefore held their management records. Others acquired papers by representing families with business interests in disputes or in the winding up of estates; while many lawyers provided a crucial service as financial intermediaries at a time when the banks and the stockmarket were in their infancy. Business records from legal practices, however, are on the whole familiar to most archivists and do not present problems of appraisal and description.

Many of the problems of appraising business records arise from the poor quality of the training of archivists in the management of business records. If the nature and purpose of the original creation of a business series is not understood, whether it be a minute book, ledger, journal, order book, plant inventory, photograph, or wage sheet, it cannot be properly appraised. It is certainly the case in the United Kingdom that a newly trained archivist will know exactly how the government of the established churches in England and Wales operated and the records that were created by their systems and how to appraise the documentation that has been generated. This is also true for records of the courts and the legal system (particularly titles to property), and to some extent for the records of landed estates and central and local government. However, the perceived view of diverse types of business management and organisation (permitted by nonrestrictive state legislation) creating unique series of records led to the belief that it was impossible to do the same for business archives. Although no two collections of business records are exactly the same, there are core records that are to be found in both, and although no two companies operated in exactly the same way, there was enough common practice for the subject to be taught to a higher standard and for it to have a higher profile among the archives training schools in the United Kingdom. Currently, it is taught most comprehensively as an option on the Society of Archivists Diploma Course taken by correspondence.

Record appraisal must include all the documentation of a business, not just those of a certain media or type. Although an in-house company archivist may also have looked after the company's reference library, museum, and art collections, it is not incumbent on an archives repository to accept a museum, library, and art collection into its holdings. Its governing authority (such as the nation, state, region, county, town, or university) may accept such a gift from a company and then disperse the distinct collections to the appropriate divisions that have the expertise to manage them. However, the records of a business should not be divided by type and dispersed unless there are valid reasons for doing so. Samples of packaging are a record of businesses marketing strategy, self-image, and response to external regulation and should not be dispersed automatically to a museum. Museums are also often the custodians of parts of business archives collections, holding the photographs, product drawings, and trade catalogues of manufacturing concerns while the remaining records are held in an archival repository in another locality. There may be aspects of preservation or access that necessitate such division—for instance, the inability to store or access or adequately catalogue films, audio tapes, or magnetic tapes. Such records may be required to be stored with separate institutions (such as a national film archives) with professional expertise in dealing with such formats and the equipment required for storage, retrieval, and access. However, these records need to be seen as part of the whole collection of a company and should appear in all finding aids with a note as to their physical location.

A contentious question is the problem of the records of subsidiaries (that may be located in any part of the world) acquired by merger and takeover by the many companies that form part or have formed part of large conglomerates. Such records have often been moved long distances to remain part of the archives of the new parent company. The current records of a merged company immediately become part of the assets of the parent company. Why not the archives? The answer is sometimes due to local feeling that part of the heritage of the area will disappear to another county, state, country, or hemisphere or due to state legislation such as in Italy[8] and France. The historical records of the HSBC Holdings Plc., the finance group founded in 1991, have been consolidated, since 1993, as a single group function in London, the head offices of the company. The formation of HSBC Holdings Plc. brought together the Midland Bank, the Hongkong Bank (Hongkong and Shanghai Banking Corporation), the British Bank of the Middle East, Marine Midland in the United States, and Samuel Montagu and Co., Ltd. Each of these banking companies had well over 100 years of financial history and scores of subsidiaries and allied companies.[9]

The bringing together of the records to form the HSBC Group Archive has resulted in the Hongkong Bank's archives being one of the best travelled in the world. It has also added to the number of major international company archives that are located within the City of London. So long as they all maintain their own archives, those concerned with business archives in the United Kingdom can sleep easy, but it is a recurrent nightmare of the Business Archives Council as to exactly how London or, indeed, the United Kingdom archives repository system would cope if a small number of theses companies began to shed their archives. Companies still active and interested in their heritage could determine where collections would be located (they would be paying for the pleasure), but defunct or uninterested companies would be effectively saying "take them or leave them." There has been an archival time bomb ticking slowly in London for many years. Crises, such as that at the archives of the Standard Chartered Bank,[10] have so far been dealt with, but often the appraisal criteria that solved the problem will not stand closer archival scrutiny.

Putting aside the particular problems of London, the decision as to whether or not to disperse a conglomerate collection when the creating/owning body disposes of it has never been adequately discussed. What is best practise? What archival criteria should come into play before recommending to a company that its final action should be to arrange for the dispersal of its subsidiary companies' records to numerous record offices around the state, country, or world? If archivists concerned with business think it matters where records are located, we should say so; if only practical considerations are to hold sway, we should say so. These are difficult areas to resolve, and there is not one solution to the problems posed, but archivists making decisions that will affect how the past may be viewed in the future should be made aware of the implications of their decisions before they make them.

There is a distinction that must be drawn between the archives still owned and actively exploited by a company and those of dead companies or those that no longer have any interest in their historical collection. An in-house company archivist appraises business records at two levels—that of a records manager, appraising record series for business purposes with a view to determine the records retention period, for instance, and at a second level, to determine the archival value of the collection. The first level of appraisal determines the administrative, legal, fiscal, and operational value and use of a record series for a live company. Some of these values will naturally change if the company ceases to exist. Equally, the archival appraisal is done within the context of a live company actively exploiting its informational assets. So the archives itself has an operational value. As soon as that link is broken, the records require reappraisal. There have

been celebrated cases where companies that once had their own archivist and archival policy have taken the decision to deposit the archives as a gift in a public repository. One of the first things that the
repository archivist undertakes is a reappraisal of the collection, a
natural response in the business world of new owners reappraising the
assets of an acquisition. Whereas a corporate archives might preserve,
at the most, between 5 and 10 percent of the total documentation
created and maintained by an organisation, it is to be expected that a
repository archivist would retain between 1 and 5 percent of the total.
It is very rare for an archivist of a long-established business to be
faced with appraising the complete documentation created as the winnowing hand of time and effective record control have usually greatly
reduced the bulk years before the archivist was born. Archival appraisal, in reality, is appraising the surviving records of a business in
relation to space constraints, the physical condition of the records,
local, regional, national, and international importance of the collection,
existing collections held, and informational value. The appraisal and
collecting policies of the long-established, pioneer centres of business
archives are being reassessed currently, and there is a need for this
work to be discussed by archivists around the world so that comments
on and suggestions about the processes can be made. It is equally
important that the users and potential users of business records are
also included in these discussions as archivists have a duty to ensure
that the corporate world memory that they intend to preserve is representative. In order to have the final responsibility for judging the
research value of records created by business, archivists must ensure
that they remain familiar with research needs in a very wide range of
subject areas. This may be possible for current needs, but when it
comes to second guessing future requisites, the reinforcement of professionals and customers from a variety of disciplines is to be actively
sought.

Despite the substantial accumulations of business records that are
now available throughout Europe, use remains disappointingly low. A
survey conducted in the United Kingdom[11] in 1994 revealed that in
the Oxfordshire Archives, which holds the important archives of Morris
Motors, the pioneer United Kingdom automobile manufacturers, and
the records of Early's of Witney, blanket makers, less than 5 percent
of researchers consulted business records in any detail. Much the same
was true in northern England at the Greater Manchester Record Office
and the West Yorkshire Archive Service, both with significant collections. The London Guildhall Library, with one of the largest and most
significant holdings of business records in the world, discovered from
an analysis of readers in May, 1993, that only 9 percent were studying
business history, compared to 63.5 percent for family history. Even the

large Erhvervsarkivet in Denmark reports a similar concern and, perhaps more than other repositories, has tried to encourage the large constituency of family historians to explore their business holdings but with mixed success. The problem with this strategy is that genealogy remains particular and parochial. Genealogists, many of whom are well qualified academically in a whole range of disciplines, are rarely interested in anything other than records that relate directly to the history of their own family. It is difficult to educate them to consult other material that might be used as a source of surrogate information about their family's economic activities or lifestyle, let alone records that might contextualise their family history. Yet, the family networks and relationships genealogists so patiently define are the selfsame networks that sustain the credit structures and business communities that are the focus of so much attention in the post-Chandler world. There is fault on both sides; archivists and academic historians affect to despise the genealogists, and genealogists remain preoccupied with filling in the boxes in tables of increasing complexity.

Although a few family historians occasionally consult certain categories of business records—for example, apprenticeship registers and wage books—the majority of users seem to be enthusiasts seeking information about a product or service that has captured their imagination. Each enthusiasm, even, seemingly, the most obscure, tends to be supported by an extensive literature, which in itself breeds subdisciplines. Some of these enthusiasms are fed and encouraged by business itself, most directly in the wine, spirit, beer, and soft drink trades and more subtly in trades associated with decorative arts and the media. Some enthusiasms are more popular than others, and some can be more easily supported by business records than others. This is largely true for the study of ships, locomotives, and road vehicles, where records tend to be kept for long periods for the later supply of parts, and where there has long been a good deal of popular interest that has spurred archivists and museum curators to rescue large collections. In the survey conducted in 1994 in the United Kingdom, archivists reported this constituency to be the most vital and demanding. At the Business Record Centre at the University of Glasgow, which holds extensive collections from the shipbuilding and locomotive building industries, 65 percent of readers in the first six months of 1994 were in this category. The Ipswich branch of the Suffolk Record Office, which houses the archives of the locomotive builders Garretts of Leiston, noted that "the usage which the records receive, or at any rate the enquiries which the office receives, are directed mainly towards products such as steam traction engines, railway locomotives or cranes, generally towards the history or technical features of a particular machine." Much the same is true of other repositories in Europe.

Moreover, many enthusiasms are truly international (shipping and railways are good example), and, as a result, requests for information, often very obscure information, come from many countries.

For the curator of business records, the enthusiast provides an opportunity in respect of the income they can generate but also a problem, both because of the narrow fraction of records they consult and the sheer quantities of what might, in most schemes of appraisal, be considered ephemeral material they want to be preserved to sustain their particular interests. For example, the ship model maker would ideally want all the hundreds and sometimes thousands of detailed drawings of a vessel preserved so that every aspect of the model will be an accurate representation. The locomotive or ship enthusiasts normally want access only to such plans, along with any accompanying photographs, and have to be persuaded to look at other classes of records even if they relate directly to the product in which they are interested. They are more concerned with the object and less concerned with how much it might have cost, who supplied components, how long it took to build, who financed it, and so on. As a result, this large community of users of business records neglects the records that make up the greater bulk of the collection they rely on. It is less difficult to encourage these users to widen their interests to encompass other aspects of the product as (unlike the sources available to family historians) other classes of records will contain information about the object of inquiry itself. For example, the ledgers of a shipbuilding company will contain costs of construction and payments from customers. These may provide vital information about the interior design and fitting-out, delivery dates, and even technical information in the textual entries. Despite the size and diversity of the enthusiast market, there are many sectors of the economy that have little appeal. Although ships and locomotives are pursued relentlessly, most mechanical and structural engineering products (stationary steam engines, machine tools, sugar machinery, bridges) are largely neglected. This presents the archivist with a problem. No one would pretend that collecting and appraisal policies are not governed to a degree by demand; the risk is that demand factors might so skew a collection that it becomes unrepresentative.

It is arguable that academic users should compensate for the enthusiast's concentration on particular sectors and the technical features of individual products. Disappointingly, there was unanimous agreement in the 1994 United Kingdom survey that readers from all backgrounds ignored the core financial series that were used both to control and manage the enterprise. Tyne & Wear Archives in Newcastle on Tyne commented, "although we regard the principal financial records as important, our readers, by and large, are rarely interested in them."

The Erhvervsarkivet in Århus reports much the same lack of interest amongst its academic users and recently an initiative has been taken by Wilfred Reininghaus, now of the Münsterstatsarchiv, to draw attention to the large holdings of merchant account books, often dating back to the seventeenth century, to be found in record offices throughout Europe. At a meeting in Dortmund to launch this initiative in the spring of 1996, there was a general consensus from all European countries that these records contain important information about the development of patterns of European continental and maritime trades (often conducted across unstable and unreliable exchanges), but that most historians lack both the accounting skills and the application to make use of them.

There is more to the lack of interest in financial records than the seeming complexity of their interpretation. The agenda for research in business history throughout the world over the last 40 years has been set by the work of Alfred D. Chandler, Jr.,[12] whose interest was in concentration and, consequently, in large, centrally managed organisations that were controlled through strong hierarchical structures, and in the papers and forms that were used to control such corporate bureaucracies. Although such records are to be found in abundance in the public archives of European *ancien régime* countries, they scarcely survived among the records of most European enterprises until relatively recent times, largely because management hierarchies were very short or effectively structured as extended partnerships. The research agenda is now changing.[13] With the increasing shift away from hierarchically controlled, large-scale enterprises and emphasis on other forms of business organisation, particularly formal and informal networks, business historians have begun to search for previous examples.[14] Not surprisingly, at least to archivists, there is in Europe an abundance of records dating back for centuries to sustain such inquiries. Unfortunately, much of the information is buried in just those financial series that all users find both daunting and difficult to approach. To exploit their potential, historians need to learn new skills that with the advent of automation even the accountancy profession no longer possesses. For the archivist charged with the care of long runs of such records and little prospect of any additional storage accommodation, the question is whether this new agenda will generate sufficient demand to prevent deaccessioning of such financial records (on the grounds that no one uses them) that has already started in the United States. Although the same pressures to deaccession obtain in Europe, no sustained programmes to destroy financial records already held in repositories has yet commenced. However, there is a noticeable reluctance to take further transmissions of such series and, if they are accepted, to subject them to rigorous appraisal (that is, weeding.)

Business records to the uninitiated are usually perceived as bulky, with long runs of incomprehensible series of accounting records, order books, files, and computer printouts. Although there is no denying that business records are often bulky, they are very rarely incomprehensible. Training in the understanding of the various classes of business records includes familiarity with accounting systems, the conditions governing their creation and preservation—in other words, their diplomatic[15]—and the uses that can be made of them by a variety of researchers. Business archives collections are also bulky because they usually do not consist of the records of one single company. This is due to the nature of corporate growth by the acquisition of other businesses or the formation of subsidiary and associated companies. The archives of a large company may contain the records of over a hundred other businesses, some of which will predate that of the parent trading company. Training in business archives is a recent feature in many European archive schools if it is included at all. Often it has been left to associations of business archivists (for example, the Business Archives Council and the Finnish Association of Business Archivists) to provide training in the form of one-day seminars and workshops or week-long training courses. Until the publication in 1991 of *Managing Business Archives*,[16] there was no United Kingdom textbook on the subject.

Archivists in European countries where there has been a more corporatist tradition are no more insulated from financial pressures than their counterparts in North America. There have, for some time, been severe constraints on the finances of government, both national and local, which provides the bulk of archives services either directly or indirectly. This has forced many archives to look for ways of exploiting the revenue-earning potential of their collections. The depositors of business records that are still trading have been approached for funds to meet the cost of storage, cataloguing, conservation, and so on. With no statutory requirement to retain most historical records, funds provided for such projects are effectively charitable donations and can qualify for relief from taxation providing the donor receives no service in return (in other words, do not exploit the collections for their own purposes). Anyway, in most repositories the bulk of business collections derive from companies that have long ceased trading. If they do still trade, they have either diversified away from their original business or exist in much reduced circumstances. Consequently, the support of the collections has to fall on the repository. In a few cases business archives are wholly funded by chambers of commerce, which draw their revenue by a direct tax on local industry and commerce (for example, the Centre rhénan d'archives d'enterprises in Alsace and the regional business archives in Germany).

The other source of revenue for all archives are users. Charges are imposed for access to only a very few archives, mostly those in private hands, largely those of great families. Businesses that maintain their own collections consider free access to historical records as good public relations. Where archives held in the public sector can earn revenue is in providing research services, particularly to users from a distance, and in selling copies of items within collections, priced on a differential scale related to the nature of the customer (private researcher or commercial inquirer) and to the ultimate use of the copy. Revenue earned in this way is marginal and does not in any way defray the cost of providing access to collections. Nevertheless, there are inexorable pressures to increase external income to compensate for the loss of public revenue. It is argued that if users pay for access to other amenities—for example, museums in many European countries—then there is no reason why access to archives should be free. Such arguments are persuasive and will probably lead to charges for access being introduced. The debate about the principle will be hotly contested, with the danger that the consequences for collection management may be overlooked. At a time when consumers are more and more aware of their rights, if charges are introduced, the relationship between the customer and the custodian will change. The majority of customers of archives are enthusiasts with very particular interests who, without education (marketing), may not be willing to subsidise through the prices they pay for access and other services the cost of keeping records for other constituencies, particularly the academic community. This will make objective appraisal difficult and threaten the long-cherished fiduciary role of the archivist. Large business collections will be at considerable risk unless mechanisms can be found for them to be funded either by commerce and industry (unlikely in many European countries where such costs, however marginal, might be deemed to reduce competitive advantage) or by the academic community. This prospect reinforces the imperative of improving dialogue with the business history community.

Throughout Europe there is complaint, echoing North America, that the archival community has lost contact with historians, who in many cases have sided with enthusiasts in criticising appraisal methods and demanding that more material be considered for permanent preservation. Archivists, particularly those responsible for large business record collections, can point to enormous stockpiles of underused holdings that are often well described in published guides. More perilously, some post-modern historians affect to condemn all archives as the tools of a dead profession on the grounds that by their very nature they are unrepresentative. By extension, history can be composed by arriving at a consensus about the past that may be based on a whole

range of subjective attitudes and responses. The root of the problem
is that the two professions, in crafting their own identities, lost contact
at a critical time. Few archivists attend historical conferences and are
therefore unaware of new developments in methodology or areas of
inquiry. As a result, they react badly to approaches that seem to
threaten their area of expertise (for example, the concept that information about the past is holistic and self-reinforcing—that all historical objects have an equivalent value whether they be buildings,
artifacts, books, or manuscripts and relate one to the other). This is
especially true in the field of business history, which, since Chandler,
has transcended sector and geographical boundaries, and which, more
than most other interpretations of the past, relies heavily on theory.
To understand how their collections could be used to inform the questions addressed by historians of enterprise, the archivists have to engage with the academic debate. The historians, for their part, need to
understand the issues that confront the archivist and to be aware that
they no longer (if they ever did) represent more than a mere fraction
of the user community; the records they need for their research are
very vulnerable to deaccessioning programmes.

No archivist anywhere in the world can be in any doubt that the
future is uncertain and problematic. In every area, particularly in the
world of business records, tried and tested methodologies are threatened by the sheer quantity of information of potential interest to future
users and by the use of new technology to create and distribute it.
Urgent attention needs to be given to the preservation and appraisal
of business records in electronic media. Since it will be possible to
provide remote access to this material in the future, it is important to
ensure that encoding, catalogue descriptions, and access protocols
conform to international standards. In an increasingly global business
community, repositories in one country already hold and will increasingly hold records of companies whose ultimate ownership is in another. In some cases, subsidiaries in one country will be of strategic
importance to that economy. Mechanisms will need to be put in place
to document the subsidiary's development and arrangements made for
preservation and access. These will be influenced by the statutory
requirements of the country in which the parent company is located.
Globalization can be expected to stimulate more international research,
such as historical exploration of the concept of comparative advantage.
A necessary prelude will be an overview of the world situation, building on the work of the Section of Business and Labour Archives of the
International Council on Archives.[17] As a next step, more will need to
be done to provide transnational guides to holdings (probably in electronic form) that will address the differing statutory and fiscal requirements for the creation and disposal of business records. An essential

feature of such guides in electronic form will be interoperability, demanding the development of agreed standards; name, subject, and record-type authority rules; and accompanying authority files.

There are only a small number of institutions and individual archivists throughout the world with expertise in the management of business record collections able to pioneer these developments. Given that trade between nations has a history stretching back to classical times, it is not remarkable that business records since at least the fourteenth century have had common characteristics. It is not difficult to recognise a *hauptbuch* or a *grand livre* as a ledger, and since at least the seventeenth century, most collections of business records contain the footprints of enterprises in other countries. This commonality of experience provides an excellent foundation for international collaboration between repositories holding business collections. Already, much has been done. It is recognised that other countries and localities have much to learn from the so-called Minnesota Method of relating acquisition policy directly to business populations and from the decision of both the Hagley Museum and Library in Delaware and the Minnesota Historical Society to deaccession large blocks of financial records. Equally, there is much to be learned from the experience of the Erhvervsarkivet in providing a comprehensive business archives service for the whole of Denmark and its efforts to promote the use of its collections by scholars and enthusiasts. The United Kingdom has more experience of surveying records within businesses than most other countries, and the Netherlands and Finland have well-developed national registers of business records in the public and private domain.

The development of shared methodologies across national frontiers is essential and will not be difficult to achieve, at least at the outset, among the major stakeholders. Contacts are well established, and these need to be formalised through staff exchanges and joint projects, particularly in addressing the problem of electronic business records, in creating transnational guides, and in exploring the complex issues of appraisal and deaccessioning. Appraisal of business records in whatever medium is almost certainly the most important issue that confronts the world archival community and one that has been addressed more objectively in North America than elsewhere. Within this context, there needs to emerge some concept of what might be termed world business collections (on the same model as world heritage sites), defined either in terms of their contribution (Bolton & Watt, Burmeister Wain, Edisons, Hoffs of Amsterdam, Krupp), or in terms of their international customer base (John Brown's Clydebank shipyard, Ford, Siemens). Clearly, the appraisal of such collections falls outside a prescriptive representative model based on even national business aggregates; is it reasonable to expect a local institution to maintain such collections, in the absence of any corporate support, out of its own resources? Progress in appraising business collections within an international context will set a wider agenda within the archives and heritage professions as nearly all collections of business records are held by institutions with much broader responsibilities. That agenda, however, can only satisfactorily be addressed through international collaboration and joint projects that focus as much on the commonality of experience as on divergence and embrace both the archival and historical sciences.

Endnotes

1. Alfred Marshall, *Industry and Trade: A Study of Industrial Techniques and Business Organisation; and of Their Influences on the Condition of Various Classes and Nations* (London, 1919).

2. Sheila Marriner, *Rathbones of Liverpool 1845–1873* (Liverpool: Liverpool University Press, 1961).

3. P. N. Davies, *The Trade Makers: Elder Dempster in West Africa 1853–1972* (London: Allen and Unwin, 1973).

4. R. H. Campbell, *Carron Company* (Edinburgh: Oliver and Boyd, 1961).

5. P. L. Payne, *Studies in Scottish Business History* (London: Cass, 1967).

6. Lesley Richmond and Bridget Stockford, *Company Archives: A Survey of the Records of 1000 of the First Registered Companies in England & Wales* (Aldershot: Gower, 1986).

7. Lesley Richmond, *Overview of Business Archives in Europe* (Glasgow: International Council on Archives/Section on Business and Labour Archives and Glasgow University Archives, 1996).

8. See articles nos., 38 and 42 of DPR no. 1409, of September 30, 1963, the main legislative text on archives currently in force in Italy.

9. Edwin Green and Sara Kinsey, "The Archives of the HSBC Group," *Financial History Review* 3 (1996): 87–99.

10. S. G. H. Freeth, "Destroying Archives: A Case Study of the Records of Standard Chartered Bank," *Journal of the Society of Archivists* 12, no. 2 (1991): 85–94.

11. Edwin Green and Michael Moss, "Reclaiming the Business Past" in *Enterprise and Management: Essays in Honour of Peter L Payne*, eds. Derek H. Aldcroft and Anthony Slaven (Aldershot: Scolar Press, 1995).

12. Alfred D. Chandler, Jr., *Strategy and Structure: Chapters in the History of the American Industrial Enterprise* (Cambridge, Mass.: MIT Press, 1962).

13. Michael Moss et Philippe Jobert, *Naissance et mort des enterprises en Europe XIXe-XXE siecles* (Carnforti: Universite de Bourgogne publication du Centre Georges Chevrier pour l'histoire du droit, 1995).

14. Mary Rose, *Business Enterprise in Modern Britain: From the Eighteenth to the Twentieth Centuries* (London: Routledge, 1994).

15. Luciana Duranti, "Diplomatics: New Uses for Old Science," *Archivaria* 28 (1989): 7–27.

16. Alison Turton, *Managing Business Archives* (Oxford: Butterworth Heinemann, 1991).

17. Lesley Richmond, *Overview of Business Archives in Europe* .

Contributors

Christopher T. Baer is assistant curator of manuscripts and archives at the Hagley Museum and Library. He is a graduate of the University of Virginia's School of Architecture. He served as appraisal archivist for the records of the Penn Central Railroad and was a fellow at the Bentley Historical Library in 1986. In his current position, he has appraised, arranged, and described many of the Hagley Library's largest corporate archives, including those of the Pennsylvania Railroad, Bethlehem Steel, Westmoreland Coal, and RCA. He is the author of many articles and several books on nineteenth-century U.S. transportation history, including *Canals and Railroads of the Mid-Atlantic States, 1800–1860; The Trail of the Blue Comet*; and *The Pennsylvania Railroad: Its Place in History, 1846–1996.*

Karen Benedict is a consultant in archives and records management with the Winthrop Group, Inc. She began her career as assistant university archivist at Rice University in Houston, Texas, and served for 11 years as the corporate archivist at Nationwide Insurance Companies in Columbus, Ohio. While with Nationwide she also was responsible for administration of the records management program and the corporate library. Benedict's professional work has included service as the secretary/treasurer of the Society of Ohio Archivists, as an elected member of the governing councils of the Society of American Archivists and of the Midwest Archives Conference, as treasurer of the Academy of Certified Archivists, and as a member of the Steering Committee of the Section of Professional Archival Associations of the International Council on Archives. She is the author of numerous articles and is the compiler/editor of both editions of the Society of American Archivist's *Select Annotated Bibliography on Business Archives and Records Management*.

Francis X. Blouin, Jr. is professor of history and of library studies at the University of Michigan. Since 1981, he has served as director of the Bentley Historical Library, a research library of the University of Michigan devoted to the history of the State of Michigan. In addition, the library houses the archives of the university. For the past 10 years he has directed a project to survey papal archives with an emphasis on the holdings of the Archivio Segreto Vaticano at the Vatican. Blouin has also served as a member of the governing Council of the Society of American Archivists and is a fellow of SAA as well. He has been a trustee and later president of the Historical Society of Michigan and serves on the board of the American Friends of the Vatican Library.

Bruce H. Bruemmer is the archivist of the Charles Babbage Institute of Computer History at the University of Minnesota. During the past 12 years, he has worked with archivists and historians in developing strategies to document the history of the computer industry. His work led him to coauthor an appraisal publication entitled *The High-Technology Company: A Historical Research and Archival Guide*. He oversaw the acquisition of the records of two major mainframe manufacturers, the Control Data Corporation and the Burroughs Corporation, as well as other, smaller firms. In addition to business records, Bruemmer has overseen the acquisition of technical literature, legal files, oral histories, and audiovisual materials. He served as an elected member of the governing Council of the Society of American Archivists.

Richard J. Cox is an associate professor in library and information science at the University of Pittsburgh, School of Information Sciences, where he is responsible for the archives concentration in the MLIS degree. Prior to his current position, he worked at a number of government and private archives. He chaired the Society of American Archivists committee that drafted new graduate archival education guidelines adopted by its Council in 1988, served for four years as a member of that association's Committee on Education and Professional Development, and was a member of the SAA's governing Council. A fellow of SAA, Cox also served as editor of the *American Archivist* from 1991 through 1995. He has written extensively on archival and records management professional issues. He is the author of four books on archival topics: *American Archival Analysis: The Recent Development of the Archival Profession in the United States*, which won the Waldo Gifford Leland Award given by the Society of American Archivists; *Managing Institutional Archives: Foundational Principles and Practices*; *The First Generation of Electronic Records*

Archivists in the United States: A Study in Professionalization; and *Documenting Localities*.

Todd J. Daniels-Howell is head of Archives and Special Collections at Indiana University-Purdue University at Indianapolis. From 1990 to 1996, he served as associate curator of manuscript acquisitions at the Minnesota Historical Society, where he appraised and acquired the papers and records of numerous individuals, organizations, and businesses, including the Soo Line Railroad, United Power Association, the Twin Cities Rapid Transit Company, and 3M Company. He serves as cochair of the Public Information Committee of the Society of American Archivists and served as public information officer of the Midwest Archives Conference in addition to other committee and task force responsibilities.

Ernest J. Dick is currently a consulting archivist, based in Granville Ferry, Nova Scotia, Canada. He is consulting archivist/historian to the Canadian Broadcasting Corporation (CBC) and was the corporate archivist for the CBC, coordinating the development and implementation of archival policy throughout the corporation. Previously, he served as a moving image and sound archivist with the National Archives of Canada from 1974, eventually becoming the acting director of the Moving Image and Sound Archives. He is a founding member of the Association of Canadian Archivists, the Association for the Study of Canadian Radio and Television, and the Association of Moving Image Archivists and has been active in the International Association of Sound Archives and the International Federation of Television Archives. He has published widely in Canadian and international archival publications, and his monographs include the *Guide to Canadian Broadcasting Corporation Sources at the Public Archives of Canada*, and the exhibition catalog *Beyond the Printed Word...Newsreel and Broadcasting Reporting in Canada, 1987-1987*.

Timothy L. Ericson is the director of Archives and Special Collections in the Golda Meir Library at the University of Wisconsin-Milwaukee. He also teaches graduate coursework in archives administration as an adjunct instructor in the university's School of Library and Information Science and Department of History. He is a fellow of the Society of American Archivists and has served both as its education officer and as its acting executive director. Ericson has also served the Society of American Archivists as an elected member both of its governing Council and its Nominating Committee. He has held similar positions in the Midwest Archives Conference, and is author of a number of publications dealing with archives administration.

John A. Fleckner is chief archivist at the National Museum of American History, Smithsonian Institution. Fleckner directs the Archives Center, a manuscripts and special collections operation with special strengths in American consumer culture, the history of technology, and American music. Before joining the Smithsonian in 1983, Fleckner held a variety of archival positions at the State Historical Society of Wisconsin. Fleckner is a past president and fellow of the Society of American Archivists and has written on Native American archives and records surveys, among other topics.

James E. Fogerty is head of the Acquisitions and Curatorial Department at the Minnesota Historical Society. The society holds one of the largest business archives in the United States, including records of Honeywell, Inc., Northwest Airlines, 3M Company, International Multifoods, Graco Inc., American Crystal Sugar Co., and the Great Northern, Northern Pacific, and Soo Line Railroads. Fogerty has directed numerous oral history projects for individual corporations, as well as oral history projects on agriculture, the environment, and the recreation industry. He currently directs the Medical Technology Oral History Project. He teaches workshops on the use of oral history and videohistory in archives, corporations, and cultural organizations. He has written numerous articles and a book on rock music producer Phil Spector. Fogerty is a fellow of the Society of American Archivists and served on its governing Council. He is a former president of the Midwest Archives Conference, and chair of the Oral Sources Committee of the International Council on Archives.

Marcy G. Goldstein is president of the Document Organization, Inc. and a consultant in knowledge management, archival administration, and records management. She is also an adjunct professor for business archives at New York University and at Drexel University. She served for more than 10 years as corporate archivist for AT&T, where she created and managed the AT&T Archives Division. Previously, she was archivist at AT&T Bell Laboratories and archivist at the New Jersey Institute of Technology.

Mark A. Greene is curator of manuscripts acquisition at the Minnesota Historical Society where he works with the appraisal and acquisition of many of the society's major corporate archives. He has negotiated acquisition of the records of companies ranging in size from major industrial corporations to a small African-American food products company. He worked at the Bentley Historical Library at the University of Michigan before becoming archivist of Carleton College. In his current position he also leads the society's acquisition of the papers of U.S. congressmen, senators, cabinet members, and diplomats born in Minnesota, as well as a large holding of the records of philanthropic organizations. Greene has published a number of archival and historical articles. He developed and teaches the Midwest Archives Conference fundamentals workshop on appraisal and has served as president of the Midwest Archives Conference, as chair of the Society of American Archivists' Manuscript Repositories Section, and as co-chair of SAA's Committee on Education and Professional Development.

Philip F. Mooney has worked as manager of the Archives Department at the Coca-Cola Company since 1977. He has served as an instructor for the Business Archives Workshop sponsored by the Society of American Archivists for over 15 years and has participated in numerous professional conferences, committees, and meetings on the subject of business archives. Among his most recent publications are chapters in *Advocating Archives: An Introduction to the Public Relations for Archivists* and *Corporate Archives and History: Making the Past Work*.

Michael S. Moss is professor of archival studies at the University of Glasgow where he is responsible for one of the largest collections of business records in Europe. Previously, he was surveying officer of the Western Survey of the National Register of Archives (Scotland) in which capacity he rescued many important business archives, including those of John Brown Shipbuilding and Engineering Co. and Fairfield Shipbuilding and Engineering Co. He has written widely on business history and business archives topics including, with John Hume, *Workshop of the British Empire: Engineering and Shipbuilding in the West of Scotland*, *A History of William Beardmore & Co: The History of a Scottish Industrial Giant*, *The Making of Scotch Whisky*, and *Shipbuilders to the World - 125 Years of Harland & Wolff PLC 1861–1986*. He contributed an article on accounting records to Alison Turton's *Managing Business Archives* and is the tutor for the business records option on the Society of Archivists diploma course. He is deputy convenor of the Business Archives Council of Scotland and a member of council of the National Trust for Scotland.

Michael Nash is chief curator, Library Collections at the Hagley Museum and Library in Wilmington, Delaware. He is also an adjunct associate professor of history at the University of Delaware where he teaches archival management and public history. His publications have appeared in the *American Archivist*, *Business History Review*, *Public Historian*, *Labor History*, and the *Journal of Social History*.

James M. O'Toole is associate professor of history at the University of Massachusetts, Boston, where he directs the M.A. program in history and archival methods. He has worked as an archivist at the New England Historic Genealogical Society, the Massachusetts State Archives, and the Archives of the Roman Catholic Archdiocese of Boston. In addition to numerous publications on American religious history, he is the author of many articles and books on archives and archival theory, including *Understanding Archives and Manuscripts*. He is a fellow of the Society of American Archivists and was a member of its governing Council. He was SAA's first publications editor and is presently a member of the editorial board of the *American Archivist*. He has also served as president of New England Archivists.

Lesley M. Richmond has been involved with business archives as a surveyor of business records on behalf of the Business Archives Council in the basements, attics, and offices of companies throughout the United Kingdom; as the corporate archivist for Racal-Chubb; and as the deputy archivist at Glasgow University Archives and Business Records Centre. She is the joint author of several guides to business archives collections, including *Company Archives, The Survey of the Records of 1000 of the First Registered Companies in England and Wales, Directory of Corporate Archives* [UK], *The Brewing Industry: A Guide to Historical Records*, and is a series editor of *Studies in British Business Archives*, which has produced volumes on the brewing, shipbuilding, chartered accountants, and banking industries. Richmond is a member of the executive committee of the Business Archives Council where she has an active role within the council's publications and company history library and industry surveys. She currently comanages a survey of the British pharmaceutical industry. She has also been a member of the steering committee of the Section on Business Archives and Labour of the International Council on Archives since 1990 and is currently the secretary of the section.

INDEX